NEURAL NETWORKS
IN THE CAPITAL MARKETS

WILEY FINANCE EDITIONS

continued on back endpaper

NEURAL NETWORKS IN THE CAPITAL MARKETS

Edited by **Apostolos-Paul Refenes**
London Business School, England

John Wiley & Sons
Chichester • New York • Brisbane • Toronto • Singapore

Other Wiley Editorial Offices

John Wiley & Sons, Inc., 605 Third Avenue,
New York, NY 10158-0012, USA

Jacaranda Wiley Ltd, 33 Park Road, Milton,
Queensland 4064, Australia

John Wiley & Sons (Canada) Ltd, 22 Worcester Road,
Rexdale, Ontario M9W 1L1, Canada

John Wiley & Sons (SEA) Pte Ltd, 37 Jalan Pemimpin #05-04,
Block B, Union Industrial Building, Singapore 2057

Library of Congress Cataloging-in-Publication Data

Neural networks in the capital markets/edited by Apostolos-Paul Refenes.
    p. cm. — (Wiley finance editions)
  Includes bibliographical references and index.
  ISBN 0-471-94364-9 (cloth)
  1. Capital market. 2. Neural networks (Computer science)
I. Refenes, Apostolos-Paul. II. Series.
HG4523.N49 1995
332′.0414 — dc20   94–37990
                                        CIP

British Library Cataloguing in Publication Data

A catalogue record for this book is available from the British Library

ISBN 0-471-94364-9

Typeset in 10/12pt Times from editor's disks by Laser Words, Madras
Printed and bound in Great Britain by Bookcraft (Bath) Ltd.

Contents

Contributors

Antony, Martin
Biggs, Norman

London School of Economics and Political Science
Houghton St. London WC2A 2AE, UK

Tsibouris, George
Zeidenberg, Matthew

University of Wisconsin
Madison, WI 53706, USA

Steiner, Manfred
Wittkemper, Hans-Georg

Westfälische Wilhelms-Universität
Am Stadtgraben 13-15, 48159 Münster, Germany

Baestaens, Dirk
van den Bergh, Willem

Erasmus University Rotterdam
PO. Box 1738 3000 DR Rotterdam, Netherlands

Grudnitski, Gary and
Quang Do, A.

San Diego State University
San Diego, California USA

Mehta, Mahendra

Citibank N. A,
Bombay (India)

Steurer, Elmar

Daimler Benz AG
Postfach 2360, 89013 Ulm, Germany

Abu-Mostafa, Yaser

Caltech and NeuroDollars Inc.
Caltech 116-81, Pasadena, CA 91125, USA

Levitt, Marc

Sunny Vale California

Hsu William, Hsu L. and
Tenorio, Manoel

Purdue University
West Lafayette, IN 47907, USA

Kingdon, Jason   *University College London*
                                    Gower Street, London NW14SA, UK

Moody, John and   *Oregon Graduate Institute*
Utans, Joachim   *P.O. Box 91000, Portland, OR 97291-1000, USA*

Singleton, J. Clay   *University of North Texas*
                                    Denton, Texas, USA

Alvin, J. Surkan   *University of Nebraska-Lincoln*
                                    Lincoln, Nebraska, USA

Poddig, Thorsen   *Universitat Bamberg*
                                    Kirschackerstrasse 39, Bamberg, Germany

Sen, Tarun   *Virginia Tech,*
                                    The R.B. Pamplin College of Business
                                    Blacksburg, VA 24061, USA

Oliver, Robert   *Arthur Andersen & Co,*
                                    1666, K Street NW, Washington DC 20006, USA

Sen, Nilanjan   *Arizona State University*
                                    Phoenix, AZ 85069, USA

Martin-del-Brio, Bonifacio   *Universidad de Zaragoza*
and Serrano-Cinca, Carlos   *E 50009 Zaragoza, Spain*

Zapranis, Achileas   *London Business School*
                                    Sussex Place, Regents Park, London NW1 4SA, UK

Francis, Gavin   *County NatWest Investment Management*
                                    43/44 Crutched Friars, London EC3NX, UK

Preface

The prevailing wisdom among financial economists is that price fluctuations not due to external influences are dominated by noise and can be modelled by *stochastic* processes. Consequently we try to understand the nature of noise and develop tools for predicting its effects on asset prices. It is, however, possible that these remaining price fluctuations, to a large extent, are due to *nonlinear* processes at work in the marketplace. Therefore, given appropriate tools, it is possible to understand much of the market's price structure on the basis of completely or partially *deterministic* but *nonlinear* dynamics.

Neural networks are a field of research which has enjoyed a rapid expansion and great popularity in both the academic and industrial research communities. Neural networks are essentially statistical devices for performing inductive inference. From the statistician's point of view they are analogous to nonparametric, nonlinear regression models. The novelty of neural networks lies in their ability to model nonlinear processes with few (if any) *a priori* assumptions about the nature of the generating process. This is particularly useful in financial engineering applications, where much is assumed and little is known about the nature of the processes determining asset prices.

The case for the existence of nonlinear dependencies in the context of financial markets can be made by using a mix of observations on market microstructure, feedback effects in market prices, and empirical observations. Dissimilar microstructures between asset markets and between spot and derivative markets, for example, could give rise to nonlinear dependence. Several financial economists have argued that price discovery takes place in the futures markets and the information is subsequently carried to the spot market through the process of arbitrage. Delays in transacting the stock-market leg of the arbitrage imply that the immediate response in the mispricing would only be partial, reflecting the change in the futures price alone. This may induce further arbitrage activity and could actually result in overshooting of the arbitrage bounds. Moreover, restrictions on short sales in the stock markets, for example, may lead to delays in executing arbitrage transactions and this, in turn, may cause nonlinear behaviour.

Nonlinear dependencies may also be explained in terms of nonlinear feedback mechanisms in price movements alone. When the price of an asset becomes too high, self-regulating forces usually drive the price down. If the feedback mechanism is nonlinear then the correction will not always be proportional to the amount by which the price deviates from the asset's real value. It is not unreasonable to expect such nonlinear corrections in the financial markets; they can be explained by the study of market psychology, where it is understood that investors and markets over-react to bad news and under-react to good news. There are many participants in the financial markets with complex motivations, reactions and interrelationships. It would be a miracle if these complexities always averaged out to give an aggregate linear feedback. Once nonlinear feedback mechanisms were introduced in the market description, many price fluctuations could be explained without reference to stochastic effects.

It is generally accepted that market imperfections, such as taxes, transaction costs and the timing of the information reaction, introduce nonlinearities in the capital markets. Although information arrives randomly in the market, market participants respond to such information with lags due to transaction costs, for example. In other words, market participants do not trade every time news arrives in the market, rather they trade whenever it is economically possible, leading to clustering of price changes. Furthermore, nonlinearities are observed when announcements of important factors are made less often than the sampling frequency. For example, weekly money supply announcements will cause nonlinearities in daily but not in monthly data.

The prevailing capital market model is based on the rationality of individual investors. In other words, it is assumed that investors are risk-averse, are unbiased when they set their subjective probabilities and always react to information as it is received. The implication is that the data-generating process is linear. In practice, however, investors may well be risk-seeking instead of risk-averse when, for example, taking gambles to minimise their losses. Moreover, they may have excessive faith in their own forecasts, thus introducing bias in their subjective probabilities, and may not react to information instantaneously but delay their response until their peers reveal their preferences. The aforementioned points question the rationality not only of individual investors but also of the market as a whole since the market is an aggregation of individuals. Therefore linear models may not be adequate in explaining the market behaviour.

Nonlinear modelling techniques are the subject of increasing interest from practitioners in quantitative asset management, with neural networks assuming a prominent role. Neural networks are being applied to a number of 'live' systems in financial engineering and have shown promising results. However, the development of successful applications with neural networks is not a straightforward task;

it requires a substantial degree of expertise both in financial engineering and in neural network engineering and dynamical systems.

This book is a primer on neural network engineering aimed at financial modelling. Part One contains introductory and tutorial material on neural networks, how to build better models, how to treat financial data series and how to develop successful testing and evaluation strategies. Parts Two to Five contain original research contributions in the field of practical applications to challenging areas within financial engineering including equity investement, foreign exchange trading, bond rating and performance prediction and some applications concerning macroeconomic and corporate performance.

Apostolos-Paul N. Refenes
London

PART ONE
NEURAL NETWORKS

1

Introduction

Apostolos-Paul Refenes, *London Business School, UK*

POSITIONING OF NEURAL NETWORKS

The recent upturn of neural networks research has been brought about by two driving forces. First, there is the realisation that neural networks are powerful tools for modelling and understanding human cognitive behaviour. This has stimulated research in neuroscience, anatomy, psychology and the biological sciences, whose primary objective is to investigate the physiological plausibility of current artificial neural models and to identify new models which will give a more accurate insight into the functionality of the human brain. Second, there is the realisation that artificial neural networks have powerful pattern recognition properties and, in many applications, can outperform contemporary modelling techniques. This has attracted researchers from a diverse field of applications including signal processing, medical imaging, economic modelling, financial engineering, and also researchers from the mathematical, physical and statistical sciences whose interest lies in the investigation of the computational properties of neural networks. This cross-fertilisation has provided added impetus in methodological developments but it has also occasionally led to exaggerated claims and expectations. Anyone even remotely connected with neural computation will testify that much more is expected from neural networks than merely a useful addition to the statistician's toolbox. With this in mind we shall attempt to elucidate the computational properties of neural networks.

The awareness of the computational properties of any new modelling methodology provides an extra degree of freedom in deciding whether or not the use of the methodology is desirable for a particular (class of) application. Figure 1.1 uses a simple taxonomy of problem-solving methodologies to position neural networks

Neural Networks in the Capital Markets. Edited by Apostolos-Paul Refenes.
© 1995 John Wiley & Sons Ltd

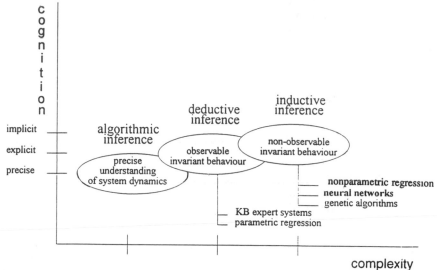

Figure 1.1   Positioning of neural networks

with respect to their established counterparts. The horizontal axis represents the complexity of the system we are trying to model. The vertical axis represents the various levels of the modeller's scientific understanding of the system's dynamics.

At the lower end of the spectrum (bottom left-hand corner), there are problems of relatively simple complexity, for which we have a precise understanding of the mathematics and physics underlying the phenomenon that we are trying to model. For problems of this nature it is possible to specify the equations of the system's dynamics and subsequently hardwire (or softwire) the algorithms to implement the required solution. Methods in this part of the spectrum are known as *algorithmic*. Algorithmic methods use strong models. Strong models make strong assumptions; they are usually expressed in a few equations with no free parameters, and are clearly the most efficient methodologies to use in the context of model-rich problems.

Further up the 'cognition' scale there are problems for which we have no precise understanding of the system dynamics — in the sense that we are not able to write down the equations of the system. However, if we observe the target system over time we can detect invariant behaviour with the naked eye, that is to say, under similar conditions the system behaves in similar ways. This enables the modeller to specify a set of *explicit* rules of a general form which describe the system's dynamics, often in conjunction with an 'expert' in the particular application. Typically, these rules are formulated in a top-down fashion which allows deductive reasoning. Deductive inference systems such as knowledge-based expert systems also use strong models with many rules and a few free parameters. Statistical inference systems such as linear regression make weaker assumptions in that, although they make strong assumptions about the nature of the relationship between the various variables, they allow the system to deduce or compute the coefficients for these variables from the observed data.

Finally, there are systems in which invariant behaviour is not observable, at least not with the naked eye. In this territory, researchers have two complementary tasks: *estimating* a model from observed data and *analysing* the properties of the results generated from the estimated model. Typically, in such data-rich but model-weak environments, model estimation is done using statistical inference techniques such as nonparametric regression. Neural networks are essentially statistical devices for performing inductive inference. From the statistician's point of view neural networks are analogous to nonparametric, nonlinear regression models. The idea of nonparametric modelling in the absence of a strong model is by no means new. Classical autoregressive moving average (ARMA) models are a good example of 'weak' modelling methods. The novelty of neural networks lies in their ability to combine much more generality with an increasing insight into how to manage their complexity.

The advantages and disadvantages of parametric versus nonparametric modelling are well known to statisticians. In principle, strong models (when available) are preferable to weak nonparametric models. Strong models make strong assumptions about the properties of the data they are trying to fit. By doing so they build a high degree of bias into the modelling process. Therefore, any errors that parametric estimators make in forecasting are almost entirely due to this bias. Weak (nonparametric) models, on the other hand, make no such *a priori* assumptions but 'let the data speak for themselves'. In trying to find an appropriate model, nonparametric estimators are exploring a much larger search space of functions to fit to the observations. This is not always an advantage, as we shall see in later sections.

With nonparametric, nonlinear inductive inference the modeller's second task — discovering the properties of the results generated from the estimated model — becomes very important. This is so because for nonlinear systems it is no longer possible to reconstruct an input signal and an independent transfer function from a given output. It is, however, possible to investigate the properties of the estimated model — for example, to quantify the sensitivity of an output to changes in each of the inputs and to estimate the relative significance of the inputs.

Much of the terminology used in neural computation traces its roots to neuroscience and psychology. The disciplines of statistics and econometrics use different terms to refer to similar concepts. For example, *inputs* are *independent variables*, *outputs* are *dependent variables*, *convergence* denotes model fitness *in sample*, *generalisation* denotes *out of sample* predictions, etc. In the following section we give a brief overview of the basic concepts underlying neural computation and explain some of the terminology.

THE NEURON AS A BIOLOGICAL ABSTRACTION AND A COMPUTING DEVICE

Neural networks attempt to mimic the way in which the human brain processes information. The basic computing device in the human brain is the *neuron*. A neuron consists of a *cell body*, branching extensions called *dendrites* for receiving input, and an *axon* that carries the neuron's output to the dendrites of other neurons (see Figure 1.2). This junction between an axon and a dendrite is called a *synapse*. A neuron is believed to carry out a simple *threshold* calculation. It collects signals at its synapses and sums them. If the combined signal strength exceeds a certain threshold the neuron sends out its own signal which is a transformation of the original input signal.

The transformation between the total input signal and the output signal is determined by a nonlinear function. Typical transformation functions are hard limiters, sigmoids and pseudolinear functions, as shown in Figure 1.3. *Hard limiter* functions produce values in the range {0, 1}, depending on whether the total input of a unit exceeds the threshold value. This type of function is used in most types of

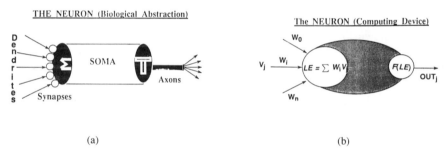

(a)   (b)

Figure 1.2 Functional block diagram of a neuron: (a) as a biological abstraction; (b) as a computing device

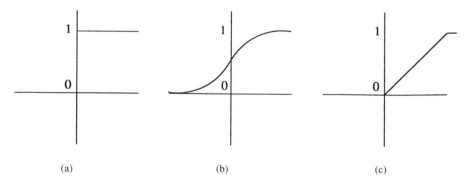

(a)   (b)   (c)

Figure 1.3 Nonlinear transformation functions: (a) hard limiter; (b) asymmetric sigmoid; (c) pseudolinear

neural learning. Its main advantage is its simplicity, which makes mathematical proofs relatively simple.

Sigmoid functions are the most widely used in all types of learning. They are more complex, differentiable, and behave well for many applications. There are two types of sigmoid function: *asymmetric* such as the one shown in Figure 1.3, and *symmetric*. A typical asymmetric squashing function:

$$x_i = f(a) = \frac{1}{1 + e^{-a}} \tag{1.1}$$

with asymptotes at 0 and 1 as shown in Figure 1.3(b).

Associated with each connection is a *weight*, and associated with each neuron is a *state* (usually implemented as an extra weight). Together these weights and states represent the distributed *data* of the network. A *neural network* is a structure made up of highly interconnected, primitive neurons. Typically neurons are organised into layers, with each neuron in one layer having a *weighted connection* to each neuron in the next layer. This organisation of neurons and weighted connections creates a neural network, also known as an *artificial neural network system* (ANNS). An neural network system learns by means of appropriately changing the internal connection strengths. This is called *weight adoptation* and takes place during the so-called *training phase*. In this phase, external *input patterns* that have to be associated with specific external *output patterns* or specific activation patterns across the networks units are presented to the network (commonly several times). The set of these external input patterns is called the *training set* (training sample); a single input pattern is called a *training vector* (observation). Furthermore, the network may receive environmental learning feedback, and this feedback may be used as additional information in determining the magnitude of the weight changes.

SIMPLE TAXONOMY OF NEURAL NETWORK LEARNING PROCEDURES

The principal goal of neural learning is to form associations between observed patterns. There are two variants of the association paradigm: *auto-association* and *hetero-association*. An auto-associative paradigm is one in which a pattern is associated with itself (cf. clustering). A hetero-associative paradigm is one in which two different patterns have to be associated with each other (cf. regression).

Depending on whether a learning procedure uses external signals *(environmental feedback)* to help form the association, one can divide the learning procedures into three classes: procedures implementing *supervised learning, associative reinforcement learning*, and *unsupervised learning*.

In supervised learning (learning with a teacher), the environmental feedback specifies the desired output pattern. Thereby the learning feedback is provided for each input–output association to be learnt by the network. The implication of this is that in each input–output pair, the exact difference between desired and actual output is known. Supervised learning is instruction-orientated. The objective of this type of learning is to eliminate differences between actual and desired output patterns by minimising a cost function or maximising an objective function.

In associative reinforcement learning (learning with a critic) the learning feedback is a scalar signal called a *reinforcement* signal which *indicates* whether or not the actual and desired patterns coincide. The reinforcement signal may be provided to the network for each input–ouput case or for sequences of input–output cases. Associative reinforcement learning is evaluation-orientated. The objective of this type of learning is to maximise some function of the reinforcement signal.

In unsupervised learning the network does not receive any environmental feedback. Unsupervised learning is self-organisation orientated. The objective of this type of learning is to capture regularities (clusters) in the stream of input patterns without receiving any learning feedback.

A secondary, but equally important classification criterion is the type of the *propagation rule*, the *nonlinear transformation function*, and the *weight adaptation rules*. Unsupervised learning procedures have no environmental feedback. Supervised learning procedures use some function of the difference between the target outputs and the desired output as a measure of how well they are doing during learning. Associative reinforcement procedures use a scalar value. Weight adaptation is performed after the unit has received a reinforcement signal.

Comprehensive reviews of these procedures and ways of converting one kind of learning procedure into another can be found in [Hinton87, Lippma87]. In this book we shall concentrate on the two most commonly used procedures in financial data, namely supervised learning by error backpropagation, and unsupervised learning by self-organising feature maps.

SUPERVISED LEARNING: THE ERROR BACKPROPAGATION ALGORITHM

Supervised learning procedures operate on regular feedforward networks of neurons. Networks typically consist of many simple neuron-like processing elements grouped together in layers. Each unit has a *state* or *activity level* that is determined by the input received from the other units in the network (see Figure 1.4). Information is processed locally in each unit by computing the dot product between its input vector $\mathbf{o}_j$ and its weight vector $\mathbf{w}_{ji}$:

$$x_i = \sum_j^n \mathbf{o}_j \mathbf{w}_{ji} - \theta_i \qquad (1.2)$$

This weighted sum, x_i, which is called the *total input* of unit i, is then passed through a sigmoid squashing function to produce the state of unit i denoted by $\mathbf{o}_i$. The most common squashing functions are the *sigmoidal*, the *hyperbolic tangent*

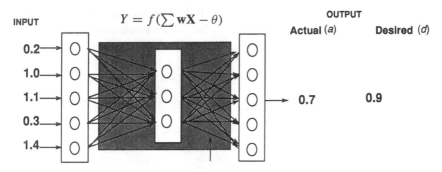

Figure 1.4 Fully interconnected network with one layer of hidden units

and the thermodynamic-like ones. All these functions can be included in the same family. In this book our attention is focused on the family of squashing functions $F_n = \{f = f(x, k, T, c) | x, k \in \mathbb{R}; T, c \in \mathbb{R} - \{0\}\}$ which are defined by (1.3):

$$f = k + \frac{c}{1 + e^{T x_i}} \tag{1.3}$$

Note that squashing functions vary according to the permissible values of k, c and T. We shall use these results later to examine the relationship between the various threshold functions, to explore the various results that we obtained, and to prove that, in general, symmetric thresholding functions in the family are capable of producing faster convergence.

Before training, the weights are initialised with random values. Training the network to produce a desired output vector $\mathbf{o}^{(r)}$ when presented with an input pattern $\mathbf{i}^{(r)}$ involves systematically changing the weights until the network produces the desired output (within a given tolerance). This is repeated over the entire training set. In doing so, each connection in the network computes the derivative, with respect to the connection strength, of a global measure of the error in the performance of the network. The connection strength is then adjusted in the direction that decreases the error. A plausible measure of how poorly the network is performing with its current set of weights is given by E in (1.4).

$$E = \tfrac{1}{2} \sum_{j,c}^{n} (y_{j,c} - d_{j,c})^2 \tag{1.4}$$

where $y_{j,c}$ is the actual state of the output unit j in input–output case c, and $d_{j,c}$ is its desired state.

Learning is thus reduced to a minimisation procedure of the error measure given in (1.4). This is achieved by repeatedly changing the weights by an amount proportional to the derivative $\partial E / \partial W$, denoted by δ_i:

$$\Delta W_{ij}(t + 1) = \lambda \delta_i y_{ij} \tag{1.5}$$

The learning rate, λ (i.e. the fraction by which the global error is minimised during each pass) is kept constant at least for the duration of a single pass. In the limit, as λ tends to zero and the number of iterations tends to infinity, this learning procedure is guaranteed to find the set of weights that gives the least mean square (LMS) error. The value of $\delta_i = \partial E/\partial W$ is computed by differentiating (1.4) and (1.2):

$$\delta_i = (d_{j,c} - y_{j,c})f^*(y_i) \qquad (1.6)$$

The LMS error procedure has a simple geometric interpretation [Hinton87]: if we construct a multi-dimensional 'weight space' that has an axis for each weight and one extra axis called 'height' that corresponds to the error measure. For each combination of weights, the network will have a certain error which can be represented by the height of a point in weight space. These points form a surface called the 'error surface'. For networks with linear output units and no hidden units, the error surface always forms a bowl whose horizontal cross-sections are ellipses and whose vertical cross-sections are parabolas. Since the bowl has only one minimum (perhaps a complete subspace but nevertheless only one), gradient descent on the error surface is guaranteed to find it. If the output units have a nonlinear but monotonic transfer function, the bowl is deformed but still has only one minimum, so gradient descent still works. However, with hidden units, the error surface may contain many local minima, so it is possible that steepest descent in weight space will be trapped in poor local minima.

UNSUPERVISED LEARNING: SELF-ORGANISING FEATURE MAPS

The most popular unsupervised learning procedure is Kohonen's self-organising maps [Kohone84]. The algorithm is based on the common belief that many parts of the human brain operate in a self-organised way. For instance, there are areas of the cerebral cortex corresponding to the sensory modalities (visual area, auditory area, somatosensory area, etc.) and to various operational areas (speech area, motor area, etc.). This means that the topographic order in which sensory signals are received at the sensory organs is the same as the topographic order in which these signals are obtained on their specific areas; different feature values of the sensory signals cause different spatial locations of the neural responses. Hence, the brain realises a topology-preserving mapping from the sensory environment to the sensory specific area; the brain forms topographically ordered (retinotopic, tonotopic, somatotopic, etc.) maps. Another central characteristic of the brain maps is that they organise themselves, that is, there is no teacher guiding their formation. Although the mechanisms of how these brain maps self-organise in a topology-preserving form are not definitely known, there is evidence for the assumption that a special kind of lateral feedback (sometimes referred to as the *Mexican-hat-type interaction*) plays an important part in their formation. Due to this neural principle of lateral feedback, a neuron excitates itself and its short-range neighbouring neurons, and inhibits its middle-range neighbouring neurons.

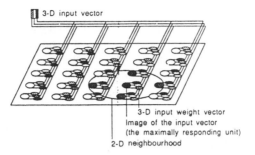

3-D input weight vector
Image of the input vector
(the maximally responding unit)
2-D neighbourhood

Figure 1.5 Self-organising feature map network. A mapping is formed from a 3-D input space onto a 2-D network. The values of the input components, weights and the unit output are shown by grey scale coding

A topological feature map [Kohone84] is a large adaptive system which consists of a number of processing units in a laminar organisation (see Figure 1.5). To form a self-organised map first, the input data is coded along a number of features, forming an input space of N-dimensional vectors. Input items are randomly drawn from the input distribution and presented to the network one at a time. All units receive the same input and produce the same output, proportional to the similarity of the input vector and the unit's parameter vector (which is also called the input weight vector of the unit). The unit with the maximum response is taken as the image of the input vector on the map. The parameter vector of this unit and each unit on its neighbourhood are changed towards the input vector, so that these units will produce an even response to the same input in the future. The parallelism of neighbouring vectors is thus increased at each presentation, a process which results in a global order.

The processing units of the resulting network are sensitive to specific items of the input space. Topological relations are retained: two input items which are close in the input space are mapped onto units close in the map. The distribution of the parameter vectors approximates that of the input vectors. This means that the most common areas of the input space are represented to a greater detail, that is, more units are allocated to represent these inputs. The dimensionality of the map is determined by the definition of the neighbourhood, that is, whether the units are laid out in a line (1-D) or on a plane (2-D), etc. If dimensionality is reduced in the mapping, the dimensions of the map do not necessarily stand for any recognisable features of the input space. The dimensions develop automatically to facilitate the best discrimination between the input items.

The basic system used by Kohonen is a single layered network whose units form an one- or two-dimensional array. The mapping from the external input patterns to the network's activity patterns is realised by correlating the input patterns with the weights of the units. This leads to a mapping which works in two phases: *similarity matching* (clustering of activity, discrimination process, and 'bubble formation'), and *weight adaptation*.

Initially the weights of the connections are set to small random values. During the similarity matching phase, the unit which is most similar to the actually presented input pattern $\mathbf{X} = (X_1, \ldots, X_n)$ at time t is located (discriminated). This most similar unit is given to the unit $\mathbf{u}_s$ whose weight vector $\mathbf{W}_s = (W_{s1}, \ldots, W_{sn})$ meets the condition:

$$|\mathbf{x}(t) - \mathbf{W}_s|_E = \min_i\{|\mathbf{X}(t) - \mathbf{W}_i(t)|_E\} \tag{1.7}$$

where $|..|_E$ is the Euclidean distance function. The next step in this phase is to define a topological neighbourhood N_s of this unit $\mathbf{u}_s$; N_s contains all units being within a certain radius centred at $\mathbf{u}_s$. This neighbourhood N_s corresponds to the centre of neural response caused by the actual input pattern $\mathbf{x}$ (often referred to as the activity bubble).

During the second phase, weight adaptation, the input weights of the units being in N_s are changed according to the rule in (1.8)

$$\mathbf{W}_i(t + 1) = \begin{cases} \mathbf{w}_i(t) + \alpha[\mathbf{x}(t) - \mathbf{w}_i(t)] & \text{if } i \in N_s \\ \mathbf{W}_i(t) & \text{otherwise} \end{cases} \tag{1.8}$$

where α is (in the simplest case) a positive scalar constant. This type of weight changing simulates the Mexican-hat-type interaction mentioned earlier.

NEURAL NETWORKS AS ADDITIVE NONLINEAR, NONPARAMETRIC REGRESSION MODELS

It is claimed that because of their *inductive* nature, neural networks can bypass the step of theory formulation and can infer complex nonlinear relationships between an asset price and its determinants. Various performance figures are being quoted to support these claims but there is rarely a comprehensive investigation of the nature of the relationship that has been captured between asset prices and their determinants. The absence of explicit models makes it difficult to assess the significance of the estimated model and the possibility that any short-term success is due to 'data mining'.

In this section we formulate neural learning in a framework similar to additive nonlinear regression [HasTib90]. This formulation provides an explicit representation of the estimated models and enables us to use a rich collection of analytic and statistical tools to test the significance of the various parameters in the estimated neural models. The formulation, when applied to modelling asset returns, can make use of modern financial economics theory on market dynamics to investigate the plausibility of the estimated models and to analyse them in order to separate the nonlinear components of the models which are invariant through time from those that reflect temporary (and probably unrepeatable) market imperfections.

Consider the family of neural networks with asymmetric sigmoids as the nonlinear transfer function. For simplicity, we consider networks with two layers of hidden connections as shown in Figure 1.6 with A and B denoting input variables,

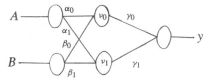

Figure 1.6 Feedforward network with two layers of hidden units

y denoting the output variable, α_0, α_1, β_0, β_1 the connection weights from the input units to the hidden layer, and γ_0, γ_1 connections from the hidden units to the output unit.

The task of the training procedure is to estimate a function between input and response vectors. The function is parametrised by the network weights and the transfer function see equation (1.1) and takes the form:

$$y = \frac{1}{1 + e^{-(\gamma_0 v_0 + \gamma_1 v_1)}} \tag{1.9}$$

where v_0 and v_1 are the outputs of the intermediate hidden units, similarly parametrised by the weights between the input and hidden layer. Ignoring the bias components, we have:

$$v_0 = \frac{1}{1 + e^{-(\alpha_0 A + \beta_0 B)}} \quad \text{and} \quad v_1 = \frac{1}{1 + e^{-(\alpha_1 A + \beta_1 B)}} \tag{1.10}$$

Let us illustrate how the task of the learning procedure can be compared to that of additive nonlinear regression by assuming, without loss of generality, that on a network with linear units at the output level:

$$y = \gamma_0 v_0 + \gamma_1 v_1 = \gamma_0 \frac{1}{1 + e^{-(\alpha_0 A + \beta_0 B)}} + \gamma_1 \frac{1}{1 + e^{-(\alpha_1 A + \beta_1 B)}} \tag{1.11}$$

In most financial engineering applications, it is common to apply smoothing transformations to the input and output variables prior to training in order, for example, to remove the effect of statistical outliers. A commonly used transformation is the logarithmic operation. Typically, instead of estimating $y = f(A, B)$ one would use the reversible transformation $\ln(y) = f(\ln(A), \ln(B))$. Using this transformation, the exponential term can be rewritten as:

$$e^{(\alpha_0 \ln(A) + \beta_0 \ln(B))} = e^{(\ln(A^{\alpha_0}) + \ln(B^{\beta_0}))}$$

$$= e^{\ln(A^{\alpha_0} B^{\beta_0})}$$

$$= A^{\alpha_0} B^{\beta_0} \tag{1.12}$$

Using (1.12) it is easy to show that (1.11) can be rewritten as the sum of two products:

$$\ln(y) = \gamma_0 \frac{A^{\alpha_0} B^{\beta_0}}{A^{\alpha_0} B^{\beta_0} + 1} + \gamma_1 \frac{A^{\alpha_1} B^{\beta_1}}{A^{\alpha_1} B^{\beta_1} + 1} \tag{1.13}$$

Overall we have six parameters $\{\alpha_0, \alpha_1, \beta_0, \beta_1 \text{ and } \gamma_0, \gamma_1\}$ ignoring the constants, i.e. biases. The task of the learning procedure is to estimate the parameters in a way that minimises the residual least square error. In the general case for networks with n hidden units and m input variables (1.13) takes the form:

$$\ln(y) = \gamma_0 \frac{A^{\alpha_0} B^{\beta_0} \cdots M^{\mu_0}}{A^{\alpha_0} B^{\beta_0} \cdots M^{\mu_0} + 1} + \gamma_1 \frac{A^{\alpha_1} B^{\beta_1} \cdots M^{\mu_1}}{A^{\alpha_1} B^{\beta_1} \cdots M^{\mu_1} + 1}$$

$$+ \cdots + \gamma_n \frac{A^{\alpha_n} B^{\beta_n} \cdots M^{\mu_m}}{A^{\alpha_n} B^{\beta_n} \cdots M^{\mu_m} + 1} \tag{1.14}$$

Thus neural learning is analogous to searching the function space defined by the terms of (1.14) and the range of the permissible values for the parameters.

This formulation is strikingly similar to the formulation of additive nonlinear nonparametric regression formulation [ReBeBu94] and it allows us to apply the analytic and statistical tools that have been developed in the field of additive nonparametric regression for the class of neural networks of a similar structure.

SUMMARY

Neural networks are essentially statistical devices for inductive inference. Their strengths (and weaknesses) accrue from the fact that they need no *a priori* assumptions of models and from their capability to infer complex, nonlinear underlying relationships. Although the future of neural networks as nonlinear estimators in financial engineering seems to be very promising, developing successful applications is not a straightforward procedure.

Substantial expertise in both the domain of neural network engineering and the domain of financial engineering is required. The choice of the variables, their significance and correlation, normalisation and optimisation of multi-parameter data sets, etc., are of extreme importance. The application development is usually a time-consuming process, involving extensive data preprocessing and experimentation with network engineering parameters.

Research in neural computation ranges from reassuring proofs that neural networks with sigmoid units can essentially fit any function and its derivative, to theorems on generalisation ability that can be obtained under very weak (nonparametric) assumptions. For such models with broad approximation abilities and few specific assumptions, the distinction between memorisation and generalisation becomes critical. The awareness of the complex interelationships between data preprocessing, fine-tuning of neural learning parameters, and generalisation is an essential element in successful application development. The purpose of the next two chapters is to explore the interrelationships among the numerous network and data engineering parameters and to highlight the importance of careful choice of the indicators used as network inputs.

2

Neural Network Design Considerations

Apostolos-Paul Refenes, *London Business School, UK*

In Chapter 1 we gave a brief introduction to supervised learning together with a simple geometrical interpretation of machine learning by gradient descent. This procedure is summarised in Figure 2.1. This chapter defines the main performance measures for neural networks and discusses the parameters that influence them.

As shown in the bottom left-hand side of Figure 2.1, we evaluate network performance as a weighted index of three metrics:

- convergence — accuracy of model fitness in-sample;
- generalisation — accuracy of model fitness out-of-sample;
- stability — variance in prediction accuracy.

The bottom right-hand side of Figure 2.1 lists a number of control mechanisms that can be used to influence the above performance measures.

- the choice of activation function;
- the choice of cost function;
- network architecture;
- gradient descent/ascent control terms;
- learning times.

In the following sections we explore ways in which the control mechanisms can be used to influence (for better or worse) the main performance measures. We start by a brief definition of the performance measures.

Neural Networks in the Capital Markets. Edited by Apostolos-Paul Refenes.
© 1995 John Wiley & Sons Ltd

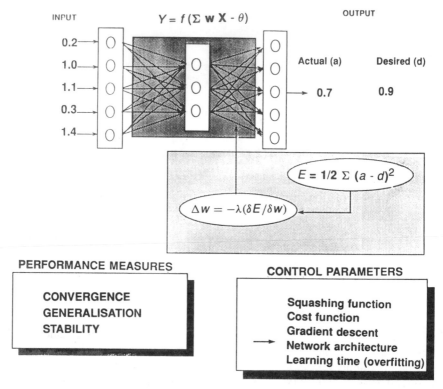

Figure 2.1 Fully interconnected network with one layer of hidden units, performance measures and control parameters

NETWORK PERFORMANCE MEASURES

Convergence is concerned with the problem of whether the learning procedure is capable of learning the classification defined in (any) data set, under what conditions it does so, and what are the computational requirements for convergence. Fixed topology networks prove convergence by showing that in the limit, as training time tends to infinity, the error minimised by the gradient descent method will tend to zero. Other (sub-optimal) methods prove convergence by showing that as training time tends to infinity the method can classify the maximum number of mappings possible with an arbitrarily large probability $p \leqslant 1$.

Generalisation is the main property that should be sought. It measures the ability of a network to recognise patterns outside the training set. Frequently, an analogy is made between learning and curve fitting. There are two problems in curve fitting: finding the *order* of the polynomial, and finding the *coefficients* of the polynomial once the order has been established. For example, given a certain data set, one first decides that the curve is second-order and thus has the form $ax^2 + bx + c$, and then somehow computes the values for a, b, c (normally by minimising the sum of squared differences between required and predicted $f(x_i)$ for x_i in the training set. Once the coefficients are computed, the value of $f(x_i)$ can be calculated for any x_i including those not present in the training data set. Choosing orders lower than the appropriate leads to bad approximation even for the points in the data set. On the other hand, choosing a higher order implies fitting a high-degree polynomial to the low-order data, and although one hopes that the high-order terms will have zero coefficients to cancel their effect, this is not the case in practice. Typically it leads to perfect fit for points in the data set, but very bad $f(x_i)$ values may be computed for x_i not in the training data (i.e. the system will not generalise well). By analogy, a network having a structure simpler than necessary cannot give good approximations even to patterns in the training set and a structure more complicated than necessary 'overfits' in that it leads to good fit for the training set but performing poorly on unseen patterns.

Stability is concerned with the consistency of the results produced by neural networks when varying the values of the parameters that influence their performance. Neural networks have been known to produce wide variations in their predictive properties. This is to say that small changes in network design, learning times, initial conditions, etc. may produce large changes in network behaviour. In theory, the only criterion for deciding whether neural networks perform better than parametric regression systems is if they converge to smaller mean squared error in-sample. In practice, however, any estimator will only *approximate* the actual structural relationship between inputs and outputs and will always contain an error element in its estimation. This error element can be divided into two components: the first is due to the estimator's *bias*, while the second is due to the estimator's *variance*.

Parametric estimators such as linear regression are *high-bias* estimators in that they assume an *a priori* model (for example, a linear relationship) but they are also *zero-variance* estimators. Neural networks, however, are analogous to nonparametric (nonlinear) regression methods in that they make no *a priori* assumptions about the problem (that is, let the data speak for themselves); the main contributor to the global error is their *high variance*, meaning that they can fit an entire family of polynomials to a given data set.

The target here is to identify intervals of values for the control parameters which give statistically stable results, and to demonstrate that these results persist across different training and test sets.

As shown in Figure 2.1, there are four mechanisms that can be used to control the values of these performance measures: first, the choice of activation function; second, the choice of cost function; third, the choice of parameters that control the gradient descent procedure; and finally, the choice of the network architecture. In the following section we discuss the influence of these mechanisms on the network performance metrics.

THE NONLINEAR TRANSFORMATION FUNCTION

The first important design consideration for neural learning is the choice of activation function for the units. The activation function is a nonlinearity, such as a hard limiter, a sigmoid or a pseudolinear, as shown in Figure 1.3. Sigmoid functions are the most widely used in all types of learning. They are more complex, differentiable, and behave well for many applications. There are two types of sigmoid function: *asymmetric* (see Figure 1.3(b)), and *symmetric*. A typical symmetric squashing function is the scaled hyperbolic tangent:

$$y = f(x) = A \tanh Sx = A \frac{e^{Sx} - e^{-Sx}}{e^{Sx} + e^{-Sx}} = A - \frac{2A}{1 + e^{2Sx}} \qquad (2.1)$$

where A is the amplitude of the function and S determines its slope at the origin, and the entire squashing function is an odd function with horizontal asymptotes $+A$ and $-A$. Symmetric functions are believed to yield faster convergence, although the learning can become extremely slow if the weights are too small [LeCun89]. The cause of this problem is that the origin of the weight space is a stable point for the learning dynamics, and although it is a saddle point, it is attractive in almost all directions. We have used this function in several non-trivial applications with parameter values similar to [LeCun89] with $A = 1.7159$ and $S = \frac{2}{3}$. With this choice of parameters the equalities $f(1) = 1$ and $f(-1) = -1$ are satisfied. The rationale behind this is that the overall gain of the squashing transformation is around 1 in normal operating conditions, and the interpretation of the state of the network is simplified. Moreover, the absolute value of the second derivative of f is a maximum at $+1$ and -1, which improves the convergence at the end of the learning session.

Before training the weights are typically initialised with random values in the range between $-2.4/I_i$ and $+2.4/I_i$ where I_i is the number of inputs of the unit to which the connection belongs. The reason for dividing by the number of input connections is that we would like the initial standard deviation of the weighted sums to be in the same range for each unit, and to fall within the normal operating region of the sigmoid. If the initial weights are too small, the gradients are very small and the learning is slow. If they are too large, the sigmoids are saturated and the gradient is also very small. The standard deviation of the weighted sum scales like the square root of the number of inputs when the inputs are independent, and it scales linearly when the inputs are highly correlated.

Refenes and Alippi [RefAli91] used the formulation in (1.3) to show that symmetric sigmoid functions are capable of improving the speed of convergence over the commonly used asymmetric sigmoids by as much as 10 times in non-trivial applications. A demonstration of this is given below. First let us consider one layered networks. Single-layer networks are important because they are linear classifiers and can be used as the building blocks in constructive techniques. Summing expressions (1.5) and (1.6) weight variation reduces to:

$$\Delta \mathbf{W}_{ij} = \lambda \mathbf{o}_j f'(x_i)(t_i - f(x_i)) \qquad (2.2)$$

The RHS of (2.2) represents the update of weights associated with connections between the output layer and the input layer. Furthermore, since the learning algorithm represents an approximation of the gradient descent algorithm, it represents the step taken along the gradient descent. We suppose that the structure of the network can successfully solve the application addressed. As we have seen, the speed of learning depends on various effects such as initial weight set, learning rate, and the properties of the squashing function chosen as mapper between input stimuli and output. If we fix the application, as well as the network design and the squashing function, the complex dependence on different parameters reduces to the initial set values and to the learning parameter.

According to the backpropagation learning rule, $\mathbf{W}(t+1)$ is related to $\mathbf{W}(t)$ as follows:

$$\mathbf{W}(t+1) = \mathbf{W}(t) + \Delta \mathbf{W}(t) \qquad (2.3)$$

After T iterations the weight values may be expressed as:

$$\mathbf{W}(T) = \mathbf{W}(0) + \sum_{t=0}^{T-1} \Delta \mathbf{W}(t)$$

If the units have a differentiable, nonlinear but monotonic output function then, if there exist weights such that $E = 0$ (the network is able to solve the implemented application), then E has no local minima and a perfect gradient descent is therefore guaranteed to find this minimum. The maximum speed for a fixed network will depend, at this stage, on the capability of the learning algorithm to discover the unique weight set minimising the error function. We have to focus our attention on the update phase and on the maximum update effect for each input–output presentation during the learning phase.

$$\max |\Delta \mathbf{W}(t)| = \max |\lambda \mathbf{o}_j f'(x_i)(t_i - f(x_i))| = \lambda \max |\mathbf{o}_j| \max |f'(x_i)(t_i - f(x_i))| \qquad (2.4)$$

Let us evaluate the two terms for both squashing functions. For the sigmoid function, the first term is $\max |\mathbf{o}_j|_s = 1$ since it is a limited function with values $\{0, 1\}$; and for the second term we have

$$\max |f'(x_i)(t_i - f(x_i))|_{t_i=0,1} = \max |(1 - f(x_i))f(x_i)(t_i - f(x_i))| = \frac{4}{27}$$

and so for the sigmoid,

$$\max |\Delta \mathbf{W}|_s = \frac{4}{27}\lambda_s \qquad (2.5)$$

where λ_s is the learning rate used for the sigmoid-based architecture.

For the tangent function the maximum update effect is made up as follows. First, $\max |o_j|_h = A$, since the output is bounded between A and $-A$. Now, for the second term we have

$$\max |f'(x_i)(t_i - f(x_i))|_{t=\pm A} = \frac{4}{27} 8SA^2$$

noting that

$$f'(x_i) = \frac{2S}{-2A}(f(x_i) - A)(f(x_i) + A))$$

from which, by substituting the obtained results in (2.4),

$$\max |\Delta \mathbf{W}_{ij}|_h = \tfrac{4}{27} 8SA^2 A\lambda_h = \frac{32A^3 S}{27}\lambda_h \tag{2.6}$$

Since the initial weight set is random and normalised in order to optimise the learning effect with respect to the activation function, we will consider the optimal case both for the sigmoidal function and for the hyperbolic tangent. The speed of convergence depends on the capacity of the net to speed up the weight update in order to reach the unique minima (that we suppose exist since the network solved the application). The capability of reaching the optimal weight set according to an 'optimal trajectory' is bounded above by the limit intrinsic with the maximum step taken. The optimal speed rate may be expressed as a ratio, using (2.5) and (2.6):

$$\frac{\max |\Delta \mathbf{W}|_h}{\max |\Delta \mathbf{W}|_s}\bigg|_{opt} = \frac{\lambda_h}{\lambda_s}\bigg|_{opt} \frac{8SA^3 \frac{4}{27}}{\frac{4}{27}} = \frac{\lambda_h}{\lambda_s}\bigg|_{opt} 8SA^3$$

For the chosen squashing function F_2, we used $A = 1.7159$, $S = \frac{2}{3}$. Typical simulation parameters for λ are $\lambda_h = 0.03$, and $\lambda_s = 0.4$ [RefAli91]. These values reduce the equation above to 2.02.

When two-layered networks are considered, the learning rule assumes two different expressions, one reflecting the propagation of the error generated into the output layer, and the other the error backpropagated along the network. So, the update phase involves two different modalities: the update of weights connecting the output layer with the hidden layer which assumes the already stated expression (2.2); and the update of the hidden layers which requires a new expression for the error in the hidden layer:

$$\delta_i = f'(x_i) \sum_{k=1}^{N} \mathbf{W}_{i,k}\delta_k \tag{2.7}$$

Likewise, in the observation utilised to prove the speed-up of the learning phase in a single-layered network we have to also consider the maximum weight update. In this case *max* may be expressed as:

$$\max |\Delta \mathbf{W}_{ij}| = \max |\lambda \delta_i \sigma_i| \tag{2.8}$$

with σ_i the input vectors $\in I$. By noting that $|f'(x_i)| \leqslant |Tc|/4$ and that $\max |\delta_k| = \frac{4}{27}|T|c^2$, we obtain the following expression for the asymmetric sigmoidal function,

$$\max |\Delta \mathbf{W}_{ij}| = \lambda_s I_l \frac{1}{27} \sum |\mathbf{W}_{i,k}| \tag{2.9}$$

while for the hyperbolic tangent (symmetric sigmoid) it becomes:

$$\max |\Delta \mathbf{W}_{ij}| = \lambda_h I_l \frac{32}{27} S^2 A^3 \tag{2.10}$$

Unfortunately the bounds strictly depend on the application. We can use a maximum update rate, defined as the percent ratio between the maximum update obtainable with the hyperbolic function and the sigmoidal one:

$$\frac{\max |\Delta W|_h}{\max |\Delta W|_s} = 32 \frac{\lambda_h I_{lh} S^2 A^3}{\lambda_s I_{ls}} \frac{\sum |\mathbf{W}_{i,j}|_h}{\sum |\mathbf{W}_{i,j}|_s}$$

If we assume that the networks are able to discover the same minimum, then the last term (that is, the ratio of sums) can be set to 1. We further note that $|I_{lh}| \leqslant A$ while $|I_{ls}| \leqslant 1$. Thus,

$$\frac{\max |\Delta W|_h}{\max |\Delta W|_s} = 32 S^2 A^4 \frac{\lambda_h}{\lambda_s}$$

In a non-trivial image classification application [RcfAli91] used the formulation above to predict a performance improvement of

$$32\frac{4}{9}(1.7159)^4 \frac{0.05}{0.6} = 10.27$$

which was confirmed with the experimental data.

COST FUNCTION

The choice of the cost function is believed to play an important role in determining the convergence and generalisation characteristics of supervised learning procedures. The most commonly used cost function is the family of quadratics given in (1.4), the least mean squared error. Several researchers suggested that instead of minimising a cost function between observed and actual values and subsequently using its output as an input to the ultimate objective function (which typically would try to maximise profit according to a specific investment strategy), it may be more useful to consider both processes in a single step and attempt to maximise the ultimate objective function in the first place. Since the mechanics of the implementation of this approach will depend on the specific objective function, we shall not deal with this approach any further. However, to demonstrate how the choice of cost function might influence network performance, let us consider a modification to the common quadratic cost function which is applicable to time-series data. The idea behind this modification is that in low-frequency financial data the structural relationship between an asset price and its determinant changes gradually with time as the economic environment evolves. Thus older observations experience exponential decay in their contribution to cost function. This is analogous to discounted least squares with discount rates determined by the parameters a and b:

$$E = \frac{1}{N} \sum_{p=1}^{N} \frac{1}{1 + e^{(a+bp)}} (t_p - o_p)^2 \qquad (2.11)$$

where N is the total number of patterns in the training data set, t_p is the target network output, o_p is the predicted network output, $a = -3$ and $b = (3-a)/N$.

The vehicle for our discussion will be a financial multivariate time-series prediction application (we shall use the same application to explore some data preprocessing considerations in later sections; see also [ReZaBe93]). The task is to predict the return of a stock, given the values $R_i(t)$ of several indicators such as *long-term interest rates* (LTR), *earnings per share* (EPS), etc. More formally, given $X_i(t)$, $(i = 1, \ldots, 6)$ we want to predict the 30-day return $Y(t)$, where $X_i(t)$ and $Y(t)$ are calculated as follows:

$$X_i(t) = \frac{R_i(t + \mathrm{d}t) - R_i(t)}{R_i(t)} \qquad (2.12)$$

$$X_5(t) = \frac{R_5(t - \mathrm{d}t) - R_5(t)}{R_5(t - \mathrm{d}t)}$$

$$Y(t) = \frac{R_5(t + \mathrm{d}t) - R_5(t)}{R_5(t)}$$

where $R_i(t)(i = 1, \ldots, 6)$ stands for the value of the econometric parameter R_i at time t, R_5 stands for the stock price, time t is counted in days, the time interval $\mathrm{d}t$ is equal to 30 days.

Specifically, we are interested in modelling stock returns as a function of six parameters:

$$\frac{\Delta S^{(30)}}{S} = f\left(\frac{\Delta LR^{(30)}}{LR}, \frac{\Delta SR^{(30)}}{SR}, \frac{\Delta EPS^{(30)}}{EPS}, \frac{\Delta \$^{(30)}}{\$}, \frac{\Delta S^{(-30)}}{S}, EPS \right)$$

where

LR = long rates

SR = short rates

EPS = earnings per share (estimated)

$\$$ = USD/FRF rate

The values of the inputs and outputs are daily closing prices of CAC-40 stocks in the Paris stock exchange. The available preprocessed data consist of 1025 patterns

Table 2.1 Unscaled data for the multivariate time-series prediction application. $X_1(t)$ to $X_6(t)$ correspond to network inputs and $Y(t)$ corresponds to the network output.

$X_1(t)$	$X_2(t)$	$X_3(t)$	$X_4(t)$	$X_5(t)$	$X_6(t)$	$Y(t)$
0.003348	0.064516	−0.004617	−0.017452	0.002174	12.900000	−0.027766
0.007804	0.064516	0.004712	−0.015734	−0.031470	12.300000	0.021049
0.007752	0.056338	0.005140	−0.008803	−0.031980	12.100000	0.063288
0.004405	0.064021	0.001852	0.001770	−0.029272	12.100000	0.001852
0.001100	0.078680	−0.001994	0.001770	0.009122	12.400000	−0.018091
−0.018559	0.014652	−0.000570	0.000000	−0.013956	11.900000	0.033024
−0.036559	0.014652	−0.004128	0.007092	−0.006136	11.800000	0.046509
−0.021529	0.022140	0.002067	0.005310	−0.011992	11.600000	0.097091
−0.022581	0.007273	0.000196	0.003527	−0.046519	11.500000	0.121959
−0.023656	−0.022673	−0.004148	−0.001758	−0.067263	11.600000	0.107456
−0.020474	−0.015403	−0.005259	−0.013913	−0.054296	11.700000	0.105268
−0.006452	−0.008353	−0.001004	−0.010417	−0.046556	12.000000	0.057271
−0.011752	−0.022353	0.005543	−0.006969	−0.047428	12.000000	0.047441

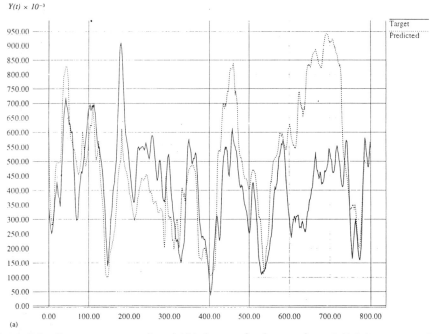

(a)

Figure 2.2 Target versus predicted $Y(t)$, **in-sample**, for topology 6-7-4-1, asymmetric activation function with range (0,1), learning rate 0.3, momentum term 0.7: (a) unmodified cost function;

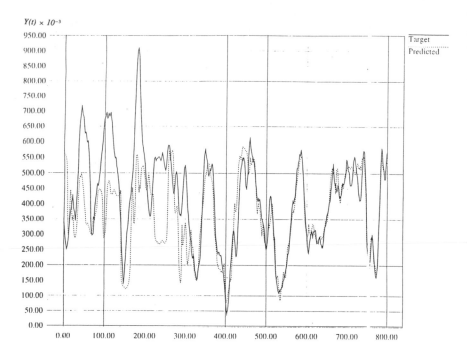

Figure 2.2   (*continued*) (b) 'time-sensitive' cost function and dt = 60 for X_4

of the form $[\bar{X}(t), Y(t)]$, where $\bar{X}(t)$ (network inputs) and $Y(t)$ (network output) are calculated from equations (2.12). Table 2.1 shows a part of the unscaled (raw) data.

We use feedforward, layered and fully connected networks. The learning algorithm is standard backpropagation with a momentum term. The activation function is the asymmetric sigmoid with a (0, 1) range. When not otherwise stated, the first 800 patterns are used for training and the remaining 225 for testing.

We experimented with a wide range of architectures, having fixed all control parameters except for the cost function. The experiments are discussed fully in [ReZaBe93]. The cost function is either the standard Ordinary Least Squares (see equation 1.4) or the Discounted Least Squares (see equation 2.11).

Figure 2.2 shows the goodness of fit of the two methods in-sample (in the best case). The solid line is the target return, the dotted line is the predicted return (in-sample) for 800 days. In Figure 2.2(a) the standard quadratic tries to minimise the error equally across all observations and makes significant overshoots with respect to the most recent data (having fitted the earlier part of the curve better). In Figure 2.2(b) the time-sensitive quadratic shows near-perfect fit for the most recent observations with most of the error appearing at the beginning of the time series as expected.

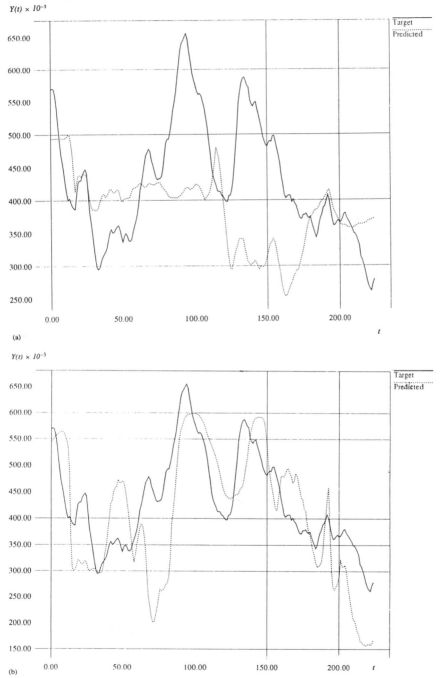

Figure 2.3 Target versus predicted $Y(t)$, **out-of-sample**, for 6-7-4-1, $\lambda = 0.3$, $\alpha = 0.7$. (a) unmodified cost function, (b) 'time-sensitive' cost function and $dt = 60$ for X_4

Figure 2.3 shows the goodness of fit of the two methods *out-of-sample*. Again the solid line is the actual return, and the dotted line is the predicted return for 200 days immediately after training. The discounted least squares cost function (Figure 2.3(b)) resulted in a substantial improvement in generalisation performance which is visible with the naked eye.

The idea behind the 'time-sensitive' cost function is for the training procedure to take into account gradually changing input–output relationships, by assigning more credit to the most recent patterns. It could be seen as an expansion of the random-walk hypothesis, which literally states that the best prediction of tomorrow's price is today's price. Generally, we expected a trade-off between reduced convergence ability and increased generalisation ability. However, the interactions between the cost function and the other parameters which influence the network performance are complicated and not easily identifiable. For a complete treatment see [ReZaBe93].

CONTROLLING THE GRADIENT DESCENT/ASCENT

A third important mechanism for controlling the performance of neural learning is the choice of control parameters for the gradient descent into the error surface. Several researchers have experimented with the addition of extra terms in the gradient descent formula (such as momentum terms and second derivatives) and have demonstrated the usefulness of the approach. An important term in the control of the gradient descent is the learning rate.

The *learning rate* λ (otherwise known as the *synaptic plasticity coefficient* or *step size*) essentially influences the magnitude of weight changes and, hence, is crucial for learning performance. However, it is difficult to find appropriate learning rates: on the one hand, a learning rate of small magnitude implies small changes of the weights even when greater weight changes are necessary (there are two reasons for requiring greater weight changes: first, speed of conversion; and second, network stability — large learning rate values may also be a way of helping the network escape from a local minimum). On the other hand, a learning rate of greater magnitude implies greater weight changes. The problem of finding appropriate learning rates can be viewed as a specific instance of the stability–plasticity dilemma which is expressed by the problem of how a learning system can be designed to remain plastic in response to significant new events, yet also remain stable in response to irrelevant events. Learning-rate adjustment constitutes an attempt to resolve this dilemma.

In principle, there are two approaches to learning-rate adjustment: first, to use one learning rate for the entire network; second, and more sophisticated, to use one learning rate for each weight. In the latter case, the general heuristics of how learning-rate update has to be performed can be described as follows. If consecutive changes of a weight have the same sign then the learning rate associated with this weight should be incremented. If consecutive changes of a weight have different signs (that is, they oscillate around the optimal change) then the associated learning rate should be decremented. A central problem arising from the use of modifiable learning rates, one for each direction, is that overall learning may degenerate to local learning. Furthermore, using modifiable learning rates leads to the distinction between two types of adaptation rule: weight adaptation rules and learning-rate adaptation rules.

Again, the ability to change the learning rate dynamically, under certain circumstances, can be viewed as an extra degree of freedom rather than an additional burden.

NETWORK ARCHITECTURE

The architecture of a neural network system is defined by the arrangement of its units, that is, the set of all weighted connections between units.

A layered or hierarchical network is one whose units are hierarchically organized into disjoint layers. Based on this hierarchical ordering, it is usual to distinguish between *lower* and *higher* layers. In a fully connected network, each unit in a layer is fully connected to every unit in the layer below and above. A bottom-up (top-down) network is a layered network whose units only affect units at the same and higher (lower) layers. An interactive network is a layered network having both bottom-up and top-down connections. A feedforward network is a layered network whose units only affect units at higher layers, whose lowest layer is an input layer, and whose intermediate layers are hidden layers.

The topology of the network is very important in determining the cognitive characteristics of the network and particularly its generalisation ability. Generalisation is the main property that should be sought from a neural network system; it determines the amount of data needed to train the system such that a correct response is produced when presented with patterns outside the training set. Although various successful applications of neural networks have been described in the literature, the conditions in which good generalisation performance can be obtained are not yet understood. Theoretical studies [Denker87] have shown that the likelihood of *correct* generalisation depends of the size of the hypothesis space (that is, the total number of networks considered), the size of the solution space (the set of networks that give good generalisation), and the number of training examples. If the hypothesis space is too large and/or the number of training examples is too small, then there will be a vast number of networks which are consistent with the training data, only a small set of which lie in the true solution space, so poor generalisation is likely. A common-sense rule is to minimise the number of free parameters in the network so that the likelihood of correct generalisation is increased. But this must be done without reducing the size of the network to the point where the desired function(s) can no longer be computed.

Reducing the number of free parameters in the network does not necessarily imply a reduction on the size of the network. Techniques such as weight sharing [RuHiWi86] can be used to reduce the number of free parameters while preserving the size of the network and specifying some symmetries that the problem may have.

Three main techniques can be used to construct a reduced-size network. The first is problem-independent and consists of dynamically deleting 'useless' connections during training. This can be done by adding a term to the cost function that penalises large networks with many parameters. Several authors have described such schemes, usually implemented with a non-proportional weight decay [Chauvi89, HanPra89] or using 'gating coefficients'. Generalization performance has been reported to increase significantly on small problems. The main drawbacks of this technique are that it requires a fine-tuning of the pruning coefficient to avoid catastrophic effects, and that the convergence is slowed down significantly.

The second technique is weight sharing. Weight sharing consists in having several connections controlled by a single parameter (weight). Weight sharing can be interpreted as imposing equality constraints among the connection strengths. An interesting feature of weight sharing is that it can be implemented with very little computational overhead.

The third technique, which is essentially a generalization of weight sharing, is called 'weight-space transformation' [LeCun89]. Weight-space transformation is based on the fact that the search performed by the learning procedure need not be done in the space of connection strengths, but can be done in any parameter space that is suitable to the task. This can be achieved provided that the connection strengths can be computed from the parameters through a given transformation, and provided that the Jacobian matrix of this transformation is known to enable the computation of the partial derivatives of the cost function with respect to the parameters.

Since reducing the size of the network will also reduce its generality, some knowledge about the task domain will be necessary in order to preserve the network's ability to solve the problem. Such *a priori* knowledge is readily available for many application domains. Figure 2.4 shows three feedforward network architectures for handwritten character recognition. The example is based on the account by [LeCun89].

The first network is a fully connected network with a single layer of hidden units. LeCun [LeCun89] reports that the network learns a randomly selected training set perfectly but it generalises badly when presented with patterns outside the training set. By using the (application-dependent) observation that the problem is basically feature extraction, it is possible to construct a second network which is performing a two-step data compression task. The generalisation performance here is reported to have improved significantly. Finally, by further constraining the network architecture to preserve shift invariant features, generalisation can be further improved.

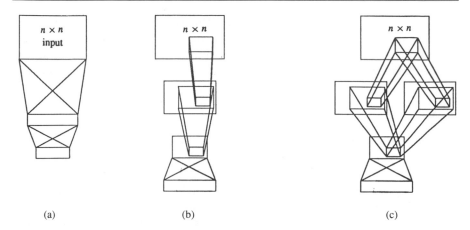

Figure 2.4 Three feedforward network architectures: (a) hierarchical fully connected; (b) hierarchical locally connected; (c) hierarchical constrained network with shared connections

TRAINING TIME AND INITIAL CONDITIONS

In addition to the main parameters discussed earlier there are two further control mechanisms worth mentioning.

Training Time

The number of presentations of the data set to the network during training is referred as the *training time*. A related term is the *epoch*, which stands for the number of training cycles after which an update of the connection weights is performed. Epoch is one of the gradient descent control terms and is typically fixed to 1. The training time is an important factor in controlling network overfitting. During the first few passes over the training set, the backpropagation algorithm extracts the main features of the data set (due to the averaging effect of the quadratic cost function). As training progresses and provided that the network has a sufficiently large number of free parameters, the procedure will start overfitting the training data. The most common way to control overfitting with the use of training time is through cross-validation and premature termination of training. The training data are randomly divided into a training and a cross-validation set. The training set is used in the normal way, while the cross-validation set is used to test the out-of-sample performance of the estimator. Training is terminated once the cross-validation error begins to rise. Typically several runs with different random splits for the training and cross-validation sets are carried out to ensure statistical stability.

Initial Weights

The backpropagation learning procedure requires unequal initial weights. If all weights start out with equal values and if the solution requires that unequal weights be developed, the system can never learn [RuHiWi86]. Furthermore, the initial weight matrix defines the starting point on the weight-error surface. Typically several training runs with different random initial weights are required to test the statistical stability.

SUMMARY

The network engineering parameters can be classified in two distinct groups according to their function during the application development. The first group comprises network architecture, cost function and activation function; together with a data set these define a weight-error surface. Given the weight-error surface, then the gradient descent control parameters, the number of iterations and the initial weights define a point (weight matrix, mean squared error) on the weight-error surface (see Figure 2.5).

It is surprisingly interesting that given the weight-error surface we can usually find a point with a near lowest mean squared error (MSE), although there are no theoretical guarantees [RuHiWi86].

The generalisation ability of the network is likely to be good, relative to its convergence ability, when the weight-error surfaces for the in- and out-of-sample data sets are very similar. It must be pointed out, that the similarity of the weight-error surfaces is not a guaranty of good generalisation in absolute terms. The

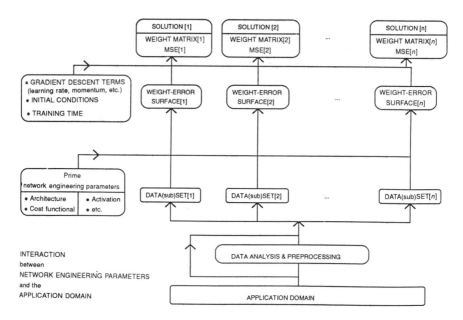

Figure 2.5   Relation between network engineering parameters and the application domain subsets

generalisation ability of the network is likely to be good in absolute terms if and only if the convergence ability is good and the weight-error surfaces in- and out-of-sample are very similar. Assuming that given the weight-error surface, there is always a proper combination of the second group's network engineering parameters describing a point with a near-lowest MSE, then the importance of cost function, activation function and network architecture ('*prime*' network engineering parameters), becomes paramount in achieving good convergence ability.

For a given set of prime network engineering parameters and any two data sets used correspondingly for in-sample training and out-of-sample testing, the magnitude of the observed dissimilarity between the two weight-error surfaces is due to two reasons. First, data sets contain a certain amount of noise. Assuming optimal prime network engineering parameters, the network during training will achieve the best possible fit to that noisy data. In effect this will degenerate the generalisation performance of the network. Second, changes in input–output relationships (very common in financial applications [ReFrZa93]) will also result in a more or less different weight-error surface out-of-sample, and consequently in reduced generalisation ability.

From the above it is clear that neural networks are not exactly 'model-free' (universal) estimators. Although, they do not need any explicit *a priori* assumption of a model, the choice of the prime engineering parameters defines a subset U^*, of specific dimensionality (*solution space*), of the universe of solutions U of all possible dimensionalities. Furthermore, a specific data set defines a subspace of the solution space. All network solutions lie in that *solution subspace*. We can distinguish two parts in the corresponding error of the 'best' solution (assuming it can be found) in that subspace (weight-error surface): the *bias* part, due to the reduction of the universe of solutions to the solution space; and the *variance* part, due to the further reduction of the solution space to the solution subspace [GeBiDo92]. The choice of the word 'variance' reflects the effect of different data sets on the stability of network solutions. Although it is possible to reduce the bias part of the error (for example, with extensive experimentation with different sets of prime network engineering parameters) the variance part of the error depends on the data. To put it simply, the optimised network solutions are 'tied' to specific data sets.

Since any data set is a subset of the application domain, it either describes partially the input–output relationship, or gives a snapshot of a gradually changing relationship. If the former is the case, then the physical size of the data set should be as large as possible, in an attempt to maximize the amount of information we use for training and consequently the generalisation ability. If the underlying input–output relationship changes gradually, then the previous recipe is not guaranteed to work, and different approaches (such as time-sensitive cost functions) should be sought.

The above describes the essence of the problem of stability of the network 'optimal' solutions across different subsets of the application domain. There are cross-validation techniques [Moody92] which attempt to tackle this problem, but they assume that the *prime* network engineering parameters are fixed. However, since optimal solutions require optimal prime network engineering parameters, the amount of work involved can be prohibiting.

Identifying the optimal prime network engineering parameters for a particular data set is not a trivial task. The 'brute force' method, of trying many different combinations of these parameters, can be extremely time-consuming. A number of sophisticated methods for deriving the optimal network architecture have been developed. In general, these fall into three broad categories: *constructive* techniques; *analytical estimation* techniques; and *pruning* techniques (see Chapter 3). Although some good results have been reported, their reliability still has to be tested and their complexity to be reduced so that they can become commonplace in everyday application development.

Having reviewed the performance measures for neural learning, and the mechanisms that can be used to control these measures, Chapter 3 reviews the main types of technique for achieving optimal performance, and discusses how these mechanisms are used. We start with analytic estimation techniques which attempt to estimate the number of hidden units required for optimal performance *a priori*, so that a good if not optimal, starting point for the network architecture can be used.

3

Methods for Optimal Network Design

Apostolos-Paul Refenes, *London Business School, UK*

Recently, several methods have been proposed which attempt to get around the problems of slow convergence and optimal network architecture. The aim of these methods is to develop learning procedures which will achieve optimum network configuration. The most common methods fall into three groups:

1. *Analytic estimation* — techniques in which algebraic or statistical analysis is used to determine hidden unit size *a priori*. By analysing the size and dimensionality of the input vector space, analytic techniques are able to give an *a priori* estimate of the number of hidden units.

2. *Constructive techniques* — where the hidden units are constructed in layers one by one as they are needed. By showing that at least one unit in each layer makes fewer mistakes than a corresponding unit in the earlier layer, eventual convergence to zero errors is guaranteed. Among these techniques are cascade correlation [FahLeb90], the tiling algorithm [MezNad89], the neural decision tree [Gallan86], the upstart algorithm [Frean89] and the CLS procedure [RefVit91].

3. *Pruning techniques* — which operate in the opposite direction by pruning the network and removing 'redundant' or least sensitive connections. These include network pruning [SieDow91] and artificial selection [HeFiZi92].

These techniques differ in complexity, convergence speed and, most importantly, in their generalisation performance. Although most, but not all, methods will guarantee to learn the classification, no realistic statement can be made about

Neural Networks in the Capital Markets. Edited by Apostolos-Paul Refenes.
© 1995 John Wiley & Sons Ltd

their generalisation performance. The novice reader may skip this section at first reading.

The investigation of methods for dynamic configuration of network architectures has wide-ranging benefits. First, the availability of reliable and accurate techniques for dynamic configuration will free the application developer from the burden of trial-and-error experimentation with differing network configurations. The second benefit is purely technical. Learning procedures with static architectures operate by attaching weights to a prespecified network so that a certain functionality is achieved. This is the classical credit assignment problem. Dynamic procedures explore approaches in which both the network and weights are generated together. It is argued that this is an easier problem to solve because the necessity of realising a solution in a fixed network is an additional constraint to the problem. Thus, the requirement of dynamically configuring the architecture is not an added burden, but an extra degree of freedom.

In the following sections we review the three main types of learning procedure outlined above. Chapter 6 outlines the principles of computational learning theory and its applicability to network design.

ANALYTICAL ESTIMATION TECHNIQUES

Recent work appears to indicate that the number of hidden nodes in the network is a function of the number of input training patterns. Several rules of thumb have been cited, based on statistical classification theory, conjecturing that the number of connections should be less than one-tenth of the sample size. It is also conjectured that the number of hidden units (H) is of the order of $(T - 1)$ and of $\log_2 T$, where T is the sample size. The following sections investigate the basis for these estimates.

Algebraic Estimation

Several researchers have reported that the number of hidden units in a network depends only on the number of input vectors (that is, sample size) [Lippma87, GorSej88]. The conjectures made above do not include effects of the input dimensionality. It has been shown subsequently [MirCao89] that input dimensionality is a factor which together with the number of hidden units, defines the maximum number of separable regions obtainable in the input space.

Consider a set of input patterns represented by vectors in d-dimensional Euclidean space $\mathbb{R}^d$. A hidden node in the first layer acts as a $(d - 1)$-dimensional hyperplane that forms two decision regions. Mirchandani and Cao [MirCao89] showed that the d-dimensional input space is linearly separable into M regions, if there exist M disjoint regions whose boundaries are composed of portions of hyperplanes. These regions can be associated with classes. That is, M regions may

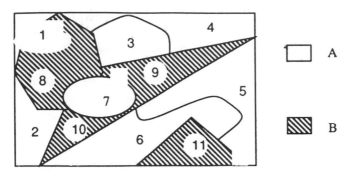

Figure 3.1   A two-class classification problem

be merged into C classes, where $C \leqslant M$. An example of a two-class problem is shown in Figure 3.1, where the two-dimensional input space is separated into 11 regions, each of which is associated with one of the two classes A and B.

The task of the connections between the hidden units and the output nodes is to associate classes with regions. The number of separable regions identifies the minimum number of training patterns, T, required for training a two-layer perceptron. Ideally, placing a training vector in each of the M separable regions (that is, $T = M$), should ensure the separation of the input space into M regions. In practice $T > M$, since the learning algorithm does not assure convergence to a global minimum.

Based on these basic notions, Mirchandani and Cao formulated a relationship between M, H and d:

$$M(H, d) = \sum_{k=0}^{d} \binom{H}{k} \qquad (3.1)$$

where

$$\binom{H}{k} = 0 \text{ for } H < k.$$

Using this formulation, Mirchandani and Cao [Mirch89] repeated several experiments which confirmed earlier results achieved by empirical estimations in common benchmarks. For example, the XOR problem in two dimensions gives $d = 2$, $M = 3$, and is seen to be solvable with this result. For $H = 2 \leqslant d = 2$, the result gives $M = 2^2 = 4$. Hence two hidden units are sufficient to solve the problem, as is well known.

The main problem with algebraic techniques is that they are static, and require a previous analysis of the dimensionality of the input vector space. This is useful for establishing a lower bound on the number of training patterns required for feedforward networks provided that the dimensionality of the problem is known. However, the solution suffers several disadvantages. First, for most real classification problems a feature space analysis is not possible. There are too many inputs, which cannot be regarded as independent. For any but trivial problems it is impossible to determine what shapes the classes would take in feature space and whether they would be disjoint, concave or simple. The second difficulty is that networks with more than one hidden layer can find solutions that do not satisfy the assumptions underlying the analysis. The third and probably the worst failure is that networks of the precalculated minimum size only rarely move to a solution.

Heuristic Estimation

Heuristic estimation techniques attempt to deal with the problems associated with non-trivial applications where the assumptions underlying rigorous algebraic techniques no longer hold true. Heuristic techniques are often developed from more rigorous approaches and observations that hold true for trivial (benchmark) problems. Typical of these is the approach proposed by Gutierrez *et al.* [Gutier89] which is based on conflict estimation.

A *conflict* is a set of input–output relationships that require incompatible weight values when the mapping is tried on a single-layer perceptron. The estimate produced is data-dependent and thus overcomes, to some extent, the difficulties of static techniques.

For an output unit O_i, the number of conflicts depends on the specific responses of O_i to the input vectors contained in the training set. For each output unit, the heuristic estimation procedure then identifies the number of conflicts present, C_{O_i}. Finally, the total number of hidden units, h, is determined by summing C_{O_i}, the numbers obtained for each individual output unit. In essence, the number of hidden units is estimated on the basis of the superposition principle whereby the overall network can be described by the sum of its individual components.

The heuristic estimation procedure developed by Gutierrez is applicable to binary-value networks and is described in Algorithm 3.I. We define the *activity*, a of a unit vector, $\mathbf{u}^r$, as the sum of its components (that is, $a = \sum_{i=0}^{r} u_i$, the number of bits set to 1). The *null* vector has activity zero. The estimation procedure requires the null vector to be included as part of the training set. An output unit is referred to as *nominally inactive* if it produces a 0 for the null input vector and *nominally active* if it produces 1 for the null input vector. The *relative activity* of an output unit with respect to a set of input vectors with a common activity level x is the number of times that the unit is active. Similarly, the relative inactivity of an output unit with respect to a set of input vectors is the number of times the unit produces 0 for the inputs in this set.

The heuristic estimation procedure normally overestimates the number of hidden units by as much as 10% [Gutier89], but very rarely underestimates it. Reported results show generalisation performance between 80% and 96% for the NETtalk benchmark which is comparable to those obtained by other researchers [SejRos87].

1 Divide the input vector space into sets of common activity levels x and count the number of input vectors for each set. These sets will be referred to as the x-active input vectors and the cardinality of the set is N_x.

2 For each output unit, determine if the unit is nominally active or nominally inactive.

3 If the output unit is nominally active, determine its relative inactivity I_x with respect to each set of x-active input vectors. Similarly, if the output unit is nominally inactive determine its relative activity A_x.

4 For each output unit determine the value of x_{low}, which is the lowest input activation level for which

$$x A_x \geqslant m/4$$

if the unit is nominally inactive, or

$$x I_x \geqslant m/4$$

if the unit is nominally active. Here m is the number of input units.

5 For the nominally active output units, determine the input activity level x_{max} which maximises I_x. For nominally inactive units find the input activity level x_{max} which maximises A_x. These two maximised values are called $I_{x,\text{max}}$ and $A_{x,\text{max}}$ respectively. The estimate for the number of conflicts expected for this output unit is:

$$C_a = \frac{A_{x,\text{max}}}{N_{x,\text{max}}}(m - x_{\text{low}})$$

for nominally inactive output unit, and

$$C_a = \frac{I_{x,\text{max}}}{N_{x,\text{max}}}(m - x_{\text{low}})$$

for nominally active units.

6 The estimated number of hidden units is then given by:

$$h = \sum_{i=1}^{n} C_{a,i}$$

where $C_{a,i}$ is the result of step 5 for the ith output unit and n is the number of output units.

Algorithm 3.I Heuristic estimation of hidden unit size

Summary

With respect to the convergence and generalisation performance measures, neither type of procedure described here can be evaluated. The reason for this is that both techniques are preprocessing techniques, and once the number of hidden nodes has been estimated, any learning algorithm can be used. Naturally, the learning algorithm will attempt to solve the problem using a fixed-size network and is subject to the constraints of traditional techniques.

The real question for analytic techniques is concerned with the accuracy to which they estimate hidden node size. Early work on algebraic techniques conjectured that hidden node size can be estimated only on the basis of the sample size. Both statistical and analytical arguments, as well as empirical results, were put forward to support this conjecture. Later work has demonstrated quite conclusively that this is not true, and at least an estimate of the dimensionality of the input vector space and feature analysis are required in order to estimate hidden unit size. Feature analysis of the input vector space is not a trivial task. Indeed, this is what the neural network is trying to achieve during learning.

Heuristic estimation procedures, such as that described earlier, attempt to give an approximate solution to the problem by preprocessing the input vector space to identify the degree of nonlinearity in the data. Even if it were possible to find exact conflict sets, the computational requirements would make the use of the technique impractical for large data sets. Nevertheless, in the absence of a strong model, analytical estimation provides a reasonable starting point.

In the following sections we discuss alternative ways of estimating hidden node size.

CONSTRUCTIVE TECHNIQUES

Constructive techniques are based on the principle that the hidden units of a network are constructed incrementally one by one as they are needed. The basic building block for constructive techniques is a *linear classifier*. This is defined as a simple node with a set of input weights w_i, a set of output weights W_o, and a simple learning rule (see Figure 3.2(a)). The components, $\langle v_1, \ldots, v_n \rangle$, of an input vector $\mathbf{V}$ which are mapped into a new vector, $\mathbf{V}^*$, whose components, V_j^*, are computed according to the following rule:

$$V_j^* = w_{o,j} f \left(\sum_{i=1}^{n} (w_i v_i) \right) \qquad (3.2)$$

A linear classifier can be trained to maximise or minimise the correlation between its outputs and some arbitrary quantity. Constructive learning starts with a fixed architecture. By showing that the addition of a new linear classifier produces less errors than the earlier architecture, eventual convergence to zero errors is guaranteed. An obvious way to use linear classifiers of this type is as mechanisms for correcting errors that the earlier network is making. This can be done by training the linear classifier to maximise the correlation between its output and the error that a specific node in the network is making. In this way, the classifier will develop corrective weights in its output connections. Once added into the network the weights of the linear classifier are frozen and the procedure is repeated.

Linear classifiers can be connected to the network in at least two ways. First, they can be inserted between the last hidden node and the output units (see Figure 3.2(b)). Second, they can be inserted in the same way but connected to all the hidden units (see Figure 3.2(c)). In the simple case where the linear classifier produces binary values, it is called a *linear discriminant*.

Figure 3.2 shows a linear classifier and two ways of constructing networks with one output unit, by repeatedly extending the output until convergence is achieved. In this case, the construction of L_i is achieved by training to minimise the error between the desired output, and the classifier's actual output. In subsequent sections we shall see how other procedures such as cascade correlation train classifiers in the opposite direction.

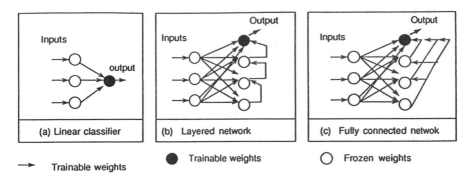

(a) Linear classifier   (b) Layered network   (c) Fully connected netwok

→ Trainable weights   ● Trainable weights   ○ Frozen weights

1 Construct a good (preferably optimal) set of weights for a linear classifier L_1. This is always possible and can be achieved using any of the gradient descent training algorithms (backpropagation, quickprop, etc.). If all (or the maximum number possible) of the training examples are correctly classified, exit. Otherwise freeze the weights for L_1.

2 Construct a good (preferably optimal) set of weights for a linear classifier L_{i+1} having inputs from the training examples and from linear classifier L_i. Depending on the training technique, it can be shown that D_{i+1} can correctly classify a greater number of training examples than D_i. Freeze the coefficients for D_{i+1}.

3 Repeat from step 2, a finite number of times until all, or the maximum number possible of training examples are correctly classified.

Figure 3.2 Generic algorithm for constructive learning

The convergence, generalisation and stability properties of these techniques depend upon the type of linear classifier used, the way in which its weights are calculated (the learning rule), the type of sub-classification it is asked to learn, and the way in which it is inserted in the network. In the following sections we review typical examples of constructive techniques.

Tiling Algorithm

The tiling algorithm operates by adding layers of hidden units, one at a time. The algorithm operates on networks with binary-valued neurons. To illustrate the operation of the tiling algorithm, Mezard and Nadal [MezNad89] use networks with only one output neuron, but the algorithm can be extended to networks with multiple output neurons.

The tiling algorithm starts with no hidden units, and this single-layered perceptron is trained until the output produces correct mappings for a subset of the training set. If no convergence is achieved, the algorithm extends the output layer by as many nodes as are necessary to divide the training set into so called 'faithful' classes. When this is done, a new output node is created and is connected to the old output layer which subsequently becomes a hidden layer. The connections from the hidden layer to the new output unit are computed (by perceptron learning) so that the newly created output input makes fewer errors than its predecessor.

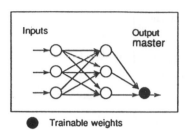

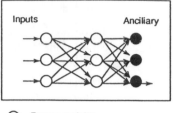

1   Forward pass on the entire data set. The master unit, m_i, divides the training set into two classes: those that it recognises correctly (*faithful*) and those still producing errors (*unfaithful*). If there are still errors, we add a set of auxiliary units at the level as m_i. The task of these auxiliary units is to form internal representations so that input patterns having different outputs should have different internal representations.

2   Add an auxiliary unit. Connect the unit to all units in the layer above. Select one of the unfaithful classes and train the newly added unit to subdivide the unfaithful class into (at least) a faithful and an unfaithful class.

3   Repeat from step 2 until no further unfaithful classes remain. This is always possible to do; in the worse case we shall have a one ancillary unit for each input pattern

4   Add a new output (master) unit. Connect the unit to all the nodes in the layer above. Train the newly added unit to learn the mapping between the internal representation and the desired output. If convergence is achieved exit, else repeat from step 1.

Figure 3.3   The tiling algorithm

The operation of the algorithm is described in Figure 3.3. Suppose we have L-layers of hidden units and one output unit (called the *master* unit). The master unit (which is the first unit in each layer) plays a special role: during the growth of the network, the master unit of the most recently built layer gives a better approximation of the desired output than the previous one, so that eventual convergence to zero errors is guaranteed. In each layer, once the master unit has been obtained, the algorithm checks to see if it gives the exact output. If not, new 'ancillary units' are added to the layer until this layer gives a 'faithful representation' of the problem. The following definitions are needed.

To each input pattern ξ_μ there corresponds a set of values of the neurons in the Lth layer. We shall refer to this set of values as the *internal representation* of pattern ξ_μ in the Lth layer. (The 0th layer is the input layer; the 0th representations are simply the input patterns themselves.) We say that two patterns belong to the same class (for the Lth layer) if they have the same internal representation, which we call the *prototype* of the class. If there are p_L distinct classes, we have p_L patterns (of $N_L + 1$ units), each of which is the representation of at least one input pattern. The problem now is to map these p_L prototypes onto the desired output.

The tiling algorithm operates on binary-valued neurons and uses the perceptron learning procedure (or any equivalent linear discriminant such as the pocket algorithm) as the building block for its convergence. It constructs a regular, layered network with full interconnections between layers.

Cascade Correlation

The cascade-correlation algorithm operates on two basic principles. The first, is the cascade-architecture principle whereby hidden units are added to the network one at a time and do not change after they have been installed. This is equivalent to building permanent feature detectors in the network. The second, is the learning algorithm which creates and installs the new hidden units. For each hidden unit created, the algorithm attempts to maximise the magnitude of the correlation between the new units' output and the residual error signal that it wishes to minimise.

The learning algorithm begins with no hidden units. The direct input–output connections are trained as well as possible over the entire training set. The weight

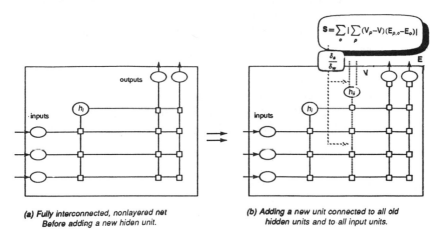

$$S = \sum_o | \sum_p (V_p - V)(E_{p,o} - E_o)|$$

(a) *Fully interconnected, nonlayered net* *Before adding a new hiden unit.*

(b) *Adding a new unit connected to all old* *hidden units and to all input units.*

1   Add a new unit H_{ji}. Connect H_{ji} to all existing hidden units H_i. This creates a new sub-network which hangs off the main network. The newly created sub-network consists of $I + H + O$ new trainable connections where I is the number of input units, O is the number of output units, and H is the number of existing hidden units.

2   Initialise the newly created connections with randomised weights. The rest of the network connections remain unchanged.

3   Forward pass. The old network reproduces the same output vector with error $\mathbf{E}^o$. The newly created sub-network produces an output vector $\mathbf{V}$. The task now is to compute the correlation, S, between these two vectors and compute the new connection strengths.

4   Backward pass. This is only done for two layers of connection weights. The outputs from H_{ji} and the inputs to H_{ji}. Repeat from step 3 until convergence.

5   Connect H_{ji} to all the output nodes. The resulting network will make less errors than before.

6   Forward pass on the entire network. If convergence has been achieved then exit, else train the entire network again.

7   Backward pass on the entire network. Train the entire network for a 'user controlled' number of iterations. If convergence is achieved then exit, else repeat from step 1.

Figure 3.4   The cascade-correlation algorithm

update rule can be any well-known algorithm for single-layered networks. At some point this training will approach an asymptote. When no significant error reduction has occurred after a (user-controlled) number of iterations through the data set, the algorithm is stopped. To reduce the error further a new hidden unit is added to the network.

The task of this newly added unit is to reduce the error at the output layer. To do so the unit is first connected to all previous hidden units and to the network's input units (that is, non-layered fully connected). The addition of the new unit produces a single sub-network which is trained independently to maximise the correlation between its own error and that of the existing network. The idea is that if the unit correlates positively with the error at a given output, then the hidden unit will develop a negative connection weight to that output unit and thus cancel some of the error. Conversely, if the hidden unit correlates negatively, the output weight will be positive. The training procedure is described in Figure 3.4.

The cascade-correlation procedure uses a combination of two learning rules. In the first stage, during the training of the entire network, any standard multi-layered perceptron rule can be used (the fully connected architecture can be reduced to a layered one by the addition of dummy units). In the second stage, during the training of the sub-network, gradient ascent is performed on the newly added unit. The cost function for this is given in Figure 3.4, and Gaussian thresholding units are used.

Constructive Learning by Specialisation

The CLS procedure combines three key ideas. The first is similar to the cascade architecture, in which hidden units are added to the network one at a time and do not change after they have been added. These units become permanent feature detectors. The second is the *constructive learning algorithm* which creates and installs the new hidden units in a way that reduces the error and also does not disturb the feature detectors. The third idea is *similarity approximation*, in which the new unit is trained to behave for future patterns in a way consistent with the remaining input vectors.

Training the network to produce a desired output vector $\mathbf{o}^{(r)}$ when presented with pattern $\mathbf{i}^{(r)}$ involves testing the network to see if the actual output vector $\mathbf{a}^{(r)}$ is in agreement with the desired output vector $\mathbf{d}^{(r)}$, and then adding a new hidden unit to correct the residual error. Only the new unit is then trained to recognise those patterns for which the network was in error. The basic idea is that a hidden unit is constructed with the purpose of correcting the mistakes at the output layer. If we are considering the family of sigmoids given by $f(x) = k + c/(1 + e^{Tx})$ then the following proposition holds:

Proposition 3.1: For all real x, c, y, ε, k, with $y - \varepsilon - k \neq 0$, if $f(x) = y$ then $\exists\ P = (1/T) \ln(c/(y - \varepsilon - k)) - x$, such that $f(x + P) = y - \varepsilon$.

Proof. The proposition is easy to verify. By definition, from (1.3),

$$f(x + P) = k + \frac{c}{1 + e^{T(x+P)}}$$

$$= k + \frac{c}{1 + e^{T(x+1/T \ln((c/(y-\varepsilon-k))-1)-x)}}$$

$$= k + \frac{c}{1 + e^{T(1/T \ln((c/(y-\varepsilon-k))-1))}}$$

$$= k + \frac{c}{1 + e^{\ln((c/(y-\varepsilon-k))-1)}}$$

$$= k + \frac{c}{1 + \dfrac{c}{y - \varepsilon - k} - 1}$$

$$= k + y - \varepsilon - k$$

$$= y - \varepsilon \qquad \qquad \square$$

We use this result as the basic building block for the constructive learning procedure. The basic idea is that neural nodes, when in error, can be corrected by the addition of an extra input P to produce the desired output and that P can be computed analytically.

The CLS procedure is illustrated in Figure 3.5. It begins with some N inputs and M outputs and at least one hidden unit. The number of inputs and outputs is dictated by the problem and by the input–output representation. Every input is connected to the unit in the hidden layer which is in turn connected to every unit in the output layer. The output units may just produce a linear threshold sum of their weighted inputs, or they may use some nonlinear activation function (cf. cascade correlation).

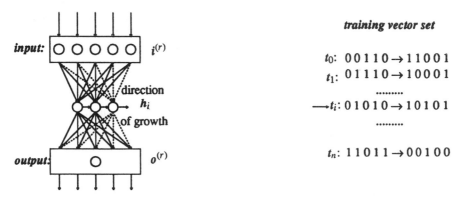

Figure 3.5 The constructive learning procedure. The network grows sideways, new units are added to correct the mistakes at the outputs, and are then trained to remain silent for those patterns for which there are other feature detectors

The learning is on-line and the algorithm begins with only a single, fully connected hidden unit with randomised connection strengths. The learning algorithm proceeds as shown below.

Step 1.   Feedforward test for training vector t_i. If the output o_r makes an error then add a new unit h_k. Connect h_k to the output unit o^r with a connection strength that corrects the error. The connection strength $w_{h,k}$ can be calculated analytically as follows. Prior to adding the new unit h_k, the output at o^r is given by:

$$\mathbf{o}_r = f \left(\sum_{i=0}^{k-1} w_{h_{i,0}}, v_{h_{i,0}} \right) = \mathbf{t}_i^d \pm \varepsilon \tag{3.3}$$

where $\varepsilon = |o^r - t_d^r|$. After adding $h_{k,0}$ the error at o^r will be eliminated. Thus,

$$\mathbf{o}^r = f \left(\sum_{i=0}^{k-1} w_{h_{i,0}} v_{h_{i,0}} + w_{h_k} v_{h_k} \right) = \mathbf{t}_i^d \tag{3.4}$$

Using $f(x) = A \tanh(Sx)$ we expand (3.4), and solving for $w_{h_k} v_{h_k}$ we obtain:

$$w_{h_k} v_{h_k} = \frac{\log_e \left(\dfrac{2A}{A - t_i^d} - 1 \right) - 2S \sum_{i=0}^{k-1} w_{h_{i,0}} v_{h_{i,0}}}{2S} \tag{3.5}$$

There are two unknowns in (3.5); the weight for h_k and its value. If we fix the value that h_k has to produce for pattern t_i, we can compute the weight and vice versa.

Step 2.   Connect the newly added unit H_k to all the input units. The connection strengths must be such that the unit recognises the current vector t_i and none of the previous vectors, $t_0, t_1, \ldots, t_{i-1}$, so that the cognitive properties of the network are not disturbed. This is achieved by training the newly added unit h_i such that:
1.   unit h_i must be trained to be active at pattern t_i;
2.   unit h_i must be trained to be inactive at patterns $t_{0,\ldots,i-1}$;
3.   unit h_i must be active for at least one other pattern in $t_{i+1}, \ldots, t_n$.
As this is not always a linearly separable problem, h_i must be a rather sophisticated unit (see text).

The main point to note here is the method of training the new units. The current unit is trained using the current pattern and all the patterns that appear before the current pattern in the training set. The new unit is trained such that it will be active for the current pattern but inactive for all the patterns that appear before the current pattern in the training set. The patterns that appear after the current pattern in the training set are not taken into consideration. It is possible that different patterns appearing after the current pattern in the training set may activate the current unit. This is done to increase the generalisation capabilities of the network.

The procedure now moves to the next pattern in the training set. Exactly the same procedure that was used for training pattern t_i is used to train pattern t_{i+1}. This carries on until the algorithm has been through all the training patterns in the training set.

The generalisation properties of the CLS procedure depend solely on the way in which hidden units are trained. For the purposes of convergence it is necessary to train a hidden unit at t_i to acquire the inhibitory and excitatory behaviour described earlier. As long as the conditions 1 and 2 in the algorithm are obeyed we could train the hidden unit in several ways.

If the hidden unit were trained to recognise only pattern t_i and no other pattern, convergence could still be possible (in fact it is much faster). However, because each unit could only recognise a specific vector, the overall network would not be able to recognise anything outside the training set. The minimal conditions for a lower bound on generalisation are as shown in step 2 above. Any arbitrary pattern would suffice for condition 3, but the higher the correlation of the unit's behaviour to the regularities within the training set, the higher the probability of good generalisation. Such behaviour can be achieved by increasing the sophistication of h_i. There are several ways of doing this. Figure 3.6 shows a construction in which h_i is composed of three subsidiary units: A, B, C. In this construction, the tasks of the subsidiary units are defined as follows:

A: is a linear discriminant; it is connected to all input units and to the previous hidden unit h_{i-1}. A is trained to produce the desired output for pattern t_i and 0 for all other patterns.

B: is a similarity approximator. It is connected in the same way as A but it is trained to minimise the least square error between its output and the desired output for pattern $t_{i+1}, \ldots, t_n$.

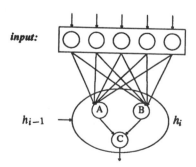

Figure 3.6 Hidden unit construction

C: is an arbitrator unit. It is connected to both A and B and sees the output of previous $A_j, j \in \{0, \ldots, i\}$. When A is active, C inhibits B and simply passes on the output of A. The connection strength between C and the output is calculated as in (3.5). When A_j is inactive C inhibits B and simply passes on the output of A ($\mathbf{o}^A$) suitably adjusted to cancel the effect of W_{h_k} by a simple division, i.e.

$$\mathbf{o}^C = \frac{\mathbf{o}^A}{w_{h_k}} \tag{3.6}$$

Convergence and generalisation proofs for the CLS procedure can be found in [RefCha92]. Broadly speaking, the CLS procedure has a simple geometric interpretation: rather than using hyperplanes to estimate class borders, it uses circles. The A unit denotes the centre of a new circle, while the B unit denotes the radius of the circle which is computed so that many observations belonging to the same class as t_i are included in the circle. Because only part of the network is retrained at each step the effective degrees of freedom in exploring the search space are reduced considerably.

Combined Linear Discriminant Techniques

An interesting technique for the dynamic configuration of networks is based on the combination of linear discriminants. A linear discriminant consists of a set of numerical weights W_i. An input vector $\mathbf{V}$ with components or 'features' $\langle V_1, \ldots, V_n \rangle$ is classified into one of two categories (true or false) according to whether the sum of its components is greater than some threshold W_0. Linear discriminants (for example, perceptrons) have been quite popular for practical applications. There are well known methods for determining good, but sub-optimal, linear discriminant weights including the pocket algorithm [Gallan86]. These algorithms also serve as the basis for the network-growing techniques discussed here.

While an individual linear discriminant has several features, it can only represent a small subset of Boolean functions, called *separable functions*. However, a network of linear discriminants can represent any Boolean function of n Boolean variables. Gallant [Gallan86] describes three algorithms for constructing networks based on linear discriminants.

The *tower-construction technique* builds linear discriminant networks in the form of a tower. Cells are added one by one and connected to the original inputs and to previous cells as shown in Figure 3.7(a). It can be shown that with arbitrarily high probability $P < 1$, the tower-construction technique will produce a network that correctly classifies a maximum number of training vectors.

The output from each level will correctly classify a greater number of training examples than the output from the previous level. This guarantees theoretical convergence to zero errors, but the training of each discriminant must first be defined so that it is possible to converge.

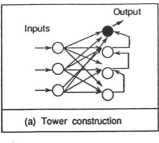
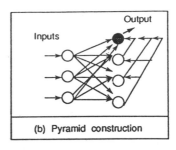

(a) Tower construction

(b) Pyramid construction

● Trainable weights   ○ Frozen weights

1   Construct a good (preferably optimal) set of coefficients for a single linear discriminant D_1. This is always possible and can be achieved by using any of the linear discriminant training algorithms (pocket algorithm, perceptron learning, etc.). If all (or the maximum number possible) of the training examples are correctly classified, exit. Otherwise freeze the coefficients for D_1.

2   Construct a good (preferably optimal) set of coefficients for linear discriminant D_{n+1} having inputs from the training examples and from discriminant D_n. Depending on the training technique, it can be shown that D_{n+1} can correctly classify a greater number of training examples than D_n. Freeze the coefficients for D_{n+1}.

3   Repeat from step 2 a finite number of times until all or the maximum number possible of training examples are correctly classified.

Figure 3.7   Network construction by combining linear discriminants

Figure 3.7(b) shows an extension of the tower-construction technique referred to as the *pyramid-construction technique*. The main difference is that in the pyramid-construction technique each new discriminant sees outputs from all the previous levels, not only the immediately preceding level. One would expect that fewer levels would be needed to solve the problem, and that this would speed up network generation. However, learning speed may be adversely affected, since each level must solve a problem in a space of higher dimensions than in the case of tower construction.

Combined linear discriminant techniques are a generic way of constructing networks dynamically. The convergence, complexity, generalisation and scalability properties of these techniques can only be assessed once the type of discriminant and training methods are known.

Other Techniques

Several researchers have been working in the field of constructive techniques. Whatever the terminology, they are in essence similar to those described here.

The *generation* method proposed by Honavar and Uhr [HonUhr88] enables a 'recognition cone' to modify its own topology by growing links and recruiting units whenever performance ceases to improve during learning by weight adjustment using backpropagation. This is typical of weight decay which is based on the assumption that nodes cannot reach convergence due to the dimensionality of the current network. This is not necessarily true as the slowness of the convergence may be due to the fact that gradient descent is performed on a long valley in the error space, where progress is extremely slow.

The *stepwise procedure* uses sub-nets of different conceptual interpretations [Kerlin92]. In this method, one first trains a one-layer network with the perceptron learning algorithm assuming that classes are linearly separable. For a class where this is not satisfied, one adds a sub-net to separate classes in a pairwise manner. For cases where this does not work either, one performs a piecewise approximation of boundaries using logical functions by additional sub-nets. As linear separability is rarely the case, one generally is obliged to separate classes in a pairwise manner two by two. The major drawback of this is that the number of hidden units increase exponentially with the number of class units.

The *dynamic node creation* method [Ash89] (explained also in Miller and Reinhardt [MilRei90]) trains networks with one hidden layer only. Given a certain net that is being trained, if the rate of decrease of error falls below a certain value, a new hidden unit is added and training is resumed when all connections continue to be modified. This is similar to the generic technique described in the Figure 3.2.

The *upstart* algorithm [Frean89] uses binary units. Like the tiling algorithm, first one unit is trained to learn the required associations using the pocket algorithm. If this is not successful, 'daughter' units are created to correct the output of this 'parent' unit, for 'wrongly on' and 'wrongly off' cases. The upstart algorithm is similar to the CLS procedure in that it uses hidden nodes to correct output units but computes the connections by the delta rule. The upstart algorithm sees the training set in batch mode, and only deals with nodes that can have up to two inputs each.

Another method proposed by [Hirose91] is quite similar to that proposed by [Ash89], in that it uses a network with only one hidden layer, adding further hidden units if the rate of decrease of error becomes small. Their contribution is that, once the network converges, the most recently added hidden unit is removed and the network is checked to determine whether the same function can be achieved by fewer hidden units. If the network cannot converge when a hidden unit is removed, the last network that converged is chosen as the final network.

NETWORK PRUNING TECHNIQUES

Pruning techniques operate in the opposite direction; they start with oversized networks and attempt to find redundant or least sensitive connection weights and remove them from the network. Some of these techniques are used as part of the run-time training algorithm, that is, merely to record sensitivity statistics, and others are used as stand-alone post-processing techniques. Three types of technique are described below.

Two-Stage Pruning

The *two-stage pruning technique* was described by Sietsma and Dow [SieDow91] and attempts to find the smallest network that will perform a particular task by 'pruning' a solution network (see Figure 3.8). When the initial network has moved to a solution, the outputs of the hidden units are analysed to determine whether any units are not contributing to the solution. If the output of a unit does not change for any input pattern, then that unit is not contributing to the solution. If the outputs of any two units are the same or opposite across all patterns, then the two units duplicate and one can be removed. It is argued that no information is lost to the next layer by removing such a unit.

Sietsma and Dow [SieDow91] demonstrate this procedure by an example network with 40 inputs, consisting of five units on the first layer, two units on the second layer, and a single output unit. The network was trained to separate smoothly varying input patterns from the same input with a perturbation added. Straight-line inputs gave an output of zero and inputs with a sine wave superimposed (at any phase delay) gave an output of one.

The first-layer outputs were approximately as given in Table 3.1. Using the two-stage algorithm, unit 1 can be discarded as its output is always close to zero. Units 3 and 5 have the same pattern of outputs with highs and lows reversed, so one of them can be discarded. This is the first stage of pruning.

The second stage of pruning is more drastic. With units 1 and 5 removed, the first-layer outputs have been changed (see Table 3.2). No unit duplicates another but it can be seen that while units 2 and 3 are essential, removing unit 4 would have no effect on the ability to separate the two classes. If unit 3 were removed the outputs on the first layer for pattern 6 would be the same as the outputs of the straight-line patterns. However, if unit 4 were cut out all patterns in the 'straight' class would still look different from all the patterns in the 'wavy' class. Unit 4 can

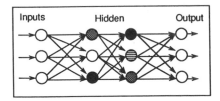
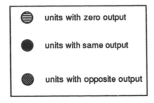

1   Determine hidden units with output close to zero for all input patterns and remove them.

2   Determine hidden units with the same or opposite outputs for all training patterns; and remove them.

3   Repeat for each layer. If the entire layer is removed, then reconnect and train again.

Figure 3.8   A two-stage pruning algorithm

Table 3.1 First-layer outputs before pruning.

Pattern	Units				
	1	2	3	4	5
Straight lines					
1	0.1	1	0	0	1
2	0.1	1	0	0	1
3	0.1	1	0	0	1
Wavy lines					
4	0.1	0	0	0	1
5	0.2	1	1	1	0
6	0.2	1	1	0	0

be removed and the network has now been pruned from 40-5-2-1 to 40-2-2-1.The first layer now reduces the number of different patterns received by the second layer from six to three. All 'straight' inputs have been reduced to a single pattern.

Examining the second-layer outputs reveals that the second layer does not reduce the number of different patterns. The output is still receiving three different patterns. One pair of inputs (0, 1) to the output unit corresponds to all the straight lines, and the two pairs of inputs (0.6 and 0, 0) indicate wavy lines. This is the same situation as holds after the first layer. Thus the second layer is not contributing to the solution and the entire layer can be removed. This is the third and most radical stage of pruning. The resulting 40-2-1 network is, of course, not a solution as the outputs of the first layer are not the same as those from the second layer, but with training it quickly becomes one.

The generalisation performance of the algorithm is based on the assumption that smaller networks can generalise better. However, this is not strictly true. The presence of low-sensitivity units may be critical in many circumstances. Consider, for example, the case in which the output of a low-sensitivity unit is combined with several others. When this combined output is multiplied by a high weight value and further combined with others, the net result may be that the internal dynamics

Table 3.2 First-layer outputs after pruning.

Pattern	Units		
	2	3	4
Straight lines			
1	1	0	0
2	1	0	0
3	1	0	0
Wavy lines			
4	0	0	0
5	1	1	1
6	1	1	0

of the network swings to a different attractor point and thus vectors in the borders between classes can be misclassified.

The two-stage procedure analyses the network by examining all units under the presentation of the entire data set. The procedure then removes each unit (along with its synaptic connections) that did not change state or replicate another unit. Thus it is possible to find a subset of the network whose performance is similar to that of the complete network, for a given training set. Unfortunately, scaling up this technique to large networks and large data sets will result in a prohibitively long training process.

The sensible use of the analysis for this procedure is dependent upon a good understanding of the problem one is trying to solve. In many large-scale, nontrivial applications, no clear understanding of the problem is readily available and thus the use of the procedure is limited.

Artificial Selection

The *artificial selection* method, due to Hagiwara [Hagiwa90] operates in two stages. During training, it records the effectiveness of hidden units and grows the network so that convergence can be achieved. In the second stage, after convergence has been achieved, the procedure makes a separate pass in which it uses the record of the effectiveness of a hidden node to remove 'bad' hidden nodes.

The artificial selection procedure starts training with a fixed number of hidden nodes. During a backward pass, the procedure computes a so called 'badness factor' for each hidden node. The idea is to record the node which is contributing the highest proportion of error in the overall least mean squared error at the output. The badness factor for the ith hidden unit, in the $(k-1)$th hidden layer is given by

$$BAD_i^{k-1} = \sum_p^n (e_i^{k-1,p})^2$$

$$= \sum_p^n \sum_j^i (w_i^{k-1} j^k \delta_j^k)^2 \qquad (3.7)$$

where δ_j^{k-1} is the error at the ith unit in the $(k-1)$th layer as computed by the error backpropagation rule. From (3.7) and Figure 3.9, the 'badness' factor indicates the degree of convergence. It is the sum of the backpropagated error component over all patterns for each hidden unit. All the weights connecting units which have large badness factors should be changed by a large amount and vice versa.

The artificial selection procedure attempts to reduce convergence times and, at the same time, creates the conditions that are required to produce optimal networks. By dynamically resetting the hidden units which contribute the most in the total error, the procedure tries to compensate for errors that are due to the gradient descent being trapped in either local minima or long valleys. By dynamically adding

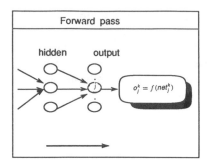

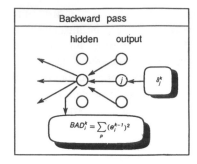

1 Compute the total squared error at the output layer; when the variation of the total squared error becomes small, detect the worst hidden unit.

2 Reset all the weights connected to the worst hidden unit to small random values; keep a count of all resets.

3 When the reset count reaches a user-controlled upper limit, add extra hidden unit to the layer.

4 If convergence reached prune the network, else repeat from step 1.

1 Continue learning for further convergence until some condition is satisfied.

2 Determine the hidden unit with the highest badness factor; and remove the unit. All weights should be copied before removing the unit.

3 Forward pass; if convergence is achieved exit, else repeat from step 1. To accelerate convergence use the algorithm defined opposite.

Figure 3.9   The artificial selection algorithm for network pruning

hidden units, it changes the shape of the error surface at the point of the highest error, hoping to find an alternative route to the global minimum. There is no guarantee that the procedure will do so; but by keeping a record of the units with worse error it would be possible to guarantee that the procedure will learn the maximum possible number of training examples with probability approaching 1 as the number of iterations increases.

Weight-Error Sensitivity

The main idea in *weight-error sensitivity* based techniques for network pruning is to estimate the sensisitivity of the error function to the exclusion of each connection, then prune the low-sensitivity connections. The sensitivity with respect to W_{ij} is defined as:

$$S_{ij} = E(w_{ij} = 0) - E(w_{ij} = w_{ij}^f) \tag{3.8}$$

where w_{ij}^f is the final value of the connection upon the completion of the training phase. This can be rewritten as:

$$S = -\frac{E(w^f) - E(0)}{w^f - 0} w^f \tag{3.9}$$

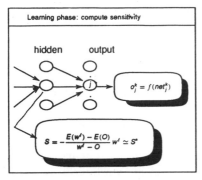 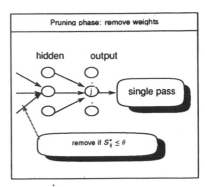

1   Compute sensitivity measures for each connection (during training) and construct a list of sensitivity measures for each connection.
2   Determine connections with $S_{ij}^* \leqslant \theta$, and remove them; θ is a user controlled parameter denoting the 'degree' of pruning.

Figure 3.10   Pruning by weight-error sensitivity

where $w = w_{ij}$ and E is expressed as a function of w assuming that all other weights are fixed (at their final states, upon completion of learning). Based on this formulation, Karnin [Karnin90] derived the following estimate:

$$S_{ij}^* = -\sum_{0}^{N-1} \frac{\partial E}{\partial W}(n) \Delta W_{ij}(n) \frac{w_{ij}^f}{w_{ij}^f - w_{ij}^i} \tag{3.10}$$

where N is the number of training epochs. This estimate for the sensitivity uses terms that are readily available during the normal course of training. The only extra computational overhead that this procedure requires is the summation, which can be implemented by maintaining a shadow array of weights that keeps track of the accumulated terms making up S_{ij}^*. The algorithm for the technique is given in Figure 3.10.

The weight-error sensitivity technique has several advantages, primarily its low computation cost, low complexity, and that it scales linearly with problem size. However, like other pruning approaches, the technique is only a heuristic that provides some reasonable estimate of the true sensitivities of weights with respect to the global error. The technique described here bases the estimate on following the learning path which may not be optimal. Otherwise each connection which is a candidate for elimination would need to be trained and retrained.

Other methods

Several researchers have studied the idea of weight *decay*. The idea is that weights that do not have much influence on decreasing the error while learning, will experience exponential time decay. Weight decay is equivalent to adding a penalty term to the cost function, changing it to

$$E^* = E + \beta^* \sum \sum w_{ij}^2 \qquad (3.11)$$

where E is the mean squared error as defined in (1.4). Thus, the global cost E^* is a weighted sum of two terms, with the relative weighting β^* being yet another free parameter to be determined. Hanson and Pratt [HanPra89] have extensively experimented with various forms of weight decay, and concluded that these penalty terms do not seem to minimise the number of units.

Mozer and Smolensky [MozSmo90] have introduced the idea of estimating the sensitivity of the error function to the elimination of each unit. In terms of (possible) connection elimination S_{ij}, the sensitivity with respect to w_{ij} is defined in (3.10). One problem with the sensitivity measure introduced in [MozSmo90] is that the partial derivative tends to zero when the error decreases. While this is a desirable property of the gradient descent learning method, it results in poor sensitivity estimation. [MozSmo90] suggested changing the cost function and demonstrated the usefulness of their estimation procedure on several examples.

SUMMARY

We have reviewed three types of technique for constructing near-optimal networks, that is to say, networks that are large enough to learn the problem but necessarily small to generalise well. All the techniques reviewed here represent an advance on fixed-geometry architectures.

The first type is based on analytic techniques that try to make an *a priori* estimate of hidden unit size. The main problem of these techniques is that they perform static analysis and can only provide a very rough estimate for hidden unit size. However, even this compares well with current experimental methods for network development.

The second type is dynamic; these methods construct the network architecture during training, and thus ease the problem of convergence at the same time. Although it is easy to reason about the convergence properties of these techniques, it is not so easy to reason about their generalisation and stability properties. Although there is no guarantee that the networks they construct are the optimum required for the training set, constructive procedures have fewer effective degrees of freedom in exploring the search space.

The third type, network pruning, operates in the opposite direction, starting with a large network and pruning it down to 'minimal' size. It is not always possible to perform optimal pruning. One cannot even reason that the removal of nodes with zero weights and duplicate nodes is desirable. First, zero-weighted nodes are almost redundant anyway and play only a small role in the generalisation performance of the system. This is analogous to polynomial fitting with zero coefficients. Second, duplicate nodes may be desirable because they provide fault-tolerance capabilities.

Chapter 6 considers recent advances in computational learning theory as an alternative to optimal network design.

4
Data Modelling Considerations

Apostolos-Paul Refenes, *London Business School, UK*

DATA REPRESENTATION

One of the most important results in neural computation research is the proof that neural networks are universal approximators. In other words, given a sufficiently large number of free parameters the learning procedure is guaranteed to find a mapping between any set of independent and dependent variables. This is a very important result as it implies that neural networks can tackle the widest possible range of problems. However, this flexibility has a severe drawback because the procedure will also lend itself to finding associations where none exist.

Therefore the selection of independent and dependent variables should be approached with great care and should be treated as a model construction process. Irrespective of the efficiency of a learning procedure in terms of convergence, generalisation or stability, the ultimate performance of the estimator will depend upon the relevance of the selected independent variables and the quality of the data used. Having too few independent variables constrains the search space, and introduces bias into the modelling process which leads to generalisation error. Having too many independent variables increases the dimensionality of the search space in which the procedure seeks the solution and will introduce generalisation error due to variance.

Approaches developed in statistical modelling methodology (such as correlation analysis and stepwise parametric regression) are often very useful. Correlation is more applicable to unsupervised learning. Once causality has been established (that is, the dependent variable identified) stepwise regression is a much stronger tool in identifying multi-collinearities and establishing the extent of the variability in the dependent variable that is explainable by each input or combination of input. Introductions can be found in the statistical analysis literature [BowOco90, KlKuMu87].

Neural Networks in the Capital Markets. Edited by Apostolos-Paul Refenes.
© 1995 John Wiley & Sons Ltd

It is also useful to establish the nature of the independent variables, some of which may be predictive and some of which may be informative (in information-theoretic terms). A predictive variable is one which alone can explain a significant part of the variability in the dependent variable. An informative variable is one which has no predictive power of its own but, when combined with others, can lead to better prediction. Consider, for example, the relationship between indicators such as volume and open-interest to the prices of futures contracts. Both indicators are thought to be predictive with respect to price movements, but they can only explain a small part of the variability in prices (typically around 12%). However, it is also believed that the relationship between volume and prices is different in bull markets than in bear markets. Thus a further informative indicator such as market trends, or indeed lagged prices would be desirable.

DETRENDING, NORMALISATION AND STATISTICAL OUTLIERS

The independent and dependent variables will, in the majority of cases, require detrending, normalisation, and attention to statistical outliers.

Detrending is a process of removing seasonal and/or general trends from the data. The existence of strong trends in the independent and/or dependent variables can lead to spurious correlations and regressions because it is easier for the network to learn the *general* features of the data than the *actual* relationship between the variables. For example, we may be trying to establish a relationship between the price of futures contracts in a commodity (say, cocoa) and technical indicators such as volume and open-interest. Using the levels of the three variables over the past ten years, the analysis will establish some relatively strong correlations. Closing prices and volume are negatively correlated (coefficient -0.44). There is an even stronger negative correlation between prices and open-interest (coefficient -0.76) which is unusually high for financial data. However, it is easy to see by simply plotting the data (see Figure 4.1) that we have found a trivial association: over the ten-year period market activity has grown steadily while the price of cocoa has fallen consistently.

Despite the relatively high R^2 produced by the regression, its usefulness as a predictor is worthless: the correlation coefficients between the *rates of change* of the three variables, for example, are less than 0.08. The reader is referred to the linear statistical analysis literature [BowOco90, KlKuMu87].

Normalisation is a process of standardising the possible numerical range that the variables can take. Normalisation is generally desirable in order to remove the possibility that the network parameters are 'tuned' for a given range of input–output data and also to bring the inputs of the activation function inside the function's normal operating region. Assuming an asymmetric sigmoid function with [0, 1] range, when its inputs fall well outside its normal operating region, then its output tends asymptotically to 0 or 1. In that case, the derivative of the sigmoid, and the activation value of the neuron tend to 0 (the derivative of the sigmoid is calculated

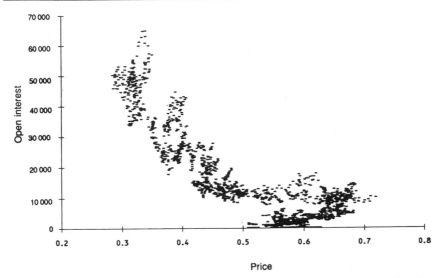

Figure 4.1 Spurious correlation due to market trends: Deutschmark/dollar futures market 1980-85. Correlation = −0.8

in terms of itself: $f'(z) = (1 - f(z))f(z)$. This is undesirable since it can bring training to a virtual standstill (known as *network paralysis*). On the other hand, since the range of the sigmoid is [0, 1], a target output which falls outside that range will constantly create large backpropagated errors and the network will be unable to learn the input–output relationship implied by the particular training pattern. Furthermore, it is undesirable to have large differences between the ranges of the network inputs, since this can diminish the importance of some otherwise useful inputs.

Typically, variables will be normalised in order to have zero mean and unit standard deviation. In the following equations $X_i^{scl}(t)$ is the scaled variable, $x_i(t)$ the original variable, σ_{x_i} the standard deviation of $X_i(t)$, and $\bar{X}_i$ the mean value of $X_i(t)$.

$$X_i^{scl}(t) = \frac{X_i(t) - \bar{X}_i}{\sigma_{x_i}}$$

$$\sigma_{x_i} = \sqrt{\frac{\sum\limits_{t=1}^{N}(X_i(t) - \bar{X}_i)^2}{N - 1}} \qquad (4.1)$$

$$\bar{X}_i = \frac{\sum\limits_{t=1}^{N} X_i(t)}{N}$$

It is also important to give due consideration to the output transfer function. If it is one with asymptotic limits such as the sigmoid, which only reaches the limits [0, 1] for inputs at infinity, then typical outputs may only reach values in the range [0.1, 0.9]. A common way of scaling the data is by a linear transformation given in equations (4.2).

$$Y^{\text{scl}}(t) = SCALE \times Y(t) + OFFSET$$

$$SCALE = \frac{MAX - MIN}{Y_{\max} - Y_{\min}}$$

$$OFFSET = MAX - \frac{MAX - MIN}{Y_{\max} - Y_{\min}} Y_{\max}$$

$$(4.2)$$

where $Y^{\text{scl}}(t)$ is the scaled variable, $Y(t)$ is the original variable, $Y_{\max}$, $Y_{\min}$ are the maximum and minimum values of the original variable $Y(t)$, and MAX, MIN are the values of the target range, that is, [0.1, 0.9] or even [0.15, 0.85].

Statistical outliers are rather extreme observations in the input–output variables. Since they cause squashing of the normalised variable into a very small range, their existence means that extreme numerical accuracy is required during training; and even worse, the majority of the observations will be 'squashed' into the linear part of the sigmoid. Usually, statistical outliers can be detected by visual inspection of the data, or by examining the frequency distributions, but more sophisticated multivariate methods can be used. A useful method for detecting statistical outliers is by calculating the Mahalanobis distance $D^2(t)$ of every training pattern $[\bar{X}(t), Y(t)]$ from the centre of the distributions of all values, taking into account all the variables of the training pattern. Mahalanobis distance is a reliable distance measure, and is calculated from the following equation:

$$D^2(t) = \sum_{i=1}^{N} \sum_{j=1}^{p} (Z_i(t) - \bar{Z}_i) V^{ij} (Z_j(t) - \bar{Z}_j)$$

$$(4.3)$$

where p is the number of variables in the training pattern, N is the total number of training patterns, $Z_i(t)$ is the ith variable of the tth pattern, $\bar{Z}_i$ is the mean value of the variable Z_i and V^{ij} is the element of the ith row and jth column of the inverse of the covariance matrix for the p variables. The reader is referred to the linear statistical analysis literature [BowOco90, KlKuMu87].

CORRELATION ANALYSIS AND MULTI-COLLINEARITIES

Correlation analysis investigates the extent to which independent variables are correlated to the dependent variable, and, if so, which one leads the other. Determining the linear correlations gives an insight into the (linear) predictive ability of the independent variables, and also determines collinearities which limit the modelling capability of any regression (including neural networks).

In the majority of cases, it is advisable to calculate the *cross-correlation* matrix between all independent variables and the dependent variable at different lags. The cross-correlation, r_{xy}, between an input time series, x, and the output time series, y, with lag k, is given by the following equations:

$$r_{xy}(k) = \frac{c_{xy}(k)}{S_x S_y} \qquad k = 1, 2, \dots. \qquad (4.4)$$

where

$$c_{xy}(k) = \frac{1}{n} \sum_{t=1}^{n+k} (x_t - \bar{x})(y_{t+k} - \bar{y})$$

$$S_x = \sqrt{c_{xx}(0)}$$

$$S_y = \sqrt{c_{yy}(0)}$$

Multi-collinearity refers to the association, measured as the correlation, between three or more independent variables. This is a data problem, and not a problem of model specification. Multi-collinearities have substantial effects on the results of any regression procedure because they limit the size of the coefficient of determination, and they make determining the contribution of each independent variable difficult to estimate. The most common method for determining multi-collinearities is the construction of the correlation matrix of the independent variables. This matrix is an array of all estimated pairwise correlations between independent variables (other methods exist, such as the computation of variance inflation factors, but we shall not consider them here; the same is true for stepwise regression). The correlation coefficients are a sensible measure of pairwise linear correlations provided that the variables are random (normally distributed). If this is not the case then the most commonly used nonparametric measure of correlation between two variables is *Spearman's rank correlation coefficient* which is the usual (Pearson) correlation coefficient applied to ranks and which satisfies the usual requirements of correlation measures (that is, it takes a value of $+1$ for perfect positive correlation and -1 for perfect negative correlation).

In the majority of cases it is desirable to decorrelate the input variables. Several methods are available in the statistical literature; two of them are principal components analysis and orthogonolisation. The reader is referred to the multivariate analysis literature, for example [KlKuMu87]. The idea is that the resultant decorrelated variables would be distinct from each other, and represent the most unique attributes of the input data as opposed to any information that might be common among all of the original variables. Principal components analysis (PCA) is very often used to reduce a relatively large number of highly correlated input variables to a small number of transformed and uncorrelated variables. PCA projects the data onto a linear subspace with minimum information loss, by a linear mapping performed by multiplying the data by the matrix of eigenvectors of the sample covariance matrix. The minimum dimensionality of the linear subspace is estimated by examining the magnitude of the corresponding eigenvalues. However, PCA can overestimate the dimensionality if the data lie on a nonlinear sub-manifold of the feature space. It has been shown [BalHor89, Kramer91] that auto-associative, nonlinear feedforward networks can perform the nonlinear analogue to PCA and extract 'principal manifolds', but the dimensionality of the hidden layers is still problematic [DemCot93].

DEALING WITH CATASTROPHIC NOISE

The presence of noise is common in financial data series, and when it exceeds certain levels it can degenerate the learning and generalisation ability of networks. There are in the statistical analysis literature many filtering techniques for smoothing time-series data to remove some of the effects of noise, such as moving averages and exponential smoothing. In this section we shall deal only with the presence of what we term *catastrophic noise* or *malicious* training vectors, which is a problem intrinsic to the mechanics of supervised learning procedures based on gradient descent.

We shall present a method for detecting malicious vectors in hetero-associative training samples (supervised learning). We define a general metric to quantify maliciousness and investigate four methods of dealing with the problem. We present an algorithm which permits the incremental augmentation of the *noise-free* part of the data set (cf. stepwise clean-up), and show that the algorithm yields faster convergence and better generalisation for small percentages of catastrophic noise in the training sample.

Malicious training vectors are those that lie very close to the true class boundaries. Arguably, these are the best ones to learn for obtaining good generalisation provided that one is able to obtain an arbitrarily large number of independent training exemplars. This is rarely the case in financial data series. Moreover, several learning procedures, including gradient descent learning, require long training times to learn training exemplars near the optimal class boundaries [DudHar73].

A graphical representation of the problem is given in Figure 4.2 depicting a simple two-dimensional classification problem. Vectors defined by (X_i, Y_i) on the left-hand side of the grid belong to class A whereas vectors on the right-hand side of the grid belong to class B. The decision surface separating the two classes is defined by an arbitrary (nonlinear) function. Training vectors in the area denoted by M are corrupted by noise obscuring the decision surface. The worse case of maliciousness is when $(X_i, Y_i) \in M$ are 'mapped' to both class A and to class B, which can have catastrophic effects on generalisation. Strictly speaking the problem is a mapping from $f : \mathbb{R}^2 \rightarrow \{0, 1\}$.

Training with all $(X_i, Y_i) \in M$ can be extremely slow and may have catastrophic effects in terms of generalisation. Removing all $(X_i, Y_i) \in M$ from the training set can improve convergence but it does not in general yield better generalisation.

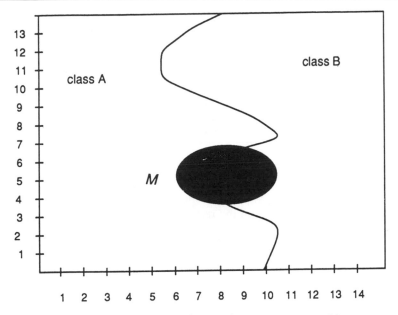

Figure 4.2   Graphical representation of the malicious training problem

When the training sample set is incomplete to the extent that adequate generalisation cannot be achieved, it is desirable to augment the available data with new vectors from the area within M. This is analogous to function completion on the decision surface by interpolating or extrapolating on the available data.

A formal definition of the problem is given below. For a given finite training set $S = (X, Y)$, where $X \subseteq \mathbb{R}^m$ and $Y \subseteq \mathbb{R}^n$, a hetero-associative learning procedure attempts to find a mapping $f : \mathbb{R}^m \rightarrow \mathbb{R}^n$. Each element in the set S has the form $s_i = (x_i, y_i)$ where $x_i \in \mathbb{R}^m$ and $y_i \in \mathbb{R}^n$ and is called an *exemplar* (or *training vector*). Let s_i and s_j be any two exemplars from the same sample set. We define the metric $m(\alpha, \delta)$ as the degree of maliciousness for exemplars $s_i \in M$. The definition of $m(\alpha, \delta)$ is such that any two exemplars s_i, $s_j \in S$ are *malicious* with degree $m(\alpha, \delta)$ if

$$d(x_i, x_j) \leqslant \alpha$$
$$d(y_i, y_j) > \delta$$

(4.5)

where $d(x_i, x_j)$ is a suitable measurement of similarity between x_i and x_j (such as the Euclidean distance). Any two exemplars s_i, s_j which are malicious m are called *malicious exemplars*. Here we concentrate on the case where both α and δ are equal to zero. We refer to this case as *catastrophic noise* since it is the worse case of maliciousness: the inputs are the same but their projections on $\mathbb{R}^n$ are different which poses an ill-defined mapping over the input training sample set. In terms of our definitions $m(0, 0)$ gives $d(x_i, x_j) \leqslant 0$ and $d(y_i, y_j) > 0$ which defines two

Table 4.1　A simple example of learning with and without malicious data.

Observation	Input	Desired output	Actual output noise-free	with noise
s_1	0.1	0.1	0.181 014	0.448 499
s_2	0.2	0.3	0.270 337	0.447 947
s_3	0.3	0.4	0.380 333	0.447 400
s_4	0.4	0.5	0.495 651	0.446 857
s_5	0.1	0.9	–	0.448 499

exemplars with $x_i = x_j$ but $y_i \neq y_j$. The further the distance between y_i and y_j the worse the problem. For brevity, in the rest of this section we use the term 'noise' to mean 'catastrophic noise'.

To illustrate the problem let us consider a simple example as shown in Table 4.1. The training sample consists of five exemplars $(s_1, \ldots, s_5)$ defined in the first two columns. The first and last exemplars, $s_1 = (0.1 \rightarrow 0.1)$ and $s_5 = (0.1 \rightarrow 0.9)$, are malicious $m(0, 0)$.

We perform two experiments with a 1-6-1 backpropagation network. In the first experiment the network (with a quadratic cost function, asymmetric sigmoid, batch update, $\lambda = 0.3$) is trained with a reduced sample (without s_5) for 10 000 iterations, and gives as actual output the values in the fourth column. This is a reasonably good approximation to the desired solution. However, if we train the same network with the entire training set including the last exemplar (s_5), we obtain a radically different output (see column 5). (The behaviour of backpropagation in such circumstances will depend on the training parameters — most importantly on the cost function and the weight update mode. Batch update tends to the average; on-line update tends to produce wild oscillations.) As the noise-to-signal ratio increases the result is becoming catastrophic in terms of generalisation.

In general, it is not always possible to determine with the naked eye which are the malicious exemplars in a training sample or which of those it is best to remove. This is a particular problem in time-series data where it is common practice to use a rolling window to model the inputs to the network. If the size of the rolling window is large (say, m) and the size of the step by which we are moving along is small (say, 1), it is easy to see how two consecutive training vectors may be malicious: the left-hand side of the training vector (the input) will be the same in $m - 2$ of the m elements but abrupt market movements may cause the right-hand sides (the two consecutive outputs) to be far apart.

Before we discuss any algorithms for dealing with the problem, let us introduce the concept of a *malicious labelled graph* (lagraph). The lagraph is a useful representation that can be employed by potential algorithms for selective removal of malicious exemplars. Let $G = (S, m, M, E)$ be a malicious labelled graph such that:

- S is a finite set of p exemplars $s_1, \ldots, s_p$; we call S the *original* sample;

- m is the malicious metric as defined in (4.5);

- $M = \{s_i | s_i \in S \text{ and } \exists s_k \text{ such that } s_i \text{ and } s_k \text{ are malicious } m\}$ — we call M a *malicious sample set*. The nodes in the graph are labelled with their associated exemplar id;

- E is the set of all malicious pairs over S, $E = \{(s_i, s_j) | s_i, s_j \in S \text{ and } s_i, s_j \text{ are malicious } m, \text{ for all } i, j = 1, \ldots, p\}$.

Note that G is an undirected graph and $(s_i, s_j) = (s_j, s_i)$. A sample set without any malicious exemplars is called a *noise-free sample*. Given any S and m, the lagraph G can be constructed as shown in the following algorithm:

proc **CONSTRUCT**-G (m, S, p)
        - S is the sample set.
        - p is the number of exemplars in S.
        - m is the malicious metric.
        - G is the required undirected lagraph which we construct and is
           composed of:
                $M(G)$ - set of nodes.
                $E(G)$ - set of edges over this set of nodes.
  for $i = 1$ to $p - 1$
      for $j = i + 1$ to p
          if $(s_i \text{ and } s_j \text{ are malicious } m)$ **then**
              $M(G) = M(G) \cup \{s_i, s_j\}$, and
              $E(G) = E(G) \cup (s_i, s_j)$

In [TuvRef93] we described a novel algorithm for detecting and removing such malicious vectors and evaluated it against three principal alternatives: first, non-removal of M which leads to the problems described earlier; second, total removal of M which is undesirable in many cases, particularly in small data sets; and third, a trivial algorithm which removes $s_i \in M$ which belong to conflicting pairs incrementally. Referring back to Table 4.1, the idea is to remove either s_1 or s_5 but not both. The criterion for selecting s_1 in preference to s_5 is not based on any prior knowledge of the mapping function; in that sense the removal process is totally random. The following algorithm (operating on G) implements a simple way of deriving G' from G such that:

- $G' = (V', E')$;

- V' is a maximum subset of M such that $E' = E \cap (V' \times V')$;

- $E' = \{\}$:

proc **MINIMAL-REMOVAL** (G)
>   -G is the malicious lagraph as constructed by the procedure
>   **CONSTRUCT**-G.
>   -Let $w(\{v\})$ be the weight of each node $v \in M(G)$.

while $E\langle\rangle\{\}$
>   select v such that min $(w(v)) \forall v \in M$
>   for all u such that $(u, v)\ i \in E$ E do
> $$M = M - u$$
> $$E = E - (u, l), \forall l \in M$$

A more sensible way to carry out the removal is incrementally to reject the *most likely* malicious exemplars. The algorithm described below implements an iterative process of augmenting the noise-free sample set (say, S_2) with new exemplars from the malicious sample set M. The selection of the set to be removed (denoted by $M - V'$) is based upon learning from an existing noise-free sample set. At the beginning of the process we use S_2 to learn the mapping $(f_2 : \mathbb{R}^m \to \mathbb{R}^n)$. This mapping, f_2, is used to identify and to extract the set $M - V'$. The malicious lagraph G is partitioned into finite set of subgraphs $C_1, \ldots, C_N$ such that each $C_i = (V_i, E_i)$ is a maximal connected graph (that is, for every $v, w \in V_i$ there is a path from v to w), and

$$G = \cup_{i=1,\ldots,N} C_i$$

In the case of $m(0, 0)$ each C_i is fully connected (i.e. for every $v, w \in V_i$ then $(v, w) \in E_i$).

We now construct S_4 to be the noise-free set S_2 augmented with N exemplars, whereby each one of them is selected from a different C_i such that:

$$\min(d(f_2(x_i), y_i)), \forall s_i \in C_i \qquad (4.6)$$

The key idea in (4.6) is to augment the training sample with the s_i which is closer to the decision surface as defined by the network trained on the noise-free sample (f_2). Referring back to Table 4.1, this will augment the training sample by s_1 rather than s_5. In practical applications this would be an incremental process and might require several training runs. There is therefore a penalty on overall convergence speed in favour of better generalisation.

Table 4.2 presents the generalisation results of the three methods for handling catastrophic noise on a benchmark data set using the well-known n-bit parity problem corrupted with random noise [TuvRef93]. Here S_1 denotes networks trained on the original data set; S_2 denotes networks trained on the original data set minus the entire subset of malicious vectors (noise-free); S_3 denotes networks trained on the noise-free data set plus the subset consisting of only one of any pair of malicious vectors (i.e. s_1 or s_5 but not both); and S_4 denotes networks trained on the noise-free subset and then used to select $s_j \in M$; and retrain recursively on the noise-free subset augmented with 'least likely' malicious vectors.

Table 4.2 Generalisation performance of ten tests of four malicious sample sets.

Set	Test										Mean	σ_n
S_1	69.9	**89.0**	80.4	77.7	82.8	71.8	63.2	83.9	84.7	**75.0**	77.84	7.49
S_2	54.2	60.1	**87.8**	**82.4**	85.1	75.7	69.9	**86.3**	86.7	72.6	76.08	11.23
S_3	**73.4**	70.3	83.2	73.0	83.5	59.3	69.9	81.2	79.2	69.9	74.29	7.20
S_4	71.4	85.5	86.3	**82.4**	**85.5**	**81.2**	**83.9**	83.2	**94.9**	69.9	**82.42**	**6.87**

Table 4.2 shows ten test runs with different training sets of 100 randomly selected vectors each containing 2% invalid malicious exemplars. The figures in the table represent percentage generalisation on the entire sample of $2^8 = 256$ observations for the 8-bit parity problem. Each column represents a different test run. Each row shows the performance of each method. The bold figures show the best performance. On average our enhanced algorithm produces better generalisation (82.4%) and also smaller standard deviation (6.86%).

From the above tests we can conclude that the preparation process which handles malicious exemplars in a training data set should adapt itself to the percentages of malicious exemplars in the training set. For a small percentage of malicious exemplars in the training sample set it is recommended to construct the training sample set in two stages. The first stage is to approximate the function f (by f_2) using the noise-free set S_2, and then in the second stage to use f_2 to augment S_2 with a subset of exemplars from the malicious set M. However, when the percentage of the malicious exemplars in the sample set increases it is better to learn the problem only from the noise-free set S_2. Learning from the original sample set is the worst solution in terms of convergence and generalisation.

We note that in this section we concentrated on the special case whereby any two samples are malicious only if their input value is the same (that is, $x_i = x_j$) but their output value is different ($y_i \neq y_j$). The procedure can be used to handle malicious sample sets which define problems of mapping with smooth functions whereby small changes in the input variables result in small changes in the output.

SUMMARY

Although the efficiency of the learning procedure in terms of convergence, generalisation and stability is the core component of any successful application, it is not necessarily the most critical one. Approaches developed in statistical modelling methodology for preprocessing the input and output data should always be given serious consideration prior to training neural networks. Although it is not essential in certain cases, it is vital in the majority of cases.

5
Testing Strategies and Metrics

Apostolos-Paul Refenes, *London Business School, UK*

While the mean squared error is a perfectly acceptable measure of performance, in practice the ultimate goal of any testing strategy is to reassure the modeller that his or her results are robust and to measure the profitability of the system. It is therefore important to design a testing strategy and metrics from the outset. This is not always carried out with the level of rigour that it merits, partly because of unfamiliarity with established methods and partly because of practical difficulties intrinsic to nonlinear systems. In this chapter we give some well-known metrics for measuring estimator performance both in absolute and relative terms.

MEASURING ESTIMATOR PERFORMANCE

The *correlation coefficient* is a popular measure of prediction accuracy in absolute terms. It measures the linear correlation between predicted values (denoted by y_i) and actual values (denoted by x_i) averaged over all observations (n):

$$R = \frac{\sum_{i=1}^{n}(x_i - \bar{x})(y_i - \bar{y})}{\sqrt{\sum_{i=1}^{n}(x_i - \bar{x})^2}\sqrt{\sum_{i=1}^{n}(y_i - \bar{y})^2}} \tag{5.1}$$

where $\bar{x} = 1/n \sum_{i=1}^{n} x_i$, and $\bar{y} = 1/n \sum_{i=1}^{n} y_i$. The square of R is often used such that $R^2 = 1$ denotes perfect correlation, and $R^2 = 0$ signifies no correlation between actual and predicted values. R and R^2 are very common measures of prediction accuracy outside the neural networks community and should always be reported.

Neural Networks in the Capital Markets. Edited by Apostolos-Paul Refenes.
© 1995 John Wiley & Sons Ltd

In the majority of cases, however, it is important to compare the accuracy of the estimator against the performance of so-called 'trivial predictors'.

The *information coefficient* (often referred to as the t-test, or Theil's coefficient of inequality) gives a good measure of the estimator's performance relative to the well-known trivial predictor based on the random-walk hypothesis. The hypothesis asserts that the best estimate of tomorrow's price is today's price. It is always desirable to measure the goodness of the predictions relative to this trivial predictor:

$$T_r = \frac{\sqrt{\sum_{t=1}^{n}(y_t - x_t)^2}}{\sqrt{\sum_{t=1}^{n}(x_t - x_{t-1})^2}} \tag{5.2}$$

The information ratio, T_r distinguishes between good and bad predictors. For $T_r \geqslant 1$ the predictor is worse than a trivial predictor; any predictor with $T_r < 1$ implies that we are making better predictions, and as T_r approaches zero the predictor is doing infinitely better than the random walk.

Another trivial predictor worth considering is *mean reversion*. This asserts that the best estimate for tomorrow's price is the historical mean value:

$$T_\mu = \frac{\sqrt{\sum_{t=1}^{n}(y_t - x_t)^2}}{\sqrt{\sum_{t=1}^{n}(\bar{x} - x_{t+1})^2}} \tag{5.3}$$

This measure is a good performance estimate for comparing different models: if we are simply predicting the mean of the observed values then the information ratio will give $T_\mu = 1$; again any prediction with $T_\mu < 1$; implies that we are making better predictions than merely predicting the mean. The T_μ statistic is sometimes referred to as the *average relative variance measure*; it measures the mean squared error normalised by the variance of the test set.

As part of an overall model construction process, modellers often have to select between models with equally good performance (cf. stepwise regression). In this case, parsimonious estimators with fewer parameters should be preferred. To account for the complexity of the estimator various metrics have been developed.

The *Akaike information criterion* is a way of adjusting the mean squared error to account for the complexity of the estimator:

$$A = \frac{1}{n}\sum_{i}^{n}(x_i - y_i)^2 \left[\frac{n+k}{n-k}\right] \tag{5.4}$$

where k is the number of free parameters in the estimator (cf. free connections in a neural network). The Akaike information criterion is similar to the conventional way of adjusting R^2 to penalise for complexity, expressed by the formula

$$\bar{R}^2 = R^2 \left[\frac{n+k}{n-k} \right]$$

The *Bayesian information criterion* is another way of adjusting the mean squared error to account for model complexity. De Groot and Wurtz [DegWur91] propose a modified normalised version of the statistic given by the expression

$$B = \ln \left[\frac{\sum\limits_{i}^{n} (x_i - y_i)^2}{n} \right] + \frac{\ln[n]}{n} k \qquad (5.5)$$

where k is the number of weights. Models exhibiting the lowest value for the B-statistic possess the best forecasting and generalisation capabilities.

Directional Change

The mean squared error clearly is a measure of the correctness of the prediction in terms of levels. Although predicting the levels of price changes (or first differences) is desirable, in many cases the sign of the change is equally important: most investment analysts are usually far more accurate in predicting directional changes in an asset price than predicting the actual level. We use the following metric:

$$d = \frac{1}{n} \sum\limits_{i}^{n} a_i \qquad (5.6)$$

where

$$a_i = \begin{cases} 1 & \text{if } (x_{t+1} - x_t)(y_{t+1} - x_t) > 0 \\ 0 & \text{otherwise} \end{cases}$$

The d-statistic has a simple interpretation: $d = 1$ implies that the estimator is predicting 100% of the directional changes; $d = 0$ implies 0% prediction in directional changes; any estimator with $d > 0.5$ is doing better than tossing a coin. The statistic should be used with care. It is advisable to normalise it with its standard deviation over at least 30 test runs with different cross-validation sets and/or initial conditions. For example, it is relatively easy to obtain a high value for d in a trending market.

Testing for Autocorrelation

Most neural network models assume that the residuals are Gaussian and uncorrelated through time. It is always desirable to investigate the properties of the residuals to see if there are any local trends and regularities which, presumably, are not predictable from the input variables. Better models can always be obtained if the data are modelled as being the sum of the network predictions and an unpredictable but autocorrelated disturbance. A simple starting point would assume Gaussian correlations between residuals, such that:

$$\beta \sum_{i}^{n} (x_i - y_i)^2 = \sum_{i}^{n} [\beta_0 (x_i - y_i)^2 + \beta_1 (x_i - y_i)(x_{i+1} - y_{i+1}) +$$

$$+ \beta_2 (x_i - y_i)(x_{i+2} - y_{i+2}) + \cdots] \qquad (5.7)$$

where β is the regularisation or 'weight decay' coefficient used to penalise network complexity by forcing redundant connections to zero values [WeHuRu91]. This would lead to simple modifications to the backpropagation rule as described in Chapter 1, so that the propagated error signal at each frame would be a weighted combination of the residuals at neighbouring frames. In the Bayesian framework the evidence would thus be used to optimise the correlation model's parameters $\beta_0, \beta_1, \beta_2, \ldots$. The result would be that the neural network would be penalised during the development stage for its complexity by forcing redundant parameters to zero or near-zero values.

MEASURING PROFITABILITY

Net Returns

The ultimate goal of any testing strategy is to measure profitability. Profitability is calculated always in the context of the trading rule and/or the portfolio management strategy. The error minimisation criteria that are used for developing the network are not necessarily the most efficient criteria. The investor is ultimately trying to maximise a different objective function than the network. The output statements from the network or the estimates of expected returns must be turned into investment actions. Let us consider a simple (technical) trading strategy in which positive expected returns are executed as long positions, and negative expected returns are executed as short positions. The net return, r, of such strategy (assuming away taxes and other market imperfections) is given by

$$r = \sum_{i}^{n} p_t^* (x_{t+1} - x_t) \qquad (5.8)$$

where

$$p_t = \begin{cases} 1 & \text{if } (y_{t+1} - x_t) > 0 \\ -1 & \text{if } (y_{t+1} - x_t) < 0 \\ 0 & \text{if } (y_{t+1} - x_t) = 0 \end{cases}$$

Typically, the profitability of the system will be evaluated against two benchmarks: a simple buy-and-hold strategy on the asset; and its distance from the ideal net profit.

The *Buy-and-hold* test is a good benchmark against which to quantify excess return. It tests whether the net profit is due to the prediction accuracy (and strategy) or merely due to general market trends. We shall define the buy-and-hold return of an asset in the context of a single period. The return r_b is comprised of an income portion (c) and a price appreciation portion:

$$r_b = \frac{c + (x_{t+n} - x_t)}{x_t} \tag{5.9}$$

The income term, c, may accrue from dividends in the case of equities, or interest in the case of bonds.

The *distance from the ideal* measures the returns of the trading system against that of a perfect predictor d:

$$r_d = \frac{\sum\limits_{i}^{n} p_t^*(x_{t+1} - x_t)}{\sum\limits_{i}^{n} |(x_{t+1} - x_t)|} \tag{5.10}$$

with p_t as defined in (5.8).

In these equations, market imperfections such as taxes and transaction costs are assumed away. In practice, however, it is always important to account for transaction costs particularly when the estimator generates trading signals frequently.

So far, we are measuring profitability in terms of *net profit*. Net profit is an overrated measure of success for several reasons. First, there is the possibility that a few large trades have skewed the results. It is unrealistic to use a system whose success depends on (probably) non-recurring events. Second, it gives no indication on the risk involved. Investors are not interested in estimates (albeit accurate) of expected returns or indeed in net profit *per se*. They are interested in risk–reward ratios. A realistic approach will always consider a portfolio consisting of different amounts invested in each of at least two assets.

The Portfolio Approach

The optimum portfolio is one which maximises risk-adjusted return within a mean-variance framework (that is, assuming quadratic utility). Thus, we may wish to choose weights of the two assets A and B so as to maximise

$$R = r_A w_A + r_B w_B - \frac{1}{T}(w_A^2 \sigma_A^2 + w_B^2 \sigma_B^2 + 2w_A \sigma_A w_B \sigma_B \rho) \tag{5.11}$$

where w_A, w_B are portfolio weights of the two assets; r_A, r_B their expected returns; σ_A, σ_B the standard deviations, ρ the correlation coefficient; and T a measure of risk tolerance.

Typically we would wish to choose optimal proportions of each asset, that is, to find w_A and $w_B = (1 - w_A)$ so as to maximise (5.11). This leads to the following result:

$$w_A = \frac{T\dfrac{r_A - r_B}{2} + \sigma_A^2 - \sigma_A\sigma_B\rho}{\sigma_A^2 + \sigma_B^2 - 2\sigma_A\sigma_B\rho} \tag{5.12}$$

This is useful because it verifies that we only need to know the difference in the two returns in order to choose portfolio weights. By holding one of the assets fixed to a risk-free asset (say, cash), equation (5.11) is simplified and we can obtain a realistic estimate of expected returns for a given level of risk tolerance. It is always advisable to implement this simple mean-variance optimisation and integrate it with the neural network framework in order to obtain more realistic estimates of the extent to which the predictive ability of the network can be transformed into better investment strategies. It may (and very often will) turn out that the payoff ratio is too low for practical use.

The mean-variance optimisation framework has its own limitations: mainly that it assumes stationarity of returns and constant variance of returns. Such an assumption is not always valid and most practitioners would wish to analyse the characteristics of the equity curves before implementing a trading system.

THE CHARACTERISTICS OF THE EQUITY CURVE

An *equity curve* is simply the total equity of an account (plotted on the vertical axis) over a period or series of trades (plotted on the horizontal axis). Figure 5.1 shows three equity curves plotted over a single period. All three lead to the same net profit at the end of the period, but they follow rather different trajectories. The characteristics of the equity curve are very important in assessing the acceptability of any investment strategy. The key characteristics are discussed below.

Drawdown

Net return and maximum drawdown are the ultimate expression of risk/reward. Of the two, drawdown is probably the most important. A system that generates an annualised percentage return of 100% over, say, five years will be unrealistic to implement if it has allowed peak-to-valley drawdowns of 50% several times during its lifetime. It would require a lot of loyalty (and deep pockets) to trade such a system with confidence. A smooth equity curve is much more desirable (and harder to obtain) than a high net return. This curve is very important as a measure of how practical the trading system will be. Most often, the systems that give the largest net profits have the largest drawdowns. If a large drawdown is compounded with a sequence of losing trades, most investors would prematurely abandon a potentially profitable trading system. The way in which drawdown is measured can

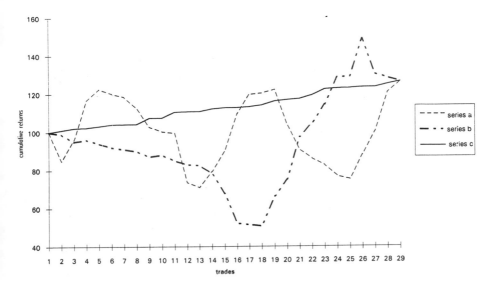

Figure 5.1 Equity curves with varying smoothness characteristics

be important. Drawdown should be measured on the equity curve plotted at the close of day and be comprised of the current closed equity plus mark-to-market equity of any open position. Drawdown is expressed as the greatest percentage retracement figured along the axis of cumulative returns.

Largest Profitable Trade

The largest positive trade can be very important if it makes a significant contribution towards skewing the net profit unreasonably. In most cases conservative system testing will ignore the largest positive trade. Let us use $R = \{r_0, r_1, \ldots, r_n\}$ to denote the ordered set of returns of individual trades. The following ratio quantifies the contribution of the largest positive trade towards net profit.

$$l = \frac{\max_l(R)}{\sum_i^n r_i} \qquad (5.13)$$

We shall term l the *luck coefficient*; it has a simple interpretation: the larger the value of l, the higher the system's dependence on a single, probably non-recurring, event. Extending this idea further we may redefine l as

$$l_\beta = \frac{\max_k(R)}{\sum_i^n r_i} \qquad (5.14)$$

where l_β denotes the contribution of the k largest profit-making trades to overall profits. For a given β (between 0 and 1), k is computed as the integer part of the product βn, that is, $k = \text{int}(\beta n)$. The second term, $\max_k(R)$ gives the sum of the returns of the k largest elements in R. For example, if your system was involved in $n = 1000$ transactions, $l_{0.05}$ denotes the contribution of the 50 largest profit-making trades ($k = 0.05 \times 1000 = 50$, or 5% of all trades) to total profit. If $l = 0.9$ then 5% of your trades account for 90% of the total profit and it is time to revisit the drawing board.

Loss-Making Trades and Relative Outperformance

The largest loss-making trade can also be especially important, particularly if it exceeds the normal risk-control measures. Any conservative testing strategy will not make specific rules to eliminate the largest losing trades. The number of consecutive loss-making trades is also an important parameter because it influences the probability of ruin (see next section). Relative outperformance is also an important consideration in any testing strategy. Any system (or investment professional) that it is seen consistently to underperform established industry benchmarks (or their peers) is unlikely to remain in action for long periods even if it yields higher net profits in the long term.

Sharpe Ratio

A popular measure of performance derived from the equity curve is the ratio developed by Sharpe [Sharpe66]. It is defined as the return, r_A, minus the risk-free rate of return divided by a volatility measure σ_A:

$$s = \frac{r_A - c}{\sigma_A} \tag{5.15}$$

where c represents a risk-free asset such as cash. The higher the Sharpe ratio, the higher the return and the lower the volatility. The ratio does have limitations (for example, increased upside volatility will result in a lower Sharpe ratio) but it is still the most common index of its type.

Sterling Ratio

Because of these limitations other statistics can be used for fair comparisons. The generalised Sterling ratio is typical of those based on the ratio of drawdown to rate of return. It is given by

$$s = \frac{\bar{r}_i}{10 - \bar{x}_i} \tag{5.16}$$

where $\bar{r}_i$ is the i-period average rate of return (for instance, the three-year average rate of return), and $\bar{x}_i$ is the i-period maximum drawdown. The main criticism of this is that it reacts too slowly to changes in performance if the recalculation period is not sufficiently frequent.

THE PROBABILITY OF RUIN

An investor is said to be ruined if his equity is depleted to the point where he is no longer able to trade. The risk of ruin is a probability estimate in the range [0,1], with an estimate of 0 suggesting that ruin is impossible and an estimate of 1 implying that ruin is inevitable. The risk of ruin, R, is a function of the following:

- the probability of success on individual trades;
- the payoff ratio — or the ratio of the average trade win to the average trade loss;
- the fraction of capital exposed to trading.

Whereas the fraction of capital exposed to trading is determined by money-management considerations, the probability of success and the payoff ratio are entirely dependent upon the accuracy of the trading system.

Let us illustrate the importance of the accuracy of the trading system with the help of a simple example adopted from [Balsar92]. Assume that we have $1 available for trading and that this entire amount is risked to trading. Further, let us assume that the payoff ratio is 1, that is, the average profit is $1 and equal to the average loss. Finally, let us assume that past trading results indicate that we have three profit-making trades out of every five trades, or a probability of success of 0.6. If the first trade is loss-making, we end up losing the entire equity of $1 and cannot trade any further. Therefore the probability of ruin at the first trade is $R = \frac{2}{5} = 0.4$.

If the first trade were to result in success we would start the next trade with an increased equity of $2. It is impossible to be ruined at the end of the second trade, given that the loss per trade is contained to $1. Ruin could occur if we lost the next two consecutive trades. The probability of this occurring is the probability of winning on the first trade multiplied by the probability of losing on each of the next two trades. This works out to be $R = 0.6 \times 0.4 \times 0.4 = 0.096$. Overall, the risk of ruin on or before the end of the three trades is the sum of the probabilities of being ruined at the end of the third or the end of the first trade. Thus $R = 0.496$. Extending this rationale, there are two possible routes to ruin by the end of the fifth trade. First assuming that the first two trades are profit-making, the next three trades would have to be loss-making to ensure ruin. Alternatively, if the first is profitable, loosing the second, winning the third and loosing the fourth and fifth will also lead to ruin. The two routes are mutually exclusive. Therefore the probability of ruin by the end of the fifth trade is:

$$R = 0.4 + 0.096 + 2(0.023\,04) = 0.54$$

The probability of ruin increases as the trading horizon expands but it does so at a decreasing rate, tending asymptotically to a fixed value, R. Under the assumption of payoff ratio of 1 and risking the entire equity on each trade this value is given by the following equation [Feller50] in the context of analysing gambling systems:

$$R = \frac{\left[\dfrac{q}{p}\right]^{\alpha} - \left[\dfrac{q}{p}\right]^{k}}{\left[\dfrac{q}{p}\right]^{\alpha} - 1} \tag{5.17}$$

where the 'gambler' has k units of capital and his opponent has $(\alpha - k)$ units of capital. The probability of success is given by p and the probability of failure is $q = (1 - p)$.

For the purposes of developing a testing strategy, we can assume that the probability of profitable trades exceeds the probability of loss-making trades leading to $q/p < 1$. Moreover, we can assume that the investor's opponent is the entire market, and that market capitalisation, α, is much larger than k making the term $(q/p)^{\alpha}$ tend to zero. Thus the probability of ruin is reduced to $(q/p)^{k}$.

For a comprehensive treatment of the evaluation of the risk of ruin under more realistic assumptions, see [Feller50, Bailey64, Balsar92].

SUMMARY

The design and execution of a comprehensive testing strategy is an integral part of application development. Its ultimate goal is to reassure the modeller that the results of his or her estimator(s) are robust, and to provide a fair measure of profitability and risk. The literature, and particularly the neural networks literature, is rich with examples of poorly tested results. This is partly because of unfamiliarity with established testing techniques, and partly because of the inherent difficulties of defining equivalent statistical tests for nonlinear models. For example, when adjusting $\bar{R}^2$ for degrees of freedom it is not clear whether one should take k to be equal to the number of all connections, or perhaps only those that are sufficiently away from zero, and if so by how much. As is often the case the number of *potential* degrees of freedom is not necessarily the same as the number of *effective* degrees of freedom. Such difficulties, however, should not be an excuse for incomplete testing strategies.

6

A Computational Learning Theory View of Economic Forecasting with Neural Nets

Martin Anthony and Norman L. Biggs, *London School of Economics and Political Science, UK*

INTRODUCTION

There has recently been an avalanche of papers in which neural network models are applied to financial and economic forecasting. In some cases surprisingly good results have been obtained. The question is no longer *whether* neural networks can make successful forecasts, but *why* they do. A recent survey [Refene92] refers to network design as a 'black art', and it is widely believed that no theoretical framework for it exists.

In fact, the subject of computational learning theory has been developed over the last decade precisely in order to provide answers to such problems. It takes a broad view of the subject, covering artificial neural networks as a special case. Among the problems discussed are: the accuracy and confidence of forecasts; the measurement of the 'expressive power' of a learning machine; and the complexity (difficulty) of algorithms for learning. In this chapter we shall discuss these matters in an economic and financial context. We shall consider their relationship with current theories of economic activity, and make comparisons with classical econometric forecasting techniques.

Neural Networks in the Capital Markets. Edited by Apostolos-Paul Refenes.
© 1995 John Wiley & Sons Ltd

A CLASSIC EXAMPLE

Around 1875 W.S. Jevons suggested that sunspot activity might affect the price of grain. An excellent account of his ideas and the ensuing debate is in the book by Morgan [Morgan90]. Although the sunspot hypothesis is not taken seriously by economists, we shall use it for the purposes of illustration because our discussion is intended to be general, rather than specific. For this reason also we shall not follow Jevons's method of testing his hypothesis, which involved a knowledge of the sunspot cycle and various *ad hoc* statistical devices. Instead, we shall discuss a simple approach which carries over to all kinds of similar situations. For example, we could use the same framework to discuss the relationship between movements in the gross national product (GNP) and the level of unemployment.

Suppose that l_t is the level of sunspot activity in month t, so that a year-long record of sunspot activity is a vector $(l_{t-1}, l_{t-2}, \ldots, l_{t-12})$. A simple version of the 'sunspot hypothesis' is that, given such a vector, we can determine the price of grain in the following period. In this context, the traditional econometric method is to look for a relationship defining v_t, the price of grain in month t: that is,

$$v_t = f(l_{t-1}, l_{t-2}, \ldots, l_{t-12})$$

The function f is assumed to belong to a particular class F of functions, involving some unknown parameters. For example, if F is the set of functions of the form

$$f(y_1, y_2, \ldots, y_{12}) = a_0 + a_1 y_1 + a_2 y_2 + \cdots + a_{12} y_{12}$$

then the parameters are $a_0, a_1, a_2, \ldots, a_{12}$. The problem is to find a particular function f in F which represents the available data and which could be used to make predictions. This means that the values of parameters are estimated by taking a number of examples $\mathbf{y} = (y_1, y_2, \ldots, y_{12})$ (where $y_j = l_{t-j}$) and the corresponding price v for each, and attempting to determine the values which best fit the data. In traditional econometrics this would be done by the least-squares method, but neural computing experts might use the 'perceptron rule'. (Both of these methods will be discussed in the examples in the following sections.) Finally, the best function obtained on the basis of past examples is used to predict future behaviour.

Although in the sunspot case there is considerable scepticism about the proposed relationship, it is not inherently impossible. Jevons himself justified it by saying that sunspot activity affects the weather, which affects the supply, which affects the price. In the case of GNP figures and unemployment, and many similar instances, there are good reasons for assuming that some such relationship does hold. In such cases it is natural to use the forecasting strategy outlined above. At the end of this chapter we shall discuss how (and if) the strategy should be altered to deal with situations where there is a strong presumption that no forecasting technique can be successful.

THE TERMINOLOGY OF COMPUTATIONAL LEARNING THEORY

In this section we shall discuss the general prediction problem using the terminology of computational learning theory. We shall continue to use the notation $\mathbf{y}$ for a sequence of data values, so that, for example, a year-long record of monthly sunspot activity is a vector $\mathbf{y} = (y_1, y_2, \ldots, y_{12})$. For simplicity, we shall begin by considering the case where the 'answer' is a Boolean variable (yes/no, or 1/0), rather than a numerical value. This corresponds to asking whether the price of grain will go up or down as a result of a given input $\mathbf{y}$, rather than attempting to find the price itself. However, it is clear that the more general situation is also more important in practice, and later in this chapter we shall describe how the theory can be applied in that case.

The discussion which follows (in this and the next four sections) is adapted from the book by the present authors [AntBig92]. The novel feature is that here we consider examples which are derived from 'economic' time series.

Our general framework consists of a 'world', W, a 'preprocessor', P, and a 'machine', M. In this context W represents a 'real-world economy', or more precisely a set of *examples*, each example being a 'snapshot' of a sector of the economy over some period of time. The preprocessor is rather like the Central Statistical Office: it takes an example and converts it into a coded form, usually a string of numbers. This coded version of the example is then presented to M, a 'machine' such as the Treasury Forecasting Section, whose function is to classify the examples. The output of M is a single bit, either 1 (if the example is recognised as belonging to a certain set), or 0 (if not). For example, M might wish to decide whether a year-long sequence of GNP figures will lead to a rise or fall in unemployment.

We need to make this rather more precise. Let $\mathbb{R}^n$ denote the set of n-tuples of real numbers, and let Y be a subset of $\mathbb{R}^n$. We define a *concept* to be a function

$$c : Y \to \{0, 1\}$$

The set Y will be referred to as the *example space*, and its members as *examples*. An example $\mathbf{y} \in Y$ for which $c(\mathbf{y}) = 1$ is known as a *positive example* of c, and an example for which $c(\mathbf{y}) = 0$ is known as a *negative example* of c.

Example 6.1. We might define the 'recession' concept $r : \mathbb{R}^3 \to \{0, 1\}$ by:

$$r(y_1, y_2, y_3) = \begin{cases} 1 & \text{if } y_1 < y_2 < y_3 \\ 0 & \text{otherwise} \end{cases} \qquad \square$$

The learning framework described above is concerned with the relationship between two sets of concepts. First, there are concepts derived from the real world, such as *recession, boom, crash*, and so on, each of which can be described in terms of a set of positive and negative examples. The other set of concepts inherent in the framework is the set which the machine M is capable of recognising. We shall suppose that M can assume various states, and that in a given state it will classify some inputs as positive examples (output 1), and the rest as negative examples (output 0). Thus each state of M determines a concept, which we may think of as a hypothesis. For this reason, the set H of all concepts which M can recognise will be referred to as its *hypothesis space*.

Example 6.2. For any $\lambda \in \mathbb{R}_+$ let $j_\lambda : \mathbb{R}^{12} \to \{0, 1\}$ be the function defined by

$$j_\lambda(\mathbf{y}) = \begin{cases} 1 & \text{if } y_1 + y_2 + \cdots + y_{12} \geqslant \lambda \\ 0 & \text{otherwise} \end{cases}$$

We may think of the set J of all such functions j_λ as the hypothesis space of a crude 'sunspot machine'. This machine predicts that the price of grain will increase if the total level of sunspot activity over the year exceeds a certain level, λ, otherwise it will decrease. The machine cannot make a more sophisticated hypothesis; only the threshold level, λ, is available for choice. The question of how to make the best choice will be discussed below (Example 6.4 *et seq.*). □

Example 6.3. For any $\mathbf{a} = (a_0, a_1, \ldots, a_n) \in \mathbb{R}^{n+1}$, and any input $\mathbf{y} = (y_1, y_2, \ldots, y_n)$, let

$$h_{\mathbf{a}}(\mathbf{y}) = \begin{cases} 1 & \text{if } a_0 + a_1 y_1 + \cdots + a_n y_n \geqslant 0 \\ 0 & \text{otherwise} \end{cases}$$

It is helpful to think of the output as a step function of the inner product $\mathbf{a}.\mathbf{y}^+$, where $\mathbf{y}^+ = (1, y_1, \ldots, y_n)$. The set P_n of all such functions $h_{\mathbf{a}}$ can be regarded as the hypothesis space of a 'machine', known as the *simple perceptron*, which operates as follows. The components y_j of an input vector are weighted by the numbers a_j, together with an 'input-independent' term a_0, and the weighted sum is then applied to a threshold unit, which implements the step function. In this case the threshold is 0, so that if the weighted sum is non-negative, the output is 'yes', otherwise the output is 'no'. It is important to observe that the weights a_i can be altered, so that by choosing suitable values we can try to make the machine perform some desired classification of inputs.

Note that, when $n = 12$, the hypothesis space P_{12} of this machine contains J, the hypothesis space of the crude sunspot machine. If we take $a_0 = -\lambda$ and $a_i = 1$ $(1 \leqslant i \leqslant 12)$, the hypothesis $h_{\mathbf{a}}$ is just j_λ as in Example 6.2. But here we have a richer hypothesis space, because by choosing unequal weights we can represent more complicated hypotheses. □

We shall discuss the situation where the hypothesis space H (or equivalently the machine M) is given, and the problem is to find a hypothesis $h \in H$, which corresponds to a 'real' concept c. Practical considerations indicate that often we have to be content with a hypothesis h which represents c only probably and approximately, in some sense to be defined. What is more, the machine M should arrive at the hypothesis h on the basis of certain partial information which, whatever it is, does not amount to an explicit definition of c. In fact, we shall assume that this information is provided by a sequence of positive and negative examples of c.

Let $Y \subseteq \mathbb{R}^n$ be the example space. A *training sample* is a sequence of labelled examples

$$\mathbf{s} = ((\mathbf{y}_1, b_1), (\mathbf{y}_2, b_2), \ldots, (\mathbf{y}_m, b_m)),$$

where the $\mathbf{y}_i$'s are examples and the b_i's are bits. Thus the value of b_i, either 1 or 0, is additional information specifying whether $\mathbf{y}_i$ is a positive or negative example. We usually think of this information as being provided by a 'teacher'. For example, the following is a training sample in which the examples have been labelled by the teacher according to their status under the 'recession' function (Example 6.1):

$$((657, 647, 689), \quad 0)$$

$$((653, 658, 661), \quad 1)$$

$$((689, 668, 671), \quad 0)$$

$$((657, 658, 669), \quad 1)$$

$$((636, 647, 654), \quad 1)$$

$$((651, 653, 659), \quad 1)$$

We can now be rather more specific about the nature of the process which controls the state of M. Suppose we are given the hypothesis space H of M. A *learning algorithm*, L, for H is a procedure for which the input is a training sample and the output is a hypothesis in H. Of course, in order to qualify as an algorithm the procedure must be effective in some sense, and we shall need to discuss this point in more detail in due course. If we ignore the problem of effectiveness, a learning algorithm is simply a function L which assigns to any training sample $\mathbf{s}$ a function $h \in H$. We shall write $h = L(\mathbf{s})$.

Example 6.4. A learning algorithm for the crude sunspot machine described in Example 6.2 is as follows. Start with $\lambda = 0$. Look at each labelled example $(\mathbf{y}_i, b_i)$ in the training sample in turn. If $b_i = 0$ and the current value of λ is less than $y_{i1} + y_{i2} + \cdots + y_{i,12}$, replace the current value of λ by $y_{i1} + y_{i2} + \cdots + y_{i12}$. If $b_i = 1$, do nothing. The value of λ, after all m labelled examples have been examined, determines the hypothesis j_λ which is the output of the algorithm, the final state of the machine. In a nutshell, the algorithm finds the largest value of the total sunspot activity which is known not to produce an increase in price.   □

Example 6.5. In the case of the simple network in Example 6.3 a possible learning algorithm is as follows. Suppose that a sequence of labelled examples is presented one at a time. Let $\mathbf{a} \in \mathbb{R}^{n+1}$ be the vector of weights immediately before the presentation of a labelled example $(\mathbf{y}, b)$. If $\mathbf{a}$ produces the 'correct' classification of $\mathbf{y}$, that is, if $h_{\mathbf{a}}(\mathbf{y}) = b$, then $\mathbf{a}$ is not altered. If the classification of $\mathbf{y}$ is incorrect, that is, if $h_\mathbf{a}(\mathbf{y}) \neq b$, then we make small changes to the weights, as follows. If the machine classifies $\mathbf{y}$ as positive ($h_\mathbf{a}(\mathbf{y}) = 1$) but it should be negative ($b = 0$), a small amount νy_j is subtracted from a_j. If the machine classifies $\mathbf{y}$ as negative ($h_\mathbf{a}(\mathbf{y}) = 0$) but it should be positive ($b = 1$), a small amount νy_j is added to a_j. This can all be summarised in a single equation:

$$\mathbf{a}' = \mathbf{a} - (h_\mathbf{a}(\mathbf{y}) - b)\nu\mathbf{y}$$

This algorithm is important in historical terms because it was the first 'incremental' algorithm and, in certain circumstances, it can be proved that it 'works'. □

Example 6.6. Recall the linear econometric model outlined in the second section of this chapter. In this situation a training sample is a sequence

$$(\mathbf{y}_1, v_1), (\mathbf{y}_2, v_2), \ldots, (\mathbf{y}_m, v_m)$$

in which the v_i's are *real* values. The network discussed in Example 6.5 is clearly related to that model, and in order to make the correspondence exact we need make only a slight modification. Instead of taking the output to be a step function of $\mathbf{a}.\mathbf{y}^+$, we take it to be the actual value of that expression, a real number. The learning algorithm described in Example 6.5 can be modified to cover this case, taking the rule to be

$$\mathbf{a}' = \mathbf{a} - (\mathbf{a}.\mathbf{y}^+ - v)\nu\mathbf{y}$$

Unfortunately, as pointed out by White [White88], in this crude form the algorithm is 'doomed to wander eternally in the netherworld of suboptimality', although an improvement can be made by allowing the learning constant ν to approach zero.

This behaviour should be compared with the classical econometric method, based on the least squares principle. Given a training sample of m ordered pairs $(\mathbf{y}_i, v_i)$ as above, that method gives the optimal weight vector as the result of a matrix calculation. Explicitly,

$$\mathbf{a} = \mathbf{v}\mathbf{Z}(\mathbf{Z}^T\mathbf{Z})^{-1}$$

where $\mathbf{Z}$ is the $m \times (n + 1)$ matrix whose rows are the augmented examples $\mathbf{y}_i^+$ and $\mathbf{v}$ is the vector $(v_1, v_2, \ldots, v_m)$. We shall return to this example later. □

The learning algorithms currently in vogue for neural networks are based on incremental rules, like the ones described in Examples 6.5 and 6.6. The idea is that by making small changes to the weights we can reinforce correct decisions and weaken incorrect ones. In the case of a network with several layers, such as a multi-layer perceptron, a combination of the 'incremental' and least-squares ideas leads to the famous *backpropagation algorithm*. It was the discovery of this algorithm, rather than the networks themselves, that provided the impetus for the practical exploitation of neural computing.

THE CONSISTENCY PROBLEM

We return to the mainstream of computational learning theory, in preparation for a more thorough discussion of the matters raised in the foregoing examples. We have already observed that the crude sunspot machine has a very restricted hypothesis space. It assumes that the relationship between a year-long sunspot record $(y_1, y_2, \ldots, y_{12})$ and an increase in the price of grain depends only on the total $y_1 + y_2 + \cdots + y_{12}$. If the 'real' relationship is more complex, the crude machine may find it impossible to represent a given training sample.

Example 6.7. Suppose that 'in reality' the price of grain increases if and only if the total sunspot activity in months 4 to 9 exceeds 6 jevons (the jevon is a unit for measuring sunspot levels which will not be found in respectable texts). If this is so, the following examples are correctly labelled:

$$(000\ 121\ 112\ 000,\ 1),\quad (111\ 001\ 111\ 210,\ 0)$$

However, any training sample containing these two labelled examples will defeat our crude sunspot machine. On the basis of the first example it will conclude that $\lambda \leqslant 8$, whereas the second example implies that $\lambda > 10$. $\square$

Example 6.8. Consider the simple neural network in Example 6.3, with $n = 2$ inputs, and the training sample

$$(00, 1),\quad (10, 0),\quad (01, 0),\quad (11, 1)$$

If there is a weight vector (a_0, a_1, a_2) which correctly classifies this training sample, then it must satisfy

$$a_0 \geqslant 0,\quad a_0 + a_1 < 0,\quad a_0 + a_2 < 0,\quad a_0 + a_1 + a_2 \geqslant 0$$

Clearly, these conditions are inconsistent, and so there can be no hypothesis h_a which represents the given training sample. $\square$

The problems illustrated in the foregoing examples are related to the idea of the 'expressive power' of a hypothesis space, which we shall discuss later in this chapter. In the meantime, the following definitions will prove useful.

Given two sets, C and H, of functions from an example space Y to $\{0, 1\}$, we shall think of C as a 'concept space' and H as a 'hypothesis space'. An algorithm for learning C by H, or a learning algorithm for (C, H), accepts training samples of the form

$$s = ((y_1, b_1), (y_2, b_2), \ldots, (y_m, b_m))$$

such that $b_i = c(y_i)$ $(1 \leqslant i \leqslant m)$ for some concept c in C, and outputs a hypothesis $L(s)$ in H. We say that L is *consistent* if $h = L(s)$ correctly classifies all the examples in s. That is, $h(y_i) = c(y_i)$ $(1 \leqslant i \leqslant m)$. This means that the algorithm produces a hypothesis which agrees exactly with all the information presented to it. As we have seen, the problem is that it may be impossible to find a function in the given hypothesis space H which does fit the training sample exactly.

LEARNING IN THE PROBABLY APPROXIMATELY CORRECT SENSE

Consider a model in which a training sample s is obtained by drawing the examples $y_1, y_2, \ldots, y_m$ from Y, according to some fixed but unknown distribution. This corresponds to the notion that the real world is producing results according to some 'laws of economics' which have not been entirely revealed to us. The examples are classified as positive or negative by means of a rule which cannot be inferred from the examples alone. In the economic context, this rule can often be thought of as being derived from hindsight. For instance, the 'teacher' might declare a 12-month sequence of GNP figures to be a positive example if unemployment decreased in the following quarter, and a negative example otherwise. In our general framework, an algorithm L for learning C by H produces a hypothesis $L(s)$ in H which, it is hoped, is a good approximation to the concept c used by the 'teacher'. More fully, we require that, as the number of examples in the training sample increases, so it becomes more likely that the error which results from using $L(s)$ in place of c is small.

In order to formalise this idea, we introduce a probability distribution μ on Y, by which we mean a function μ defined on an appropriate family of 'measurable' subsets of Y and satisfying the usual axioms. It must be emphasised that, in the applications we have in mind, we make no assumptions about μ. The situation we are modelling is that of a world of examples presented to the machine according to some fixed but unknown distribution. The 'teacher' is allowed to classify the examples as positive or negative, but cannot control how the examples are presented.

Given a 'target' concept c in C we define the *error* of any hypothesis h in H, with respect to c, to be the probability of the event $h(\mathbf{y}) \neq c(\mathbf{y})$. That is,

$$\mathrm{er}_\mu(h, c) = \mu\{\mathbf{y} \in Y | h(\mathbf{y}) \neq c(\mathbf{y})\}$$

We refer to the set on the right-hand side as the *error set*. In order to streamline the notation, we suppress the explicit reference to c when it is clear from the context, and we write $\mathrm{er}_\mu(h)$ in place of $\mathrm{er}_\mu(h, c)$.

Example 6.9. Suppose the sunspot algorithm produces the hypothesis $h = j_\lambda$, whereas 'in reality' the threshold at which sunspot activity increases the price of grain is κ (that is, $c = j_\kappa$). Then the error set is the set of $\mathbf{y}$ in $\mathbb{R}^{12}$ such that

$$\lambda \leqslant y_1 + y_2 + \cdots + y_{12} < \kappa$$

The probability assigned to this set will depend on the distribution of total yearly sunspot activity, which may or may not be known. Fortunately, as we shall see, it is possible to make non-trivial assertions which are valid for any distribution. $\square$

Given a probability distribution μ on the example space Y, the product set Y^m inherits a probability structure from Y. This construction allows us to regard the components of a sample $\mathbf{x} = (\mathbf{y}_1, \mathbf{y}_2, \ldots, \mathbf{y}_m)$ as 'independent' variables, each distributed according to the probability distribution μ on Y. This probability distribution on Y^m is denoted by μ^m. Informally, for a given $A \subseteq Y^m$ we can interpret the value $\mu^m(A)$ as 'the probability that a sample of m examples drawn from Y according to the distribution μ belongs to A'.

Suppose we are given a target concept c. Any sample $\mathbf{x} \in Y^m$ uniquely determines a training sample $\mathbf{s}$ in which the examples are labelled according to their classification by c. That is, if $\mathbf{x} = (\mathbf{y}_1, \mathbf{y}_2, \ldots, \mathbf{y}_m)$, then $\mathbf{s} = ((\mathbf{y}_1, c(\mathbf{y}_1)), (\mathbf{y}_2, c(\mathbf{y}_2)), \ldots, (\mathbf{y}_m, c(\mathbf{y}_m)))$. We write S_c^m for the set of all such training samples of length m. Given c, we can interpret the probability that $\mathbf{s} \in S_c^m$ has some given property P as the μ^m-probability that the corresponding $\mathbf{x}$ is in some set, and a minor abuse of notation allows us to write it as $\mu^m\{\mathbf{s}|\mathbf{s}$ has $P\}$.

When the example space Y is equipped with a probability distribution μ, we can now give a precise interpretation to the notions of the error of the hypothesis produced when a learning algorithm L is supplied with a training sample $\mathbf{s}$; and the probability that this error is less than ε. The first quantity is just $\mathrm{er}_\mu(L(\mathbf{s}))$. The second is the probability, with respect to μ^m, that $\mathbf{s}$ has the property

$$\mathrm{er}_\mu(L(\mathbf{s})) < \varepsilon$$

Putting all this together, we can formulate the notion that, given a *confidence* parameter δ and an *accuracy* parameter ε, the probability that the error is less than ε is greater than $1 - \delta$. The resulting definition was formulated first by Valiant [Valian84a, Valian84b] and, using this terminology, by Angluin [Anglui88].

We say that the algorithm L is a *probably approximately correct* (pac) algorithm for learning the concept space C by the hypothesis space H if, given real numbers δ and ε ($0 < \delta, \varepsilon < 1$), there is a positive integer $m_0 = m_0(\delta, \varepsilon)$ such that, for any concept $c \in C$, and any probability distribution μ on Y,

$$\mu^m\{\mathbf{s} \in S_c^m | \mathrm{er}_\mu(L(\mathbf{s})) < \varepsilon\} > 1 - \delta \text{ whenever } m \geqslant m_0.$$

The fact that m_0 depends upon δ and ε, but not on c and μ, reflects the fact that the learner may be able to specify the desired levels of confidence and accuracy, even though the target concept and the distribution of examples are unknown. The reason why it is possible to satisfy the condition for every possible distribution μ is that it expresses a relationship between two quantities which involve μ: the error er_μ and the probability with respect to μ^m of a certain set.

Theorem 6.1. The learning algorithm for the crude sunspot machine, as described in Example 6.4, is probably approximately correct when considered as an algorithm for learning J by J.

Proof. The following is a sketch, ignoring some technical details, which may be found in [AntBig92].

Suppose that δ and ε are given. For any target concept j_κ, let $\mathbf{s}$ be a training sample of length m labelled by j_κ, and suppose $L(\mathbf{s}) = j_\lambda$. As in Example 6.8, the error set is the set of $\mathbf{y}$ in $\mathbb{R}^{12}$ such that

$$\lambda \leqslant y_1 + y_2 + \cdots + y_{12} < \kappa$$

For the given value of ε, and any μ, let β be such that the μ-probability that $z = y_1 + y_2 + \cdots + y_{12}$ lies between β and κ is ε. Thus if $\lambda \geqslant \beta$, the error of $L(\mathbf{s}) = j_\lambda$ is less than ε. Now, the event $\lambda \geqslant \beta$ occurs when at least one of the examples in $\mathbf{s}$ has z greater than β. What is the probability of this happening?

The probability that any one example has z *not* greater than β is at most $1 - \varepsilon$, so the probability that all m examples have z not greater than β is at most $(1 - \varepsilon)^m$. The probability that at least one example has z greater than β is thus at least $1 - (1 - \varepsilon)^m$. Note that this is independent of the target concept j_κ and μ. Furthermore, we can make it greater than $1 - \delta$ by taking m sufficiently large. In fact,

$$m \geqslant m_0 = \left\lceil \frac{1}{\varepsilon} \ln \frac{1}{\delta} \right\rceil$$

will do.   □

The proof provides an explicit formula for the number m_0 of labelled examples sufficient to ensure prescribed levels of confidence and accuracy. Suppose we require $\delta = 0.001$ and $\varepsilon = 0.01$. Then the value of m_0 is $\lceil 100 \ln 1000 \rceil = 691$. This means that if we supply at least 691 examples classified by the 'correct' concept, and take the output hypothesis as a substitute for the correct one, then we can be 99.9% sure that at most 1% of future examples will be misclassified, provided they are drawn from the same source as the training sample.

Of course, all this depends on the assumption that the correct concept is indeed a member of the hypothesis space J of the crude sunspot machine. We might expect that a larger and more 'expressive' hypothesis space would not allow us to use an algorithm which is so simple and so effective.

HOW CAN WE PROVE THAT AN ALGORITHM IS PAC?

Learning in the pac sense is a property of an algorithm. Given any algorithm, we can try to prove directly that it is pac, but that might require a very specific argument, as in the case of Theorem 6.1. Consequently it is desirable to approach the problem more generally.

Recall that a learning algorithm L for (C, H) is consistent if it always produces a hypothesis $L(\mathbf{s}) \in H$ which agrees with the training sample $\mathbf{s}$, provided that $\mathbf{s} \in S_c^m$ for some $c \in C$. For the sake of simplicity we shall confine the ensuing discussion to the case $C = H$, although this is not strictly necessary. We make the obvious abbreviations, such as referring to a learning algorithm for H, instead of (H, H).

For a given $\mathbf{s} \in S_c^m$ and $h \in H$, define the *observed error* of h with respect to $\mathbf{s}$ to be

$$\text{er}_{\mathbf{s}}(h) = \frac{1}{m}|\{i\,|\,h(\mathbf{y}_i) \neq c(\mathbf{y}_i)\}|.$$

Thus L is consistent if and only if $\text{er}_{\mathbf{s}}(L(\mathbf{s})) = 0$. We shall show that in order to ensure that a consistent learning algorithm is probably approximately correct, it is sufficient to put a condition on the relationship between the observed error and the 'actual' error $\text{er}_\mu(h)$ for all $h \in H$.

As before, we assume that there is an unknown probability distribution μ on Y. Suppose we fix, for the moment, a target concept $c \in H$. Given $\varepsilon > 0$, the set of hypotheses whose actual error $\text{er}_\mu(h)$ is greater than ε may be described as the set of ε-*bad* hypotheses for c. A consistent algorithm for H produces an output for which the observed error is 0, and the pac property requires that such an output is unlikely to be ε-bad. This prompts us to say that H is *potentially learnable* if, given real numbers δ and ε $(0 < \delta, \varepsilon < 1)$, there is a positive integer $m_0 = m_0(\delta, \varepsilon)$ such that, whenever $m \geqslant m_0$,

$$\mu^m\{\mathbf{s} \in S_c^m\,|\text{ for all } h \in H, \text{er}_{\mathbf{s}}(h) = 0 \implies \text{er}_\mu(h) < \varepsilon\} > 1 - \delta$$

for any probability distribution μ on Y and any $c \in H$.

Theorem 6.2. If H is potentially learnable, and L is a consistent learning algorithm for H, then L is pac.

Proof. It is sufficient to recall the observation that if L is consistent, then $\text{er}_{\mathbf{s}}(L(\mathbf{s})) = 0$. Thus the condition stated means that the actual error of $L(\mathbf{s})$ is less than ε, as required for pac learning. $\qquad\square$

In the following sections we shall investigate the relationship between potential learnability and the expressive power of a hypothesis space. The culmination of this investigation will be a set of results which have direct applicability to econometric forecasting. The following theorem is an important first step in this direction, but it is essentially irrelevant to our present concerns, so we shall omit the proof. (See [AntBig92].)

Theorem 6.3. Any finite hypothesis space is potentially learnable. $\qquad\square$

THE 'EXPRESSIVE POWER' OF A HYPOTHESIS SPACE

The proof of Theorem 6.3 is fairly simple, but it depends critically on the finiteness of H. Most economic and financial models require an infinite hypothesis space, and it is desirable to extend the theory to cover this case. For example, even the hypothesis space J of the crude sunspot machine contains infinitely many functions j_λ, one for each non-negative real number λ.

The key to extending Theorem 6.3 to infinite spaces is to formalise the notion of 'expressive power' of a hypothesis space H. To introduce some of the ideas, consider P_n, the hypothesis space of the simple neural network illustrated in Example 6.3. In the case $n = 2$, P_2 consists of the Boolean-valued functions h_a for which

$$h_a(y_1, y_2) = 1 \iff a_0 + a_1 y_1 + a_2 y_2 \geqslant 0$$

The example $\mathbf{y} = (y_1, y_2)$, considered as a point in the plane $\mathbb{R}^2$, is a positive or negative example of h_a according to which side of the line $a_0 + a_1 y_1 + a_2 y_2 = 0$ it lies on. Given a sample of points in $\mathbb{R}^2$, P_2 can only achieve certain classifications of the sample into positive and negative examples: precisely those for which the positive examples are separated from the negative examples by a line in the plane. That is why the sample given in Example 6.8 cannot be classified by P_2. The fact that relatively few samples can be separated by a straight line is an indication of the restricted 'expressive power' of P_2.

Suppose that H is a space of hypotheses defined on the example space Y, and let $\mathbf{x} = (\mathbf{y}_1, \mathbf{y}_2, \ldots, \mathbf{y}_m)$ be a sample. The *number of classifications* of $\mathbf{x}$ by H is the number of distinct 'classification vectors' of the form

$$(h(\mathbf{y}_1), h(\mathbf{y}_2), \ldots, h(\mathbf{y}_m))$$

as h runs through all hypotheses of H. Although H may be infinite, we observe that the number of classifications is finite. Indeed, there are at most 2^m possible classification vectors for an m-sample, because each component is either 1 or 0. We define $\Pi_H(m)$ as the maximum, over $\mathbf{x} \in Y^m$, of the number of classifications of $\mathbf{x}$ by H.

Example 6.10. Let $Y = \mathbb{R}^{12}$ and take $H = J$, as in Example 6.2. Let $\mathbf{x} = (\mathbf{y}_1, \mathbf{y}_2, \ldots, \mathbf{y}_m)$ be a sample, and let $z_i = y_{i1} + y_{i2} + \cdots + y_{i12}$ for $1 \leqslant i \leqslant m$. Observe that any rearrangement of the examples within the sample will not alter the number of distinct classification vectors. Thus we may assume that the examples are arranged in strictly increasing order of z,

$$z_1 < z_2 < \cdots < z_m$$

Then the functions $j_\lambda \in J$ can produce only classification vectors of the form

$$(111 \ldots 11), \ (011 \ldots 11), \ (001 \ldots 11), \ \ldots, (000 \ldots 00)$$

of which there are $m + 1$. (If not all the examples are distinct, there will clearly be fewer possible classifications.) Thus the maximum number of classifications by J is given by $\Pi_J(m) = m + 1$. $\qquad\qquad\qquad\qquad\qquad\qquad\qquad\qquad\qquad\qquad\qquad\quad\square$

We noted above that the number of possible classifications of a sample of length m is at most 2^m, this being the number of binary vectors of length m. We say that a sample $\mathbf{x}$ of length m is *shattered* by H, or that H shatters $\mathbf{x}$, if this maximum possible value is attained; that is, if H gives all possible classifications of $\mathbf{x}$. Note that if the examples in $\mathbf{x}$ are not distinct then $\mathbf{x}$ cannot be shattered by any H. The *VC dimension* of H is the maximum length of a sample shattered by H. That is,

$$\text{VCdim}(H) = \max\{m \,|\, \Pi_H(m) = 2^m\}$$

where we take the maximum to be infinite if the set is unbounded. (The letters VC stand for Vapnik and Chervonenkis, who introduced this definition in the early 1970s [VapChe71, Vapnik82].

For example, when $H = J$ we have already seen that $\Pi_J(2) = 3$, whereas there are $2^2 = 4$ possible classification vectors for a 2-sample. Thus $\text{VCdim}(J) < 2$. It is trivial that J shatters any sample consisting of just one example, and therefore $\text{VCdim}(J) = 1$. A more substantial example is given in the next theorem.

Theorem 6.4. For any positive integer n, let P_n be the hypothesis space of the simple network with n inputs. Then

$$\text{VCdim}(P_n) = n + 1$$

Proof. We show that P_n shatters a sample of length $n + 1$. Let $\mathbf{o}$ denote the origin of $\mathbb{R}^n$ and, for $1 \leqslant i \leqslant n$, let $\mathbf{e}_i$ be the point with a 1 in the ith coordinate and all other coordinates 0. We shall show that P_n shatters the sample

$$\mathbf{x} = (\mathbf{o}, \mathbf{e}_1, \mathbf{e}_2, \ldots, \mathbf{e}_n)$$

Suppose that S is a subset of $\{\mathbf{o}, \mathbf{e}_1, \ldots, \mathbf{e}_n\}$. Let

$$a_0 = \begin{cases} \frac{1}{2} & \text{if } \mathbf{o} \in S \\ -\frac{1}{2} & \text{if } \mathbf{o} \notin S \end{cases}$$

and, for $i = 1, 2, \ldots, n$, let

$$\alpha_i = \begin{cases} 1, & \text{if } \mathbf{e}_i \in S \\ -1, & \text{if } \mathbf{e}_i \notin S \end{cases}$$

Then it is straightforward to verify that, with this choice of $\mathbf{a}$, the set of positive examples of $h_\mathbf{a}$ is precisely S. Therefore $\mathbf{x}$ is shattered by P_n and, consequently, $\text{VCdim}(P_n) \geqslant n + 1$.

The fact that P_n shatters no sample of length $n + 2$ is a consequence of Radon's theorem (see [AntBig92]). From this we conclude that $\text{VCdim}(P_n) = n + 1$. $\square$

An immediate application of this result is to make precise the observation (Example 6.3) that the hypothesis space P_{12} is more expressive than J. Indeed, we have $\text{VCdim}(P_{12}) = 13$, whereas $\text{VCdim}(J) = 1$.

Using this idea, we can begin to throw some light on the mysterious properties of artificial neural networks. Consider a typical 'multi-layer perceptron' composed of linear threshold units. Suppose that there are u units with fixed thresholds, connected by l links with variable weights, and that there is a single output unit producing a Boolean value. Altering the weights allows the machine to compute a set of functions which comprise its hypothesis space H. Then it is known [BarHor89] that the VC dimension of H is bounded above in terms of u and l as follows:

$$\text{VCdim}(H) \leqslant 2l \log_2(eu)$$

where e is the base of natural logarithms, $2.718\ldots$. If the number of links which feed in to each unit is bounded, l is bounded by a constant multiple of u. In this case Maass [Maass93] has proved that the upper bound is asymptotically optimal; that is, for some constant K, there are arbitrarily large networks of this type satisfying

$$\text{VCdim}(H) \geqslant Kl \log_2 l$$

Typical of recent work on lower bounds for the VC dimension of neural networks is a result of Bartlett [Bartle93]. He shows that all two-layer perceptrons composed of linear threshold units, and a large family of three-layer networks of this type, have VC dimension at least proportional to the number of links.

Roughly speaking, Maass's result gives a 'super-linear' lower bound for the VC dimension, which means that the expressive power of a neural network can increase more than linearly with the number of connections in it. Thus it is no surprise that a haphazard concoction of units and interconnections will often represent quite complicated hypotheses. The problem arises, as we shall see in the next section, when we come to study the effectiveness of learning algorithms for such networks.

Anthony and Holden [AntHol93] investigated the VC dimension of a more general type of network, first introduced in the 1960s, which includes 'radial basis function networks' and 'polynomial discriminators'. A *linearly weighted* neural network, with n real inputs and a single Boolean output, is defined by a fixed set $\phi_1, \phi_2, \ldots, \phi_k$ of *basis* functions, each of which maps $\mathbb{R}^n$ to $\mathbb{R}$. The state of the network is determined by a variable weight vector $\mathbf{w} = (w_1, w_2, \ldots, w_k)$. The output corresponding to input $\mathbf{x} \in \mathbf{R}^n$ and state $\mathbf{w}$ is 1 or 0 according as the weighted sum

$$\sum_{i=1}^{k} w_i \phi_i(\mathbf{x})$$

is positive or not.

For example, a *polynomial discriminator* is obtained when all the functions ϕ_i are monomials, that is, products of the components of $\mathbf{x}$ such as $x_1^2 x_3 x_n^3$. The *degree* d of a polynomial discriminator is the maximum total degree of any ϕ_i, in the usual sense. Anthony and Holden showed that the VC dimension of a polynomial discriminator is at most $\binom{n+d}{d}$. They also obtained a better bound for the case when the network is given only Boolean-valued inputs.

The *radial basis function networks* are another important class of linearly weighted networks. Here each ϕ_i is defined in terms of the distance of the input from a fixed 'centre' $\mathbf{y}_i$:

$$\phi_i(\mathbf{x}) = \phi(\|\mathbf{x} - \mathbf{y}_i\|)$$

where ϕ is a fixed function and $\|\mathbf{z}\|$ is the usual Euclidean norm of $\mathbf{z}$. Anthony and Holden showed that the VC dimension of a radial basis function network is equal to k, the number of basis functions, if $\phi(r)$ takes any one of the forms

$$r, \quad \exp(-cr^2), \quad (r^2 + c^2)^{1/2}, \quad (r^2 + c^2)^{-1/2}$$

We conclude our discussion of the VC dimension by stating what is perhaps the most basic theoretical result in computational learning theory. This is the promised extension of Theorem 6.3 to the case where the hypothesis space is infinite.

Theorem 6.5. A hypothesis space H is potentially learnable if and only if VCdim(H) is finite.

Proof. See [Blumer89] or [AntBig92]. $\qquad\qquad\qquad\qquad\qquad\qquad\qquad$ □

It follows from this result and Theorem 6.2 that if H has finite VC dimension then any consistent learning algorithm for H is probably approximately correct. In fact, as shown by Blumer *et al.* [Blumer89], if there is a pac learning algorithm for H, then H must have finite VC dimension. This has the interesting consequence that potential learnability is equivalent to the existence of a pac learning algorithm, and is not a stronger condition as one might at first expect. It is possible to give explicit bounds for the sample size $m_0(\delta, \varepsilon)$ ensuring that, with probability at least $1 - \delta$, the actual error of any hypothesis whose observed error is zero is less than ε. In [Blumer89] it is proved that a suitable value is

$$\frac{K}{\varepsilon}\left(d \log\left(\frac{1}{\varepsilon}\right) + \log\left(\frac{1}{\delta}\right)\right)$$

where d is the VC dimension of H, and K is a known constant not depending on H.

EFFICIENT COMPUTATION

Economists now recognise that economic agents affect the outcome of the processes in which they participate by making their own predictions about them. This is called the *rational expectations* scenario. From our point of view the relevant question concerns the ability of an agent to make the required calculations within a realistic time-scale. For example, in order to forecast electricity demand one hour ahead it is no use having a program which takes more than an hour to run. In the financial context (see the final section of this chapter) it may well be the case that seconds, rather than hours, are vital.

Over a period of twenty years mathematicians have developed the subject of complexity theory, which addresses questions about the running time of algorithms. This subject figures prominently in the seminal papers of Valiant [Valian84a, Valian84b], and it has been crucial in the subsequent development of computational learning theory. The central idea of complexity theory is that an algorithm is 'efficient' if its running time is a polynomial function of the size of the problem.

Example 6.11. Consider the computation of the optimum 'least-squares' weight vector **a** by the matrix formula

$$\mathbf{a} = \mathbf{vZ}(\mathbf{Z}^T\mathbf{Z})^{-1}$$

given in Example 6.6. Here the size of the 'input' is measured by the number m of examples and the number n of variables in each one. In order to work out the answer we have to carry out some matrix operations — specifically, three matrix multiplications and an inversion. It is customary to regard the number of arithmetical multiplications required as an indicator of the running time for matrix algebra, and it is known that multiplying matrices of size $p \times q$ and $q \times r$ can be done with pqr multiplications, and inverting a $p \times p$ matrix with p^3 operations. Thus, in order to compute **a** by this method, the number of multiplications required is

$$m(n + 1) + 2m(n + 1)^2 + (n + 1)^3$$

Since this is a polynomial function of the input size, we can regard the least-squares method as an efficient algorithm.   □

It is a sad fact that many important problems cannot (apparently) be solved by an algorithm which runs in 'polynomial time'. These problems are classified as *NP-hard*. Very roughly, NP-hard problems are those which become impossible to solve in practice when the problem size is doubled. For the details, the reader is referred to the now classic book by Garey and Johnson [GarJoh79], as well as [AntBig92] and the references given therein.

In the case of a pac learning algorithm, we require the learning procedure to be efficient, that is, to run in polynomial time, with respect to several measures of the problem size. These are:

- the number of input variables, measured by n such that $Y \subseteq \mathbb{R}^n$;
- the required level of confidence, measured by δ^{-1} in the notation used earlier;
- the required level of accuracy, measured by ε^{-1} in the notation used earlier.

The main result is that a pac learning procedure is efficient with respect to these parameters provided that the running time of the learning algorithm is polynomial in n and the sample size m; and that the VC dimension of the hypothesis space is polynomial in n (see [AntBig92]).

This result is reassuring, up to a point. For example, it tells us that increases in confidence and accuracy can be obtained without impossible computational loads, provided that the running time is polynomial in n and m, and the VC dimension is polynomial in n. This result seems to be adequate for certain kinds of econometric problem, such as that discussed in Example 6.11. The reason is basically that the VC dimension of P_n is $n + 1$, although strictly speaking we need an extended definition of dimension here, because we are dealing with a real-valued output. This will be covered in Example 6.14.

But there is a difficulty. There are theorems which say that finding a consistent hypothesis is NP-hard when the hypothesis space represents certain kinds of 'machine', including quite simple neural networks [BluRiv88], [AntBig92]. From this it is a short step to the conclusion that pac learning is also NP-hard in these situations. Indeed, it seems that there may be some kind of trade-off between the expressive power of the machine and the difficulty of any learning algorithm for it [Biggs92]. This means that the power of a neural network to represent a wide range of hypotheses may have to be set against the fact that training the network is intractably hard.

EXTENSIONS OF THE PAC MODEL AND APPLICATIONS TO FORECASTING

In this section we shall review several extensions of the pac model which are relevant to forecasting problems. Work is still in progress on these extensions, which are very important from the practical point of view, because they make the model correspond more closely with realistic problems. Fortunately, there is now some evidence that, in certain respects, the theoretical properties of extended models do not differ fundamentally from those of the basic model described above.

As we have already noted on several occasions, it is essential to deal with hypotheses whose values are real numbers, rather than the Boolean values 0 and 1. This is often the situation in practice: for example, we need to predict the actual level of unemployment, not just whether it will rise or fall.

Another practical problem is that the classification provided by the 'teacher' may not be completely reliable. Even in the Boolean case, it may be a matter of opinion (for example) as to whether a given economic situation is or is not classified as a 'recession'. Thus for a given $\mathbf{y} \in Y$, both $(\mathbf{y}, 0)$ and $(\mathbf{y}, 1)$ might occur in a training sample. In the real case the value of v in a labelled example $(\mathbf{y}, v)$ is usually subject to some degree of uncertainty, and is not a deterministic function of $\mathbf{y}$. In such circumstances we cannot expect to find a hypothesis which agrees with the training sample, for the simple reason that the training sample itself may not define a functional relationship between an example and its label.

In order to discuss such problems, the relevant notion is that of a 'stochastic' concept. This will be a simultaneous extension of c and μ, where c is a deterministic concept, and μ is a probability distribution on the example space. We need to define it in such a way as to cover real-valued concepts as well as Boolean-valued ones, so we let $V \subseteq \mathbb{R}$ be the set of values, where the Boolean case corresponds to $V = \{0, 1\}$. Then a *stochastic concept* is simply a probability distribution σ on $Y \times V$.

Example 6.12. Let $Y \subseteq \mathbb{R}^{12}$ be the set of possible year-long sunspot records $\mathbf{y}$, and $V \subseteq \mathbb{R}$ be the set of possible grain prices v. Any probability distribution σ on $Y \times V$, such as the one which presumably exists in the 'real world', is a stochastic concept, and there is a corresponding density $\mathrm{d}\sigma$. In traditional econometric thinking the stochastic nature of the relationship between $\mathbf{y}$ and v is modelled by writing down an equation which includes a 'white noise' term η, thus:

$$v = f(y_1, y_2, \ldots, y_{12}) + \eta$$

Clearly, this is equivalent to assuming a particular form for the probability density $\mathrm{d}\sigma(\mathbf{y}, v)$. In practice, we are interested in whether, given a finite number of examples of σ, we can construct a hypothesis which represents it with given levels of confidence and accuracy. □

We shall now extend our discussion of deterministic Boolean-valued concepts to real-valued stochastic concepts. Some of the extensions are immediate. For example, we can speak of the probability that a training sample of length m has some given property, by referring to the product distribution σ^m on $(Y \times V)^m$. In order to define the error of a hypothesis $h : Y \to V$ with respect to a stochastic concept σ on $Y \times V$, we need a little preparation. In the real-valued case we need to know more than simply whether $h(\mathbf{y}) = v$ or not; we are interested in the discrepancy between $h(\mathbf{y})$ and v. This discrepancy can be measured by a 'loss function' in several ways [Haussl92]. For our purposes the most appropriate is the quadratic loss, which is simply the square of the difference. The *error* of h with respect to σ can now be defined as the expected value of the loss, that is

$$\mathrm{er}_\sigma(h) = \int_{Y \times V} (h(\mathbf{y}) - v)^2 \mathrm{d}\sigma$$

As in earlier sections, in addition to this 'actual' error we must consider the *observed error* of h on a training sample $\mathbf{s}$ of m labelled examples $(\mathbf{y}_i, v_i)$. Here the definition is

$$\mathrm{er}_\mathbf{s}(h) = \frac{1}{m} \sum_{i=1}^{m} (h(\mathbf{y}_i) - v_i)^2$$

We can now formulate the property of a hypothesis space which extends the idea of 'potential learnability' defined above. We say that a hypothesis space H of functions from Y to V has the *uniform convergence of errors* (UCE) property if the following holds. Given real numbers δ and ε ($0 < \delta, \varepsilon < 1$), there is a positive integer $m_0(\delta, \varepsilon)$ such that, for any stochastic concept σ on $Y \times V$,

$$\sigma^m \{\mathbf{s} | \forall h \in H | \mathrm{er}_\mathbf{s}(h) - \mathrm{er}_\sigma(h) | < \varepsilon\} > 1 - \delta \qquad \text{whenever } m \geqslant m_0.$$

Roughly speaking, this says that by taking a large enough training sample we can be confident that the observed error is close to the actual error, even though we do not know the actual distribution of labelled examples. We shall see that, as with potential learnability, the UCE property of H can be linked with a measure of its expressive power.

But first we need one other piece of the jigsaw. Suppose that L is a learning algorithm which produces a hypothesis $L(\mathbf{s})$ in H. As we have seen, it is futile to expect that $L(\mathbf{s})$ will 'agree with' a training sample $\mathbf{s}$ generated by a real-valued stochastic concept. It is more realistic to ask for an output hypothesis that is, in some sense, optimal. Precisely, if

$$\mathrm{opt}_\sigma(H) = \inf\{\mathrm{er}_\sigma(h)|h \in H\}$$

then we would like $L(\mathbf{s})$ to be close to $\mathrm{opt}_\sigma(H)$. Now, if H has the UCE property then a hypothesis which is optimal with respect to the observed error will be close to optimal with respect to the actual error. In other words, the output $L(\mathbf{s})$ of an algorithm which minimises the observed error on the training sample $\mathbf{s}$ will, with probability close to 1, have actual error which is close to optimal, provided the length of sample is big enough. This is just an extended form of the pac property: we shall refer to it as the *probably approximately optimal* property. The link with the UCE property shows us how to establish that the classical optimisation procedures of econometrics are probably approximately optimal algorithms.

Example 6.13. The least-squares algorithm (Example 6.6) produces a weight vector **a** which minimises the observed error

$$\frac{1}{m}\sum_{i=1}^{m}(\mathbf{a}.\mathbf{y}_i^+ - v_i)^2$$

Thus, if we can show that the relevant hypothesis space has the UCE property, then it will follow that L is probably approximately optimal. $\qquad\square$

We now proceed to establish the promised relationship between the UCE property and the expressive power of a hypothesis space. We begin by generalising the VC dimension to the case when the hypotheses have real values. Given a hypothesis $h : Y \to V$, and $t \in \mathbb{R}$, define

$$h^t(\mathbf{y}) = \begin{cases} 1 & \text{if } h(\mathbf{y}) \geqslant t \\ 0 & \text{otherwise} \end{cases}$$

For any m-sample $\mathbf{x} = (\mathbf{y}_1, \mathbf{y}_2, \ldots, \mathbf{y}_m)$ and any $\mathbf{t} = (t_1, t_2, \ldots, t_m) \in \mathbb{R}^m$, define the $\mathbf{t}$-classification vector of $\mathbf{x}$ to be

$$(h^{t_1}(\mathbf{y}_1), h^{t_2}(\mathbf{y}_2), \ldots, h^{t_m}(\mathbf{y}_m))$$

Observe that this is a $\{0, 1\}$-valued vector, and so the hypotheses in H can provide at most 2^m different $\mathbf{t}$-classification vectors for any given $\mathbf{x}$. Following [Pollar84] and [Haussl92], we define the *pseudo-dimension* of H to be the maximum value of m such that there is a $\mathbf{t}$ and an $\mathbf{x}$ for which the number of distinct $\mathbf{t}$-classification vectors of $\mathbf{x}$ is 2^m. It is clear that when $V = \{0, 1\}$ the pseudo-dimension is equal to the VC dimension. Also, it can be shown that when H is a vector space over $\mathbb{R}$, the pseudo-dimension of H is equal to its dimension as a vector space. Details are given by Haussler [Haussl92].

Example 6.14. In the case of the linear econometric model, there is a hypothesis $h_{\mathbf{a}}^*$ for each $\mathbf{a} \in \mathbb{R}^{n+1}$, defined by $h_{\mathbf{a}}^*(\mathbf{y}) = \mathbf{a}.\mathbf{y}^+$. In this case it is clear that the hypothesis space is a vector space of dimension $n+1$, and so the pseudo-dimension is also $n + 1$. (A direct proof can be constructed along the lines of the proof of Theorem 6.4 sketched above.) $\qquad\square$

Haussler also defines a notion of ε-capacity of H, and establishes an upper bound for it in terms of the accuracy ε, the pseudo-dimension d of H, and the value M such that all hypotheses in H take values in the interval $[0, M]$ (provided such a value exists). This leads to the following fundamental result.

Theorem 6.6. If H is a hypothesis space with finite pseudo-dimension then H has the UCE property. $\qquad\square$

The final conclusion is as follows:

Theorem 6.7. Provided that the hypothesis space H has finite pseudo-dimension, a learning algorithm which produces a hypothesis in H minimising the observed error on a training sample is probably approximately optimal. $\qquad\square$

As an application of the theory, [Haussl92] obtains explicit bounds on the size of sample required so that, with high probability, the observed error and actual error of a real-valued multi-layer perceptron are close. More precisely, to illustrate his results, consider a multi-layer perceptron with l links whose weights are bounded in absolute value by some constant k. Suppose that the activation function of each unit is the standard sigmoid function

$$f(x) = \frac{1}{1 + e^{-x}}$$

Haussler's theory shows that there is a constant $c > 0$, depending on k, and a corresponding sample size

$$m_0 = \left\lceil \frac{c}{\varepsilon^2} \left(l \log \left(\frac{1}{\varepsilon} \right) + \log \left(\frac{1}{\delta} \right) \right) \right\rceil$$

such that the following is true. Suppose a training sample s of size m_0 is presented to the network and that the weights of the network are altered by some means so that the resulting function computed by the network is h. Then, with probability at least $1 - \delta$, the actual error $er_\mu(h)$ of the network is within ε of its observed error

$er_s(h)$. Thus, for example, if the observed error is at most ε then, with probability at least $1 - \delta$, we can be confident that the actual error is at most 2ε. Recent work of Macintyre and Sontag [MacSon93] has removed the need for a constraint on the weights, although they do not give an explicit expression for the required sample size.

Although these results are highly satisfactory, we ought not to conclude without mentioning another problem. It cannot always be assumed that the probability distribution which produces the examples is the same as that for which forecasts are required. Traditionally, it has been held that advances in 'technology' may change the laws of economic behaviour, whatever those laws might be. This difficulty, too, is currently the subject of mathematical analysis. For details, the reader is referred to two recent papers, on learning under a slowly changing distribution [Bartle92], and learning 'drifting concepts' [HelLon91].

It must be admitted that there is still a considerable amount of work to be done before we can claim that the foundations are sound — but the same could be said of classical econometric theory. The outline, at least, is clear, and it is certainly worth taking account of the insights it provides.

ARE THE MARKETS EFFICIENT?

Some financial time series are notoriously resistant to forecasting techniques. Here we shall ask if the foregoing discussion can throw any light on financial markets, where there is a strong body of opinion which holds that any forecasting technique is doomed to failure.

Let us denote the 'return' from investing in stocks and shares on a particular financial market by the sequence $\{r_t\}$. The precise definition of r_t should include such matters as the appropriate time interval, transaction costs, and comparison with the return on risk-free investment. Although such things are important in practice, for our purposes the details are irrelevant. We shall simply think of r_t as the 'net return at the end of the day'. In this light, the crucial question is: if we know the values r_s for $s < t$, can we decide whether or not $r_t \geqslant 0$?

In certain circles it is an article of faith that the answer is 'no', and this is called the *efficient market hypothesis* (EMH). (Of course, the word 'efficient' is not intended in the same sense as we used it when we were discussing 'efficient computation' although there are connections, as we shall see.) In fact there are several versions of the hypothesis. The weakest, as presented by Malkiel [Malkie87], asserts that 'prices fully reflect the information contained in the historical sequence of prices. Thus investors cannot devise an investment strategy to yield abnormal profits on the basis of past price patterns'. One argument for this form of the EMH is, roughly speaking, that if it is possible to predict a profitable opportunity, then people will do it, prices will adjust as a consequence of their expectations, and the opportunity for profit will thereby disappear.

On the other hand, it might be suggested that people who have access to sophisticated algorithms and machines can do better than those who do not. In the past, individuals have been able to make relatively small amounts of money on the stock exchange by employing simple and informal algorithms. There is every reason to think that nowadays larger groups are using more formal procedures, requiring considerable computing power, and that they are doing quite well. Until recently these procedures were based on classical econometric methods, but neural computing methods are now entering the scene.

So what can computational learning theory tell us about all this? We should like to put forward two ideas for consideration. The first is that in order to make predictions it is not necessary to use very detailed hypotheses based on economic theory. A typical example of that approach is the work of Sentana and Wadwhani [SenWad91] on the Japanese stock market. They start by assuming a relationship between r_t and volatility σ_t^2; although σ_t^2 is unobservable, there are several observables that can serve as proxy for it. Using a proxy variable together with some other 'explanatory variables' (such as a measure of liquidity), they apply econometric techniques to estimate the coefficients of a linear relationship. From our point of view, this procedure amounts to choosing a restricted hypothesis space, for which there is a very well-tried learning algorithm. As we have seen, it is quite likely that any neural net of moderate size would provide a hypothesis space capable of representing the suggested relationships between the variables. Furthermore, in order to construct a suitable network we do not have to make specific assumptions about the form of these relationships.

The second point is that the speed of computation may well play a part in financial forecasting. It could be suggested that the EMH holds only in the sense that forecasting in the relevant context is NP-hard. In order to make a reliable and accurate forecast, we need so much information that it is impossible to process it in the time available for it to be useful. One could regard this argument as an elaboration of Simon's *bounded rationality* theory [Simon82]. The simplest form of bounded rationality hypothesis allows opportunities for profit to those who have advanced technology, as [White88] points out. On the other hand, the advocates of the EMH would argue that such opportunities will disappear as the technology becomes publicly available. The implications for the EMH of more sophisticated forms of bounded rationality, such as we have outlined, are not straightforward. This topic deserves a separate discussion.

In conclusion, it is worth stressing the point that some algorithms are better than others, even if they are all inherently inefficient. A similar situation occurs with the travelling salesman problem: although the problem is NP-hard, it is nevertheless possible to make a successful attempt at fairly large instances of it, provided one has a big enough computer and the right algorithms [Lawler85]. This situation almost certainly has parallels with current developments in financial forecasting.

PART TWO
EQUITY APPLICATIONS

7

Modelling Stock Returns in the Framework of APT: A Comparative Study with Regression Models

Apostolos-Paul Refenes, A.D. Zapranis, *London Business School, UK* and
G. Francis, *County NatWest Investment Management, UK*

INTRODUCTION

A great deal of effort has been devoted to developing systems for predicting stock returns in the capital markets. Limited success has been achieved. It is believed that the main reason for this is that the structural relationship between an asset price and its determinants changes over time. These changes can be abrupt. For example, one month a rise in interest rates will strengthen sterling, while the next month a rise will weaken sterling. This phenomenon of unstable structural parameters in asset price models is a special case of a general fundamental critique of econometric and statistical models. A relationship might be established, for example, between consumer spending and personal income. A tax cut could then be analysed via its effect on personal income. Critics, however, assert that this cannot be done, because a change in policy (the tax cut) will change not only the level of income, but also the relationship between spending and income.

Neural Networks in the Capital Markets. Edited by Apostolos-Paul Refenes.
© 1995 John Wiley & Sons Ltd

Neural network architectures have drawn considerable attention in recent years because of their interesting learning abilities. They are capable of dealing with the problem of structural instability. Several researchers have reported exceptional results with the use of neural networks [DutSha88, White88, Schoen90, Refene92, Refene93]. Neural networks are generally believed to be an effective modelling procedure when the mapping from the input to the output vector space contains both regularities and exceptions. They are, in principle, capable of solving any nonlinear classification problem, provided that the network contains a sufficiently large number of free parameters (hidden units and/or connections) [Hinton87].

In this chapter we investigate the performance of neural networks in the non-trivial application of stock performance modelling. The problem consists of a universe of stocks whose returns are linked to three factors. The idea is to model how the structural relationship between a stock's return and its determinants changes over time. The model can then be used in three ways: to predict the relative outperformance of each stock in the universe, six months in advance, given the current values of its determinant factors; to test the hypothesis that excess returns required by investors for factor exposures, change *slowly* over time as the economic environment evolves, and that a period of six months is a reasonable time frame for dynamic remodelling; to analyse the factors which determine stock performance and to identify how the relative significance of these factors changes over time.

The whole process is part of a dynamic version of the arbitrage pricing theory (APT) model. Currently the modelling is done by linear regression. Our target is to outperform linear regression with respect to three performance metrics:

- goodness of fit *in-sample* (convergence);

- goodness of fit *out-of-sample* (generalisation);

- stability of results with varying network parameters and different data sets.

We show that neural networks give better model fitness in-sample by one order of magnitude and outperform linear regression in out-of-sample forecasting. We identify intervals of values for the parameters that influence network performance over which the results are stable, and show that the same performance figures persist across different training/test sets. We show that by using sensitivity analysis, neural networks can provide a reasonable explanation of their predictive behaviour and can model their environment more convincingly than regression models.

In the next section of this chapter we give a brief overview of the stock performance modelling application. Then we discuss the neural network set-up. We also define the metrics for evaluating the convergence and generalisation ability of different network configurations and comparing with multiple linear regression. We discuss our results using multiple linear regression (MLR) as a benchmark. We then perform sensitivity analysis on the model and discuss its use as a stock modelling tool.

A DYNAMIC MULTI-FACTOR MODEL OF STOCK RETURNS

The Arbitrage Pricing Theory

The arbitrage pricing theory (APT) [RosRos90] is widely used in portfolio management as an alternative to the capital asset pricing model (CAPM) [Sharpe64]. APT has the benefit of being a more powerful theory; it requires less stringent assumptions than the CAPM, yet it produces similar results. The difficulty with APT is that it shows that *there is* a way to forecast expected asset returns but does not specify *how* to do it.

The key idea of the theory is that there exists a set of factors such that *expected returns* can be explained as a linear combination of each asset's exposure to these factors.

The APT model is based on a *no-arbitrage* assumption that can be stated as requiring an upper limit on the ratio of the *expected excess return* so that any risk investment divided by the *volatility* of that same investment is bounded. If this ratio were not bounded then it would be possible to get positive expected excess returns for very low levels of risk. With the no-arbitrage assumption there always exists a portfolio that we call portfolio Q which is efficient and has the highest ratio of expected excess return to volatility. In this case any asset's (or portfolio P's) expected excess return will be proportional to its covariance with portfolio Q. For portfolio P we have:

$$E(r(P)) = \gamma(n)E(r(Q)) \tag{7.1}$$

where $\gamma(n)$ is the 'beta' of the asset with respect to portfolio Q, $E(r(P))$ is the expected excess return of portfolio P, and $E(r(Q))$ is the expected excess return of portfolio Q.

The advantage of this is that it does not require any special assumptions in order to arrive at the result. The disadvantage is that we do not know portfolio Q. The effort to uncover portfolio Q usually takes the form of searching for *attributes* of Q rather than the actual portfolio holdings. The idea is that the particular portfolio Q will depend on the universe of assets we are considering and the properties of those assets at that time. The main proposition of the APT model is the following:

Proposition 7.1: Stock returns can be explained in terms of a set of factors. Traditionally, it has been assumed that the return is a linear combination of each stock's exposure to these factors:

$$R_i = \alpha_i + \sum_{j=1}^{n} f_{ij}\beta_j + \varepsilon_i \tag{7.2}$$

where R_i is the return on stock i; α_i a constant for stock i; f_{ij} the exposure of stock i to factor j; β_j the return attributable to factor j; and ε_i a random error with mean zero. $\square$

Using data on a universe of stocks, it is possible to estimate a model of the following form for the expected return on stock i, where λ_j is the estimate of β_j.

$$\bar{R}_i = \lambda_0 + \sum_{j=1}^{n} f_{ij}\lambda_j \qquad (7.3)$$

In the framework of APT, the λ's represent the excess expected return required by investors because of a security's sensitivity to the particular factor. By subtracting the mean from both sides of the equation above, one obtains the expected return of stock i above the average of all stocks.

$$\bar{R}_i - \bar{R} = \sum_{j=1}^{n} (f_{ij} - \bar{f}_j)\lambda_j \qquad (7.4)$$

So a stock's return relative to the average is assumed to be a linear function of its relative exposure to various factors. These factors are chosen subjectively and are typically based on information derived from the balance sheet of the individual companies.

According to the ATP framework, three stages are necessary during the investment process:

- preprocessing of data to calculate relative values for the factors involved;
- ranking the stocks;
- constructing the portfolio.

In order to rank the stocks in the universe, it is necessary to estimate the λ coefficients. However, before this can be done, the appropriate time frame has to be selected. The ATP model makes no proposition about the time frame over which λ coefficients are to be estimated, with practitioners often using static time-frames. In our case, the appropriate time-frame is determined by the DynIM^{TM} model.[1]

The DynIM^{TM} Hypothesis

DynIM^{TM} is a dynamic version of ATP. The main proposition of the model is the following:

Proposition 7.2: The excess returns required by investors for factor exposures tend to change slowly over time as the economic environment evolves.

For example, small companies tend to be hit hard during a recession, but they do very well in a buoyant economy. Therefore, the DynIM^{TM} model is designed to be 'dynamic' in the sense that relationships are recomputed each month using sample data over the previous six months.

The purpose of stock ranking is the construction of a portfolio. Stock ranking is defined as the task of assigning ratings to different stocks within a universe.

This is actually a classification problem: given a set of classes and a set of input data instances, each described by a suitable set of features, assign each input data instance to one of the classes. In our case the different stocks form the set of input instances and the various ratings form the possible classes to which the input stocks can belong. Each stock instance can be described by a set of features which represent important financial information about the company which the stock represents.

More formally, the problem statement is as follows. Let S represent the space of stocks, $s_1, s_2, s_3, \ldots, s_n$, and R be the set of possible (mutually exclusive) stock ratings, $r_1, r_2, r_3, \ldots, r_m$. Let F represent the k-dimensional feature space, $f_1, f_2, f_3, \ldots, f_k$, describing each of the stocks. Each stock s_i can be considered as a k-tuple $(c_1, c_2, c_3, \ldots, c_k)$ in the Cartesian space $f_1 \times f_2 \times f_3 \times \cdots \times f_k$. Rating the stocks involves finding the one-to-one mapping function g [DutSha88]:

$$g : f_1 \times f_2 \times f_3 \times \cdots \times f_k \rightarrow R \qquad (7.5)$$

In the application described we have an average of 143 stocks updated on a monthly basis. Each stock is described in a three-dimensional feature space by three factors (A, B, C) and the ranking is based on the predicted relative outperformance of each stock six months ahead.

So far, the DynIM^{TM} has been applied quite successfully to UK stocks. For the purposes of estimating the λ coefficients, DynIM^{TM} uses multiple linear regression. A natural extension to this work is to relax the first assumption of the model to allow for a more general nonlinear relationship between factors and resultant return. In this chapter we show that neural networks are a superior substitute for linear regression.

EXPERIMENTAL SET-UP

Training and Test Sets

The training and test sets consist of data provided in a preprocessed form and presented as factor A, factor B, factor C and resultant outperformance Y. The factors A, B and C are parameters extracted from the balance sheets of the companies in the universe of UK stocks. Details of these factors are not specified. Table 7.1 gives an example of the training data set we use in this application.

The rightmost column is a code for each stock in the said universe. A, B, and C are the inputs to the network with Y being the target output (the outperformance of the stock). The outperformance of stock P in the tth month is the result of the application of an unknown function g on P_t/P_{t+6}, where P_t is the price of the stock P in the tth month, and P_{t+6} is the price of stock P after six months (in the $(t + 6)$th month). More formally:

$$Y_t^P = g\left(\frac{P_t}{P_{t+6}}\right) \qquad (7.6)$$

where Y_t^P stands for the outperformance of the stock P in month t.

Table 7.1 Sample training data.

Y	A	B	C	Stock code
−0.203553	+1.268286	−0.128681	+0.616215	6811.000000
−0.066618	−0.272814	−0.187851	−0.124382	6842.000000
+0.170599	+0.175118	+0.331097	+0.420197	6870.000000
−0.078946	−0.061965	−0.181817	+0.309313	6926.000000
+0.193520	−0.342653	+1.379686	+0.215267	8118.000000
+0.112259	+0.792553	−0.417726	+0.066999	8320.000000
−0.190763	+1.016654	+0.270754	+1.166889	8800.000000
−0.104398	−0.194282	+0.169641	−0.036239	8846.000000
−0.124752	−0.021836	+0.900211	+0.338135	9344.000000
−0.070049	−0.135540	−0.064680	+0.599856	9601.000000
−0.087188	+0.156639	+0.410285	−0.001720	9616.000000
+0.049878	+0.286707	+0.124161	−0.280837	10585.000000
−0.049638	+0.611714	+0.072714	+0.160638	10812.000000
+0.020342	+0.000000	−1.085925	−0.174620	11052.000000
+0.135470	+0.658805	+0.213187	+0.307542	11144.000000
+0.011012	+0.417831	−0.363035	−0.139603	13302.000000

The data set covers the period from May 1985 to December 1991 on a monthly basis, and concerns 143 stocks. The overall size of the data set therefore is given by: $143 \times 12 \times 6 = 10\,296$ training vectors.

In accordance with the DynIM^{TM} proposition, the networks are trained on six monthly batches of data and evaluated for the next six-month period. Thus each training/test run consists of $143 \times 6 = 852$ training vectors. The intermediate size for each training run makes the problem non-trivial and allows for extensive tests on convergence and generalisation.

Network Set-up

The learning algorithm used is the standard backpropagation learning algorithm with a momentum term. All simulations are run on SUN4 workstations; convergence is reached within 30 000 iterations typically requiring three to four days of CPU time.

The need for statistical stability in the results requires extensive experimentation with the parameters that influence network performance. Our target here is to identify intervals of values for these parameters which give statistically stable results, and to demonstrate that these results persist across different training and test sets. Below we give a list of these parameters and how they are varied in the simulations.

- *Network architecture*. We examine layered, fully connected, feedforward networks. The numbers of neurons of the input and output layers are defined by the application and they are three for the input layer (one for each factor

A, B and C) and one for the output layer (representing the outperformance Y). The parameters with respect to network topology are the number of hidden layers and the number of neurons of each layer. The aim is to identify network topologies for which the results show small standard deviation (from a mean value higher than MLR's).

- *Gradient descent terms.* The parameters here are the learning rate and the momentum term. The epoch is kept always equal to one, meaning that the weights are updated after each presentation of a training pattern. This is the 'on-line' or 'stochastic' version of backpropagation, as opposed to the 'batch' version where the weights are updated after the gradients have accumulated over the whole training set. Also there is no offset added to the derivative of the transfer function. The objective is to find the ranges of the momentum term and learning rate that yield stable performance for a given network architecture, as a function of the training time.

- *Training time.* The training time is the number of presentations of the entire training set to the network (iterations). This parameter is of great importance since the effect of any network configuration on network performance must be seen as a function of the training time. The aim is to identify the largest possible intervals of network topology for which the results show small standard deviation.

- *Transfer function, cost function, and initial conditions.* The transfer function is not a parameter; for all simulations we use the common asymmetric sigmoid. The cost function used for all simulations is the common quadratic error function, and we test the stability of the results with varying initial conditions.

The network architecture consists of three inputs (corresponding to A, B and C) and one output (corresponding to Y). We experiment with several configurations of hidden units. The best configuration in terms of the trade-offs involved between convergence and generalisation and also giving a conveniently stable network is a 3-32-16-1 configuration. By 'convenient stability' we mean a network whose generalisation performance remains stable (high mean, low standard deviation) for a wide range of values of control parameters. For example, a network whose generalisation is consistent for training times of, say, 15 000–30 000 iterations is preferable to a network in which small variations in training times produce wide variations in outcome.

Figure 7.1(b) shows the architecture of the 3-32-16-1 network. The notation used here will be useful for our discussion in the sensitivity analysis section. The network shown in Figure 7.1(a) is solely depicted for the purposes of the analysis in the next section but one.

Performance Metrics

It is apparent from the ATP and DynIM^{TM} models that the main requirement on the estimator (MLR and/or the neural network) is to estimate the λ coefficients as

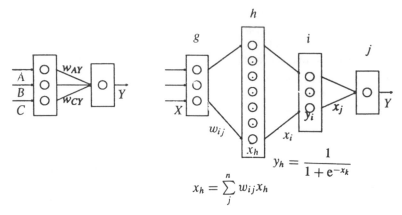

Figure 7.1 (a) Single-layer network; (b) three-layer feedforward network with 3-32-16-1 connectivity

accurately as possible, that is, to fit an accurate model in the universe of stocks for the previous six months. The accuracy of fit is typically measured by the mean squared error of observed against actual values for Y in-sample. The DynIM™ hypothesis guarantees that the results of the estimator remain accurate for at least the trailing six months.

In theory, therefore the only criterion concerning whether neural networks perform better than regression is if they converge to smaller mean squared error in-sample. In practice, however, any estimator will only *approximate* the actual structural relationship. Even if the DynIM™ hypothesis holds, the estimator will still contain an error element in its estimation. This error element can be divided into two components. The first component is due to the estimator's *bias*, while the second component is due to the estimator's *variance*.

Parametric estimators such as linear regression are *high-bias* estimators in that they assume an *a priori* model (for example, a linear relationship) but they are also *zero-variance* estimators. Neural networks, however, are analogous to nonparametric regression methods in that they make no *a priori* assumptions about the problem (that is, they let the data speak for themselves); the main contributor to the global error is their *high variance*.

So, it is always possible that although neural networks may have produced better fit in-sample, their actual estimation of the λ coefficients might be quite wrong. To avoid this problem we consider the following performance measures when comparing with MLR:

- *Convergence*. The *in-sample* performance of the network is important because it determines its convergence ability and sets a target of feasible *out-of-sample* performance which can be achieved by fine-tuning the network parameters and training discipline. The target here is to achieve a better model fit than MLR but without penalising generalisation.

- *Generalisation*. This is the main property that should be sought. The aim here is to achieve (out-of-sample) generalisation performance (that is, prediction of relative stock outperformance) which is better than that of linear regression. If the networks are capable of making better (out-of-sample) predictions, then this is the most objective metric that they have indeed managed to capture the structural relationship between a stock's performance and its determinant factors more accurately than MLR and any subsequent analysis is thus more reliable.

- *Stability*. Neural networks have been known to produce wide variations in their predictive properties. This is to say that small changes in network design, learning times, initial conditions, etc. may produce large changes in network behaviour. Our target here is to identify intervals of values for these parameters which give statistically stable results, and to demonstrate that these results persist across different training and test sets.

- *Sensitivity*. The ultimate performance metric is the usefulness of the estimator as a qualitative decision-making tool in portfolio management. This involves analysing the sensitivity of a stock's exposure to changes in the values of its determinant factors, the ability to simulate 'what-if' scenarios, and the ability to have a formal framework for reasoning about the model's prediction. Later in this chapter we give an analytic framework for factor analysis and its practical application to this problem. We show that, using this framework, the network can provide a reasonable explanation of its decisions.

To quantify the convergence and generalisation performance of the two methods (linear regression and neural networks) we use two metrics. The first metric is the common root mean square (RMS) error. The RMS error is clearly a measure of the correctness of prediction in terms of absolute values and can sometimes be misleading because of its averaging properties. Another metric that could be used instead is the percentage of change in direction (POCID).

In terms of stock ranking, POCID is a measure of the relative outperformances in the stock universe. It provides an approximation of the 'shape' of one's portfolio six months ahead. If our stock universe were a time series, then POCID would give a metric of the direction of change. POCID is calculated by comparing the first differences $(t_2 - t_1)$, $(t_3 - t_2)$, ..., $(t_m - t_{m-1})$ and $(o_2 - o_1)$, $(o_3 - o_2)$, ..., $(o_m - o_{m-1})$, where the t_i are the desired values and the o_i the predicted values of the outperformance, and m is the total number of patterns in the training set for each pair of adjacent training patterns one by one. The POCID metric is defined as the number of pairs $((t_i - t_{i-1}), (o_i - o_{i-1}))$ which have the same sign for both differences $(t_i - t_{i-1})$ and $(o_i - o_{i-1})$, expressed as a percentage of the total number of such pairs $(m - 1)$.

POCID is, to a certain extent, sensitive to the order in which the training patterns are presented, and therefore that order should remain the same for all simulations.

Furthermore, it cannot be regarded as a measure of correct prediction in the direction of change of the outperformance, but as an indication of how well the network predicts the 'shape' of the universe of outperformances.

STOCK PERFORMANCE MODELLING: RESULTS

Comparison with Multiple Linear Regression

The first target of this work is to show that the in-sample performance of the network gives a better fit than linear regression. The in-sample performance of the network is important because it determines its convergence ability and sets a target of feasible out-of-sample performance which can be achieved by fine-tuning the network parameters and training discipline. Figure 7.2 shows two scattergrams depicting the target versus predicted outperformance for MLR and for a neural network with topology 3-32-16-1, learning rate $\eta = 0.3$ and momentum rate $m = 0.3$, trained for 25 000 iterations.

The ideal shape in both scattergrams in Figure 7.2 would be a straight line with a slope of 45 degrees, which crosses the origin. The reason is obvious; if the desired outperformance is, say, 0.2 the ideal would be that the predicted is also 0.2; if the desired is -0.1 the predicted should be the same. The points $(0.2, 0.2)$, $(-0.1, -0.1)$ define the line just described. We see in Figure 7.2 that in the scattergram for MLR the dots are scattered all over the place; in contrast, to the scattergram for the neural network where they resemble the shape of a straight line. This is reflected in the RMS values. The conclusion is evident: the neural network yields much better in-sample fitness than MLR.

Generalisation: Testing the DynIM™ Hypothesis

The second network performance metric is generalisation. Our goal here is to achieve out-of-sample performance comparable to or if possible better than MLR. This would confirm that the model is indeed capable of producing better estimates for the λ coefficients. There are two 'out-of-sample' periods. The (six-month) period immediately trailing the training period and the subsequent six months. For instance, if we are training from May to October 1985 we are using the values for A, B and C available at the time. However, in order to calculate Y there is a delay of up to six months until these values become available. So we would not know $Y_{Oct} = g(y_{Oct}/y_{March})$ until March 1986. In April 1986 we can use the model in one of three ways:

- By supplying the network with the values of $(A, B, C)_{April}$ we can obtain a prediction for October 1986.
- By supplying the network with the values of $(A, B, C)_{Nov\ 85}$ we can obtain a prediction for May 1986.

Predicted Y

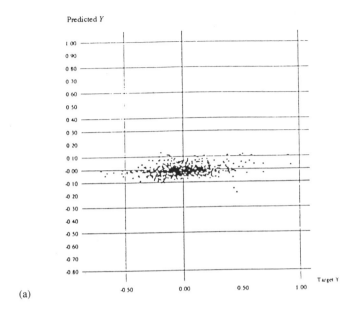

(a)

$Y \times 10^{-3}$

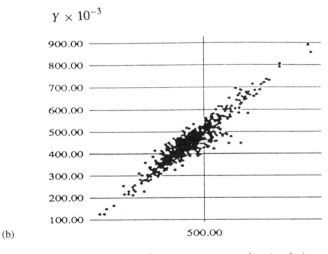

(b)

Figure 7.2 Target versus predicted outperformance, in-sample simulations (May–October 1985), with (a) MLR and (b) a 3-32-16-1 network with learning rate $\eta = 0.3$, momentum $m = 0.7$, trained for 25 000 iterations. For (a) RMS = 0.138; for (b) RMS = 0.044

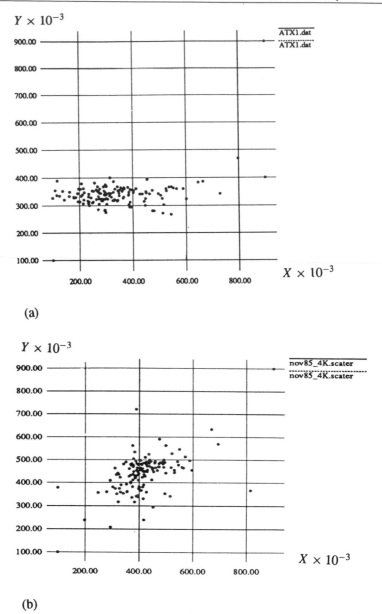

Figure 7.3 Target versus predicted outperformance; out-of-sample (A, B, C) for November 1985, with (a) MLR and (b) a 3-32-16-1 network with learning rate $\eta = 0.3$, momentum $m = 0.7$, trained for 25 000 iterations. For (a) RMS = 0.128; for (b) RMS = 0.066

- By supplying the network with the values of A, B, C from November 1985 to April 1986 we can obtain predictions for the period from May 1986 to October 1986.

Assuming that the DynIM™ hypothesis holds, we are able to plot the relative outperformance of each stock up to six months in advance. Any further predictions will be less valuable as the relationship has changed according to the DynIM™ hypothesis. The accuracy of these predictions (that is, using A, B and C, values from November 1985 to April 1986) gives us the most objective criterion of the accuracy of the approximation that the network has made of the structural relationship between May 1985 and October 1985.

Figure 7.3 depicts the target versus predicted outperformance for MLR and the 3-32-16-1 neural network, for out-of-sample testing with factor values for November 1985.

Evidently the network has produced results that are much better than regression. Although not as good as in-sample, the prediction is reasonably accurate and certainly better than regression. The RMS error for this prediction is 0.066 compared to 0.128 for MLR.

Figure 7.4 shows the RMS error (predicted versus actual) for each subsequent month up to and including April 1986. The solid line shows the RMS given by the neural network, while the dotted line shows the RMS given by MLR.

MLR starts with an in-sample RMS error of 0.13 and remains practically unchanged, which indicates that the model captures only major features of the market, averaging out important trends and variations. The neural network, on the other hand, starts with an RMS error of 0.04 in-sample, which immediately increases to 0.066 for the following month and remains broadly unchanged for a further five months before it starts rising again. This type of behaviour is consistent with the second proposition of the DynIM™ framework which argues that the relationship between a stock's performance and its determinants changes over time, but relatively slowly.

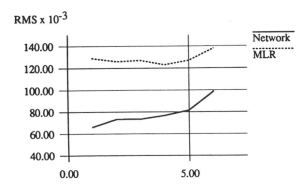

Figure 7.4 MLR versus network RMS error with A, B, C values from November 1985 to April 1986

The results presented above clearly outperform MLR. However, for a real-life application such as that described here it is important to examine how these results vary with network parameters. The objective is to identify intervals of statistical stability for these parameters. This is analysed extensively in [Zapran92] and summarised in the following sections.

Stability with Network Architecture

We experimented with the architecture of the network, varying the number of hidden layers from one to three. The numbers of neurons of each layer were also varied. For all these simulations the learning rate (η) and the momentum rate (m) were fixed ($\eta = 0.3$ and $m = 0.7$). The number of iterations varied from 500 to 30 000. At the high end of training times, the RMS error in-sample remained very stable, varying from 0.044 to 0.072. Single-layer networks give RMS error outside this range.

The out-of-sample performance also remained stable, varying from around 0.06 to around 0.10 for networks with two layers of hidden units; POCID also remains stable around 85% [Zapran92] with a standard deviation of 7%.

Stability with Gradient Descent Control Terms

A detailed analysis of the network performance stability can be found in [Zapran92]. In summary, learning rates in the range 0.2 to 0.4 when combined with a momentum term of less than 0.7 yield better convergence (see Figure 7.5).

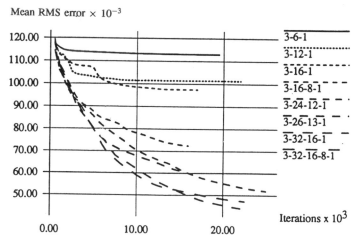

Figure 7.5 RMS (in-sample), for momentum $m = 0.7$, topology 3-16-1, different learning rates, and different numbers of iterations

In general, one- and two-layered networks with a learning rate $\eta = 0.2$ and a momentum term $0.3 < m \leqslant 0.5$ yield the best combination of convergence and generalisation.

Stability with Training Time

For simple networks with one layer of hidden units, 5000 iterations were sufficient to stabilise the RMS to a virtually unchanged (with the number of iterations) value. For more complicated networks with two or more hidden layer, training times in excess of 15 000 iterations are necessary. The POCID metric behaves like the RMS, tending asymptotically to a maximum which is generally found after the 25 000 iterations limit, although the shape of the curve is noisier.

For out-of-sample performance, we obtained best results for large numbers of iterations. In general, there is a smooth improvement in out-of-sample (generalisation) performance. The generalisation performance of the network improves steadily from 5000 to 30 000 iterations. Even at the bottom end at 5000 iterations, the network predicts significantly better than linear regression.

There are, however regions with temporary performance drop-offs (both in terms of increased RMS and decreased POCID). We do not think, however, that these can be interpreted as signs of *overtraining*, because they appear rather early (mainly between 5000 and 10 000 iterations). Probably their existence implies that the network is still *undertrained*, and the better solutions are yet to come for larger numbers of iterations. This behaviour persists across different data sets.

Stability of Results with Different Training Samples

All the simulations mentioned so far were performed for the same training and testing data sets. The training data set contained monthly data for the period from May 1985 to October 1985, and the testing data set contained data for November 1985 to April 1986 inclusive. In order to examine the effect of the data set on the performance of the network, we carried out simulations for the topology 3-32-16-1, using the mean values for the learning and network parameters.

The convergence and generalisation performance of the network does not alter significantly. It appears that the performance of the network is slightly worse than the mean performance in the previous data set but well within the range of the standard deviation (7% in terms of POCID, 0.005 in terms of RMS). Figure 7.6 shows RMS and POCID metrics for the new and old data sets. The profiles of the two curves are much the same.

Stability with Initial Conditions

Backpropagation is known to be sensitive to the values of initial conditions, that is, randomised initial weight values. It is always desirable to observe the mean

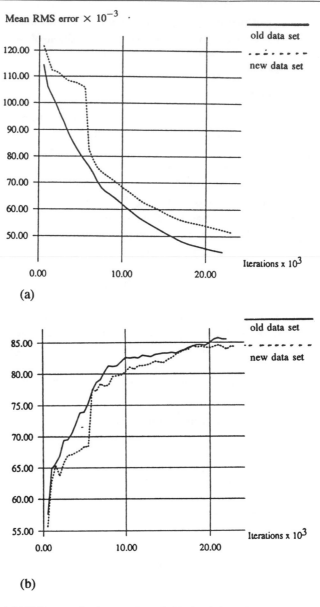

Figure 7.6 (a) RMS in-sample, for topology 3-32-16-1, learning rate $\eta = 0.3$, momentum rate $m = 0.7$, old training data set May to October 1985, new training data set January 1986 to June 1986, old testing data set April 1986 and new testing data set December 1986. (b) POCID in-sample, for topology 3-32-16-1, learning rate $\eta = 0.3$, momentum rate $m = 0.7$, old training data set May to October 1985, new training data set January to June 1986, old testing data set April 1986 and new testing data set December 1986

and standard deviation of the network performance measures for a large number of different initial conditions. We have so far performed only two random sampling runs for the same network configuration but with different initial conditions.

In-sample the curves for the RMS are very much the same, but for all other comparisons in- and out-of-sample the first set of initial weights marginally outperforms the second one. We believe that some adjustment to the network configuration while using the second set of initial weights, or if we insist on harder training, might help to bridge that gap in performance. It is clear that the starting point of the training phase can make a difference (perhaps not a great one) but it should be a consideration when training the network.

STOCK MARKET ANALYSIS

Factor Significance Estimation

In the framework of quantitative asset allocation, it is useful to have an estimate of the degree of impact that a factor has on the relative outperformance. As the structural relationship between factors and outcome changes over time, an accurate estimate of current degree of impact that each factor has (in the present economic environment) can be a very useful tool in asset reallocation. Suppose, for example, that *market capitalisation* were one of the factors. If it were observed that this factor is starting to become significant (with respect to other factors) then the portfolio could be restructured to contain a larger component of assets with high or low market capitalisation as appropriate.

In order to interpret the relative significance of the various factors, the change in output (outperformance Y) relative to the change in an input variable (factor X), $\partial Y / \partial X$, $X \in \{A, B, C\}$, needs to be determined. Several researchers have attempted to interpret the network dynamics in similar ways [GorSej88]. Here we perform parameter significance estimation in a way similar to [KlGuPe89] and [SeOlSe92]. The notation relates to Figure 7.1.

If the network is simple, with no hidden layers, it is trivial to compute the partial derivative, $\partial Y / \partial X$. We know that the output Y is given by the sigmoid function $f(z) = (1 + e^{-z})^{-1}$ where $z = w_{AY} + w_{BY} + w_{CY} + \theta$, and θ is an internal threshold (see Figure 7.1(a)). We also know that $f(z)$ is continuous and differentiable.

For multi-layered networks, the partial derivative $\partial Y / \partial X$, can be computed by applying the chain rule for derivatives repeatedly through the paths that connect the output node Y to the input node X. Starting from the output layer we know that $x_j = \sum_{w_{ij} y_i}$, therefore $\partial x_j / \partial y_i = w_{ij}$. Using the chain derivative rule:

$$\frac{\partial Y}{\partial y_i} = w_{ij} \frac{\partial Y}{\partial x_j} \tag{7.7}$$

Proceeding to the next layer on the left and continuing until the input layer, with similar applications of the chain rule we obtain:

$$\frac{\partial Y}{\partial X} = w_{gh} K_h \tag{7.8}$$

where h denotes the nodes in the middle hidden layer, g denotes nodes in the input layer, and K_h is given by:

$$K_h = \frac{\partial y_h}{\partial x_h} w_{hi} \frac{\partial y_i}{\partial x_i} w_{ij} \frac{\partial Y}{\partial x_j} \tag{7.9}$$

Like [SeOlSe92] we use this notation to emphasise the fact that K_h is a function independent of any parameters in the input layer. The node at the output layer and the nodes in the input layer g are connected via multiple paths through the hidden layers. To obtain the partial derivative over all paths G connecting the nodes Y and $X \in \{A, B, C\}$ we sum all such $\partial Y / \partial X$. Using the notation in (7.8) we obtain:

$$\frac{\partial Y}{\partial X} \rfloor_G = \sum_h w_{gh} K_h \tag{7.10}$$

We note that the K_h's are the same for all input variables, X_g, since all changes reflected from the outer layer through the hidden layers pass through the same paths for all input variables. We note that this does not include the input layer weights. Therefore a relative change in Y with respect to a change in a factor (A, B or C) is influenced primarily by the weights in the input layer. If the absolute values of the weights in the input layer for a particular factor are high, then it is reasonable to expect that the result in Y will be very sensitive to changes in this input. The magnitude of this change cannot be determined since it depends upon the sign and magnitude of K_h, but an approximation can be estimated by considering a linear combination of the weights in the input layer. [KlGuPe89] and [SeOlSe92] note that this approximation is necessary only when the K_h's are not all of the same sign.

Figure 7.7 plots the values of the input layer weights for each factor. The sums of the absolute values of the input layer weights for each factor A, B, and C are 103, 110 and 91, respectively. The two factors with the highest significance for the period under consideration (May to October 1985) are A and B. This is a very important finding, and we can use it as an integral part of the asset allocation process (see also later sections).

The estimates for $\partial Y / \partial X$ produced here are only approximations. Better estimates can be produced if the K_h's are known. However, the K_h's depend not only upon the weights in the hidden layers but also upon the input vector. The K_h's change with each input vector. [SeOlSe92] propose an approach for obtaining better estimates for the K_h's based on a weighted mean for K_h which can be obtained by combining all the weights and the inputs. The weighted mean can then be used in (7.10) to obtain a better estimate of $\partial Y / \partial X$. A complementary approach would be experimentally to analyse the sensitivity of the output as the values of each factor are varied while holding the other factors constant at some fixed point in their range. This is very useful for simulating 'what-if' scenarios in asset management.

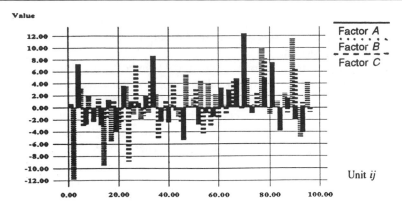

Figure 7.7   Factor significance estimation

Sensitivity Analysis

To perform sensitivity analysis we first determine the ranges of factors A, B and C. For each factor, the minimum, maximum and the mean value of the range are determined. The values of each factor are then varied one at a time, while holding the values of the other factors constant at their mean (or median) value. For each factor being varied we step through its range smoothly using a relatively small step size. In our case the ranges for A, B and C are $[-2.37, 1.50]$, $[-2.733, 3.86]$ and $[-1.44, 1.67]$, respectively. We generate approximately 300 values (A^*, B^*, C^*) for each factor. These 'hypothetical' values are then fed into the neural network model which is used to compute the output. This output is treated as the likelihood of the sample being a target. Wan [Wan90] shows that the output of a multi-layer network classifier can be considered to be a nonparametric estimate of a posterior probability of the sample belonging to a particular class.

For all three variables, the network outcome is plotted against the value of the factor. The plot for factor A is shown in Figure 7.8. It should be noted that the

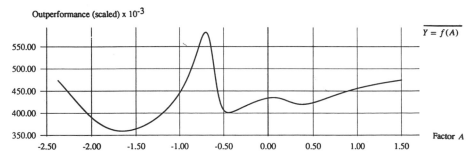

Figure 7.8   Sensitivity plots for factor A^*, with $B = -0.11$, $C = 0.05$

absolute value of the predicted outperformance Y, is not as important as the *change* in the network output. As expected, the relationship between Y and factor A is a complex nonlinear function.

The sensitivity plots for a factor are interpreted to indicate that if all other factors were held constant at around the mean value, changes in this factor would affect the relative outperformance in the manner shown by the plot. For instance, Figure 7.8 shows that the outperformance is very sensitive to changes in factor A. For large negative values of A, stock performance is very low, and it increases with A in a nonlinear manner. The plot is consistent with general expectations. Regression models are unable to capture such information.

Factor B also shows a similar nonlinear behaviour. Factor C appears to be the least sensitive of all, in that only changes in its values at the extreme end of its range have a significant influence on outcome (see Figure 7.9).

These observations confirm the expectations predicted by the analysis in the previous section.

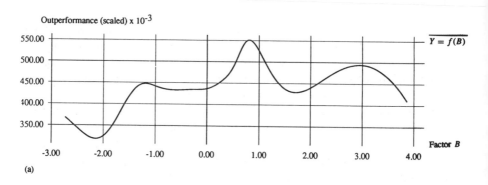

(a)

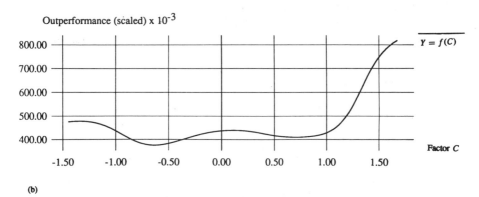

(b)

Figure 7.9   Sensitivity plots for (a) factor B^*, with $A = -0.06$, $C = 0.05$; (b) factor C^*, with $A = -0.06$, $B = -0.11$

Market Profiling

The justification for the sensitivity analysis lies in the argument that if the model captures the relationship between predictor variables and the outcome accurately, then the relationship is very likely to be meaningful at least for the training sample. Sen *et al* [SeOlSe92] assert that the 'quality' of the model can be relied upon if the predicted behaviour is not counter-intuitive. We argue that it is possible to quantify the 'quality' of the model by observing its prediction accuracy for the out-of-sample period immediately following the training period. Earlier in this chapter we used the out-of-sample RMS error to show that the quality of the neural model is superior to that of current 'best practice'.

In this section we extend the sensitivity analysis to produce a more complex profile of the stock market by keeping the least significant factor fixed at its mid-point and varying the most significant factors from the minimum to the maximum values in their range. We repeat this process for consecutive time frames to produce a three-dimensional visualisation of how the market evolves as the economic environment changes.

In Figure 7.10 we fix the least significant factor C at its mean value and vary the values of factors A and B using approximately 60 equal intervals (each) over their whole range. The neural network model is then used to compute the output. For both factors A and B (X- and Y-axis) the predicted outperformance is plotted on the Z-axis. The estimated decision surface is viewed from an angle of 60, 30 degrees. The network was trained with data from May to October 1985.

As expected, the relationship between outperformance and the determinant factors is a complex nonlinear function. It is interesting to note the effects of the nonlinear combination of factors A and B. In particular, in the low end of the ranges $[-2, -1.5]$ the nonlinearly combined values of A and B have an overall positive effect.

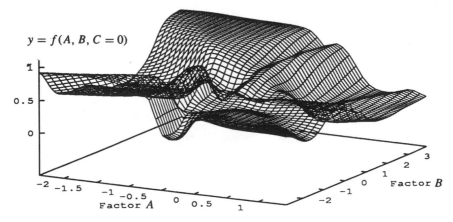

Figure 7.10 Estimated outperformance surface for factors A and B (May to October 1985); C remains fixed at its mean value

Again, it should be noted that the *absolute* value of the predicted outperformance is not as important as the predicted *changes* in the outperformance. However, the fact that, when we tested the predicted output against the actuals, we only found a relatively small RMS error provides important evidence that the predicted surface can be treated as being quite accurate even in absolute terms.

We now move on to the next six-month period and repeat the process with a retrained network. Figure 7.11 shows the estimated outperformance surface produced by a network trained with data from November 1985 to March 1986. A slightly different surface is now predicted, with stocks in the far corner being the best suggested outperformers. Stocks in the left-hand corner ($A \in [-2, -1]$, $B \in [-2, -1]$) which were good performers started to drop off.

Figure 7.12 shows the estimated outperformance surface produced by a network trained with data from January to June 1986. There is now a definite concentration

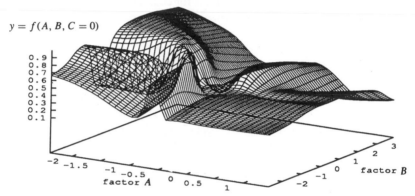

Figure 7.11   Estimated outperformance surface for variables A, B (November 1985 to March 1986)

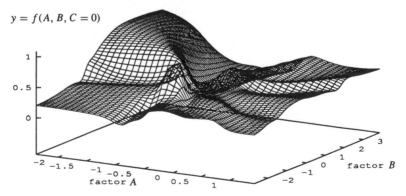

Figure 7.12   Estimated outperformance surface for variables A, B (January to June 1986); C remains fixed at its mean value

of 'good' stocks in the far corner and the 'bubble' between $A \in [0, 0.5]$ and $B \in [1, 3]$ is starting to migrate to the back right-hand corner.

It must be noted that since the relationship will be continuously recalculated every month, the evolution of the market profile will be much smoother than shown in Figures 7.9 and 7.10. In fact, we deliberately produced the estimated outperformance surfaces such as to cover both non-overlapping periods (May to October 1985 and November 1985 to March 1986) and overlapping periods (November 1985 to March 1986 and January 1986 to June 1986). It can be seen from Figures 7.11 and 7.12 that the overlapping period shows a smoother transition.

Testing the DynIM™ Hypothesis

The estimated outperformance surfaces support the DynIM™ hypothesis that the structural relationship between an asset price and its performance changes

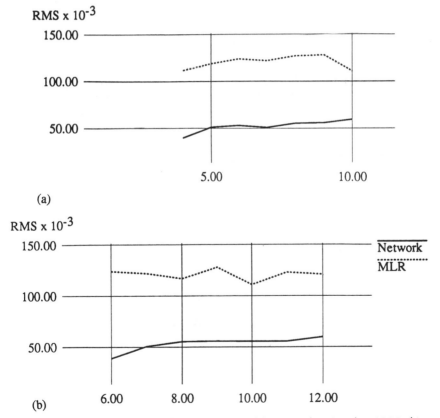

Figure 7.13 (a) Out-of-sample RMS for the period from April to October 1986; (b) out-of-sample RMS from June to December 1986. It should be noted that in the overlap, predictions are made by two different networks

dynamically over time, but they do so relatively slowly. However, in order to test the DynIM^{TM} hypothesis more rigorously, we need to ensure that the network predictions are accurate and reliable.

This is an impossible task since we have no way of confirming that the predicted outperformance for *all* simulated triples (A^*, B^*, C^*) is in fact the same as the actual one. The most objective way of doing so is to test the RMS error of the predicted against the actual outperformance for those out-of-sample triples (A, B, C) for which we know the outcome. If the network error for these triples is low, then there is every chance that the network approximates the outperformance surface quite accurately. Earlier in this chapter (Figures 7.3 and 7.4) we tested the DynIM^{TM} hypothesis for the period from May to October 1985 by comparing the RMS error between predicted and actual for the subsequent six months. The findings supported the DynIM^{TM} hypothesis and showed that the networks are more accurate than MLR. The RMS error was satisfactorily low. So there is every chance that the predicted outperformance surface following May to October 1985 (as shown in Figure 7.9) is quite accurate.

We now repeat the process for the periods from November 1985 to March 1986 and from January 1986 to June 1986. Figure 7.13(a) shows the RMS error for out-of-sample predictions from April to October 1986 on a month-by-month basis. Likewise, Figure 7.13(b) shows the RMS error for out-of-sample predictions from June to December 1986. Like Figure 7.3, in both cases the RMS error starts with a level close to 0.04 in-sample, which increases to 0.055 for the trailing month and remains low for a further six months.

CONCLUSIONS AND FURTHER WORK

Classical statistical techniques for prediction reach their limitations in applications with nonlinearities in the data set. Most forecasting methods are only capable of picking up general trends and have difficulty in modelling cycles that are by no means repetitive in amplitude, period or shape. Despite their inadequacies, techniques such as multiple linear regression have proved to be a useful tool in the capital markets and are used routinely.

We showed that even simple neural learning procedures such as the backpropagation algorithm far outperform current 'best practice' in a typical application for stock ranking within the framework of the arbitrage pricing model. Their smooth interpolation properties allow neural models to fit better models to the data and to generalise significantly better.

We believe that the performance measures obtained here can be improved further with careful network design and preprocessing of the data. As far as the data are concerned there is at least one obvious area of improvement. This is concerned with the existence of malicious vectors in the training set. These are vectors which lie close to the borders between classes (one-to-many mappings) and which the quadratic cost function used here finds difficult to learn (at best it averages). We have developed an algorithm for detecting such malicious vectors [Zapran92] and applied it to the training set. We found that up to 13% of the training data were classified as such vectors, and we are currently experimenting with various strategies for dealing with such vectors [TuvRef93].

NOTE

1. DynIM™ (Dynamic Multi-Factor Model of Stock Returns) is a Trade Mark of County NatWest Investment Management Ltd.

8

Testing the Efficient Markets Hypothesis with Gradient Descent Algorithms

George Tsibouris and Matthew Zeidenberg,
University of Wisconsin, USA

INTRODUCTION

Accurate modelling of economic phenomena has always been one of the main concerns of economists. Most attempts to understand the economy have been either model-driven, statistical, or both. A theory based on optimising behaviour is formulated and a testable hypothesis derived from the theoretical model is checked against economic data. Statistical tests enable economists to reject incorrect hypotheses to the desired degree of confidence. Specification of financial models has traditionally been done in partial equilibrium. Both capital asset pricing models (CAPM) and arbitrage pricing theory (APT) derived models attempt to describe asset price behaviour based on optimisation in partial equilibrium. Such models have been very useful in expanding our understanding of stock price behaviour. Nevertheless, many empirical financial anomalies have remained unexplainable. It is possible that this may be due to the partial equilibrium nature of these models. Attempting to model financial markets in a general equilibrium framework still remains analytically intractable.

Stock prices, because of their highly chaotic nature, are notoriously difficult to model with standard methods such as least-squares regression. In recent years, there has been great interest within the scientific community in discerning patterns in such highly chaotic data, since such data are present not only in economic time

Neural Networks in the Capital Markets. Edited by Apostolos-Paul Refenes.
© 1995 John Wiley & Sons Ltd

series but also in the behaviour of other dynamical systems such as weather patterns and ecological models. Models that reveal systematic trends in economic data may be generalized to other domains.

Because of their inductive nature, neural networks, like other statistical models, can bypass the step of theory formulation altogether, or can be combined with prior knowledge of the characteristics of the system. They can infer complex nonlinear relationships between variables that are given as their input and variables that are given as their output. There are four types of neural network that suggest themselves for the modelling of time-series data: feedforward backpropagation networks; recurrent backpropagation networks; cascade-correlation networks; and networks based on the temporal difference method of Sutton. We explore the use of feedforward backpropagation networks, temporal difference models, and cascade-correlation networks in the case of stock-market time-series data.

Neural network models are fitted to daily stock prices. The estimated parameters are used to obtain one-step-ahead forecasts. Learning achieved by this system is compared to traditional statistical techniques.

The next section sets out the econometric methodology that is commonly used. Then the estimation results are presented and discussed, and possible directions for further study outlined.

ECONOMETRIC METHODOLOGY

The efficient markets hypothesis (EMH) has found broad acceptance in the financial community. In its weak form, the EMH asserts that an asset price is a reflection of all the information that can be gleaned from past price behaviour. This implies that the movement of an asset's price is completely unpredictable given its history. Thus, technical analysis cannot provide a financially profitable investment strategy. The intuitive reason behind the unpredictability of asset price returns is similar to the reason why one rarely finds money lying on the ground. Nobody disputes the fact that money does indeed fall out of people's pockets but, when it does, it tends to be picked up fairly quickly. Profit opportunities in financial markets are exploited at their inception.

Traditional tests of the EMH have involved estimating a linear autoregressive model of asset returns and testing the joint null hypothesis that the coefficients of the lagged returns are equal to zero. Nevertheless, the inability to refute the null hypothesis does not imply an affirmation of the EMH. It simply may be that eventual underlying nonlinear patterns are undetectable using linear methods.

Neural networks are a rich class of functional forms that are capable of approximating arbitrary Borel measurable functions [HekrPa91]. This property allows us to exploit nonparametric estimation methods based on these neural networks. These models can be viewed as an input–output system of a particular form. A general neural network describes a mapping between a vector of inputs and a vector of outputs. The simplest model is constructed in the following form: define a $1 \times r$

vector of inputs $\mathbf{X}$ and a $1 \times p$ vector of outputs $\mathbf{Y}$. Their interaction can be described as:

$$\mathbf{Y} = \mathbf{X}\boldsymbol{\beta}$$

where $\boldsymbol{\beta}$ is the connection strength matrix of size $r \times p$. If we assume that one of the input neurons exhibits a value of one at all times, we then have the multivariate linear statistical model with an intercept term. In theory, each of the $\mathbf{X}$ inputs could be processed in parallel, which is one of the main analogies between this model and the brain.

The family of models described above is only capable of approximating quasi-linear models. Even with a slightly more sophisticated underlying structure (say, quadratic terms), it performs poorly. This led to the development of more complex networks by applying further analogies with neural function in the cerebral cortex. Intermediate processing layers were introduced between the input and output. These layers are called 'hidden' since it is not possible to obtain empirical observations on them. The output of this network model can be described as follows:

$$Y_k = \psi_k \left(\sum_{j=1}^{q} \alpha_j \left(X \gamma_j \right) \beta_{kj} \right) \equiv f_k(X, \theta),$$

where $\boldsymbol{\beta}' = \left(\beta_1, \ldots, \beta_p \right)$ and $\boldsymbol{\gamma}' = \left(\gamma_1, \ldots, \gamma_q \right)$ are the connection strengths, ψ_k and α_j are known functions, and $\boldsymbol{\theta}' = (\boldsymbol{\beta}', \boldsymbol{\gamma}')$.

In backpropagation, a member of the family of smooth and monotonically increasing functions, for example the sigmoid function

$$\alpha_j \left(\mathbf{X}\gamma_j \right) = \frac{1}{1 + e^{-X\gamma_j}}$$

is used as the activation function α_j. Without loss of generality and for computational simplicity we define the output processing function ψ_k to be the identity function.

Alternative choices of activation function are possible. One example that time-series econometricians are familiar with is letting α_j equal the sine function. We therefore get the spectral analysis model where a linear combination of sine functions at different frequencies can approximate any function arbitrarily closely.

The backpropagation method is implemented on θ using recursive m-estimation, namely:

$$\theta_{t+1} = \theta_t - \eta_t \nabla_\theta f_k(\mathbf{X}, \boldsymbol{\theta})'(\mathbf{Y} - f_k(\mathbf{X}, \boldsymbol{\theta}))$$

where η_t is the learning rate, ∇_θ is the gradient and θ_0 is an arbitrary starting value.

EMPIRICAL RESULTS

For our estimation, we selected six stock price data sets from different industries in an attempt to avoid sector-specific idiosyncrasies. They are the stock prices of

Citicorp (CCI), John Deere (DE), Ford (F), General Mills (GIS), GTE, and Xerox (XRX). We use daily temporal aggregation. The observations span the period from 4 January 1988 to 31 December 1990. The total number of daily observations is 758. All our data are from the Center for Research in Security Prices (CRSP).

We divided each data set into two portions. The first portion, which, following general practice, we call the training set, is used to construct the network model and spans the period from 4 January 1988 to 29 December 1989. The second portion is used to test the validity of the model on data not used to produce the model, that is, what is commonly referred to as 'generalisation' performance. The dates for this portion span the period from 2 January 1990 to 31 December 1990.

Table 8.1 presents summary statistics of the data. It shows the division of each data set into two portions, with dates, sample means and standard deviations for the training and test sets in each of the six cases. The variables in Table 8.1 are one-day returns for holding the stock in question. The closing values are used to represent the daily price.

The average daily return of the six stocks, CCI, DE, F, GIS, GTE, and XRX for the training period is 0.0010% and for the test period is −0.0009%. The most volatile stock during the training period was CCI, with a standard deviation of 0.0202%. The most volatile stock during the test period was also CCI, with a standard deviation of 0.0267%. The least volatile stock, for both the training and test periods, was GIS, with standard deviations of 0.0127% and 0.0158%, respectively.

We implemented the backpropagation algorithm using the signs of stock returns as inputs and outputs. A similar technique was used in a previous paper by the authors using different stocks and a different sample period. For each of the six data sets CCI, DE, F, GIS, GTE, and XRX, we used a network of nine input units, five hidden units and one output unit. This represents a model of $(9 \times 5) + (5 \times 1) = 50$ weights or parameters. Backpropagation is more parsimonious in number of parameters than the equivalent linear polynomial expansion with $2^9 - 1 = 511$ parameters. As a side note, an alternative specification using signed magnitudes as

Table 8.1 Summary statistics of the data set.

Variable	Sample	Start date	End date	Mean	Std. Dev.
CCI	Train	4/1/88	29/12/89	0.0013	0.0202
	Test	2/1/90	31/12/90	−0.0026	0.0267
DE	Train	4/1/88	29/12/89	0.0013	0.0158
	Test	2/1/90	31/12/90	−0.0008	0.0190
F	Train	4/1/88	29/12/89	0.0006	0.0150
	Test	2/1/90	31/12/90	−0.0015	0.0169
GIS	Train	4/1/88	29/12/89	0.0010	0.0127
	Test	2/1/90	31/12/90	0.0014	0.0158
GTE	Train	4/1/88	29/12/89	0.0017	0.0135
	Test	2/1/90	31/12/90	−0.0004	0.0168
XRX	Train	4/1/88	29/12/89	0.0003	0.0135
	Test	2/1/90	31/12/90	−0.0015	0.0167

inputs and signs and magnitudes as two separate outputs was attempted. It did not perform very well.

As an illustrative example, to predict the value of CCI at period (day) t (corresponding to the output unit), we used the signs of the returns for the past five periods $t - 1$, . . . , $t - 5$, as well as the return between t and $t - 10$ (two weeks), $t - 22$ (one month), $t - 132$ (about six months), and $t - 264$ (about one year), for a total of nine inputs. Positive asset returns are coded as a 1, while negative asset returns are coded as a 0. We have experimented with varying the number of hidden units and found five to be an adequate compromise. General experience has led researchers to choose a number of hidden units less than or equal to the number of inputs.

We performed backpropagation learning on the training set for 200 iterations or epochs, where an iteration represents one complete pass through the input data, altering the weights in the network. We recorded the total error sum of squares (TSS) of all the training patterns. We considered, as is general practice, the output unit to be predicting a positive sign for the subsequent return if it (a sigmoid unit) output above 0.5, and negative below 0.5. The performance is the percentage of the time that the predicted output agrees with the true output. We also calculated the RMS error, the number correctly predicted, and the average output of the network for each set. Table 8.2 presents the results of the neural network estimations on the financial data series. The TSS error and the RMS error are reported for all the asset price measures for both the training set and the test set. The average direction of asset price change, which corresponds to the average value of the output, is also presented. For the daily asset prices, the average output in the training set equals 0.4412 and in the test set equals 0.4148. This means that the neural network model predicts an upward movement approximately 44.12% of the time and a downward movement the remainder of the time (in the training set). This is broadly consistent with one of the implications of the random-walk hypothesis in which upward asset price movements should occur just about as frequently as downward movements.

The lower portion of Table 8.2 presents the actual performance statistics of the backpropagation algorithm in- and out-of-sample. The number of correct signs of the asset price returns coming from the model is compared to the actual data series. The percentage of correct signs is calculated for both the training and test runs. Standard deviations are also calculated for the percentage of correct signs under the null hypothesis of the model actually having a 0.5 probability of estimating the direction of change correctly. The probability of a type I error, namely the probability that we would get the percentage of correct signs that we report given that the model was providing absolutely no explanatory power, is also presented.

The percentage of correct responses ranges from 48.22% for the DE test set to 60.87% for the CCI test set. The average percentage of correct responses for the training sets was 60.20% and the average percentage for the test sets was 55.01%. As is usually the case in many such experiments of this type, the performance on the training set (after training) usually exceeds that on the test set. This is

Table 8.2 Empirical results for backpropagation.

Variable	Set	Sample size	TSS	RMS error	Avg. est.	No. correct	% correct	Std. Dev.	Probability of type I error
CCI	Train	505	65.6505	0.3606	0.2358	327	64.75%	6.6304	0
	Test	253	39.2403	0.3938	0.2456	154	60.87%	3.4578	0
DE	Train	505	60.5288	0.3462	0.6953	265	52.48%	1.1125	0.1335
	Test	253	47.6768	0.4341	0.7237	122	48.22%	−0.5658	0.7123
F	Train	505	67.1428	0.3646	0.3404	304	60.20%	4.5834	0
	Test	253	34.6182	0.3699	0.3356	152	60.08%	3.2063	0
GIS	Train	505	69.0926	0.3699	0.2263	307	60.79%	4.8504	0
	Test	253	41.7974	0.4065	0.2229	135	53.36%	1.0688	0.1446
GTE	Train	505	65.7384	0.3608	0.4492	313	61.98%	5.3844	0
	Test	253	35.8668	0.3765	0.4666	135	53.36%	1.0688	0.1446
XRX	Train	505	67.5382	0.3657	0.5203	308	60.99%	4.9394	0
	Test	253	44.1531	0.4178	0.4904	137	54.15%	1.3203	0.0934

because the training process tends to fit characteristics of the training set that are not generalisable (so-called 'overfitting'), that is, it fits 'noise' in the training set as well as signal. Therefore, it is not desirable to train the training set beyond a certain number of iterations, since in the early stages of learning it learns the 'first-order' characteristics of the training data, which are more likely to correspond to the true model. In subsequent iterations, the model learns 'second-order' characteristics which vary from data set to data set and would prove to be of no help in attempts to generalise.

The estimated percentages of correct responses for the training sets are all more than two standard deviations from the value maintained under the null hypothesis, with the exception of DE. The standard deviations range from 1.1125 for DE to 6.6304 for CCI. These values correspond to very low probabilities of type I errors in the training set, with the highest value for all stock measures being 13.35% for DE (all the rest are virtually zero).

In the test sets, the estimated percentages of correct responses range from −0.5658 to 3.4578 standard deviations from the null of 0.50. The probability of a type I error in the test set ranges from a high value of 71.23% for DE to 0% for CCI and F.

These results provide evidence that backpropagation models are able, using previous asset returns, to provide some predictive power for future returns. This result is evidence against the weak form of the EMH. With respect to DE, GIS, GTE and XRX, the test sets did not provide evidence of prediction abilities. This result is in accordance with the result of White [White88] who was unsuccessful in forecasting IBM daily stock prices using neural networks.

Viewed jointly, all six asset prices give a chi-square statistic of 13.21, with five degrees of freedom. This statistic is significant at the 2.5% level. This represents a reasonable confidence level that our technique is doing significantly better than chance overall.

We also ran the learning algorithm for 850 iterations, after which there was no appreciable decrease in the TSS error, signifying that the network had reached a minimum in error space. The gradient descent algorithm does not ensure a global minimum. Nevertheless, multiple runs from different randomly selected initial parameter values did converge to the same minimum. This would suggest either a global minimum or a local minimum with a large basin of attraction. Simulated annealing on the learning rate has been shown to ensure convergence to the global minimum. Nevertheless, this technique is very costly in terms of computing time. This documented the overfitting effect, since performance on the test sets was uniformly better (in one case, the same) in the case of 200 iterations of training than in the case of 850. Also, performance on the training sets was uniformly worse in the case of 200 iterations than in the case of 850, as would be expected given the hypothesis of overfitting.

We also ran the TD(0) algorithm for the same training and test sets and for the same stocks. The results are shown in Table 8.3. The percentage of correct

Table 8.3 Empirical results for TD(0).

Variable	Set	Sample size	TSS	RMSE	Avg. est.	No. correct	% correct	Std. Dev.	Probability of type I error
CCI	Train	505	63.2321	0.3539	0.3870	280	55.45%	2.4475	0.0073
	Test	253	30.3577	0.3464	0.3870	152	60.08%	3.2063	0.0007
DE	Train	505	71.2646	0.3757	0.3430	240	47.52%	−1.1125	0.5438
	Test	253	34.0338	0.3668	0.3430	131	51.78%	0.5658	0.2877
F	Train	505	62.8760	0.3529	0.4510	270	53.47%	1.5575	0.0606
	Test	253	30.8235	0.3490	0.4510	149	58.89%	2.8291	0.0023
GIS	Train	505	75.9399	0.3878	0.2400	269	53.27%	1.4685	0.0722
	Test	253	37.4637	0.3848	0.2400	137	54.15%	1.3203	0.0934
GTE	Train	505	69.3214	0.3705	0.3070	268	53.07%	1.3795	0.0853
	Test	253	34.1236	0.3673	0.3070	138	54.55%	1.4460	0.0749
XRX	Train	505	82.5044	0.4042	0.1750	275	54.46%	2.0025	0.0228
	Test	253	36.7052	0.3809	0.1750	152	60.08%	3.2063	0.0007

responses ranged from 47.52% for the DE training set to 60.08% for the CCI and XRX test sets. The average percentage of correct responses for the training sets was 52.87% and the average percentage for the test sets was 56.59%. This is a bit unusual in that performance on the test sets consistently exceeded that of the training sets. Sutton claims that the TD(0) algorithm is particularly adept at generalisation.

There were only two estimated percentages of correct responses for the training sets that are more than two standard deviations from the value maintained under the null hypothesis, namely CCI and XRX. The standard deviations ranged from -1.1125 for DE to 3.4475 for CCI.

In the test sets, the estimated percentages of correct responses range from 0.5658 to 3.2063 standard deviations from the null of 0.50. The probability of a type I error in the test set ranges from a high value of 28.77% for DE to 0.0007% for CCI and XRX.

Viewed jointly, all six asset prices gave a chi-square statistic of 16.35, with five degrees of freedom. This statistic was significant at the 1% level. This is comparable to the result achieved with backpropagation. However, this algorithm actually learned to output a constant value for each of the stocks, under both training and test sets (a different constant for each stock). Why it did this is still a puzzle to us, and a subject of further investigation.

We also attempted to use the cascade-correlation algorithm, but were unable to get it to converge for our data. We suspect that this is because the cascade-correlation algorithm does not explore as wide a volume in the parameter space as the other two algorithms, since it freezes the weights between input and hidden units.

DIRECTIONS FOR FURTHER WORK

In backpropagation learning, or, for that matter, in any algorithm that searches a parameter (or weight) space for an optimal set of parameters, the learning time increases with the number of parameters. Moreover, as Weigend *et al.* [WeHuRu91] and others have pointed out, Occam's razor would lead us to prefer models with fewer parameters. Several researchers have proposed methods for reducing the number of parameters in backpropagation learning and variants thereof. In particular, Weigend *et al* have found that using one such method, which they call weight elimination, can yield improved performance in forecasting tasks such as the one that we have attempted in this chapter. They add to the error a term that is roughly a normalised sum of the squares of the weights. Since we are minimising the error, the backpropagation algorithm will attempt to send to zero some of the weights at the expense of others, to minimise the total sum of squares of the weights. We have not yet tried this algorithm on our data sets, but it looks promising.

We plan to investigate the cascade-correlation algorithm further, possibly extending it to a recurrent version. This algorithm has proven effective in other empirical studies, and it is possible that we can adapt it for testing the EMH.

We also plan to perform a factor and/or cluster analysis of each of the backpropagation networks that we have developed, to attempt to account for its performance in terms that are theoretically understandable, instead of simply viewing the network as a 'black box'. It may instruct us as to which input data are most relevant to the network.

CONCLUSION

We estimated two models, a backpropagation model and a temporal difference model, on six stock returns. With both models, we found some evidence against the null hypothesis that the stock market is weakly efficient.

Two particularly important observations emerge from this study. Traditional tests of the efficient market hypothesis have focused on linear models of asset prices. It is only recently, with the advent of nonlinear modelling techniques, that this hypothesis has been put to a more stringent test. These new tests have provided some contradictory evidence to the efficient market hypothesis. Secondly, neural networks have been shown to be a rich class of nonlinear optimisation models. Their relatively simple and intuitive architecture has been able to model fairly complex dynamic behaviour.

ACKNOWLEDGEMENTS

We would like to thank Yoshiro Miyata for developing his excellent PlaNet neural network simulation package which we have used extensively. This chapter is a revised and updated version of a paper presented at an earlier conference.

9

Neural Networks as an Alternative Stock Market Model

Manfred Steiner and Hans-Georg Wittkemper,
Westfälische Wilhems-Universität, Germany

INTRODUCTION

In recent years, artificial neural networks have become mature tools for capital market analysis in finance. They have successfully been applied to areas such as stock price prediction [Kamijo90, Baba92], option trading [Bailey88], bond rating [DutSha88], forecasting financial distress [Humper89, Coats92, Erxleb92, RehPod92], forecasting several economic indexes [Windso90, Hoptro91, Wong92] and more complex tasks such as security trading systems including portfolio optimisation [Kosaka91].

Much current research in finance has focused on analysing the relation between asset price, risk and return. Important milestones in understanding the nature of asset pricing are the basic studies of the market model [Sharpe63], the capital asset pricing model (CAPM) [Sharpe64] and arbitrage pricing theory (APT) [Ross76]. While these studies promise great benefit from a theoretical point of view, their utility in practice, if tested empirically, is often limited [Perrid93]. Some of these limits result from very restrictive underlying assumptions about the behaviour of capital markets, which are far from reality.

Artificial neural networks (ANNs) can be used as an alternative approach for modelling the dynamics of capital markets. Typically, studies of the capital market

Neural Networks in the Capital Markets. Edited by Apostolos-Paul Refenes.
© 1995 John Wiley & Sons Ltd

are based on a deterministic relationship between several factors, which in a second step should be proved empirically by simple statistical procedures such as regression or factor analysis. ANNs can create their own representation of the relation between influencing factors and asset return based on historical training data. They can infer a complex nonlinear model about the relationships on the capital market, not requiring a detailed economic model about the underlying relations formulated in advance.

OBJECTIVES

In the following we try to investigate the performance of several models to forecast the return of a single stock. On one hand, we use ANN models of varying architecture in order to model future stock returns, and, on the other hand, we use traditional least-square regression techniques as benchmarks. As measurement criteria we use the mean absolute difference (MAD):

$$\text{MAD} = \frac{1}{n} \sum_{t=1}^{n} |R_{it} - R_{it}^*| \tag{9.1}$$

where R_{it}^* is a proxy for the return of stock i at time t.

The sample data consist of the daily prices and turnovers from the Frankfurt stock exchange, starting 1983 and ending 1986, and the returns of three different indexes, the DAX Index, the WestLB Index and the Index der Frankfurter Wertpapierbörsen. These indexes differ because of distinctive sets and weightings of the included stocks and the way they handle dividends and stock subscription rights.

The stock data are divided into two groups. The first consists of Siemens, BASF and Kaufhof, later referred to as dax-values. These are blue-chip stocks, well represented and weighted in the DAX Index. The second group consists of stocks from smaller companies, Didier, PWA and KHD, later referred to as ndax-values, which are not included in the index.

In general, the use of weekly returns seems to be preferable to the use of daily returns, because surveys have shown that weekly returns are more likely to be normally distributed than daily returns [BaBeFe92]. On the other hand, the use of weekly returns does not guarantee normally distributed data and for the training of ANNs it is more important to have enough representative sample data than to worry about their distribution [TamKia90].

TESTED MODELS

In an exploratory experiment we have selected some ANN architectures which seemed to be worthy of further analysis. ANN architectures with more than two hidden layers, context layer [Elman90], or more complex recurrent net structures have been eliminated from this study, because it seems that they consume considerably more resources in the form of time and storage without delivering results

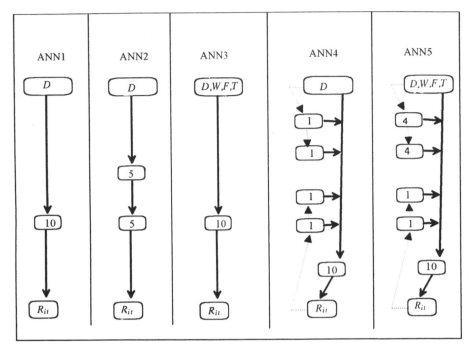

Figure 9.1 Architectures of ANNs 1–5

significantly better than or sometimes even comparable to those structures investigated here. The remaining ANNs differ in the number of units, their arrangement and the number of feedback layers (see Figure 9.1).

The squares in Figure 9.1 denote layers, digits within a square denote the number of units in that layer; D stands for the daily return of the DAX Index as input value, W for the daily return of the WestLB Index as input value, F for the daily return of the Index der Frankfurter Wertpapierbörsen as input value, T for the logarithmic turnover of the specific stock on that day as input value. Thick lines represent fully connected feedforward links between consecutive layers, and dotted lines show feedback connections to recurrent layers. A description of the basic dynamics, including learning principles and specific features, of these recurrent nets is given in [RuHiWi86, Jordan89, Servan89, Mozer93].

It is necessary to transform all input and output data for the ANNs into a range from 0 to 1. A recommended method is the use of a simple mapping function:

$$R_{it} = \frac{X_{it} - \min(X)}{\max(X) - \min(X)} \qquad (9.2)$$

with X_{it} as source value and R_{it} as ANN value. This function requires the maxima and minima for all data. For a realistic forecast it is not possible to know them beforehand, so we make two assumptions. First, we assume that all returns are within the range from -3.75% to $+3.75\%$. In order to take precautions against irregular turnover values we calculate a range for the turnover which holds 97.5% of all training and holdout data. The borders of this 97.5% interval are expected to be a good estimate for the range of future turnovers. This procedure assumes stationarity for the ranges of returns and turnovers over a time-scale of two years.

The ANNs were trained according to the error-backpropagation algorithm with a learning rate of 0.0075, no momentum term and the initial weights randomly chosen from the interval $[-0.65, +0.65]$. The 250 data from year Y were used to train the ANNs; after finishing the training phase the nets were used to calculate the estimates for the returns of year $Y + 1$.

During the training phase we kept a record of the changes of every single weight in the ANNs, in order to allow only those changes leading to the recognition of a systematic relationship within the training data to prevail. Changes which might result from fitting noise were eliminated by setting the specific connection to zero. The significance of each link was calculated according to the technique developed by [FinZim91, HeFiZi92, RehPod92]. Another tool used to avoid overtraining was a cross-validation technique. We reserved a proportion of the training data as holdout data which were not used in the learning epoch. The ANN was trained as long as the quality of the forecast for the training and holdout data increased. As soon as the slope of a regression function for the MAD of the training data for each epoch became smaller than a critical value or the quality of the forecast for the holdout data decreased, we stopped the training and started the forecasting phase.

Because the training of an ANN began with randomly chosen initial weights, the forecasts of the trained net varied randomly to some extent. In order to avoid nonrepresentative results we repeated each ANN experiment twice and used the average over these three experiments as the final result. To compare and evaluate the ANN forecasts we used four regression models as benchmarks. The first model (linreg) is based on a simple linear least-square regression. The coefficients a and b were estimated using the sample data from year Y and later used to forecast the proxies for the returns in year $Y+1$. The second benchmark (linreg $a = 0$) is similar to the first, except that we set the coefficient a to zero. This can result in better forecasts. Our exploratory experiment has not been able to refute the hypothesis that a, the market-independent component of the stock return, differs significantly from zero. A multiple least-squares regression (multreg), with returns of the three indexes and the logarithmic turnover of the stock as input data, was used as the third benchmark. The data from one year were used to calculate the coefficients $b_1, \ldots, b_4$ in order to determine the MAD of the forecast for the following year.

The last model (progreg) is not a forecast model but a real benchmark. The 250 daily data of year $Y + 1$ were used to derive a and b of a least-squares linear regression in order to calculate the MAD for year $Y + 1$. This model should by definition deliver the smallest mean squared errors of all investigated models.

Starting with the daily data from 1983, the parameters for the regression models were estimated and the ANNs trained. Then these adapted models were used to estimate the 250 daily stock returns in 1984. Finally, the MAD between the model forecasts and the real stock returns were calculated. This procedure was carried out three times until all MAD for all years were recorded.

RESULTS

To show all the results of this test in detail would result in a confusing collection of tables and diagrams. Table 9.1, as an example, shows the MAD results of one run for forecasting the stock return of the KHD shares.

Table 9.2 lists the average MAD over the three years and the specific group. For easier reading the ranking of the models based on the columns of that table is also included. All ANNs with the exception of ANN 2, show a better performance than the standard linear regression models linreg and linreg $a = 0$. As expected the regression model linreg $a = 0$ leads to a smaller MAD than the standard model linreg.

The ranking in Table 9.2 shows that ANN models can benefit by using recurrent feedback layers. ANN 5 achieves a better ranking than ANN 3 and ANN 4 outperforms ANN 1. The ANN 2 model achieves the worst performance overall, this may

Table 9.1 MAD of the KHD stock return forecasts.

Model	MAD 1984	MAD 1985	MAD 1986
linreg	0.008 627 819	0.013 806 292	0.014 481 676
linreg $a = 0$	0.008 666 947	0.013 775 482	0.014 484 178
progreg	0.008 311 657	0.013 580 990	0.014 217 510
multreg	0.009 144 964	0.012 933 076	0.014 141 152
ANN 1	0.008 590 915	0.013 806 606	0.014 539 008
ANN 2	0.008 604 944	0.013 825 383	0.017 492 600
ANN 3	0.008 483 986	0.012 985 924	0.013 952 082
ANN 4	0.008 473 968	0.013 492 698	0.014 366 783
ANN 5	0.008 248 313	0.013 074 743	0.013 989 005

Table 9.2 Summary of the MAD for the specific groups and the resulting rankings.

Model	dax-value MAD	ndax-value MAD	Total MAD	dax-values rank	ndax-values rank	Total rank
linreg	0.0 081 259	0.0 123 370	0.0 102 314	8	8	8
linreg $a = 0$	0.0 081 138	0.0 123 136	0.0 102 137	7	7	7
progreg	0.0 080 028	0.0 120 792	0.0 100 410	5	4	5
multreg	0.0 071 830	0.0 121 974	0.0 096 902	2	6	3
ANN 1	0.0 080 565	0.0 121 543	0.0 101 054	6	5	6
ANN 2	0.0 089 707	0.0 127 085	0.0 108 396	9	9	9
ANN 3	0.0 071 961	0.0 118 060	0.0 095 010	3	2	2
ANN 4	0.0 078 866	0.0 120 313	0.0 099 590	4	3	4
ANN 5	0.0 071 732	0.0 116 660	0.0 094 196	1	1	1

be either because the model is too complex for this specific task or because our learning technique is not sufficiently well suited for that kind of ANN. Therefore we exclude ANN 2 from further discussion of the results.

In order to give a more detailed view of the differences between the MAD of the tested models we calculated the relative performance difference between every model and the standard regression model linreg (see Figure 9.2):

$$\text{rdiff} = \frac{\text{MAD (linreg)} - \text{MAD (model)}}{\text{MAD (linreg)}} \tag{9.3}$$

The standard procedure for estimating the parameters of the underlying market model linreg produces the most inaccurate proxies for the stock returns. The ANN 1 model uses the same data and performs a kind of nonlinear univariate regression which results in much smaller MAD than the standard regression model. In some cases the proxies of ANN 1 are even more precise than the estimated returns from the benchmark progreg, not only in terms of MAD but also in terms of the mean squared error. This should be impossible if the assumption about the underlying linear market model is correct. Therefore we compared the returns of the PWA stock in 1984 to the return estimates from the ANN 1 and linreg $a = 0$ (Figure 9.3).

Using artificial DAX index returns in the interval from -3.75% to 3.75% we recorded the resulting estimates for the PWA stock return from linreg $a = 0$ and ANN 1 (Figure 9.4).

The nonlinear relationship assumed by ANN 1 seems to give a better fit to the observed stock returns, measured in terms of MAD, than the linear market model. From an economical point of view, this nonlinear structure seems to be plausible.

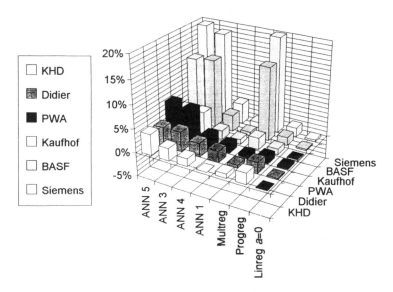

Figure 9.2 Relative MAD difference between each model and the linreg model

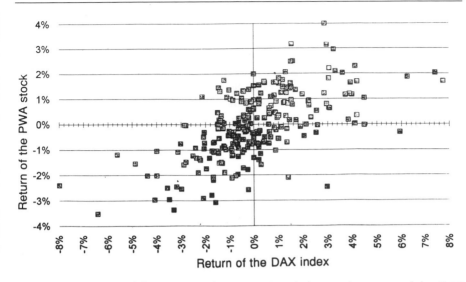

Figure 9.3 Returns of the PWA stock in 1984 in relation to the return of the DAX index

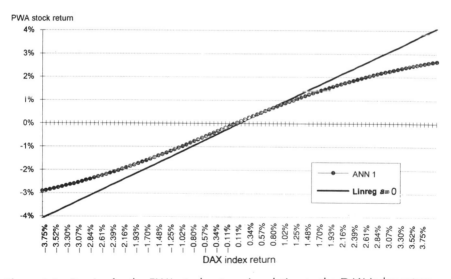

Figure 9.4 Proxies for the PWA stock returns in relation to the DAX index return

It postulates that very high (low) index returns lead to only smaller increases (decreases) in stock return.

Believing in a linear market model becomes harder if we take a closer look at the performance of ANN models 3 to 5. Giving an ANN feedback layer allows the ANN to use these layers as a short-term memory for detecting structures in time. The simplest structure in time would be an autoregressive process such as $\beta_1 = a + b\beta_{t-1} + u_t$.

On average, recurrent ANNs perform better than comparable ANNs without feedback layers. This points to the fact that a model describing the true capital market relationships should contain dependencies in time. In order to get some idea about how proxies of an ANN are influenced by structures in time, we compared the proxies from ANN 4 and linreg $a = 0$ for the Siemens stock in 1986. We recorded the return estimates from the two models, calculated the residuals and the difference between both residuals.

$$\text{diff} = e_{\text{linreg}} - e_{\text{ANN 4}} = (R - R^*_{\text{linreg}}) - (R - R^*_{\text{ANN 4}})$$

Testing for systematic relations between these differences and previous changes in the DAX return gives the plots shown in Figures 9.5 and 9.6.

These plots show that changes in the DAX return from the two previous trading days have an impact on the ANN proxies. In order to see the direction of this impact, we analysed how the proxies of ANN 4 changed if the actual DAX return were 0 and the DAX return of the two previous days varied within an interval from -0.015 to 0.015. The resulting stock return forecasts can be seen in Figure 9.7.

Because ANN models can detect nonlinear relations and structures in time, they allow a better modelling of the real relations and dependencies on the capital market which influence the stock return and deliver better proxies than simple least-squares regressions. Using more input data dramatically improves the accuracy of

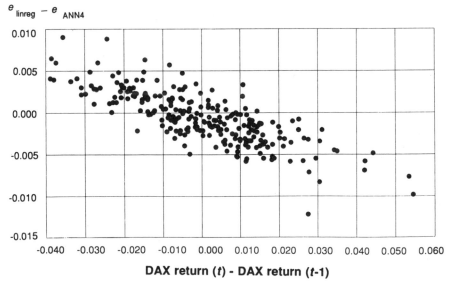

Figure 9.5 Residual differences related to the changes of the index return between days $t-1$ and t

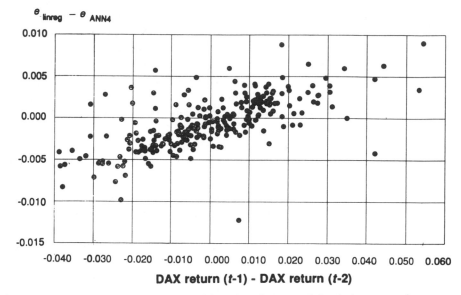

Figure 9.6 Residual differences related to the changes of the index return between days $t - 2$ and $t - 1$

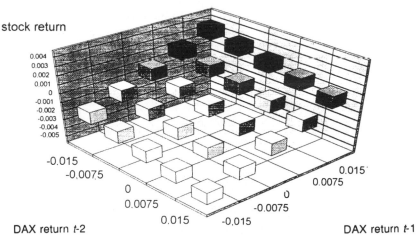

Figure 9.7 Hypothetical stock returns in relation to previous DAX returns

the models in terms of MAD. This effect is especially strong for dax-values. The multreg model leads to a much better fit than the linreg model. For the ndax-values multreg leads only to a slight improvement over the linreg models.

Using more input data also improves the performance of the ANN models. ANN 3 delivers a smaller MAD than ANN 1 and the recurrent version, ANN 5, shows the best performance of all models on average. From an economical point of view the additional inputs seem to be either redundant, because they are similar indexes, or meaningless, because turnovers should not impact the market model.

A t-test for the coefficients of the multiple regression multreg reveals that there is no significance for the turnover coefficients and, on the other hand, the sign of that coefficient is not stable over the different stocks and years. The ANN models have found a reproducible stable relationship between the expected stock return and the turnover of that stock.

ANNs can build nonlinear high-dimensional models for the relationship between the input and output variables. At present it is not possible to visualise the real dependencies of these models with easily understandable two-dimensional plots [WejTes90]. Showing only some of these dimensions means cutting down some of the nonlinear interdependencies and ignoring or distorting the true dynamics within the ANNs.

To analyse the impact of the turnover for the ANNs avoiding the above-mentioned problem, we built an ANN similar to ANN 1 but with one additional input neuron for the stock turnover. This ANN has been trained with the KHD data from 1984. After the training the ANN had to estimate the expected stock returns with given artificial DAX returns, varying from -0.0375 to 0.0375, and the logarithm of the stock turnover varying from 5.6 to 10.1. Finally the estimated stock returns are shown as a hyperplane in Figure 9.8.

The stock returns estimated with respect to the regression model linreg would all reside on a plane orthogonal to the Z-axis and with a slope (β) of 0.891. The b

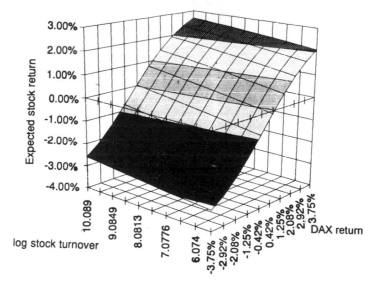

Figure 9.8   Hypothetical stock returns in relation to DAX return and stock turnover

coefficients from the multreg model for the same data are: for the DAX Index, 1.22; for the WestLB Index, 0.0329; for the F/M Index, -0.589; and for the logarithmic turnover, 0.000 007. The forecasts of the ANN model differ significantly from those of the linreg and multreg model. Because the ANN proxies result in much smaller MAD and sum of squares of the residual, we assume that this ANN model has more in common with the true relationships on the capital market which determine the expected return of a stock than the inferior regression models.

CONCLUSIONS

This study shows that ANNs outperform comparable statistical techniques for estimating the return of a single stock. Normally applied regression techniques allow only a coarse modelling of the underlying relations on the capital market. ANNs build a more precise model of the interdependencies based on historical sample data than based on economic considerations. The resulting model of the relationship between the return of a stock and factors of the capital market is usually nonlinear, may contain dependencies in time and multiple connections between several influencing factors. Therefore ANNs can give more reliable forecasts for stock returns than the comparable statistical techniques.

Although the learning technique used works very well in this study, it may not be applied to other problems without major changes. Further research has to be carried out on how to adapt ANN models to the specific tasks or problems and how to set up the various parameters in order to obtain a near-optimal network structure.

Further research by the authors indicates that more complex ANN systems, consisting of several smaller recurrent networks using data from national and international economies, from the capital market, balance sheets and similar sources may lead to a better approximation and a better understanding of the real dynamic relationships on the capital market.

10

Tracking the Amsterdam Stock Index Using Neural Networks

Dirk Emma Baestaens and Willem Max van den Bergh, *Erasmus University, Netherlands*

INTRODUCTION

Recent studies of the time-series properties of various financial variables have indicated the presence of nonlinear dynamics. For example, Larrain [Larrai91] discovered chaotic behaviour in US ·T-bill rates and Peters [Peters91] detected a chaotic attractor in the S&P 500 series. The upshot of such discoveries is that the random-walk hypothesis has come under fire, as already demonstrated by the effort devoted to tactical asset allocation and market timing strategies [Mandel71, DeGooi89]. Moreover, the chaotic behaviour that can be best described over time by short bursts of large-amplitude excursions questions the validity of autocorrelation and spectral tests [Brock86]. While most returns appear to be generated by a white-noise process, when analysed by linear time-series techniques these authors found that they also contain small though significant nonlinear dependencies [HinPat85].

The formal proof of the presence of deterministic chaotic nonlinear dynamic behaviour leads to the question of the model behind these systemic dynamics. Unfortunately, this question has not been resolved conclusively [Chen86, Hsieh91]. To be relevant to decision-makers, the model should incorporate sufficient detail, that is, it should be a multivariate approach that is able to deal with time-dependent, possibly non-recurring patterns within the data.

Neural Networks in the Capital Markets. Edited by Apostolos-Paul Refenes.
© 1995 John Wiley & Sons Ltd

Neural networks, are thought likely to be a fruitful avenue of research [White88]. It is argued that they bypass the disadvantage embedded in standard large-scale econometric models, namely their inability to deal with structural change within the system under observation.

This chapter attempts to analyse the Amsterdam stock-market return by means of a novel nonlinear technique based on insights in human cognition and to evaluate the results with respect to those generated by more traditional regression and multiple discriminant analysis (MDA). Our primary objective is not to look for a point predictor of next month's stock return but rather to unravel the forces behind the directional change in the return.

VARIABLE CONSTRUCTION

Our aim is to detect relationships between the so-called 'contextual variables' and the monthly return on the Datastream Amsterdam general stock index for the period from November 1979 to March 1991. The choice of the contextual variables is somewhat arbitrary as there does not appear to exist any theory that accounts for stock returns as a function of micro- and macroindices. Therefore we constructed our data set using those variables, notably non-equity-related return variables as well as macroeconomic indicators, identified by Chen et. al. [Chen86] as well as Ferson and Harvey [FerHarv91] as systematically affecting stock returns (Table 10.1).

To take the peculiarities of the Dutch economy into account, we added a few characteristic variables such as terms of trade (TERMS) and the guilder/dollar spot exchange rate (FUS). Serial correlations in the returns of the index are not expected. However, it may be the case that a very specific context may give rise to a lagged return (bandwagon effects) or that extreme levels of the index may influence future returns (additional uncertainty, contrarian investment opportunities, etc.). For these reasons, our data set also comprises the return as well as the level of the stock index, lagged by one period. All raw seasonally adjusted monthly series were extracted from Datastream, creating a data set consisting of 134 observations (cases).

In Table 10.1, an asterisk denotes derived variables that warrant further explanation. Regarding ECPI, the actual inflation rate was split into an anticipated and an unanticipated or error component on the basis of a simple ARIMA $(1,1,0)$ time-series model. We believe that the application of a more sophisticated interest-rate model [FamGib84] may not be imperative since the inflation components represent within sample forecasts. Serious difficulties in constructing the risk-premium variable (RISKP) were encountered. Traditionally the premiums represent the difference between the BAA and under bond portfolio return (t) and a long-term government bond return (t). Unfortunately the BAA index is unavailable for the Dutch corporate bond market, so we had to develop a proxy as follows. The BAA proxy equals the unweighted mean of the returns calculated from seven bond price indices for a reasonably representative subset of corporations. Finally, the nondurables variable

Table 10.1   Selected variables.

SYMBOL	VARIABLE	DEFINITION
1. CALLRATE	call money rate	percentage
2. LTGOVB	interest on long-term government bonds	percentage
3. M2	money supply stock	index rebased to 1978, SA
4. TBNLUS	NL treasury bill rate minus US T-bill rate	percentage
5. TESTRU	term structure, LTGOVB minus T-bill rate	percentage
6. ECPI*	anticipated inflation rate	index SA
7. UCPI	unanticipated inflation	percentage
8. DECPI	changes in anticipated rate	percentage
9. RISKP*	risk premium	percentage
10. FUS	guilder/dollar average exchange rate	ln of variable relative
11. TERMS.	terms of trade (export prices/import prices, inc. BLEU & Oil)	actual value
12. NONDUG*	change in consumption of non-durables	ln of variable relative
13. INDPRO	total industrial production	index SA
14. ORDANO	opinion variable on activity: total orders received, judged as above normal	actual value
15. ORDBNO	total orders received, judged as below normal	actual value
16. RETLAG	stock index return, lagged by one period	ln of index relative
17. LEVELLAG	stock index level, lagged by one period	actual value
18. RETIN (=dependent variable)	Datastream Amsterdam stockindex return	ln of index relative

(NONDUG) attempts to capture the real growth of personal consumption expenditure, and was derived by differencing the change in the value index for total household expenditure and the change in the index for durable goods expenditure.

EVALUATION OF THE MULTILAYER BACKPROPAGATION NETWORK

We will present four exploratory means of analysis with a view to determining the relative contribution of neural networks to uncovering hidden regularities in seemingly randomly distributed data series. First, we compare a within-sample forecast on the basis of ordinary least-squares (OLS) regression to a fit generated by a trained multi-layer backpropagation network (MBPN) architecture, with 17 inputs, one layer of hidden units and direct connections from input to output units. Then we present out-of-sample forecasts generated by the same techniques for the last 10 months (April 1990 to January 1991). Next, the contribution of the variables will be discussed at individual and generic level using a slightly adapted MBPN network that generates binary output. Finally, we evaluate the misclassifications of the MBPN model. As a yardstick the classification procedure was replicated on the basis of the cases' highest posterior probabilities generated by simple linear multivariate discriminant analysis (MDA).

Within-Sample Estimations

Figure 10.1 compares the actual returns and the two within-sample estimations yielded by OLS and MBPN techniques. The latter have been generated by our customised model described earlier and have been obtained after just a single presentation of the input vector series (134 observations). The actual return served as the target variable. The benefit implicit in this very short training period lies in the adaptability of our trained network to structural changes within the economy; it is hoped to contribute positively in the out-of-sample exercise. Obviously, repeated presentation (overtraining) of the input vector series would have resulted in an improved goodness of fit of our model but at the cost of flexibility, the so-called grandmothering effect.

Table 10.2 shows a (relatively) low R^2 but Figure 10.1 clearly indicates the regression model's aptitude at identifying the direction of change in the returns. However, MBPN appears to outperform OLS on both magnitude and direction. The 6% standard error may appear large, but it must be noted that the actual returns lies in the range $[-0.35, 0.18]$.

More noteworthy is the highly significant contribution of just a few variables, notably NONDUG, RISKP, FUS, LTGOVB, ORDBNO and M2 (see Table 10.3). Observe that both real and monetary variables play a role. Incidentally, LEVELLAG (the level of the last index) and RETLAG (the return from $t-2$ to $t-1$) contribute

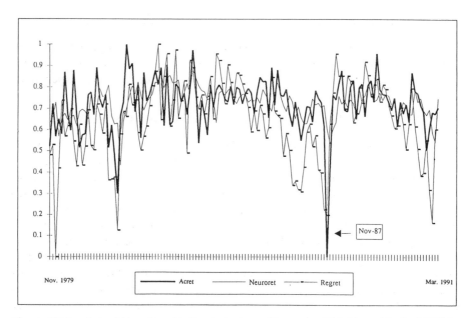

Figure 10.1   Actual (Acret) and estimated returns (Regret by OLS; NeuroNet by MBPN). All returns scaled to the range [0,1]

Table 10.2   OLS diagnostics.

Multiple R	0.53922
R squared	0.29076
Adjusted R squared	0.19294
Standard error	0.06282
D.W.	1.95
$F = 2.97224$ Signif $F = 0.0004$	

Table 10.3   Within-sample regression coefficients.

Variable	B	SE B	Beta	T	Sig T
LEVELLAG	−2.35939E-04	2.20307E-04	−0.289463	−1.071	0.2864
NONDUG	0.177788	0.068151	0.231448	2.609	0.0103
RETLAG	0.090429	0.093299	0.091278	0.969	0.3344
RISKP	0.591860	0.263718	0.198018	2.244	0.0267
UCPI	0.023022	0.017045	0.121848	1.351	0.1794
ORDANO	0.004554	0.003064	0.191811	1.487	0.1398
DECPI	0.012599	0.016250	0.071985	0.775	0.4397
TESTRU	−0.011533	0.009478	−0.177978	−1.217	0.2262
TERMS	0.003657	0.003371	0.124667	1.085	0.2802
FUS	0.064569	0.026916	0.478108	2.399	0.0180
TBNLUS	−0.006989	0.004965	−0.176313	−1.408	0.1619
LTGOVB	−0.018569	0.006729	−0.467076	−2.760	0.0067
INDPRO	−0.001343	0.001956	−0.093946	−0.687	0.4936
ORDBNO	0.003367	0.001584	0.514027	2.125	0.0357
ECPI	−0.006575	0.004530	−0.617383	−1.451	0.1493
M2	0.002061	7.77734E-04	1.189411	2.650	0.0092
(Constant)	−0.008910	0.435031		−0.020	0.9837

very little, as could be expected since the dependent variable seems to follow if not a random walk then certainly a martingale process [LeRoy89].

OLS regression is a static technique, that is, it is unable to cope with structural changes in the sample, whereas the Dutch economy can be safely assumed to have evolved considerably between 1979 and 1991! As noted earlier, MBPN represents a more dynamic approach as the training procedure may explicitly account for the sequential character of the input vector series. Furthermore, MBPN allows us to measure the dynamics in the contribution of the selected contextual variables to its output. We believe tomorrow's returns to be a function of the marginal variable contributions (that is, consisting of *today's* variable constellation) rather than of the average variable (that is, comprising the *total* sample period) contribution as OLS implicitly assumes.

Out-of-sample Results

We now assess the predictive power of both traditional OLS and ANS techniques by comparing the predicted returns for the last ten months (up to March 1991) based on

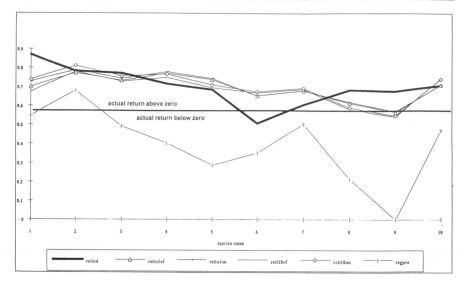

Figure 10.2 Out-of-sample predictions for OLS (regpre) and MBPN; retind equals the actual return. MBPN results yielded after various training procedures. '1of' = one presentation of the total sample (124 cycles) and learning disabled; '10on' = ten presentations (1240 cycles) and learning enabled

a regression model estimated on the first 124 cases and the MBPN network trained with the same 124 cases. The MBPN estimations are produced by continuously adjusting the network weights (delta rule) after each of the ten predicted cycles. The regression could also have benefited from continuous feedback on past estimates but only when more weight is given to the most recent cases. We prefer not to enter into the discussion of attributing these weightings, but we do appreciate the edge taken by the MBPN module. Figure 10.2 plots the results. The regression output has been rescaled to fit in the [0, 1] range to facilitate comparison with the ANS output that by definition falls within that range. It can be observed that although the regression estimates more or less track the actual return, their direction is often erroneous. Note that a scaled zero return equals 0.58 in the [0, 1] interval. It follows that just one of the regression estimates is positive (case 2), whereas the real return turns out to be positive except for case 6. A misjudgment in the sign of the return matters more than one in magnitude! The conclusion may then well be that the ANS seems to beat regression with respect to this data set.

Considering the regression's lack of feedback on recent performance we have also chosen to disable ANS to learn from its most recent errors during the out-of-sample period. But even then, as the RETIN1OF and RETI10OF variables demonstrate, ANS still outweights the regression performance. ('-of' means training disabled whereas '-on' means the reverse.) We also checked for the impact of varying training periods, but the finding here suggests that the first training round already picks up a lot of the returns characteristics ('-1' signals one training period of 124 cycles, whereas '-10' signals ten periods or 1240 cycles).

Individual versus Systematic Variable Contributions

As it is often claimed that neural networks do not present the user any insights into the problem under study, that they represent a black-box approach in contrast to the various statistics on the variables in regression, this section will present an exploratory decomposition of the forces influencing network decisions. It is our assertion that an adapted network specification offers much more insight into the *evolution* of the individual variable's relative importance than traditional statistical tools and may provide a useful complementary tool.

The MBPN network used in the previous analyses had a single output node generating a numeric signal representing the decided value of the index return given a specific determinant input vector. This network specification does not allow a proper analysis of the contribution of each determinant. A method to compute the contribution made by each input item towards the decision has been developed by Hecht Nielsen for MBPN networks that produce one or more binary outputs. A binary output node is trained to generate a signal that is either TRUE or FALSE. We can apply this method if we use a network that is able to decide on the classification of the index returns over time. Each return class is represented by one binary output node. We have specified four classes of index return: class 0, with very low (strongly negative) returns; class 1, with moderately low returns; class 2, with moderately high returns; and class 3, with strongly positive returns. Class borders have been determined by letting classes be of approximately equal size. To allow for four different classes we need two binary nodes that may produce the following output (0=FALSE, 1=TRUE): 00, 01, 10, 11. We used the same 17-element input vector specification as in the previous tests and one single nine-node hidden layer connected to the two-node binary output layer. Each binary output node is able to generate an internal signal between 0 and 1, and the decision boundary is set at 0.5. Internal signals above 0.5 are considered TRUE and under 0.5 FALSE. This network has been trained to produce a classification of index returns over time by consecutively offering the actual *ex post* return class as a training signal.

After the training of the network it should be able to track the actual return classification for each input determinant vector. For each time period we can calculate the decisiveness of the classification. Decisiveness is the strength of both internal output signals based on their distance from the decision boundary. We simply compute the average strength of both signals. Since each distance must lie between 0 (0%) and 0.5 (100%), decisiveness values range from 0 to 100. It is now possible to determine the contribution to the decisiveness of each determinant over time. This is done by temporarily assuming the determinant value is unknown and examining the change in the output decisiveness. If an unknown input value is assumed for a numeric item the arithmetic mean of the input item (the unconditional expectation) is presented to the internal neural network. After each input's contribution is calculated, these contributions are scaled so that the largest absolute value of any contribution is 100.0.

Results of the classification and variable contribution over time by the trained network (during the training the complete time-series was presented 100 times, i.e. 13 400 training cycles) for the first 40 cases are listed in Table 10.4. This time slice is representative for the whole sample period.

Table 10.4 Classification and variable contribution over time to the decisiven‥

Case	Year	Month	Output	DECISIVN	TARGET	ABSERR	CALLRATE	INDPRO	LTGOVB	M^2	ORDA
1	79	12	0	96.52	0	0	25.7	−5.8	−10.2	100.0	−5.
2	80	1	0	10.43	1	1	5.6	7.4	−9.3	10.8	−5.
3	80	2	0	1.12	0	0	2.4	0.5	−14.0	10.9	−3
4	80	3	1	22.27	1	0	−3.2	−15.3	100.0	−62.4	51.
5	80	4	1	18.54	0	1	3.0	−1.3	81.4	−90.6	13.
6	80	5	3	88.45	3	0	−12.5	−0.9	−13.1	57.0	−1
7	80	6	1	81.28	1	0	12.5	3.4	81.3	−25.6	−11.
8	80	7	0	44.88	0	0	48.8	−21.3	5.4	100.0	55.
9	80	8	3	98.22	3	0	−7.7	24.1	10.6	11.8	5.
10	80	9	1	86.31	1	0	−13.0	84.0	59.0	−43.6	−33.
11	80	10	0	24.99	0	0	26.2	−34.7	−29.3	100.0	64.
12	80	11	0	40.01	0	0	28.1	5.3	26.6	62.4	22.
13	80	12	0	36.79	0	0	15.3	−17.9	−0.5	57.1	33.
14	81	1	0	25.94	2	2	10.1	−12.5	−38.8	39.7	25.
15	81	2	3	13.38	2	1	−17.3	−8.2	−100.0	21.3	18.
16	81	3	1	92.22	1	0	0.5	5.4	100.0	−12.2	−9.
17	81	4	3	0.38	3	0	−8.4	7.3	−56.0	16.4	10.
18	81	5	1	2.35	2	1	2.0	0.1	26.3	−7.5	−3.
19	81	6	1	1.00	1	0	14.2	−1.9	93.0	−21.7	−7.
20	81	7	1	3.03	2	1	2.9	0.6	15.7	−18.3	−6.
21	81	8	3	11.70	0	3	−72.0	23.2	−100.0	36.1	24.
22	81	9	1	100.00	1	0	2.5	9.0	100.0	−4.8	−3.
23	81	10	1	13.72	0	1	9.8	1.0	66.9	−34.4	−13.
24	81	11	3	27.50	0	3	−48.3	17.2	−100.0	31.4*	23.
25	81	12	0	8.41	1	1	14.8	−7.5	−0.9	13.5	7.
26	82	1	0	1.83	1	1	6.6	0.9	−2.2	7.1	4.
27	82	2	3	10.98	3	0	−18.5	6.7	−100.0	16.0	10.
28	82	3	1	11.87	3	2	0.3	2.1	14.9	−17.1	−5.
29	82	4	3	3.24	3	0	−10.6	9.2	−100.0	20.7	17.
30	82	5	1	2.05	1	0	3.2	0.5	27.0	−12.0	−15.
31	82	6	3	21.30	2	1	−9.9	31.0	−100.0	26.7	23.
32	82	7	1	4.17	0	1	3.7	−0.1	−100.0	18.7	−6.
33	82	8	3	70.09	3	0	−1.4	38.9	47.0	100.0	43.
34	82	9	1	100.00	1	0	−0.3	37.3	13.5	−6.8	−1.
35	82	10	1	18.39	2	1	1.0	−9.9	67.2	−51.5	−16.
36	82	11	2	48.72	2	0	0.1	16.0	−0.3	−41.9	−18.
37	82	12	3	65.12	3	0	15.4	48.8	10.4	100.0	35.
38	83	1	2	98.98	2	0	−0.8	30.8	9.0	−28.6	−4.
39	83	2	3	7.50	3	0	−9.7	−13.7	−23.8	73.0	26.
40	83	3	1	33.51	1	0	−1.0	7.6	−17.8	−6.2	−2.

The OUTPUT column in Table 10.4 contains the classification by the network, while the TARGET column refers to the actual class. ABSERR is the absolute classification error, that is, the distance from the actual class, and DECISVN is the decisiveness value as described above. The other 17 columns show the contribution to the decisiveness of each determinant. Look, for example, at the classification of December 1979 in the first row. The decided class is correct (that is, a large positive return) and the decisiveness is high. The table shows that M2 and ECPI are the determinants that contribute mostly to the decisiveness while there is only slight negative contribution of LTGOVB and TESTRU.

coefficient (DECISIVN)

ORDBNO	TBNLUS	TERMS	NONDUG	ECPI	UCPI	DECPI	RISKP	TESTRU	FUS	RETLAG	LEVELLAG
0.0	4.0	-1.4	0.0	96.2	11.9	6.7	-0.5	-12.0	40.0	52.0	17.8
-1.3	1.2	-0.5	-8.2	10.9	1.0	-0.1	1.5	-100.0	9.8	7.6	-41.8
-0.9	1.1	-4.6	23.9	6.3	0.3	0.0	-0.2	-100.0	4.1	0.0	-21.0
-1.3	-43.6	54.0	33.7	-29.6	1.5	2.8	35.6	-16.7	-0.7	-6.1	-0.1
7.3	33.3	45.5	27.9	-18.9	0.0	-58.0	28.5	45.8	16.0	-51.1	-100.0
17.9	22.1	-0.6	-4.2	15.5	-2.4	83.2	97.0	80.4	-9.6	46.8	100.0
14.9	100.0	33.6	-21.4	-7.2	0.5	0.4	-10.9	89.9	25.8	66.7	4.0
21.4	26.9	-7.3	13.7	81.0	-2.6	73.0	-1.7	-98.4	89.5	5.9	-22.2
19.9	-3.3	5.7	22.8	-9.2	1.4	51.5	4.3	100.0	-13.9	1.6	96.3
-30.5	-1.9	20.8	11.8	-42.2	3.2	10.6	-2.4	75.1	-34.7	44.1	100.0
40.9	77.6	-20.2	60.2	71.3	-9.1	-79.9	31.4	-41.5	62.7	27.0	-59.7
35.2	-16.9	-26.5	-23.0	68.3	-17.1	-19.1	8.8	10.1	62.4	27.7	-100.0
27.0	-31.7	-31.9	-23.7	58.1	-16.8	0.9	5.0	44.6	42.7	23.8	-100.0
24.5	-46.7	-24.4	-7.5	38.5	-8.4	10.3	9.9	10.4	23.7	20.2	-100.0
22.1	-28.7	13.5	23.2	8.7	8.9	28.6	19.8	-7.9	-4.0	-9.5	59.0
6.6	-2.3	58.7	69.8	-6.6	0.4	4.9	-3.4	-2.7	-1.1	8.1	31.0
2.2	100.0	5.8	-9.3	3.0	2.4	34.3	-3.8	-2.1	-1.2	6.6	71.5
2.1	-100.0	3.9	-3.9	-0.8	0.1	-12.2	-1.7	0.0	-0.9	6.7	-41.1
1.6	-38.2	7.9	-43.6	-3.2	2.1	-9.3	2.4	-2.4	-4.8	3.3	-100.0
3.8	-100.0	9.3	-4.8	-1.2	1.0	4.7	0.2	6.1	-5.0	-2.3	-88.7
24.5	-11.4	6.3	60.8	12.1	-18.8	26.8	8.6	14.1	9.1	-13.4	29.5
4.3	-1.1	5.0	82.6	-1.6	0.0	-0.5	-1.9	4.3	0.4	-5.5	9.3
11.8	8.6	-19.0	23.6	-2.2	3.2	-77.5	10.1	2.0	-1.6	-34.8	-100.0
28.6	16.9	-4.9	22.9	8.4	-11.4	29.2	6.1	17.1	0.1	35.0	48.8
6.3	1.0	2.0	1.4	11.7	0.9	-6.1	30.7	-27.0	-2.2	31.1	-100.0
3.3	-4.2	2.0	-13.1	5.9	-0.7	6.6	0.4	-2.1	-2.8	1.5	-100.0
16.0	-7.4	0.9	11.8	4.5	2.3	15.7	5.1	0.7	2.9	-1.3	19.6
7.9	-100.0	-6.5	13.5	-1.2	-1.5	-7.5	2.2	-0.3	-3.3	16.4	-66.8
21.4	14.6	0.0	-13.8	5.1	10.4	24.2	13.4	-4.0	5.8	-71.5	44.1
6.1	-47.7	0.4	2.5	-1.3	-2.2	-4.0	5.9	0.0	-2.9	25.5	-100.0
33.3	-28.4	-1.5	2.1	5.4	16.3	17.2	28.6	-16.1	8.9	9.4	44.0
19.9	2.7	9.1	-79.4	3.1	-2.8	4.2	5.6	1.6	-8.1	12.0	-92.2
93.7	23.7	-0.3	24.7	12.0	6.3	35.8	-36.6	0.4	-3.8	50.1	52.3
-4.7	-0.6	0.1	100.0	-3.4	4.0	-1.9	0.2	-3.7	12.5	10.7	49.8
11.3	25.8	14.8	60.7	-3.6	-18.4	-44.5	41.7	8.5	-24.7	8.1	-100.0
-46.8	2.1	1.1	17.3	-8.2	12.9	-18.8	100.0	-1.4	43.8	12.9	33.9
89.1	-5.2	-0.2	1.7	7.2	44.8	-19.6	57.4	-0.5	12.6	-17.3	91.8
-31.7	17.6	0.3	42.6	-6.5	28.3	66.0	43.9	5.5	21.1	66.0	100.0
100.0	-22.5	-8.5	-95.8	13.6	-32.3	-25.5	93.7	12.2	-56.8	-25.9	-37.7
13.7	-45.9	9.0	100.0	-0.8	-2.4	-0.1	10.2	3.9	-4.1	26.7	-26.7

In case of a misclassification (ABSERR > 0), interpreting the marginal contributions becomes a fruitless activity. In all other cases, the fluctuation over time of the variables' contribution may be revealing since OLS regression may not always be able to capture the relevant functional relationships between independent and dependent variables. Assume, for instance, a variable that contributes to the decision (return category) in one state of the business cycle only (for instance, when the market falls but not when it rises, or vice versa). Since the overall (average) contribution may be trivial, OLS is unlikely to identify this variable as significant. The decisiveness analysis, however, as described above, will mark both significant and insignificant contributions over time, allowing the decision-maker to categorise the variables' contextual behaviour over time, thereby enhancing his or her understanding of the variables' economic relevance. Next, assume a variable is active during all states of the business cycle but in the opposite direction (for instance, a variable amplifying the direction of the market both in periods of very high and low market). This typical nonlinear behaviour may be completely overlooked by OLS[1] but probably not by MBPN. Lastly, assume that a variable is active during all states of the business cycle but in the same direction as the market (for instance, a variable amplifying returns during upturns and contracting it during downturns). Both the decisiveness and OLS techniques may be expected to detect the variable's overall relevance. In short, classifying contextual variables according to their contribution (behaviour) over time may yield valuable insights in stock return generating mechanisms.

Table 10.5 Comparison between OLS and ANS variable evaluation.

Variable symbol	Significant t-statistic	Abs. mean contribution to decisiveness
LEVELLAG		44.8961
NONDUG	2.6	43.0376
FUS	2.39	36.5214
LTGOVB	−2.76	34.1018
M2	2.65	30.5773
TBNLUS		18.7009
UCPI		17.0864
ORDBNO	2.12	14.3678
RISKP	2.24	12.7107
RETLAG		12.5518
INDPRO		11.0301
TESTRU		11.0278
ECPI		11.0169
DECPI		10.3479
TERMS		8.17229
CALLRATE		7.68186
ORDANO		7.51555

It is interesting to compare the variable contributions over the total sample period with the overall regression coefficient estimates as shown in Table 10.5. The second column contains the significant t-statistics of the OLS coefficient estimations. The third column shows the average of the absolute contributions to the decisiveness.[2] The mean significance over time of the variables seems to coincide. A major exception is LEVELLAG. This leads to the conclusion that the level of the index may be an important leading indicator of expected returns. The fact that OLS does not identify this coefficient suggests that some asymmetry prevails in the way returns react to the index level. This finding may intuitively lend weight to the contrarian investment hypothesis as suggested by [Chan88]. Potential mean-reverting behaviour implicitly refutes the efficient markets hypothesis.

It can be seen that RETLAG contributes on average to the return of the index, somewhat surprisingly given that the first-order serial correlation of the index returns was found to be minor (see the Durbin–Watson (DW) statistic in Table 10.2). A closer look at Table 10.4 depicts RETLAG as cyclically active. Overall, more analysis of the variables' cyclical behaviour is called for.

MBPN's Classification Accuracy

Analysis of the marginal variable contributions is only sensible when a high decisiveness coefficient (DECISIVN) is coupled to a low (*ex post*) misclassification value (ABSERR), signalling the number of classes between the actual and predicted category. To put it another way, when the classification has been successful we expect a significant negative relation between the decisiveness and the classification error. Figure 10.3 shows the absolute error plotted against the decisiveness values, sorted in ascending order. It is obvious that both the number of classification errors and the magnitude rise when the decisiveness falls, which is in line with expectation.

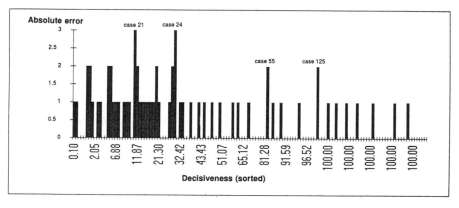

Figure 10.3   MBPN misclassifications sorted in ascending order of decisiveness

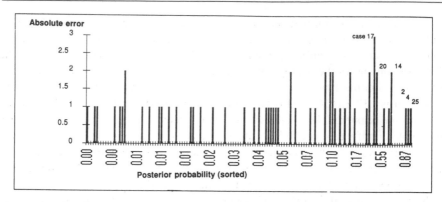

Figure 10.4 MDA misclassifications

To see how well the MBPN classification compares with traditional linear MDA, Figure 10.4 plots the absolute error coefficient against the posterior probability coefficients, derived from setting the prior probabilities equal to the observed sample proportions of cases in each group.

It is worth contrasting the Figures 10.3 and 10.4. Relatively larger MDA misclassifications tend to appear on the right-hand side, implying larger errors being predicted with increasing probabilities, whereas the larger neural misclassifications tend to be located on the left hand-side. However, the number of relatively large misclassifications appears to coincide quite well. We feel, however, that the two techniques *complement* each other in the sense that the largest misclassifications relate to different observations (see the inserted case numbers in both figures), with the notable exception of cases 20 to 26. These observations cover the period from July 1981 to January 1982 which appears to exhibit extremely unusual behaviour since neither ANS nor MDA succeeded in correct classification. Further investigations are called for.

CONCLUSIONS

What constitutes the advantage of neural networks over other, more traditional techniques for the investor? Neural networks seem to contribute mostly in those circumstances where one is able to specify a set of indices that account for a certain phenomenon without being able to describe the exact underlying relationships. The application of regression techniques becomes improper in the absence of a clear-cut conceptual model.

The high degree of correspondence between the outcomes in terms of variable contributions of both ordinary regression and multi-layer backpropagation analysis is obvious. This harmony inspires confidence but simultaneously indicates that at least the linear component of the relationship between index returns and the selected determinants has been successfully captured by the neural network. The selected network architecture with direct connections between inputs and outputs may be a contributory factor.

The out-of-sample predictions produced by the MBPN model appear to outweigh those generated by OLS in terms of both magnitude and direction. The question remains as to how far this finding can be generalized. Our results look attractive. The challenge of beating the market with neural networks may be enticing, but the issue of discerning the 'true' model behind stock returns is even more stimulating from an academic point of view. Box–Jenkins, VAR, ARCH, GARCH and EGARCH routines are all extremely well suited to obtaining an exact fit of time series but do not contribute much to the conceptual understanding of the phenomenon under study.

In this respect, neural networks are not necessarily the black-box tool they are usually taken to be. We have shown that MBPN analysis is able to unravel dynamic functional relationships between stock-market returns and contextual variables and may be helpful in increasing our understanding of the working of financial markets.

NOTES

1. Of course, nonlinear regression models may alleviate this issue. However, model specification is very problematic as theoretical insights in stock-return patterns remain very diffuse.

2. Note that this approach considers an *average* variable behaviour that neglects the additional dynamic information contained in the decisiveness analysis!

11

Important Factors in Neural Networks' Forecasts of Gold Futures Prices

Gary Grudnitski and A. Quang Do,
San Diego State University, USA

INTRODUCTION

One of the general criticisms levelled at neural networks is that their complexity makes them difficult to understand. This means that for potential users to trust the results of neural networks, the knowledge learned by the networks in the training process must be revealed to confirm its correctness. The purpose of this chapter is to address this criticism by using the neural networks derived by Grudnitski and Osburn [GruOsb93] to examine the relative importance of four input factors. Specifically, through a sensitivity analysis, we attempt to discover the critical or irrelevant features of the input data set in the neural networks' forecasts of gold futures prices.

Towards accomplishing this purpose, the remainder of the chapter is organised as follows. In the next section, relevant portions of Grudnitski and Osburn's paper are presented. Included in this section is a rationale for the factors they selected to forecast price changes of gold futures, a description of the factors they used to produce the forecasts, and a synopsis of the results they obtained. The third section of this chapter describes the method used to investigate the importance of the inputs to the forecast networks. The fourth section reports and discusses the results of our sensitivity analysis. A summary is given in the chapter's last section.

Neural Networks in the Capital Markets. Edited by Apostolos-Paul Refenes.
© 1995 John Wiley & Sons Ltd

FORECASTING GOLD FUTURES PRICES USING NEURAL NETWORKS

Forecasting futures prices is integral to a profitable futures trading strategy. Current research suggests that the standard random-walk assumption of futures prices may actually be only a veil of randomness that shrouds a noisy nonlinear process (see, for example, [Savit90] and [Tvede92] for an explanation of the apparent randomness in these price time series, and [FraSte89, Blank91, DeCost92] for evidence of the existence of nonlinear structures of rates of return).

Grudnitski and Osburn [GruOsb93] attempted to remove part of this veil by using neural networks to forecast monthly gold futures price changes based on past price changes, historical open interest patterns held to represent the beliefs of a majority of the traders in the gold futures market, and a barometer of general economic conditions. They trained 41 different network models of the Commodity Exchange (COMEX) Gold Futures market for the period from December 1982, to September 1990 using the following factors:

1. The change in, and volatility of, gold futures prices. Grudnitski and Osburn's price inputs coincided with the availability of commitments information (described next). Accordingly, using *Barron's* weekend closing prices for the most widely held gold futures contract, they derived month-end prices, which included the weekend closing prices two weeks before and two weeks after the end of the month. First differences were then calculated, and are graphed in Figure 11.1. Additionally, the monthly volatility of gold futures prices was represented in Grudnitski and Osburn's study by using the centred mean and weekend closing prices around the centred mean to compute a standard deviation of prices for each month.

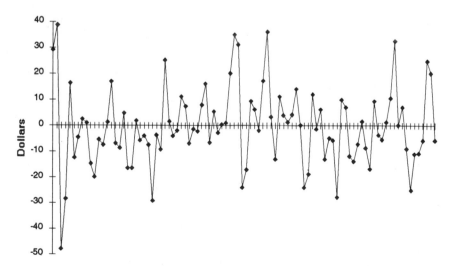

Figure 11.1   Gold futures price changes, January 1983 to September 1990

2. Commitments of major trading groups. An important input to the forecast of futures prices emanates from several studies [Band86, Hadady87a, Hadady87b, Kaufma87, and TewJon87], which indicate that, over time, small traders lose money and large traders make money in a futures market. To capture the trading strategy (i.e., traders' expectations about what will happen) of both small and large trading groups, Grudnitski and Osburn gathered data from a publication[1] of the Commodity Futures Trading Commission (CFTC) on end-of-month net percentage commitments[2] of large speculators, large hedgers, and small traders. They obtained these data from monthly volumes of the *Commitments of Traders in Futures Reports*.

3. The monthly growth rate of M1. Certain underlying economic conditions are another important factor held to influence futures prices [Stein89]. This influencing tendency may manifest itself as a seasonal (or longer) futures-specific, cycle-driven positioning of traders. What results is an exaggeration of or a reduction in the short-term patterns of price behaviour in the futures market, and, may be accounted for by including a variable that evidences significant correlation with the futures' price movements. To represent an underlying economic factor that influences the gold market, Grudnitski and Osburn used *Barron's* to obtain M1, the monthly growth rate of the aggregate supply of money.[3]

A Description of the Forecast Networks

Grudnitski and Osburn's forecast networks had 24 input-layer neurons. These input-layer neurons represent six inputs per month (price change, volatility, commitment percentages of the three trading groups, and M1) presented four months at a time. Grudnitski and Osburn's basic assumption was that the sequence of values of fixed size n in the window $I_0, \ldots, I_n$, is related to the following sequence of output values $O_0, \ldots, O_n$, and is defined entirely within the data set [Refene93]. More formally, the compositions of these patterns are as follows:

$$t_0 : I_0 = \{V_0 \ldots V_3\} \;\; \rightarrow \; O_0 = \{V_4\}$$

$$t_1 : I_1 = \{V_1 \ldots V_4\} \;\; \rightarrow \; O_1 = \{V_5\}$$

$$\ldots$$

$$t_j : I_j = \{V_j \ldots V_{j+3}\} \rightarrow O_j = \{V_{j+4}\}$$

For example, this meant that in the Grudnitski and Osburn study the August 1989, forecast (O_0) was produced from the April (V_0), May (V_1), June (V_2), and July (V_3), 1989, inputs of the price change, volatility, and the three trading groups' commitments.

Forecast Results

The feedforward, backpropagation forecast networks of Grudnitski and Osburn had two hidden layers of neurons and one output-layer neuron. Their networks were designed with eight neurons in the first hidden layer, and two neurons in the second hidden layer. Applying a similarity-based selection process, Grudnitski and Osburn adaptively trained 41 networks from different 15-month training sets. A forecast was then produced and a trade initiated based on the sign of the forecasted price change for 41 out of the 75 possible trading periods.

Grudnitski and Osburn's networks forecasted the correct direction of the next month's gold futures price change 61% of the time. Based on the networks' forecasts, total and average gains per trading period for a single futures contract were $17 525 and $427, respectively. Considering transaction costs and margin requirements, Grudnitski and Osburn's 41 trades of a futures contract resulted in an average per period (cumulative) return on investment of 16.36% (670%). When they adjusted these returns for risk, they found that the networks' forecasts yielded not only positive returns above risk, but also returns that were statistically significant above a return to market risk.

FURTHER ANALYSIS OF THE FORECAST NETWORKS

In this section, we discuss the procedure employed to assess the importance of the input factors to Grudnitski and Osburn's forecast networks. We also describe the extent to which the input values to the networks were simulated.

Alternative Procedures for Evaluating the Importance of Inputs

When a rule-based expert system produces output, the exact line of reasoning it used to reach these conclusions from the input data can usually be traced. But when a multiple, hidden-layer neural network produces an output value, all that remains is a large number of weights that have modified signals from connecting neurons. Interpreting these weights to discover how the network arrived at its answer and to find what input data features it considered to be important in that process, is tenuous at best.

One method of assessing the importance of the inputs to a network suggests that we examine the magnitude of the weights that connect the input-layer neurons to the hidden-layer neurons. Generalising classical statistical wisdom to the size of these weights, tells us that inputs that produce large absolute connecting weights are important, while inputs that generate connecting weights near zero are unimportant.

But certain conditions exist that might cause us to be grossly misled by drawing conclusions from the size of the weights. For example, in the presence of a large connecting weight from an input-layer to a hidden-layer neuron, perhaps the hidden-layer neuron has a very small absolute weight connecting it to the next hidden-layer neuron, making its own activation unimportant. Or, the input with the large connecting weight may connect strongly to one or more other hidden-layer neurons, which, in turn, may connect to the next hidden-layer neurons in opposing ways. The different values of that input might then cancel each other by the time the output-layer neuron is reached, meaning that the input, for all practical purposes, is ignored. Finally, if neither pair of highly correlated inputs is important in determining output values, they both might have large weights connecting them to hidden-layer neurons. This could occur when one of the input's weights becomes trapped with a large absolute value in the training process, thereby forcing the other input's weight to be large so that a balancing or cancelling influence is exerted [Master93].

Similarly, small connecting weights do not necessarily mean an input is unimportant. For example, several small connecting weights from an input neuron can add up to a significant effect. Or, the connecting weights from a neuron in the first hidden layer to a neuron in the second hidden layer, and from that neuron in the second hidden layer to the output layer, may be large, thus causing an input to have a significant effect on the output values.

Because of the above problems associated with focusing on connecting weights to assess the importance of the input factors, we chose instead to adopt a form of sensitivity analysis, wherein we documented the degree to which various simulated values of the inputs changed the forecasts of the networks. In practice, this involved presenting a base case to the trained neural network, and then observing the effect on its output when individual input values were systematically varied. Large differences from the base-case forecasts were held to evidence inputs or factors that had a marked effect; small differences were ascribed to inputs or factors that were thought to have little or no effect.

Simulated Data

The base case consisted of median or neutral values for all 24 inputs. This meant that for the four periods preceding the forecast ($V_0, \ldots, V_3$), the change in prices was set to zero, the volatility of the weekly prices during the month was set to $4.46, the change in M1 was set to 0.51, and the net commitments positions for large hedgers, large speculators, and small traders were set to zero (that is, no trading group was either short or long). Because the input data were normalised to lie between a range of 0 and 1,[4] the base case then consisted of all input factors taking on a value of 0.5 (except, of course, the input being varied).

The simulated values of prior price changes of a futures contract varied from −$25 to +$25 in increments of $1, the volatility of monthly prices of a futures contract ranged from $1.00 to $9.00 in increments of $0.10, and the change in M1 varied from −1.0 to 2.0 index points in increments of 0.1 index point. Because the sum of net commitments positions of the three trading groups had to equal zero each month, three different 'opposing position' data subsets were created. In the first data subset, small traders held net commitments positions between −15% and +15%, varying in increments of 1%, against large speculators. In the second subset, small traders held these same net positions, but this time against large hedgers. And in the third subset of simulated cases, large speculators took the place of small traders in terms of holding these net positions against large hedgers.

RESULTS AND DISCUSSION

In this section we focus on analysing the extent to which each of the six inputs in the four-month window influences the change in forecasted gold futures price of the networks. Here we look at both the magnitude and the directional relationship of the price change forecast *vis-à-vis* simulated values of each of the four factors.

Prior Prices

As can be seen from Figure 11.2, for all but period V_1, the change in the networks' forecasted price is both large and negatively related to the change in prices of prior periods. This derived relationship between the change in prior prices and forecasted price change is consistent with the propensity of the price-change series itself to oscillate in a somewhat sawtoothed fashion (see again Figure 11.1).

Figure 11.2 indicates that the networks appear to use prior price-change patterns to forecast a price retracement, wherein the magnitude or the likelihood of the price reversals themselves is related to the number and direction of the prior periods' price changes. Further, the incorporation of prior prices by the networks in this manner is consistent with a technical trading strategy predicated on price changes being both trend determined and trend determining [Marsha89]. For example, if the sign of the price change in all three prior periods (V_3, V_2, V_0) is consistent, the

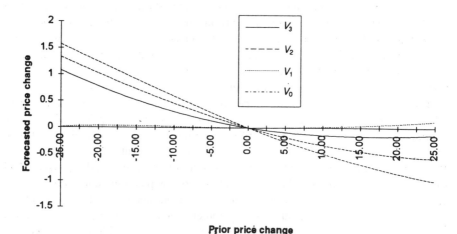

Figure 11.2   Forecasted price change as a function of prior price changes

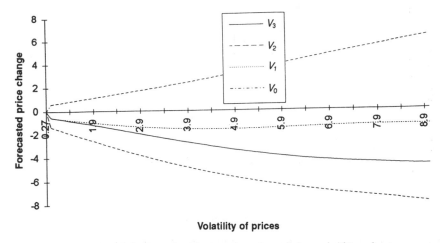

Figure 11.3   Forecasted price change as a function of the volatility of prices

networks appear to be teasing from the input data that a large (or highly likely) price retracement will occur. Moreover, especially for large prior price changes, the networks forecast that the size or likelihood of a positive price change will be greater than the size or likelihood of a negative price change based on equal but opposite prior price changes.

Price Volatility

As can be seen from Figure 11.3, for all but the oldest measure of monthly volatility, the networks forecast that prices will change negatively whenever the previous months' prices are highly volatile. This relationship is consistent with the notion held by some market moves that the short-term volatility of prices represents, to an extent, trader confusion about short-term price movements and uncertainty in the market. A greater amount of uncertainty and its accompanying pessimism about prices on the part of market participants appears to be captured in the price volatility factor and translated by the networks into negative price-change forecasts.

General Economic Conditions

Figure 11.4 depicts the networks placing little short-term emphasis, for three out of the four preceding periods, on general economic conditions in their forecasts of price changes. One reason for this factor's lack of significance is the differences in the rate of change and direction between it and the price-change series. Specifically, while the rate of change of M1 is small — about 1 index point per month on average

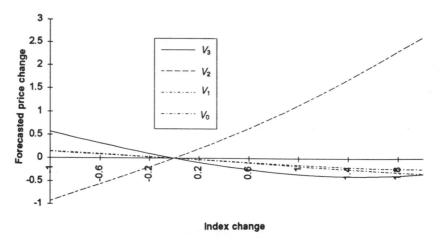

Figure 11.4   Forecasted price change as a function of the change in M1

and then mostly positive[5] — the price-change series had not only a larger rate of change but also a pattern of changes that went up and down.

Positions of Trading Groups

Figures 11.5, 11.6 and 11.7 show the price changes that were forecast by the networks when different net commitments positions are held by the three major trading groups. These figures seem to illustrate clearly that the networks place substantial weight not only on the extent of a trading group's holding but also against which trading group this position is held. Specifically, Figures 11.5 and

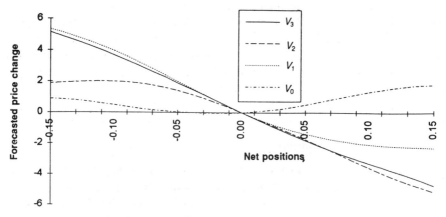

Figure 11.5   Forecasted price change as a function of net commitments positions of small traders against large speculators

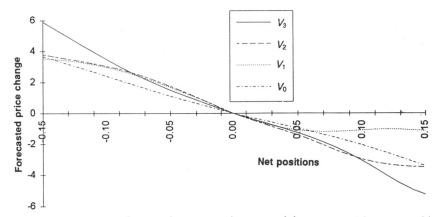

Figure 11.6   Forecasted price change as a function of the net commitments positions of small traders against large hedgers

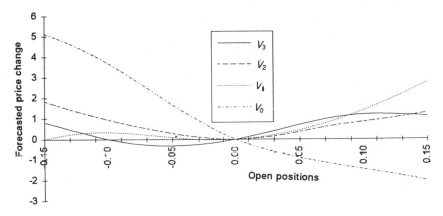

Figure 11.7   Forecasted price change as a function of the net commitments positions of large hedgers against large speculators

11.6 indicate that when small traders hold positions against large speculators and hedgers, the networks forecast the occurrence of large price changes that are contrary to the small traders' positions. Additionally, Figure 11.7 appears to indicate that when large speculators take positions against large hedgers, the neural networks forecast that mixed price changes will result.

One popular explanation [Zaremb90] for these derived relationships between forecasted price change and net commitments positions of these trading groups is that amateur (that is, small) traders lose money to professional traders (large hedgers and speculators). This loss occurs because amateur traders initiate and terminate trades haphazardly. They also seem unable to manage risk capital judiciously. They often assume they can beat the odds too easily, and they are too ready to commit their resources fully. Eventually, small traders who are successful join the ranks of the professional trading groups, while the rest drop out only to be replaced by eager new small traders, who enter the competition with the same inexperience and resource disadvantage as their predecessors.

SUMMARY

This investigation used 41 previously developed neural networks to examine the importance of four input factors on the networks' forecast of monthly changes in gold futures prices. To assess the importance of the factors, a form of sensitivity analysis was adopted, wherein the effect on the networks' output when individual input values were systematically varied was observed. Large differences in forecasted prices were held to evidence factors that had a marked effect, while small differences were ascribed to factors that were believed to have little or no effect.

Of the four factors, the networks appeared to place the greatest differential emphasis on the net commitments positions of the various trading groups. This was especially true for the situations where the group categorised as small traders held long or short positions. For example, a 5% short or long position taken by small traders in the four months directly preceding the forecast, resulted in a change in the networks' forecast of approximately ±$2.00.

The volatility of monthly prices was another factor that appeared to have a marked effect on the forecasts produced by the neural networks. The networks appear to have constructed a relationship wherein any significant degree of volatility in monthly prices for the three periods immediately preceding the forecast, results in a forecasted price decrease of from $1.00 to $5.00.

Third in importance among the four factors were changes in prior-period prices. For large prior price changes (Over ±$15.00), the networks forecasted a gold futures price change that was in the opposite direction and of a magnitude from $0.50 to $1.50. For lesser and more frequently occurring prior price changes, (±$5.00) the networks forecasted a price retracement of less than $0.50.

General economic conditions, as represented by M1, seemed to be of least importance among the four factors, and of little absolute significance to the forecast networks. One explanation for this factor's lack of effect is the differences in the consistency of the direction and the rate of change between M1 and the price-change series.

In concluding, it is important to note that our assessment procedure has a limitation, which could adversely affect the ability of potential capital markets users to generalise our findings about the relative importance of the input factors. The results we obtained from the application of this form of sensitivity analysis are very much a product of the base case selected (that is, that all input values except the one under inspection were set to 0.5). Were we to present the networks with different and perhaps more extreme base cases by setting input values to 0.1 or

0.9, for example, the results may have been dramatically altered as various hidden- and output-layer neurons went in and out of saturation [Master93].

NOTES

1. This monthly report first published in 1983, lists the size and nature of the open interest positions for large and small traders.

2. The reporting level for gold futures is 300 contracts. Net percentage commitments are the long minus short positions of the trading groups divided by the total open interest.

3. M1 was indexed at 100 for December 1982 and was changed each month according to the following formula:
$$\text{Index}_{t+n} = \text{M1}_{t+n}/478.5t_0$$

4. The inputs of price change, price volatility and M1 were normalised separately, and the three commitments inputs were normalized as if they were one factor. This meant applying the following transformation to the input values:

$$i_{norm} = (i - min)/\text{range}$$

       where i_{norm} vector of normalised values of the input,

            i vector of original values of the input,

            min = minimum original value of the input, and

            range = range of the original values of the input.

5. For the 75 possible trading periods (that is, months from July 1984 to September 1990) the change in M1 was negative only 16 times.

PART THREE
FOREIGN EXCHANGE APPLICATIONS

12
Foreign Exchange Markets

Mahendra Mehta, *Citibank N.A., India*

INTRODUCTION

Our discussion of the application of neural network learning methods to forecast and trade in the foreign exchange (FX) market commences with some useful facts and statistics about this market. This chapter is divided into twelve different sections. The first section deals with the background of global market activity in the FX world, including major statistics on global turnover, trading volume by currency pairs, the prominence of the US dollar (USD) and Deutschmark (DEM), players in the FX market, etc. In the second section principal characteristics of the FX market are discussed. The third section reviews some popular viewpoints of technical analysis and related methods. The fourth section considers an argument in favour of the possibility of successfully learning about FX time series since they are a man-made process. The fifth section discusses several issues and problems associated with modelling FX time series as a mathematical process. The sixth section explores why totally data-driven analysis, such as neural network learning procedures, is meaningful for FX time-series forecasting and trading. The seventh section addresses the importance of data reliability and validation aspects as an important requirement for undertaking any neural network related investigation. In the eighth section, data sampling frequency is studied and several suggestions made to address this problem and to obtain good results while trading with FX spot time series. The ninth section deals with the different types of input which can be considered for a FX time series for neural network studies. This section also deliberates on the necessity of filtering the FX data before using them to learn some patterns using neural networks. The tenth section deals with various aspects of

Neural Networks in the Capital Markets. Edited by Apostolos-Paul Refenes.
© 1995 John Wiley & Sons Ltd

neural network configuration, training procedures and parameters, learning vector creation, network update strategy, etc. The eleventh section discusses some trading strategies and other important related considerations using neural networks. The final section briefly reviews various issues relating to the pitfalls and limitations of neural network based learning and trading in the FX market with a view to cautioning users on a few important points before employing these techniques to trade in the marketplace. This section also includes suggestions on the direction of further research and development in this area.

THE GLOBAL FOREIGN EXCHANGE MARKET

Global Turnover

Global net turnover in the world's FX market is estimated to be about US $1 trillion per business day. According to a survey conducted by the Bank of International Settlement [BIS93], the daily turnover in April 1992 was estimated at $880 billion (Figure 12.1). According to this study, the FX trading volume doubled from 1986 to 1989. It grew about 42% in the years 1989 to 1992. This is partly due to sizeable increase in trading volume in other FX market segments, particularly futures, options and swaps. These instruments experienced relatively slower growth in previous periods. According to the survey, the spot market has the highest trading volume, followed by the swap market. Though the FX options market has shown the sharpest increase since around 1989, it accounts for only about 4% of the total daily trading volume.

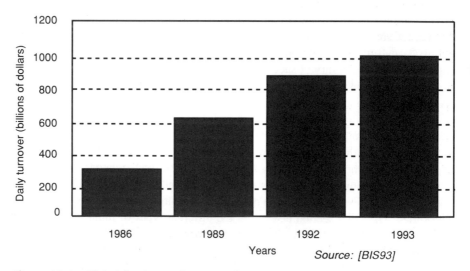

Figure 12.1   Global foreign exchange market turnover

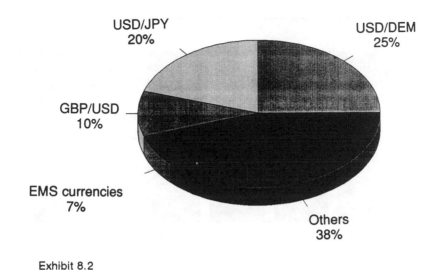

Exhibit 8.2

Source: [BIS93]

Figure 12.2   Global foreign exchange market turnover by currency pairs

Trading Volume by Currency Pairs

Foreign exchange market activity cannot logically be broken down by single currencies alone. It can, however, be broken down in terms of the proportion of total turnover in which any given individual currency figures on one side of total transactions. By currency pairs, US dollar/Deutschmark transactions account for over 25% of the total reported net turnover. US dollar/yen and US dollar/sterling transactions approximately account for 20% and 10%, respectively. Direct transactions between EMS currencies account in total for an additional 7% of all reported net turnover (Figure 12.2)

The Prominence of the US Dollar

The US dollar remains by far the most important currency in the world's FX market. It figures on one side of over 80% of net reported turnover, and seven of the ten most heavily traded currency pairs have the US dollar on one side. Its role is more pronounced in the swap market, where it is involved in 95% of total turnover — indicating the use of the US dollar as the main hedge currency. Despite its dominance, the US dollar now seems to play a less significant role than it did three years ago. At that time, about 90% of identified gross swap transactions involved the US dollar on one side.

Although the US dollar remains the single most actively traded currency, partly because of its role as a vehicle currency, its significance varies among currency

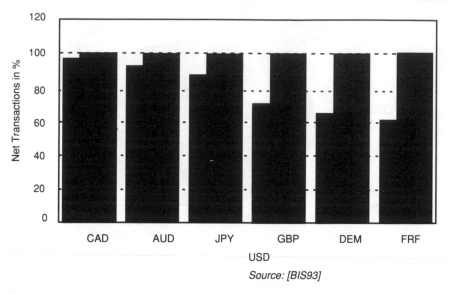

Source: [BIS93]

Figure 12.3   Volume of transaction in currencies against the US dollar

counterparts. For example, 98% of all deals involving the Canadian dollar have the US dollar on the other side. Similarly, it is present in 93% of deals involving the Australian dollar and in 87% of deals involving the Japanese yen. However, there are strong indications that, in respect of the Australian dollar, the volume of deals in which the US dollar figures on one side of the deal will decrease. The US dollar figures less prominently in deals involving European currencies such as sterling, the Deutschmark and the French franc, with shares of 70%, 64% and 60% respectively (Figure 12.3).

The Deutschmark

The Deutschmark is now clearly the second most widely traded currency in the FX market. Evidence strongly suggests that its importance rose sharply between 1989 and 1992, mostly at the expense of the US dollar, and to a lesser extent of the Japanese yen. The Deutschmark now figures on one side of nearly 40% of total transactions and is involved in four of the ten most heavily traded currency pairs. It is the only currency, apart from the US dollar, traded in large quantities against a wide range of other currencies. Together the US dollar and the Deutschmark account for 95% of all trading against the Japanese yen, the pound sterling, the Swiss franc, the Australian dollar, the Canadian dollar and the French franc.

The focus in direct cross-trading against the Deutschmark (that is, without involving the US dollar as a trading currency) is clearly European, with the yen being the only non-European currency bought and sold against the Deutschmark to any notable extent.

It seems none the less justified to conclude that the relative importance of the Deutschmark in the FX market has increased considerably over the past three years and is expected to increase further in the next few years.

Despite the extensive use of the Deutschmark in the total FX market, the nature of trading in it differs substantially from that in the US dollar. Business involving the Deutschmark is much more heavily concentrated on spot transactions. Over 60% of the total cross-currency deals involving the Deutschmark are in this category, in contrast to only 42% in the case of the US dollar. This difference once again reflects the extensive use of the US dollar in hedging operations taking place in the swap, futures and options markets.

Players in the Foreign Exchange Market

Dealers (mainly banks) account for the bulk of FX market transactions (known as interbank transactions), whether located in the same or in different countries. The evidence seems to suggest that transactions with other market participants have expanded more rapidly than those between interbank dealers in the most recent three-year period. This includes pension funds, corporate, large investors, fund managers and other non-banking financial institutions. Over half of all reported net transactions were cross-border in April 1992, and nearly 60% in the case of inter-dealer business. The latter proportion appears to have increased moderately since 1989.

Geographical Distribution of Trading

In geographical terms, FX trading appears to have become somewhat more concentrated than in 1989 and previous years. This was almost entirely the result of the above average growth of trading in the United Kingdom, which took its share of global trading up from 25% in 1989 to nearly 30% in 1992. The combined share of the three major countries (the United Kingdom, the United States and Japan) is about 60%. The next four most important centres, Singapore, Switzerland, Hong Kong and Germany, accounted together for around a further 25% of the total FX volume. Among the smaller countries, the three Scandinavian countries excluding Norway, together with Spain and Greece, all registered large percentage increases in turnover.

The Role of Brokers

About one-third of FX trading is conducted through brokers, and their role is especially notable in the spot and swap sectors of the market. With the main exception of Italy, the role of brokers appears to have declined somewhat since around 1989. Trading through brokers in Japan, the United States and the United Kingdom has recorded the most significant fall.

PRINCIPAL CHARACTERISTICS OF THE FOREIGN EXCHANGE MARKET

To begin, it will be useful to examine the general characteristics of the FX market. This will facilitate understanding as well as productive modelling of the related time series. Most of our discussions will centre around the spot market as this market is the most important segment of the FX market.

The FX spot market has the following important characteristics:

- Among all the financial markets, the spot-market segment of the FX market can be technically regarded as the most *efficient*. This attribute makes it very difficult to apply conventional modelling techniques to forecast the dynamic behaviour of the FX time series with a view to taking profitable trading positions.

- Spot transactions on the FX market are carried out 24 hours a day using an electronic network such as the dedicated dealing system offered by Reuters, telex, telephone, etc. The absence of any formal *exchange* makes it very easy to trade on the spot market. However, transactions on the futures market are made using exchanges.

- Ignoring credit-related issues, another important reason for very high trading volume on this market is the possibility of high leverage, This feature attracts even small-time speculators and investors to enter and trade on this market. The entry to trade on the FX market has been facilitated by the highly leveraged margin trading facilities offered by financial companies, banks and brokers all over the world.

- The FX market is perhaps the only market which is open virtually 24 hours a day, five days a week. The market opens early in New Zealand and Australia, followed by Japan. A little later, several trading centres in the Far East, such as Hong Kong and Singapore, enter the global market. As market closes in Japan, it opens in the Middle East and Europe, closely followed by the United Kingdom. While the UK is still actively trading, North America enters the market, and when it is time for North America to close, New Zealand and Australia return to the market and the next 24-hour cycle begins. On Saturday and Sunday very limited trading is reported from the Middle East markets.

- Trading volumes are very heavy, as already discussed, particularly in four major currency pairs DEM/USD, CHF/USD, USD/GBP, and JPY/USD and also some cross-currency pairs such as DEM/GBP, JPY/GBP, JPY/CHF. Therefore the market is considered deep and very liquid for the purpose of initiating any trade and closing the trade at any time of the day. In general, FX spot-market trades can be completed in a few seconds.

- Funding costs for overnight FX trading positions are based on the interest differentials of the two currencies involved in trading. These are normally low unless a high interest rate currency is sold against a low interest rate currency.

Therefore, in general, it does not cost much (in terms of funding charges) to hold trading positions in this market.

- Bid and offer spread, and therefore transactions costs associated with spot transactions, are generally very low compared to any other market — of the order of 0.03–0.05% for each transaction carried out on the interbank market. To give an example, an interbank 1 MM US $ round (buy and sell against DEM) transaction may typically incur a transaction cost of US $500. This cost is very low compared to costs incurred in other market instruments.

- With increasingly efficient communication and rate distribution systems available from various rate and market information vendors around the world, the trading network has expanded at a very rapid pace — dependable and consistent spot rates are available in every geographical location with almost equal efficiency. Therefore an FX market does not provide any geographical locational arbitrage such as one sometimes finds in other markets.

- If positions are not held overnight, there is almost no funding cost, except for the operational costs necessary for effecting the transaction and the fixed cost associated with back-office operations related to settlements, etc.

- Foreign exchange markets can react almost instantaneously following the breaking of any political, economic or other news which might affect investor, trader or large fund managers' sentiments. The market is generally very fragile and is very often seen to react to statements by prominent policy-makers or even rumours. It is this phenomenon which suggests that in general, the FX market should be sampled many times during the day, as discussed later in this chapter.

- Recent events have proved that the FX spot market cannot be easily manipulated by any single participant, however big. This includes central banks. Most central banks intervene from time to time in the market with a view to influencing or controlling exchange rates. Very often such attempts are unsuccessful (witness the breakdown of the ERM in September 1992) as well as extremely costly, and it is natural to question whether such interventions make sense. It is clear that the FX market is extremely deep, efficient and non-manipulative. It is the collective thinking of the majority of market participants alone that determines the dynamic relationship between various currencies. The inability of central banks to bend FX markets to their will in accordance with national monetary and economic policies does appear to be on the increase.

- One very significant point which relates to volatility in the FX market is sudden and sometimes large movements which are caused immediately after the release of some economic data relating to the US and other major economies of the world. The exact time of release of these data is precisely known, and thus it may be useful if ways can be studied to incorporate this fact into the neural modelling.

- Another significant reason for the increase in trading volume and deep liquidity in FX market is the rapid liberalization of several economies in the world. As more and more economies open up and their currency is floated on the world market, traders, speculators, investors and currency fund managers see increased opportunity to trade on this market, making the market deep and perhaps efficient.

- Annualised daily volatility (standard deviation of first differences of the exchange rates observed daily) in respect of most currencies lies between 10% and 15%. Sometimes, for a short period, it is quite possible that the volatility in respect of some major currencies may even go as high as 18–20%. But for most major currency pairs, a reasonable estimate of the value of the volatility is generally between 10% and 15%. For some less active currencies, it even lies between 5% and 10%.

TRADING USING TECHNICAL ANALYSIS

Trading on FX and other financial markets using some sort of simple or advanced technical analysis is extensively practised by dealers, traders, investment managers and portfolio managers. These tools are taken from conventional technical analysis and charting techniques such as moving average techniques, stochastics, Relative Strength Index (RSI), Moving average convergence and divergence (MACD), Elliott wave theory, market profile technique, point and figure chart, candlestick method, resistance and support levels, momentum indicators, etc.

In spite of its widespread use, technical analysis has until now met with considerable disapproval from most academics. As [Malkie87] bluntly puts it:

> Obviously, I am biased against the chartist. This is not only a personal predilection, but a professional one as well. Technical analysis is anathema to the academic world. We love to pick on it. Our bullying tactics are prompted by two considerations: a) the method is patently false; and b) it's easy to pick on. While it may seem a bit unfair to pick on such a sorry target, just remember: it is your money we are trying to save.

In spite of such sentiment technical analysis has been enjoying a renaissance on Wall Street as well as most other world financial centres. All investment advisers and major brokerage firms world-wide regularly publish technical commentaries on the market and individual securities, currencies, commodities and bonds, and many of the newsletters published by various experts are based on technical analysis. There is convincing evidence that since the late 1970s or early 1980s the number of practitioners of technical analysis has grown considerably, while the number of practitioners of fundamental analysis (a technique for modelling market movements based on the fundamental economic variables, discussed below) has fallen sharply. This suggests that among practising traders, dealers, investment managers and portfolio advisers technical analysis is creating sustained interest and value added.

From the statistics, research work reported [Treyno86] and other available evidence based on experience, it is appropriate to conclude that if technical analysis related studies have something to offer in the financial markets, modelling and associated forecasting using neural network learning procedures are all the more likely to give productive results.

There is a strong futures, options and swap market in foreign exchange. It is also quite possible to use neural network techniques in the futures and options markets. There is little difference between the approach to be used for the spot and other markets except relating to data preparation and problem identification associated with learning, etc.

In the context of neural network applications, it is very important to mention that application of neural network learning procedures cannot work well with any problem unless the problem is correctly posed and all related variables identified to a large extent and understood in the context of the neural network problem-solving framework. The neural network is an excellent tool but, unlike many other tools, considerable background and data preparation work has to be done very carefully and intelligently before the given problem can be tackled to give useful and productive results.

FOREIGN EXCHANGE TIME SERIES: A MAN-MADE PROCESS

It will be meaningful and important to delineate certain distinctive idiosyncrasies of financial markets and in particular FX time-series movements (from the point of view of modelling the series) resulting from the market activities carried out by different market participants. A closer understanding of these attributes will facilitate more decisive modelling. Foreign exchange time series are primarily a man-made process, which is to say that movements are basically caused by activities undertaken at irregular or regular intervals by dealers, traders, market-makers, importers, exporters, investors, fund managers and central banking agencies, and by a number of other economic parameters.

Natural processes are inherently difficult to model and predict. Foreign exchange time series should be relatively more amenable to some form of systematic modelling procedure compared to various other complex non-stationary and random processes which are caused naturally. Some of the characteristic features discussed below are the outcome of close examinations of the typical behaviour of FX time series:

- Generally series are discretely continuous and movements are usually between one and five pips (movements in the fourth decimal place in most currency pairings with the US dollar and the second decimal place against the Japanese yen) except when the market is volatile and movements are caused by an unanticipated political or economic event. Most often market volatility is high when major US economic data are released, as mentioned earlier.

Table 12.1   Intra-day movements of major currency pairs.

Currency pair	Average high–low differences in 24 hours (pips)
DEM/USD	221
CHF/USD	183
JPY/USD	138
USD/GBP	170
ITL/USD	1822
FRF/USD	560
USD/AUD	63
JPY/DEM	94

- The bid/offer spread is generally a very good indicator of short-term market volatility and high liquidity. The usual bid/offer spread for most active currencies is around 0.05–0.08%.
- Total average movements for Deutschmark/US dollar rate are typically around 230 pips in any 24-hour window. Some important statistics pertaining to intraday movements of major currencies for a given period are shown in Table 12.1.

MODELLING OF FOREIGN EXCHANGE TIME SERIES: ISSUES AND PROBLEMS

One important focus of several scientific investigations in the study of naturally occurring complex phenomena is forecasting. Given knowledge about a system and its past behaviour, what predictions can be made regarding its future evolution? Two common approaches to the making of such predictions are the model-based approach and the statistical approach.

The *model-based approach* assumes that there is sufficient *a priori* information in the form of physical conservation laws or system dynamics such that a first-principle derivation may be made to construct an accurate or quasi-accurate model of the observed processes. If an accurate model can be constructed, it is indeed possible mathematically to forecast the future behaviour of the system state using standard and sufficiently matured techniques. Where an accurate model cannot be constructed and only quasi-accurate models are available, techniques such as Kalman filtering and several other techniques based on estimation theory may be employed. Using the Kalman estimation algorithm, it is possible to model uncertain components of the system dynamics by incorporating what is known as *process noise* or process uncertainty. But there are two difficulties with this approach. One is that it is not often possible to identify a model because the underlying laws may not be clearly understood, as is the case with FX time series. Another is that, even if an accurate model can be constructed, the specification of the current state from which the model can predict, may require much more information than is practically obtainable. There are many practical problems which cannot be modelled easily using conventional modelling techniques. Faced with the above limitations, recently reported research work [Narend90] suggests that neural learning methods can be employed to solve many such problems to estimate and forecast unknown variables, identify systems and variables and also for control applications in nonlinear problems.

Experience and the initial study show the behaviour of FX time series to be a problem which can be addressed by neural network learning methods. Systematic study and application of neural network techniques in forecasting FX time series can give very promising results. Neural network related studies have opened another vast discipline for financial analysts. Study of financial time-series forecasting, identification of arbitrage opportunities on the financial market, overpricing and underpricing of instruments, hedging, risk management, credit risk evaluation and even correct pricing for complex securities using neural network techniques can provide promising results. Under the current state of problem-solving tools for nonlinear problems, many problems can only be addressed by neural network learning methods with effective results.

WHY DATA-BASED ANALYSIS IS ATTRACTIVE IN THE FOREIGN EXCHANGE MARKET

Quantitative methods for estimating and forecasting trends in various financial market (time series) movements and investment and trading decision-making are increasingly becoming an indispensable part of market analysis. Continuous monitoring of the condition of the market and its constant diagnosis using systematic and organised techniques have become extremely important tools in analysing today's complex financial markets.

Systematic and suggestive analysis of various financial time series with the help of paradigms, patterns, charts, graphs and related statistics with a view to comprehending possible market movements is rapidly growing as an important discipline.

Predominantly, there are two ways of analysing market movements: fundamental analysis and technical analysis. There was a time when the only acceptable practice was to understand and follow the fundamental variables and factors that make prices move. This conviction is undergoing a significant change primarily for the following reasons:

- The increasing inability to define and comprehend the fundamental variables and study the effects of changes in these on prices or trends in a systematic manner.
- The rapid flow of financial, political, commercial and other types of information, and the rapid shift in the demand and supply pattern, which have significant influence on market movements.
- The need to be able to take fast and timely trading and investment decisions in briskly moving markets.

- The increasing interaction and application of more mature scientific, engineering and statistical techniques in financial markets to analyse and understand the phenomena of market movements. Some of the techniques include neural learning procedures, genetic optimisation procedures, chaos theory and adaptive estimation procedures.

- The rapid evolution of computer technology in terms of cost, speed, power and flexibility in its ability to address multi-dimensional problems.

- Increased short-term volatility in several financial time series and new opportunities in the marketplace.

DATA RELIABILITY AND VALIDATION

In neural network and technical analysis related studies, since analysis is totally based on data, it is very critical that the data to be used for analysis are absolutely clean. Since the learning of patterns, structures and complex formations is totally data-dependent, it is extremely vital and important that data used are free from any errors whatsoever.

Availability of reliable and clean data is the basis of neural network experiments; without it neural network experiments should not be performed. Further, all data points which it is proposed to use for learning should be very carefully graphed and examined individually before any systematic neural network learning study is undertaken. In ensuring this, it may also be relevant to scrutinise if the source from which data are obtained is totally dependable. If two or more currencies are to be studied simultaneously, then it may also be necessary to get synchronous data for as many currencies.

Data Errors: Causes and Remedies

During the process of data collection, validation and trade execution, it is sometimes the case that rates quoted by data distribution services (Reuters or Telerate, for example) are not only non-tradable but also incompatible with the market rate at that point in time. This error is very common for DEM/USD and other active currencies and happens many times during the active hours. There can be many reasons for this.

The tick by tick exchange rates that are supplied to the news services by major financial institutions are intended for use by market participants as a general indication of where exchange rates stand at any given time and do not necessarily represent the true rate at which transactions are actually being conducted. It has been noticed that some participants do occasionally try to manipulate indicative prices to send a signal or create a favourable market movement. Sometimes this results in erroneous quotes, but most often, since a bank's reputation and credibility as a market-maker emerges from favourable relationships with other market participants, it is generally the case that these indicative prices match closely the true prices experienced in the market. As mentioned earlier, the FX market has no geographical location and no business-hour limitations, and most of the popular data distribution services are widely subscribed, so any market-maker can submit new bid and ask prices. In addition, deliberate attempts to move the market in some particular way, as discussed above, data error can take place as a result of data-entry problems. As quotes are submitted manually via computer keyboard and other similar data entry mechanisms, it is quite possible that data entry errors also might crop up from time to time, resulting in erroneous quotes particularly during volatile market conditions. But this can easily be detected and it is generally the case that these types of incorrect quote are very quickly rectified.

DATA SAMPLING FREQUENCY FOR NEURAL NETWORK LEARNING

One significant issue in the study of FX time-series forecasting problems, particularly of intra-day data, using neural network learning procedures, is the data sampling frequency — the rate at which data from the market should be sampled. This influential variable requires some consideration.

In most other markets which have business-hour limitations and less intra-day volatility, most conventional technical analysts normally use daily opening, high, low and closing prices from the underlying time series. There are two reasons for doing this: first, noise in the time series is reduced considerably; and second, the difficulty experienced in systematically recording the intra-day data and in handling noise in it.

Most FX traders and analysts give scant consideration to intra-day data for systematic analysis except in looking for favourable rates to enter and exit the market. But because of high intra-day volatility in the FX spot market, it is more appropriate to sample the market more often than once a day. The other reasons are as follows:

- Because of low transactions costs, it is easy to identify good trades during intra-day market movements. Also it is sometimes possible to turn around two or three good trades during the day itself. This is not possible if only open, high, low and closing prices are monitored. As discussed earlier, the FX market never closes and so opening, high, low and closing prices are less meaningful.

- In addition, for actively managing positions and for risk-control purposes, it is a good idea to sample more often than once in a day.

- Identification of intra-day patterns and forecasting of movements are more likely to be recognised by neural network learning methods, giving us additional opportunities.

However, intra-day sampling of the FX market increases noise in the time series considerably. Therefore to keep the noise low and identify good trends, it is necessary either to use some sort of filtering (discussed later in the chapter) or to find some optimum sampling frequency, or both.

The identification of the appropriate sampling frequency is a difficult problem. One possible method is to use correlation analysis. In this method the time series is sampled at different frequency intervals and autocorrelation is used to arrive at the required sampling frequency. In addition to this, it is possible to vary the sampling frequency depending upon the volatility of the market. Systematic study needs to be carried out to identify variable sampling frequency parameters for different currencies. Experience and the study performed suggest that for four major currencies and three cross-currencies, it is sufficient to sample the market at intervals of between 5 and 60 minutes, depending upon the currency pair. It is also a good idea to use some sort of simple averaging to smooth the data sampled at higher sampling rates. As far as less active currency pairs are concerned, it may still be a good idea to sample two or three times a day.

A uniform sampling frequency has its own problems when using intra-day data. One problem which is often encountered if the market is sampled at very high frequency and at uniform rate is repetition of the same price at different points in time. This is generally seen during the lunch interval (particularly in Japan and Far East) or when trading is thin. This causes the set of learning vectors to be malicious and generally has an undesirable influence on the learning process. It is therefore suggested that the sampling frequency should be selected in such a manner that production of malicious vectors is minimised. It is also possible to use data compression procedures to avoid malicious vectors altogether.

From close study of the data, market movements and volume of trades, it appears that the FX market is generally more volatile when both UK and US markets are open and less volatile for Far East and Asia business-hours trading; this suggests the use of two or three different sampling frequencies depending upon the time of day.

TYPES OF INPUT FOR NEURAL NETWORK STUDY

This is the most decisive part of the neural network study phase. As can be seen from the typical minute-by-minute plot shown in Figure 12.4, intra-day time series can be extremely noisy. There is little doubt that filtering or smoothing of data such as these needs to be carried out before the data can be used to enable neural network learning. We examine a few possible approaches to addressing this issue. One of the simplest approaches is to compute a moving average of the raw data (sampled at some predetermined interval) and form a series of learning vectors to be given to the neural network for supervised or unsupervised learning. Some of the different inputs which can be considered are as follows.

Price Input

Series of raw prices sampled at regular time intervals and filtered by some means can form one set of possible inputs. However, application of this type of inputs

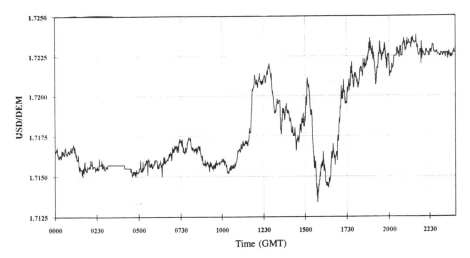

Figure 12.4 USD/DEM spot rate (mid-rate), 1 December 1993, sampled every minute

in the FX market has many problems. First, FX price movements are generally nonstationary and quite random in nature, and therefore not very suitable for learning purposes. Second, raw price inputs give rise to scaling problems; however, this issue is less serious and can be addressed with little manipulation. In addition, since intra-day price changes in most currencies tend to affect only the second or fourth decimal place (depending upon the currency pair) the sensitivity of the price changes is very low and this generally results in poor learning. Therefore for most neural network studies and analysis concerned with the FX market, price inputs are not a desirable data set. Results of extensive experiments using raw prices as network inputs show that the learning process improves by using other types of input.

First Difference Input

If $P_1, P_2, \ldots, P_t$ is a price sequence sampled at regular intervals, then $P_2 - P_1, P_3 - P_2, \ldots, P_t - P_{t-1}$ are defined as the *first differences* of the price sequence. First differences are perhaps the most effective way to generate data sets for neural network learning. This is true both for intra-day and inter-day data series. Two advantages of taking first differences can be cited here. First, it helps in making the time series stationary, which is a useful statistical property. Second, it overcomes the scaling problem which is associated with rates.

Rate of Return Input

Rates of return differ only slightly from first differences. Given the price sequence $P_1, P_2, \ldots, P_t$ sampled at regular intervals, we form the rate of return at time $t + 1$

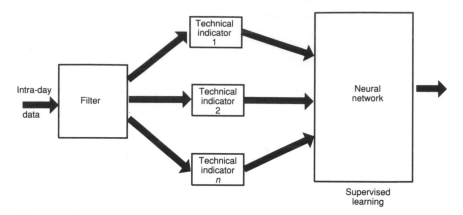

Figure 12.5   Neural network learning strategy based on technical indicators

by dividing the first difference at that time by the price at time t:

$$\frac{P_{t+1} - P_t}{P_t} \tag{12.1}$$

A sequence of this kind has properties similar to those of first differences.

Inputs based on the technical indicators

It is also a good idea to process raw FX time series and generate a series of technical indicators [Kaufma87] such as moving averages, oscillators and stochastics, to input to the neural network with the aim of producing a short- or medium-term forecast for the time series (see Figure 12.5).

NEURAL NETWORK LEARNING DESIGN

An important objective of most learning procedures relating to financial time series, which can potentially result in profitable trading positions, is to learn to identify the market conditions prevailing just before a trend is established. Generally, a forecasting algorithm must be able to capture trending market conditions quickly, along with major turning points. Neural network learning design of the following steps:

- network configuration design;
- learning vector selection;
- learning parameter selection;
- learning and testing data selection;
- update strategy and problems.

Network Configuration Design

By using one of the many commercially available software packages or writing a flexible computer program, it is simple to configure a neural network for learning purposes. There is no clear hard and fast rule for determining the network configuration for optimal learning for a given problem. The choice of number of layers and nodes in each layer is a crucial factor for good network design. For FX time series data, the following considerations will help identify a suitable network. While selecting the network configuration, it is important to consider what number of nodes is appropriate so as to avoid close fitting of the training data. A complex network having too many weights will fit the training vector data more or less exactly, but exact fitting of the learning data is more likely to cause problems because it is less likely to do well in its out-of-sample performance. For all financial time-series forecasting applications the objective is to learn generalised patterns existing in the data rather than specialised patterns. To design a neural network, a reasonable strategy is to start with a one layer and a few nodes and increase the complexity while monitoring generalisation by testing (out-of-sample) at each epoch. The most common index of generalisation for backpropagation is the mean squared error, calculated by squaring each error, summing the squares, then dividing the sum by the number of outputs and data patterns. A good technique for preventing overtraining is to stop when the mean squared error, yielded by the testing sets, stops improving.

Learning Vector Selection

As mentioned, most intra-day data and even inter-day data require a certain amount of smoothing before they can be considered for training a neural network. A simple and very effective way to filter data is to use a moving average over an appropriate period of time. This period should be selected such that filtering should not give rise to too great a lag between the actual price and the filtered price while reducing the noise to a reasonable extent in the data set,

Another effective way to reduce noise is to use a series of technical indicators, since each of the technical indicators essentially represents some sort of filtering algorithm.

One effective appealing approach is to use Kalman filters (Figure 12.6). Figure 12.7 shows the DEM/USD time series of Figure 12.4 after processing through the Kalman filter. The process has been modelled as first-order Markov process in the given example.

From the close study of intra-day data for four major currencies and three other cross-currencies, it appears that it will be reasonable to consider a learning input vector data set going back approximately two to three hours, taking a reasonable number of data points in between, and training the network in supervised mode so as to forecast future conditions (derived from technical indicator or rate of return)

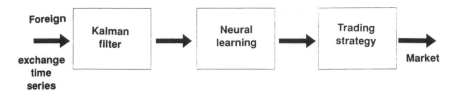

Figure 12.6   The Kalman filtering and learning approach

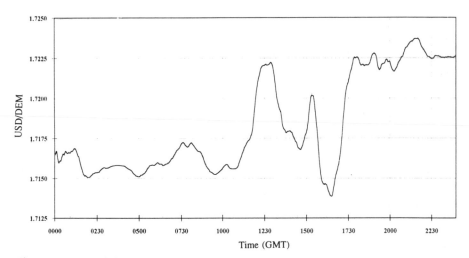

Figure 12.7   USD/DEM spot rate, 1 December 1993, after Kalman filtering

and by optimising certain performance criteria. For the daily time series for the currency pairs mentioned, it will be reasonable to take data going back 1–20 days and filter the data using some suggested methods (Figures 12.6 and 12.7).

Learning Parameter Selection

The backpropagation algorithm is one of the most popular choices for network training. It is also possible to use the random optimisation method for the selection of the weights instead of backpropagation. In this method, the weights are perturbed every iteration in some programmed random manner and an objective function (say minimisation of RMS error) is computed. With the new weights, if the error is reduced, the weights are considered valid weights. If the new weights do not reduce the error, the old weights are once again perturbed and the error is once again computed and checked. The search continues till the error is minimised. This process of error minimisation is more likely to find global minima than the gradient descent method associated with backpropagation, which is quite prone to finding local minima.

It is also necessary to have a sufficient number of examples to train the network — typically, for daily time series at least four or five years and for intra-day series four to six months of data points, depending upon the sample period, should be considered.

The best performer is the network with the fewest weights needed to process the training data accurately. In practice, this size is a function of the quantity and quality of the training data [Hammer93].

Many methods have been described for eliminating weights, including pruning out those that do not contribute to accuracy, omitting them between some nodes, and sharing them among certain connections. The simplest is to limit the number of nodes, since each node has many weights. The number of input and output nodes depends on the data and is fixed during training. As a result, choosing the number of weights is the same as choosing the number of hidden nodes.

Learning and Testing Data Selection

If the performance of the network is statistically significant when measured on out-of-sample data, then we can say that learning has taken place.

Test-set (out-of-sample) and training-set mean squared error both typically fall rapidly at the beginning of training as the network moves its weights away from their original random positions. In time, both curves become flatter. Typically, training-set error continues to decline, but test-set error eventually begins to increase. This increase shows that the network has stopped learning what the training patterns have in common with the test patterns and has started to learn meaningless differences. This overfitting of the training data harms the network's ability to generalise, since it is merely memorising the noise in the training data. As a result, the mean squared error measured with the training set can be a deceptive index of performance. In fact, a network with a falling training-set error may be deteriorating on test-set performance. Again, for best generalisation, training should stop when the test-set mean squared error reaches its lowest point (usually identified *ex post*). Further learning offers no benefit, and the fact that one configuration ultimately reaches a lower training-set mean squared error than another is no basis of choice between them. The real basis of choice is the error remaining at the best test-set performance. This residual error varies with configuration. The network with the least residual error is assumed to be the best one for the problem.

The number of hidden nodes influences the residual error. Ideally, there is some optimum number of hidden nodes producing the smallest residual error, with larger and smaller number of hidden nodes both producing larger errors. Real networks trained with real data do not always exhibit this behaviour cleanly. Nevertheless, monitoring error measured with a separate test set while varying the number of hidden nodes is a key strategy for optimising performance with backpropagation training.

Some of the simple network configurations that can be explored for intra-day forecasting are as follows:

- Ten to fifteen input nodes, and data input sampled at half- to one-hour intervals. First differences of the prices should be considered. The configuration may be one hidden layer with as few nodes as possible (to be decided after a number of experiments).

- Five to ten input nodes, with first difference of hourly rates as the input. The training should be performed on the next hour's first difference price.

- Simultaneously, test using out-of-sample data set is required to be carried out in accordance to the procedure mentioned above to make sure that the network has learned properly and not overfitted.

Network Update Strategy and Problems

It is necessary and important to design a network update strategy and to address other issues related to this problem. It is quite a difficult problem to arrive at a good and appropriate network update strategy. We discuss two approaches here.

In *periodic training* the network designed and selected is periodically trained using the most recent data exactly as done while selecting the network initially. This procedure can be carried out in two ways. In the first method, only incremental training may be carried out using the latest data received from the market. In the second procedure, the entire data set can be used to train the network once again to arrive at the new set of weights but following the learning procedure as suggested earlier in the previous subsection. This procedure should be carried out at least every two to three months in the case of daily data and monthly in the case of intra-day data.

It is also possible to have a moving window (sufficient number of data has to be taken in the window) of learning data set and *use the latest data set only to train the network*. This can be done periodically for intra-day data. For daily data, incremental learning seems to be a better idea.

Both the above procedures have advantages and disadvantages. Only experience and repeated experimentation can determine the network update strategy. It is obviously necessary to resolve this issue before entering the market to trade using neural networks.

TRADING STRATEGY USING NEURAL NETWORKS

After training the network on either long-term or short-term market movements, the next task is to use the network and its forecasting abilities to trade in the marketplace. In the short-term forecasting network, since it is costly to enter the market to trade many times in a day (primarily because of the transactions costs involved and the imperfect forecasting accuracy of the trained network), it is necessary to design a trading strategy which takes this into account. A reasonable trading strategy is to set up a trading value threshold. If the trained neural network suggests that in a given forecast interval, the forecasted rate will be greater than the set threshold value, a long position (buy) is initiated. Similarly, if, in the given forecast interval, the trained network suggests that the forecasted rate will be less than the set threshold value, a short position (sell) is initiated. These positions can be kept either till a stop-loss is hit or a take-profit situation is encountered. The stop-loss and take-profit levels have to be designed based on the movements of the underlying time series. Another possibility is keep the long or short position intact until the reverse takes place.

There are several other ways to design a trading strategy. Most of these will be based on the individual's own perspective on FX time-series movements and other trading variables. It may also be a good idea to integrate the trading strategy with neural learning itself. This, however, has to be done by taking several neural learning issues into account.

Trading with Several Neural Nets

If the selected network configuration is complex then every new learning sequence starting from the random weights will terminate in a different set of weights for the same FX learning data set. One possible reason is that weights terminate in local rather than global minima. This happens because of the very complex search surface. One possible way to exploit this is to use all the trained nets (having different final weights) and take a majority decision to trade. This can evolve into a more robust trading strategy both for intra-day data and also inter-day data.

LIMITATIONS OF NEURAL NETWORKS IN FOREIGN EXCHANGE TRADING

The neural network learning procedure is not a very transparent methodology and therefore it takes quite a lot of understanding, experience and plenty of experimentation to come up with a stable set of networks to trade in the marketplace. One other issue is judging the stability of the trained network and reliance on the selected network to take risks in the marketplace. This requires considerable firmness and can become difficult at times. It still remains an open question whether neural network trading methods can continuously outperform the very simple technical rules currently employed on the FX market by traders and dealers.

In spite of this, it is quite clear from the literature and the problem-solving abilities of neural networks that they have a lot to offer to model and forecast the short-, medium- and long-term behaviour of FX time series. Once proved successful, neural networks will constitute an extremely useful technique for trading in several currencies in a similar manner.

FUTURE WORK

One of the research and application areas which could potentially give good results is neural network learning on multiple currencies simultaneously and trading in one currency only, for example, learning on DEM/USD and CHF/USD and trading in CHF or DEM only. Another area is forecasting long-term FX movements using a neural network with the help of both fundamental financial data such as interest rates, money supply, inflation data and balance-of-payment figures, and time-series related data, and training the neural network to forecast long-term trends. But it is in the areas of hedging, risk management, arbitrage, mispricing, estimation of volatility, that neural learning is likely to produce much better and quicker results.

13

Nonlinear Modelling of the DEM/USD Exchange Rate

Elmar Steurer, *Daimler Benz AG, Germany*

INTRODUCTION

In recent years there has been growing interest in the search for evidence of nonlinear dynamical systems and chaotic processes in financial markets. One aspect of these models is their tendency to display very complex, apparently random behaviour, even when simple cases are analysed. In consequence it is difficult to predict the correct behaviour of a chaotic system. The purpose of this chapter is to use the BDS test to check for chaotic behaviour and apply nonparametric forecasting methods based on chaos theory to predict the short-term development of the Deutschmark/dollar (DEM/USD) exchange rate. Nonlinearities in daily exchange-rate changes should yield improvements in forecasting in comparison with the random-walk concept by using a nonparametric method. Therefore a nonparametric method, the nearest-neighbour technique, is used for this study. Empirical results for the DEM/USD exchange rate will be presented and discussed. Concerning the prediction of direction (increase/decrease), an accuracy rate up to 6% better than provided by the simple random-walk concept was achieved. As this model is superior to the random walk, the above-mentioned time series could be chaotic.

Nonlinear Dynamics and Chaos

A nonlinear, deterministic dynamical system is a time series in which, starting at some initial condition, the values of the series are fixed, nonlinear functions of the

Neural Networks in the Capital Markets. Edited by Apostolos-Paul Refenes.
© 1995 John Wiley & Sons Ltd

previous states. A deterministic (discrete-time) dynamical system produces a time series x_t, where x_0 is an initial condition, and the time evolution of the process is dictated by the relation $x_{t+1} = f(x_t)$ for some function f.

Briefly, chaos is a deterministic, nonlinear process which looks random and is characterised by the following points:

- Chaotic patterns are enormously dependent on small changes in the initial conditions or parameter specifications.
- These patterns have self-similarity. That is, they appear to be repeating. If we examine a chaotic graph or system under a microscope, simple shapes or characteristics will appear over and over again.
- It is impossible to predict the process in the long run.

Searching for nonlinear dynamics is important for the following reason. If the dynamics is nonlinear, using linear models will not lead to good prediction, because nonlinear systems can display behaviour better from that produced by the commonly used linear stochastic models. Of course, if the dynamics is chaotic, then long-term prediction is impossible even if the correct structure is known, because of the errors in observation of initial conditions or parameter specifications and because of computer rounding error; however, shorter-term prediction remains plausible. Given the potential importance of nonlinear modelling, the first step is to see if nonlinear dynamics can be detected in data.

Previous Work

The statistical properties of the returns on financial assets have been extensively studied in the finance literature. The empirical findings, in some cases, support the validity of the random-walk concept that successive price variations were uncorrelated. The most comprehensive work dealing with stock prices is the study by Fama [Fama65] on 30 Dow Jones Industrial stocks for a five-year period (1956–61); for all intervals (from daily to monthly), the serial correlation coefficients were small and generally not significantly different from zero. In further studies in the literature [Kon84, AffMcD89, Hsieh89] the consensus is that the distribution of these changes is unimodal and has fatter tails than the normal distribution.

Previous work has explored the properties of deterministic systems that exhibit apparently random dynamic behaviour, or chaos. Most relevant to the work presented here, [SchLeB89, LeBaro89] have found empirical evidence that the time path of stock-market returns is consistent with nonlinear deterministic models rather than purely stochastic behaviour. Furthermore [Hsieh89, Hsieh91] applied (G)ARCH models to the analysis of the returns of exchange rates and stock returns (x_t). In the autoregressive conditional heteroscedasticity (ARCH) process developed by [Engle82], the conditional variance h_t depends autoregressively on past residuals e_t whereas the unconditional variance remains constant. With x_t as the change of a financial time series, an ARCH process is defined by

$$e_t / f_t \sim N(0, h_t)$$

$$h_t = \alpha_0 + \sum_{i=1}^{q} \alpha_i \varepsilon_{t-i}^2$$

$$e_t = x_t - m_t$$

where m_t and h_t are the mean and the conditional variance of the process at time t. The mean may be assumed constant with regard to time: $m_t = m$. f_t is the information set at time t consisting of the lagged values e_t and of h_t. [Bollers86] extends Engle's approach to a generalized ARCH (GARCH) process in that also lagged values of the conditional variance h_t itself determine the conditional variance in the actual period:

$$e_t / f_t \sim N(0, h_t)$$

$$h_t = \alpha_0 + \sum_{i=1}^{q} \alpha_i \varepsilon_{t-i}^2 + \sum_{i=1}^{p} \beta_i h_{t-i}$$

$$e_t = x_t - m_t$$

p and q denote the order of the process. (For more details, see [Bollers86], and, for a survey, [Bollers92].) It is noticeable that x_t is not stochastically independent of x_{t-1}. Traditional tests of linear dependence (such as the autocorrelation coefficient) will not detect the nonlinear dependence. Time series generated by (G)ARCH models exhibit low autocorrelation for the changes, and high autocorrelation for the changes squared. This phenomenon has been empirically observed in many financial time series [Hsieh89, LeBaro90, KugLen90, DieNas90, Bollers92]. Furthermore, (G)ARCH models imply that large (low) movements in price are followed by large (low) movements *in either direction*. So great attention is paid in the econometric literature, especially in applications to financial data (see [Bollers92]). The results of these studies show that models with conditional heteroscedasticity are able to capture the statistic properties of the daily changes.

[KugLen90] report evidence of nonlinearity in exchange rates. They were able to rule out linearly autoregressive conditional heteroscedasticity as a possible explanation of the structure for the JPY/USD exchange rate, strengthening the possibility that a truly chaotic process was being observed.

Using the same data as Scheinkman and LeBaron, Ramsey *et al.* [ScLeRa89] come to the conclusion that there is virtually no evidence for chaos in the stock-market data. Other factors, such as non-stationarity in the time series and small-sample bias, might cause nonlinearity. After correcting for non-stationarity and bias, Ramsey *et al.* find no evidence of a chaotic attractor in stock returns. To summarise, 'it is widely agreed that a variety of high-frequency asset returns are well described as *linearly* unpredictable, conditionally heteroskedastic and unconditionally leptokurtic' [DieNas90].

Implication of Chaos for the Financial Markets

On the other hand, the implication of chaos theory for the financial markets is that price movements are not random, but follow a pattern which, although complex, is predetermined. In other words; chaos theory is an attempt to prove what chartists already suspected — that there is an order to the apparent randomness of the market. But this order is so complex that the random-walk concept is proven by the standard linear statistical tests of Fama *et al.* The assumption of linearity is only an approximation to the real world. Therefore an innovative statistical test, the BDS test of Brock, Dechert and Scheinkman [Brock87], is used to detect the presence of nonlinear structure in the DEM/USD exchange rate in the third section of this chapter.

The difficulty of forecasting the precise value of chaotic processes does not mean that chaos is useless in predicting market prices. Once a pattern is established, it can be used to make predictions about future results. Chaos theory, then, is a search for patterns. One method of search is the nearest-neighbour technique which is described and applied to the DM/Dollar exchange rate in the fourth section of this chapter. When random behaviour is caused by low dimensional chaos the short term forecast of such a method should be better than the simple random walk.

The Data Used

The data base consists of daily DEM/USD spot rates. The time period covered is from 1 January 1975 to 31 December 1991. Returns r_t were computed on a daily basis by taking the logarithmic difference between the closing values of two successive trading days. There are a total of 4260 daily observations. Figure 13.1 is a plot of the natural logarithms of these daily changes S_t/S_{t-1}.

Table 13.1 provides some summary statistics of the data. The mean is almost zero. The range of daily change, however, is relatively high, the largest being

Table 13.1 Summary statistics of log price changes, $r_t = \ln(S_t/S_{t-1})$. Sample period: 1 January 1975 to 31 December 1991. Significance levels in parentheses.

Observations	4260
Mean	−0.00011
Median	0.00000
Std. dev.	0.006562
Skewness	0.121844
Kurtosis	4.94692
Maximum	0.0657
Minimum	−0.0453
Kolmogorov D	0.064094
H_0 : Normality	(<0.01)

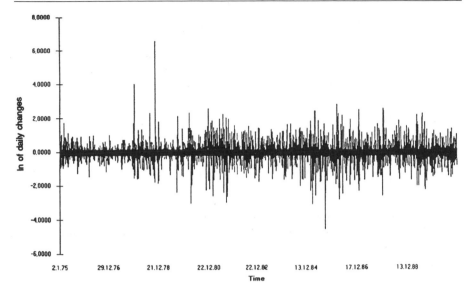

Figure 13.1 Natural logarithms of daily changes in the DEM/USD exchange rate, 1 January 1975 to 31 December 1991

6.57% on 1 November 1978, the lowest -4.53% on 23 September 1985. The data are unimodal and approximately symmetric, with a higher peak and fatter tails than the normal distribution. Non-normality is confirmed by the coefficient of kurtosis being 4.9469, which is larger than the kurtosis of 3 for a normal distribution. Furthermore the Kolmogorov D-statistic of less than 1% shows that the distribution of the DEM/USD exchange-rate changes is significantly different from the normal distribution at the 5% level. The null hypothesis of normality can be rejected.

TESTING FOR AUTOCORRELATION

Table 13.2 shows the autocorrelation of the DEM/USD exchange rate changes. As expected, there is negligible linear dependence in the data. Standard errors and the Box–Pierce Q-statistic are adjusted for heteroscedasticity according to [Hsieh88]: under the null hypothesis that the data are white noise with a constant variance, the standard error for each sample autocorrelation coefficient is $1/\sqrt{n}$. This is 0.0153 for this time series. 'Heteroscedasticity may cause the standard error of each sample autocorrelation coefficient to be underestimated by $1/\sqrt{n}$. [Diebol86] gives a heteroscedasticity-consistent estimate of the standard error for the tth sample autocorrelation coefficient:

$$S(\tau) = \sqrt{(1/n)(1 + \gamma_{x^2}(\tau)/\sigma^4)}$$

$\gamma_{x^2}(\tau)$ is the tth sample autocovariance of the squared data, and s is the sample standard deviation of the data.' These adjusted standard errors are reported in

Table 13.2   Autocorrelation coefficients.

Lag l	Auto-correlation coefficient $\rho(t)$	Significance level $\rho(t) = 0$	Hetero-scedasticity-consistent standard error	Adjusted Box–Pierce Q-statistic	Adjusted Box–Pierce Q-statistic: significance level
1	0.03893	0.0111*	0.01876	4.3043	0.0381
2	−0.00692	0.6517	0.02018	4.4218	0.1096
3	0.02904	0.0582	0.01875	6.8186	0.0779
4	−0.00037	0.9808	0.01889	6.8190	0.1458
5	0.01150	0.4534	0.01928	7.1747	0.2080
6	0.03477	0.0233*	0.01923	10.4415	0.1073
7	−0.00564	0.7130	0.01817	10.5377	0.1601
8	0.02675	0.0812	0.01886	12.5490	0.1284
9	0.01662	0.2786	0.01778	13.4220	0.1445
10	0.00784	0.6094	0.01784	13.6151	0.1913
11	0.01484	0.3334	0.01789	14.3026	0.2167
12	−0.01237	0.4202	0.01743	14.8059	0.2523
13	0.00376	0.8064	0.01752	14.8519	0.3167
14	0.04333	0.0047*	0.01755	20.9418	0.1032
15	0.00677	0.6591	0.01849	21.0758	0.1345
16	−0.0291	0.0576	0.01745	24.0500	0.0884
17	−0.00262	0.8647	0.01722	24.0731	0.1175
18	−0.00387	0.8009	0.01681	24.1261	0.1510
19	−0.00662	0.6664	0.01695	24.2785	0.1857
20	0.01963	0.2012	0.01679	25.6439	0.1857
21	0.01267	0.4094	0.01722	26.1850	0.1995
22	0.01075	0.4842	0.01681	26.5939	0.2271
23	−0.01146	0.4557	0.01696	27.0505	0.2539
24	−0.02897	0.0594	0.01623	30.2358	0.1771
25	−0.01026	0.5046	0.01703	30.5985	0.2027
26	−0.00583	0.7044	0.01676	30.7189	0.2390
27	0.00592	0.7003	0.01694	30.8410	0.2778
28	0.00886	0.5645	0.01803	31.0825	0.3135
29	0.00392	0.7985	0.01667	31.1377	0.3590
30	−0.02470	0.1082	0.01733	33.1675	0.3154

* Significantly different from zero at 5% level.

column 4 of Table 13.2. In column 3 the significance level of the null hypothesis that one autocorrelation coefficient $\rho(t)$ is zero, is shown. The significance level is computed by the ratio of the autocorrelation coefficient $\rho(t)$ and the standard error $1/\sqrt{n}$. This ratio is asymptotically distributed as standard normal. The significance level is computed by a two-tailed test.

The significance level of the ratio of the autocorrelation coefficient $\rho(t)$ and the standard error show that only few $\rho(t)$ are statistically different from zero. The null hypothesis of serial independence is rejected at the 5% significance level in only three cases: For the lags $l = 1$, $l = 6$ and $l = 14$.

Moreover, the joint test that the first K autocorrelation coefficients are zero can be conducted using the Box–Pierce Q-statistic, adjusted for heteroscedasticity [Hsieh88]:

$$\sum_{\tau=1}^{K}[\rho(\tau)/S(\tau)]^2$$

This statistic is asymptotically distributed as chi-square with K degrees of freedom. In Table 13.2 the test for the first 50 autocorrelation coefficients is presented. The adjusted Box–Pierce statistics do not indicate significant deviations from an uncorrelated process for the daily changes when calculated for lags from $l = 1$ up to $l = 30$. To summarise: the results of this section show that there is no linear dependence in the observed DEM/USD exchange rate changes time series.

EMPIRICAL APPLICATION OF THE BDS TEST

The BDS test [Brock87] has been applied to the time-series data of the DM/Dollar exchange rate to search for occurrences of systematic nonlinearity. The results of the BDS test are presented in Table 13.3. I use N-histories with $N = 2, \ldots, 8$, and a distance of e which depends on the standard deviation of the data. For example: $e = 1$ means that the distance e is equal to the standard deviation of the data. For a given N, e cannot be too small because $C_N(e)$ will capture too few points; also e cannot be too large because $C_N(e)$ will capture too many points. The test has been performed for $e = 0.5$, 1.0 and 1.5.

The data strongly reject the null hypothesis of independently and identically distributed (iid) data. There is considerable evidence of nonlinear structure, as the BDS statistics are all over 4. With increasing dimension N and larger distance e the BDS statistic increases. This means that the nonlinear structure is more evident for higher dimensions. One may note that the values of $w_N(e)$ for $e = 0.5$ and the N-histories $N = 6$, $N = 7$, and $N = 8$ are negative. The reason is that $C_N(e) = 0$. No pair from a series of N successive points is between the distance equal to half of the standard deviation of the data.

But rejection of the null hypothesis does not provide direct evidence of chaos. As [Hsieh91] pointed out, the BDS test has good power to detect four types

Table 13.3 BDS test.

N	e	$w_N(e)$	e	$w_N(e)$	e	$w_N(e)$
2	0.5	9.21	1.0	12.00	1.5	11.89
3	0.5	18.78	1.0	21.20	1.5	21.07
4	0.5	53.56	1.0	39.18	1.5	36.17
5	0.5	75.10	1.0	73.96	1.5	66.31
6	0.5	−12.95	1.0	202.22	1.5	138.04
7	0.5	−9.63	1.0	831.04	1.5	421.02
8	0.5	−7.40	1.0	2653.7	1.5	1256.7

of non-iid behaviour: linear dependence; non-stationarity; chaos; and nonlinear stochastic processes. In this case linear dependence can be ruled out, as shown in the previous section of this chapter.

Under the assumption that structural changes occur infrequently [Hsieh91] showed that non-stationarity or structural changes are not the reason for the rejection of the null hypothesis because 'by going to higher and higher frequency data in shorter and shorter time periods, we should remove the effects of structural changes'. According to him, the time horizon of daily changes is short enough to avoid these structural changes. 'This makes it unlikely that infrequental structural changes are causing the rejection of iid in weekly returns'. What is more interesting now is the presence of low-complexity chaotic behaviour in the DEM/USD exchange rate changes. Therefore in the next section I take an approach using a nonparametric method to show direct evidence of chaotic behaviour.

As substantial nonlinear dependence in the data is indicated by the BDS test, the next step is to implement a nonparametric method to construct a forecast better than the simple random walk which will give and to have an indication that the DEM/USD exchange rate is governed by low-complexity chaotic behaviour. In this study I use the nearest-neighbour technique. Other examples of nonparametric methods are kernel estimation, series estimation and neural networks [Hsieh91]. The nearest-neighbour technique used in this chapter is the simplest method. If a trivial nonparametric technique leads to forecasting results better than the naive prediction, then a good indicator of low-complexity chaotic behaviour is obtained.

USING THE NEAREST-NEIGHBOUR TECHNIQUE TO PREDICT THE DEVELOPMENT OF EXCHANGE RATES

Description of the Nearest-Neighbour Technique

If low-complexity chaotic behaviour causes the rejection of the null hypothesis of the BDS Test in the previous section, then a nonparametric method should yield better forecast results than the simple random walk. The random walk is the best prediction in an efficient market in which price movements are stochastic. The fundamental statement of the random-walk theory is that the best estimate of the future price S_{t+1} is the present price S_t. This approach is called the *naive prediction*. The introduction of the nearest-neighbour technique as a prediction method for chaotic time series is founded on the following idea. If x_t is a chaotic process, it can be written as:

$$x_{t+1} = f(x_t)$$

where $f(\ )$ is nonlinear function which can be smoothed by a nonparametric method. In the case of chaotic behaviour the probability of any two N-histories $x_t^N = (x_t, x_{t+1}, \ldots, x_{t+N-1})$ and $x_s^N = (x_s, x_{s+1}, \ldots, x_{s+N-1})$, being 'close together' is higher than the Nth power of the probability of any two points, x_t

and x_s, being together. This means that some clustering is occurring in an N-dimensional space (see above). This geometrical structure is called an *attractor*. In other words, some 'patterns' of exchange-rate movements occur more frequently compared with a truly random process.

There are many ways to implement a nonparametric method. In this study I choose the nearest-neighbour technique as a simple example. The first step of this method is to look for similar situations in the past and to select those points which have the nearest distance to the actual situation. The method used here is the first-order approximation. This means simply looking through the time series for the k nearest neighbours, and predicting that the system will exhibit a similar behaviour in the future. I approximate $x(t + 1)$ by $x(t' + 1)$, where $x(t')$ is the nearest neighbour of $x(t)$. For example, to predict tomorrow's exchange-rate the exchange rate pattern most similar to that of today is sought. The forecast is that tomorrow's exchange rate will be the same as the average of the neighbouring pattern one day later.

Therefore two parameters have to be determined. One is the dimension d of the chaotic process. If the dynamics take place on an attractor with dimension D, then the selected dimension d has to be larger than the dimension D of the attractor. The other parameter is k, the number of the nearest neighbours to be selected. [Abrams84] suggested that k should be set proportional to $n^{4/(d+4)}$.

To employ the nearest-neighbour technique we must have a distance function $\lambda(x_i, x_j)$. In this case let the distance function $\lambda(x_i, x_j)$ be the Euclidean distance between the actual d-dimensional vector x_i and a historical d-dimensional vector x_j:

$$\lambda(x_i, x_j) = \sqrt{\sum_{k=1}^{d}(x_{i-k+1} - x_{j-k+1})^2}$$

The method used here can be characterized by saying that the closeness is determined by a measure on past returns. Close sets of points will be determined using a group of k nearest neighbours, where the 'distance' between two points i, j is measured using the Euclidean norm over the d lagged values. These k nearest-neighbour vectors are used to construct a forecast of tomorrow's exchange-rate change by taking the mean of the values one day later of the k nearest-neighbour vectors. There are many modifications possible for such a forecasting rule. A few important modifications are explored here to examine their impact on forecast performance.

The first is the use of the median instead of the mean. The second is to weight the local forecasts. Each point in the neighbourhood can be weighted according to its distance from the actual vector x_t; points close to x_t have large weight, and points far from x_t have small weight:

$$w = \frac{\lambda(x_i, x_t)}{\lambda(x_m, x_t)}$$

where x_m is the farthest point in the nearest-neighbour group. This normalization leaves w between zero and one. In this chapter the method used by Diebold and Nason [DieNas90] and recommended by [Clevel79] is applied where the weight is determined by a tricubic function:

$$f(w) = (1 - w^3)^3$$

The Error Measures of Prediction Used

Observations 3801–4260 are used for out-of-sample forecast comparison with the random walk. For each point of this interval the previous 3800 observations are used for searching the k nearest neighbours. Then a prediction is constructed by taking the mean; taking the median; and evaluating the tricube function.

The forecast is used to compute the mean squared error (MSE), the Theil coefficient of inequality (T) and the accuracy rate for the case of predicting direction of change. The third measure of the quality of prediction is the accuracy rate. The accuracy rate measures the correct increase/decrease forecast. Only the tendency has an impact on this measure. In the long run the naive prediction method should have an accuracy rate of 50%.

The Results

The results of taking the different methods of prediction are presented in Tables 13.4–13.6. Table 13.4 covers the results obtained by taking the mean, Table 13.5 by taking the median and Table 13.6 by using the tricube function weighting scheme. The first column of each table specifies the dimension d, the first row specifies the number of the selected nearest neighbours k.

The diagnostic indicators are: the MSE; the T-coefficient; and the accuracy rate of increase/decrease prediction. Each table contains selected examples of possible combinations of the dimension d and the number of nearest neighbours k, which show the general behaviour of this nonparametric method in a representative way. The following features of the results are worth pointing out.

- Concerning the forecasting method by taking the mean, MSE values are obtained in the range [0.531, 0.595]. The values of the T-coefficient are between 0.734 and 0.777. The accuracy rates have obtained a level up to 54% and are better than the accuracy rate of the naive prediction (the accuracy rate of the naive prediction is 48.04% in this case). To summarise, this means that the nearest-neighbour technique outperforms naive prediction. As this nonparametric method is superior to the random-walk process, the DEM/USD exchange rate changes could be chaotic.

- The forecasting method by taking the mean (Table 13.4) and the median (Table 13.5) deliver similar results. Concerning the MSE and the T-coefficient, the use of the mean provides better outcomes. In 26 of the 30 cases considered

Table 13.4 Forecasting results by taking the mean.

Dimension	Nearest neighbours k					
d	5	10	15	20	40	60
(a) MSE						
5	0.590	0.551	0.540	0.537	0.532	0.533
7	0.588	0.576	0.549	0.550	0.532	0.531
10	0.586	0.554	0.548	0.534	0.536	0.534
14	0.573	0.562	0.546	0.544	0.539	0.538
18	0.595	0.560	0.551	0.541	0.535	0.537
(b) Theil coefficient of inequality						
5	0.774	0.748	0.741	0.738	0.735	0.735
7	0.773	0.765	0.747	0.747	0.735	0.734
10	0.771	0.750	0.746	0.737	0.738	0.736
14	0.763	0.755	0.744	0.743	0.739	0.739
18	0.777	0.754	0.748	0.741	0.737	0.738
(c) Accuracy rate of increase/decrease prediction (%)						
5	52.61	52.39	53.04	51.30	51.09	51.74
7	48.91	51.74	50.65	50.43	52.39	50.65
10	48.70	51.96	54.78	54.13	51.52	49.35
14	51.74	49.35	52.61	51.09	53.91	53.26
18	52.83	51.74	53.26	51.96	51.96	53.04

Table 13.5 Forecasting results by taking the median.

Dimension	Nearest neighbours k					
d	5	10	15	20	40	60
(a) MSE						
5	0.692	0.552	0.551	0.549	0.544	0.541
7	0.591	0.587	0.571	0.562	0.534	0.538
10	0.605	0.563	0.560	0.547	0.537	0.542
14	0.634	0.555	0.554	0.540	0.541	0.538
18	0.613	0.563	0.551	0.541	0.543	0.542
(b) Theil coefficient of inequality						
5	0.838	0.750	0.748	0.747	0.743	0.741
7	0.775	0.772	0.761	0.756	0.737	0.739
10	0.784	0.756	0.754	0.745	0.738	0.742
14	0.802	0.751	0.750	0.740	0.741	0.739
18	0.789	0.756	0.748	0.741	0.742	0.742
(c) Accuracy rate of increase/decrease prediction (%)						
5	53.48	55.43	53.26	50.00	52.83	51.30
7	50.43	48.91	51.52	50.87	53.04	53.91
10	50.65	53.26	53.7	54.70	53.91	49.35
14	52.61	52.39	52.83	52.17	50.65	51.30
18	52.83	51.96	51.09	53.26	51.09	48.91

Table 13.6   Forecasting results by taking a weighting scheme.

Dimension d	Nearest neighbours k					
	5	10	15	20	40	60
(a) MSE						
5	0.797	1.096	1.468	1.843	3.467	5.320
7	0.667	0.811	0.996	1.266	2.085	2.890
10	0.608	0.711	0.810	0.897	1.247	1.615
14	0.542	0.580	0.616	0.650	0.811	0.980
18	0.547	0.564	0.581	0.598	0.819	0.749
(b) Theil coefficient of inequality						
5	0.899	1.055	1.221	1.368	1.876	2.324
7	0.823	0.908	1.005	1.134	1.455	1.713
10	0.786	0.850	0.907	0.954	1.125	1.280
14	0.742	0.767	0.791	0.812	0.907	0.998
18	0.745	0.757	0.768	0.779	0.827	0.872
(c) Accuracy rate of increase/decrease prediction (%)						
5	53.04	56.74	54.13	54.78	53.48	53.70
7	48.04	49.57	51.09	50.00	49.35	50.22
10	51.52	51.96	50.87	49.78	50.00	50.87
14	51.52	51.52	51.52	50.00	52.61	52.39
18	54.35	56.52	54.78	54.78	52.39	53.91

the MSE by taking the mean is lower than the MSE by taking the median. On the other hand, with regard to the accuracy rate the use of the median seems to be better. The accuracy rate by taking the median was higher on 19 of the 30 occasions. The weighting scheme used does not appear to improve forecast performance here.

- Particularly noticeable are the following properties of the selected combinations of the dimension d and the number of nearest neighbours k. The criterion concerning the selection of k as described in [Abrams84] represents a useful additional criterion (see above). According to him, the optimal value of k depends on the dimension d. The general trade-off is: for higher dimensions better forecasting results are obtained with a smaller value of k.

- The nearest-neighbour technique performs best for following d–k combinations: $d = [5, 7]$ and $k = [40, 60]$.

Finally, it is worth noting that values of d greater than 20 and of k greater than 60 provide poorer results. A possible explanation is that with numbers of nearest neighbours k more than 5% of the available data possible clusters cannot be fitted and a supposed chaotic attractor cannot be matched and used for prediction.

CONCLUSION

This study shows that daily exchange-rate changes are not independent of past changes. I have used the BDS test to search for evidence of nonlinear dynamic structure in the DEM/USD exchange-rate changes. One can argue that the evidence in this work supports the findings of [Hsieh89] that there is considerable evidence of nonlinear structure in the DEM/USD exchange rate.

Furthermore, this chapter reports the results of a comparison of the performance of a nonparametric forecasting method and the naive prediction applied to data on the DEM/USD exchange rate. The results consistently indicate a low-complexity chaotic behaviour. The reason for this is that the nonparametric method used the nearest-neighbour technique, outperforms the forecasting results of the random-walk model and the naive prediction, respectively. Forecasting results are measured by the mean squared error (MSE), the Theil coefficient of inequality (T) and the accuracy rate of increase/decrease prediction. The T-coefficient has values of approximately 0.74, and accuracy rates of up to 54% were obtained. These results lead to the conclusion that the nearest-neighbour technique can considerably improve the short-term prediction of the DEM/USD exchange rate changes. Furthermore, in this work attempts have been made to improve forecasting results by variations of the nearest-neighbour forecasting method. The results suggest, however, that forecasting by taking the median of the k nearest neighbours delivers similar results and using a weighting scheme with respect to the distance obtains no improvement in comparison to the simple method by using the mean of the k nearest neighbours as a predictor of the future exchange rate.

To summarise, in economics the potential of forecasting methods using nonparametric techniques has probably been underestimated. The empirical results of this study suggest that in the case of the DEM/USD exchange rate there is low-dimensionality chaos and the use of nonlinear nonparametric techniques can produce significantly better results.

14

Managing Exchange-Rate Prediction Strategies with Neural Networks

Apostolos-Paul Refenes, and A. Zaidi,
London Business School, UK

INTRODUCTION

Commonly used techniques for exchange-rate prediction and trading include moving averages, oscillators and mean value. Each of these techniques has complementary advantages. For example, the moving-average technique performs quite well when the market is in a trend but performs rather poorly around turning points and/or oscillations. Likewise, oscillator techniques tend to perform well on oscillations but poorly on trends. Currently there is no decision rule for dynamically selecting strategies in order to avoid losses.

This chapter describes a neural network back-end system which uses the predictions of a portfolio of strategies, and also contextual information, in order to switch between trading strategies. The key idea is to predict (on the basis of past performance) which of the strategies is likely to perform best/worse in the current context, and thus minimise losses.

The network is trained on daily currency exchange data from 1984 to 1986, and is tested out-of-sample on from 1986 to February 1992. Its annual returns outperform the best classical techniques by an average of 6 percentage points on a $1 million position (including transactions costs).

Neural Networks in the Capital Markets. Edited by Apostolos-Paul Refenes.
© 1995 John Wiley & Sons Ltd

In the next section of the chapter we give a brief overview of the techniques which are commonly used for currency exchange-rate prediction. Then, we describe the experimental set-up and network architecture. Finally, we discuss the results.

COMPUTER TRADING STRATEGIES

Several computer trading strategies have been developed over time, and are routinely used in the capital markets. Among them moving averages and mean-value based strategies are well known [Brown63, Menden89].

The *moving-averages strategy* is quite simple. Given a time series on k points $(v_1, \dots, v_k)$, the system computes two moving averages for the $(k + 1)$th point. The long moving average (LMA) is given by:

$$\text{LMA}_{k+1} = \frac{1}{n} \sum_{i=1}^{n} v_i \qquad (14.1)$$

Likewise, the short moving average (SMA) is given by:

$$\text{SMA}_{k+1} = \frac{1}{m} \sum_{i=1}^{m} v_i \qquad (14.2)$$

with $m < n < k$. Depending on the relative lengths of the two moving averages (n and m), the LMA gives a much smoother curve than the SMA. The decision rule for taking a position in the market is straightforward, and is based on the characteristics of the lines drawn from v_k to $v_{\text{LMA}_{k+1}}$, and v_k to $v_{\text{SMA}_{k+1}}$.

Positions are taken if the two lines intersect (see Figure 14.1). If the LMA line is intersected from below the system takes a *long* position (buys the asset at the current price). Conversely, if the LMA line is intersected from above the system takes a *short* position (sells at the current price).

The moving averages technique performs quite well when the market is in a state of trend but performs rather poorly around turning points and/or oscillations, because it receives delayed signals of the abrupt changes.

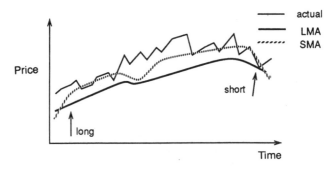

Figure 14.1   Trading with simple moving averages

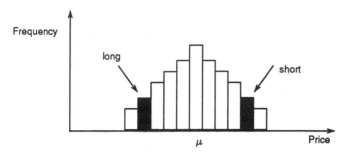

Figure 14.2   Trading with simple mean value (market profiling)

The *mean-value strategy*, however, has some significant differences. The idea is to build a profile of the market along two axes — the horizontal axis plotting prices, and the vertical axis plotting frequency of transactions at the corresponding price (see Figure 14.2).

The key idea is that the commodity trades around a mean value, with occasional (standard) deviations. If the hypothesis is true, the distribution of the time series over a fixed time period will be normal. The decision rule for taking a position in the market is straightforward. If the price of the commodity takes a value higher than the mean value (μ) the system takes a *short* position, and if the commodity takes a lower value than μ the system takes a long position.

The mean-value strategy performs quite well when the market is in an oscillatory state. When the market enters a trend, the histogram is rather flat and the strategy breaks down. Similarly, it is not possible to construct a normal distribution near turning points.

It is clear from the above that the two techniques have complementary advantages. Although both strategies perform badly around turning points, it is possible to avoid some of the losses by alternating strategies as the market changes from a trendy to an oscillatory behaviour and vice versa.

In this chapter we describe a neural network system which uses the predictions of these techniques, along with contextual information, in order to make use of the (perceived) best strategy. The key idea is to predict (on the basis of past performance) which of the strategies is likely to perform best/worse in the current context, and thus minimise losses.

EXPERIMENTAL SET-UP

System Architecture

The neural system described uses the following indicators as inputs. The first and second input are the recommendations (prediction) of the two techniques at time t (see Figure 14.3). Each of these can be 0 or 1, denoting a *short* or *long* position, respectively. The two indicators may be in agreement or they may give conflicting

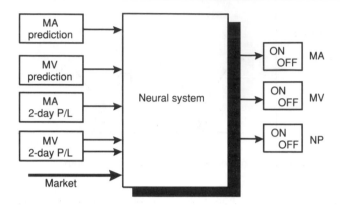

Figure 14.3 System architecture

signals. The third and fourth indicators are related to the performance (profit or loss) of the two strategies over the past two days. Each indicator gives two inputs. The final indicator is directly related to the market — the rate of change over the past n days; this is implemented as n separate inputs to the network (for the results reported here $n = 3$).

The output of the system gives three options for trading at time $t + 1$. Namely:

- MA: use the recommendation of the moving-averages strategy;
- MV: use the recommendation of the mean-value strategy; and
- NP: take no position.

These are implemented as three different signals (outputs). Each signal can take values in the range $[0, \ldots, 1]$ which is interpreted as the relative level of confidence. If both MA and MV are ON (greater than 0.5 plus a small user-controlled bias δ) the largest of two signals is chosen. If the NP signal is ON all others are ignored.

Training and Test Sets

The network is trained on daily data from 1984 to 1986. We used several architecture configurations and learning algorithms including standard error backpropagation networks [WeHuRu92] and the constructive learning procedure [RefCha92]. With both procedures, the best results were obtained with networks of two layers of hidden units. Networks with no hidden units could not converge to sufficiently low RMS levels. Networks with a single layer of hidden units produced solutions similar to two-layer networks but the consistency of the results varied significantly with the values of the control parameters (choice of learning rates, initial conditions and topology). The results with the error backpropagation network (9-12-6-3) are given in the following section.

RESULTS

Figure 14.4 shows the cumulative profits on a daily basis from 1986 to 1992 for the moving-averages and mean-value strategies, respectively. On an annual basis the returns are an average of 12.3% and 13.1% for the simple moving averages and mean value, respectively.

Figure 14.5 shows the cumulative profits for the backpropagation network; clearly the network outperforms both strategies. Its total cumulative return is $1.45 million compared to $0.98 million and $1.19 million for the moving-averages and mean-value strategies, respectively. On an annual basis the network gives an average return of 18% on a $1 million position, compared to 12.3% and 13.1% for the moving-averages and mean-value strategies, respectively.

The network is a multi-layer perceptron (9-12-6-3). It was trained on daily data from 1984 to 1986 for 2000 epochs. The standard deviation from this performance (with training times varying between 1000 and 5000 epochs) is 0.24.

The decision rule is to select the strongest signal from the three network outputs, as explained in the previous section. Alternative options (bias towards either strategy if the signal strength differs within small $\delta = 0.1$) were also examined, and although they give similar results on average, the profile of the rolling returns is substantially different.

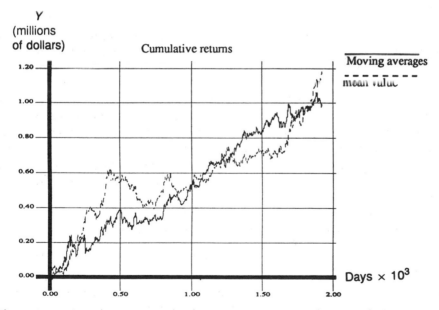

Figure 14.4   Cumulative returns for the moving-averages and mean-value strategies

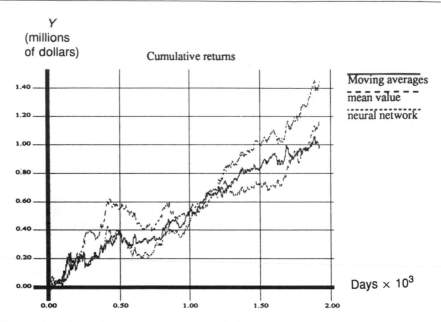

Figure 14.5 Cumulative returns for the neural network

DISCUSSION

One of the major disadvantages of neural systems, at this stage of development, is the inability to explain their reasoning. This is very important for safety-critical or risk-aversive systems. To obtain an explicit understanding of the system's behaviour we analysed the attractor points in the network dynamics. Weight sensitivity analysis was used similar to [GorSej88]. This provided the basis for an explicit formulation of the 'rules' that the network has learned about the market, and the trading strategies. The idea here is to see if these explicit rules make sense and, if so, to replace the network with the analytical model.

To simplify the problem we ignored the market contextual input to the network (that is, the rate of change over the past n days). The resulting model was quite simple.

At any time t we are using either the moving-average (MA state) or the mean-value (MV state) indicators. The decision rule is as follows:

- *In the MA state*: If you lost at $t - 1$ and the indicators at t (for $t + 1$) agree, then switch to the mean-value strategy;

- *In the MV state*: If you lost at $t - 1$ and $t - 2$ and the indicators at t (for $t + 1$) disagree, then switch to the moving-averages strategy.

To evaluate this heuristic rule discovered by the network, we computed the P/Ls for the moving-average, mean value and the heuristic from 1984 to 1992. The heuristic rule gives a 3 percentage points gain on the mean-value strategy and a 3.2 percentage points gain on the moving-averages indicator.

CONCLUSION

We presented a hybrid system for managing trading strategies in the foreign exchange markets. The results obtained for the USD/DEM exchange rate are superior to those of classical techniques such as moving averages and mean value. We believe that the system is applicable both to managing a larger number of trading strategies, and also to other currencies and markets.

15

Financial Market Applications of Learning from Hints

Yaser S. Abu-Mostafa,
Caltech and Neuro Dollars Inc., USA

INTRODUCTION

When a neural network learns its target function from examples (training data) it knows nothing about the function except what it sees in the data. In financial market applications, it is typical to have a limited amount of relevant training data, with high noise levels in the data. The information content of such data is modest, and while the learning process can try to make the most of what it has, it cannot create new information on its own. This poses a fundamental limitation on the learning approach not only for neural networks but also for all other models. It is not uncommon to see simple rules such as the moving average outperforming an elaborate learning-from-examples system.

Learning from hints [AbuMos90, AbuMos93] is a technique that enhances learning from examples by boosting the information content in the data. The method allows us to use prior knowledge about the target function, from common sense or expertise, along with the training data in the *same* learning process. Different types of hint that may be available in a given application can be used simultaneously. In this chapter, we give experimental evidence of the impact of hints on learning performance, and explain the method in some detail to enable readers to try their own hints in different markets.

Neural Networks in the Capital Markets. Edited by Apostolos-Paul Refenes.
© 1995 John Wiley & Sons Ltd

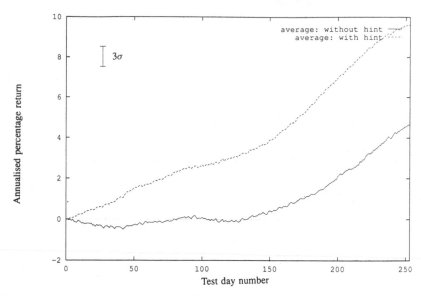

Figure 15.1   Learning performance with and without hint

Even simple hints can result in significant improvement in the learning performance. Figure 15.1 shows the learning performance for foreign exchange (FX) trading with and without the symmetry hint (see below). The plots are the annualised percentage returns (cumulative daily, unleveraged, transaction cost included), for a sliding one-year test window in the period from April 1988 to November 1990, averaged over the four major FX markets with more than 150 runs per currency. Only the closing price history is used for training.

The error bar in the upper left-hand corner is three standard deviations long (based on 253 trading days, assuming independence between different runs). The plots establish a statistically significant differential in performance due to the use of hints. This differential holds for all four currencies, as we will see. Since the goal of hints is to add information to the training data, the differential in performance is likely to be less dramatic if we start out with more informative training data. Similarly, an additional hint may not have a pronounced effect if we have already used a few hints in the same application. There is a saturation in performance in any market that reflects how well the future can be forecast from the past. (Believers in the efficient market hypothesis consider this saturation to be at zero performance.) Hints will not make us forecast a market better than whatever that saturation level may be. They will, however, enable us to approach that level *through learning*.

This chapter is organised as follows. The next section characterises the notion of very noisy data by defining the '50% performance range'. We argue that the need for extra information in financial market applications is more pronounced than in other pattern recognition applications. Then we begin the discussion of our method for learning from hints. We give examples of different types of hint, and explain how to represent hints to the learning process. The fourth section of the chapter gives more experimental results on the use of the symmetry hint in the four major FX markets. The fifth discusses different algorithms for scheduling hints in the learning process. The sixth then provides experimental evidence that it is indeed the information content of the hint, rather than the incidental regularisation effect, that results in the performance differential that we observe.

FINANCIAL DATA

This section provides a characterisation of very noisy data that applies to the financial markets. It sets the stage for the need to use hints, but it is not a prerequisite for the next section.

Consider the market as a system that takes in a lot of information (fundamentals, news events, rumours, who bought what when, etc.) and produces an output (an up/down price movement, for the sake of simplicity). A model, such as a neural network, attempts to simulate the market (Figure 15.2), but it takes an input x

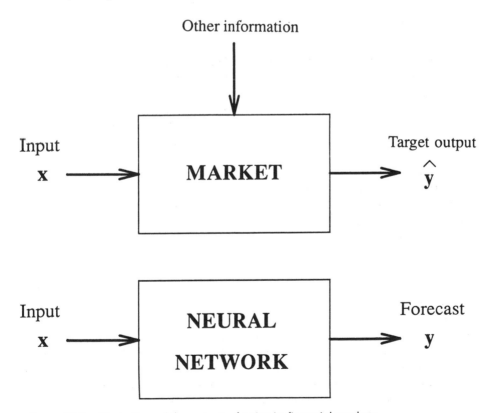

Figure 15.2 Illustration of the nature of noise in financial markets

which is only a small subset of the information. The 'other information' cannot be modelled and plays the role of noise as far as x is concerned. The network cannot determine the target output $\hat{y}$ based on x alone, so it approximates it with its output y. It is typical that this approximation will be correct only slightly more than half the time.

This is what makes us consider x 'very noisy'; y and $\hat{y}$ agree only $\frac{1}{2} + \varepsilon$ of the time (50% performance range). In a typical pattern-recognition problem, such as optical character recognition, y and $\hat{y}$ would agree $1 - \varepsilon$ of the time (100% performance range). It is not the poor performance *per se* that poses a problem in the 50% range, but rather the additional difficulty of learning in this range. Here is why.

During learning, we use a limited set of N examples to train (and validate) a neural network to forecast the market. In the 50% performance range, we want y to agree with $\hat{y}$ on $(\frac{1}{2} + \varepsilon)N$ examples. The number of functions on N points that do that is huge. Too many random functions look like good candidates based on the limited set of examples. This is in contrast to the performance range where the functions need to agree with $\hat{y}$ on $(\frac{1}{2} + \varepsilon)N$ examples. The number of functions that do that is limited. Therefore, one can have much more confidence in a function that was learned in the 100% range than in one learned in the 50% range.

It is not uncommon to see a random trading policy making good money for a few months, but it is very unlikely that a random character-recognition system will read a paragraph correctly. Of course, this problem would diminish if we used a very large set of examples, because the law of large numbers would make it less and less likely that y and $\hat{y}$ can agree $(\frac{1}{2} + \varepsilon)$ of the time just by 'coincidence'. However, financial data have the other problem of non-stationarity. Because of the continuous evolution in the markets, old data may represent patterns of behaviour that no longer hold. Thus, the relevant data for training purposes are limited to fairly recent times. Put together, noise and non-stationarity mean that the training data will not contain enough information for the network to learn the function. More information is needed, and hints can be the means of providing it.

HINTS

In this section, we give examples of different types of hint and discuss how to represent them to the learning process. We describe a simple way to use hints that allows the reader to try the method with minimal effort. Later, we will describe more sophisticated ways to schedule different hints for learning, which may become necessary if several hints of different types are involved. As far as our method is concerned, a hint is any property that the target function is known to have. For instance, consider the symmetry hint in FX markets as it applies to the USD/DEM rate (Figure 15.3). This simple hint asserts that if a pattern in the price history implies a certain move in the market, then this implication holds whether you are looking at the market from the US dollar viewpoint or the Deutschmark viewpoint.

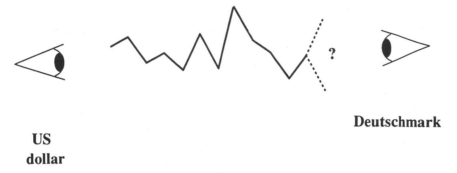

Deutschmark

US dollar

Figure 15.3   Illustration of the symmetry hint in FX markets

Formally, in terms of normalised prices, the hint translates to the target function being invariant under inversion of these prices.

Is the symmetry hint valid? The ultimate test for this is how the learning performance is affected by the introduction of the hint. The formulation of hints is an art. We use our experience, common sense, and analysis of the market to come up with a list of what we believe to be valid properties of the market. We then represent these hints in a canonical form, as we will see shortly, and proceed to incorporate them into the learning process. The improvement in performance will only be as good as the hints we put in. Later we will discuss the adaptive minimisation algorithm that allows us to schedule the hints taking into consideration how much confidence we have in them. The canonical representation of hints is a more systematic task. The first step in representing a hint is to choose a way of generating 'examples' of the hint. For illustration, suppose that the hint asserts that the target function $\hat{y}$ is an odd function of the input. An example of this hint would have the form $\hat{y}(-x) = -\hat{y}(x)$ for a particular input x. One can generate as many examples as needed by picking different inputs.

After a hint is represented by examples, it is ready to be incorporated into the learning process along with the examples of the target function itself. Notice that an example of the function is learned by minimising an error measure, say $(y(x) - \hat{y}(x))^2$, as a way of ultimately enforcing the condition $y(x) = \hat{y}(x)$. In the same way, an example of the oddness hint can be learned by minimising $(y(x) + \hat{y}(-x))^2$ as a way of ultimately enforcing the condition $y(-x) = -\hat{y}(x)$. This involves inputting both x and $-x$ to the network and minimising the difference between the two outputs. It is easy to show that this can be done using backpropagation [RuHiWi86] twice.

The generation of an example of the hint does not require knowing the value of the target function; neither $\hat{y}(x)$ nor $\hat{y}(-x)$ enters the equation for the oddness hint. In fact, x and $-x$ can be artificial inputs. The fact that we do not need the value of the target function is crucial, since it was the limited resource of examples for which we know the value of the target function that led to our interest in hints in the first place. On the other hand, for some hints, we can take the examples of the target function that we have, and employ the hint to duplicate these examples. For instance, an example, $\hat{y}(x) = 1$, can be used to infer a second example, $\hat{y}(-x)$, using the oddness hint. Representing the hint by duplicating the examples of the function is an easy way to try simple hints using the same software that we use for learning from examples.

Let us illustrate how to represent two common types of hint. Perhaps the most common type is *the invariance hint*. This hint asserts that $\hat{y}(x) = \hat{y}(x')$ for certain pairs x, x'. For instance, '$\hat{y}$ is shift-invariant' is formalised by the pairs x, x' that are shifted versions of each other. To represent the invariance hint, an invariant pair (x, x') is picked as an example. The error associated with this example is $(y(x) - \hat{y}(x))^2$. Another related type of hint is the *monotonicity hint*. The hint asserts, for certain pairs x, x', that $\hat{y}(x) \leqslant \hat{y}(x')$.

FOREIGN EXCHANGE TRADING

We applied the symmetry hint in the four FX markets of the US dollar versus sterling, the Deutschmark, the Japanese yen, and the Swiss franc. In each case, only the closing prices for the preceding 21 days were used for inputs. The objective (fitness) function we chose was the total return on the training set, and we used simple filtering methods on the inputs and outputs of the network. In each run, the training set consisted of 500 days, and the test was done on the following 253 days. Figures 15.4–15.7 show the results of these tests averaged over all the runs. The returns are annualised, unleveraged, and include the transaction cost.

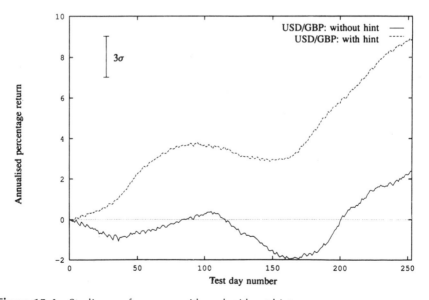

Figure 15.4 Sterling performance with and without hint

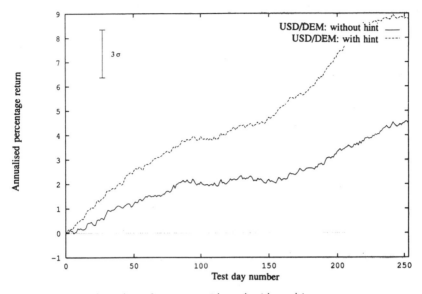

Figure 15.5   Deutschmark performance with and without hint

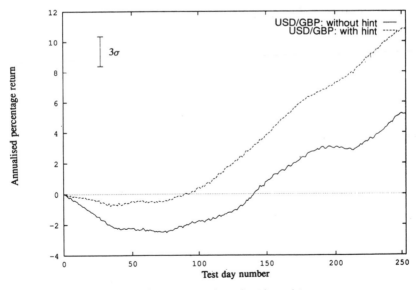

Figure 15.6   Japanese yen performance with and without hint

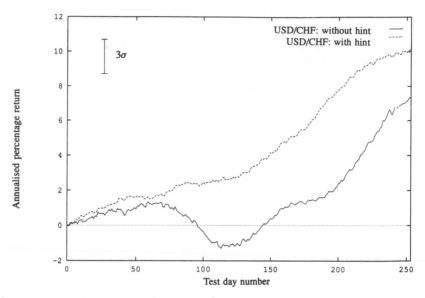

Figure 15.7   Swiss franc performance with and without hint

Table 15.1   Statistics of trades: without hint.

	APR	Hit rate (%)	Position in market (% of time)	Number of trades	Trade length
Average	4.6	50.1	45.8	29	4.0
USD/GBP	2.4	49.8	51.5	27	4.8
USD/DEM	4.5	49.1	47.6	34	3.6
USD/JPY	5.2	50.8	48.9	27	4.7
USD/CHF	7.3	50.8	35.1	28	3.1

Table 15.2   Statistics of trades: with hint.

	APR	Hit rate (%)	Position in market (% of time)	Number of trades	Trade length
Average	9.6	51.5	53.2	32	4.1
USD/GBP	8.9	51.8	59.1	31	4.7
USD/DEM	8.7	49.4	54.1	36	3.8
USD/JPY	10.9	52.8	53.4	29	4.6
USD/CHF	10.1	51.9	46.2	32	3.6

All four currencies show an improved performance when the symmetry hint is used. Tables 15.1 and 15.2 show the average statistics of the trades for the cases without hint and with hint, respectively, for each currency and for the average of the four currencies. Listed in these tables are the annualised percentage return, the percentage daily hit rate, the percentage of time there is a position in the market, the number of trades per year, and the average length of a trade in (trading) days. Roughly speaking, we are in the market half the time, each trade takes four days, the hit rate is close to 50%, and the APR without hint is 5% and with hint is 10%. Notice that having the return as the objective function resulted in a fairly good return with a modest hit rate.

LEARNING SCHEDULES

In this section, we discuss how to schedule different hints in the learning process. Scheduling becomes an important issue if several hints of different types are involved in one application. We assume that an error measure on the training data E_0 and error measures on the different hints $E_0, E_1, \ldots, E_M$ have been defined (the dual case of 'objective functions' instead of error measures, with maximisation instead of minimisation, can be dealt with in a similar way).

The most a learning algorithm can do given the training data and the hints is to achieve zero error on $E_0, E_1, \ldots, E_M$ simultaneously. It is seldom the case that this all-zero error can be reached because either it does not exist (that is, no configuration of the network weights can satisfy all the hints and the training data simultaneously), or it is difficult to reach (the computing resources do not allow us exhaustively to search the space of weights looking for the perfect configuration). In either case, we will have to settle for a point where the E_m are 'as small as possible'.

How small should each E_m be? It is the job of the learning schedule to strike a balance among the $\dot{E}_m$, otherwise some E_m may become very small at the expense of the others. This would mean that some hints are overlearned while the others are underlearned. Different criteria for balancing the errors result in different schedules. A schedule is tantamount to a method for simultaneous minimisation of a number of interdependent quantities [WisCha78].

The implementation of a given schedule goes as follows:

1. The algorithm decides which hint to work on next according to some criterion.

2. The algorithm requests a batch of examples of this hint.

3. It performs its descent on this batch.

4. When it is done, it goes back to step 1.

The descent method can be simple backpropagation, but another descent method, or even another learning model, can be used with the same schedule.

The simplest class of schedules is *fixed* schedules, where each hint has a predetermined turn in the descent. Figure 15.8 shows a fixed schedule for a problem that uses two hints in addition to the training data. The schedule puts twice as much emphasis on the training data as it does on either hint.

Another class of schedules is *adaptive* schedules, where the turns of different hints are decided based on what happens as the algorithm runs. For instance,

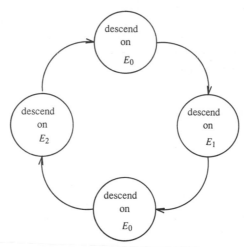

Figure 15.8 A fixed schedule

the schedule may choose the hint which happens to have the largest value of the error E_m at the current iteration. Adaptive schedules attempt to answer the question: given a set of values for the E_m, which hint is the most underlearned? As we deal with more and more hints, this question becomes more subtle. The *adaptive minimization* schedule determines which hint is the most underlearned by relating the individual errors E_m on the hints to estimates of the actual test error E.

Given $E_0, E_1, \ldots, E_m$, adaptive minimization makes $m + 1$ estimates of E, each based on all but one of the hints:

$$\hat{E}(\bullet, E_1, E_2, \ldots, E_M)$$

$$\hat{E}(E_0, \bullet, E_2, \ldots, E_M)$$

$$\hat{E}(E_0, E_1, \bullet, \ldots, E_M)$$

$$\cdots$$

$$\hat{E}(E_0, E_1, E_2, \ldots, \bullet)$$

and chooses the hint for which the corresponding estimate is the *smallest*, to descend on. The idea is that, if ignoring E_m resulted in the most optimistic expectation of the test error, then E_m must be too large.

The form of the estimator function $\hat{E}(\bullet)$ depends on the types of hint [CatMos94], and can be tailored to different applications. For instance, it is possible to underemphasise a hint in the learning process (to reflect a lack of confidence in its validity, for instance) by picking an estimator that has a threshold for the corresponding E_m below which it treats E_m as zero.

CROSS-CHECKS

In this final section, we report more experimental results aimed at validating our claim that the information content of the hint is the reason behind the improved performance. Why is this debatable? A hint plays an incidental role as a constraint on the neural network during learning, since it restricts the solutions the network may settle in. Because overfitting is a common problem in learning from examples, any restriction may improve the generalisation performance by reducing overfitting [Akaike69]. This is the idea behind regularisation.

To isolate the informative role from the regularising role of the symmetry hint, we ran two experiments. In the first experiment, we used an uninformative hint, or 'noise' hint, which provides a random target output for the same inputs used in the examples of the symmetry hint. Figure 15.9 contrasts the performance of the noise hint with that of the real symmetry hint, averaged over the four currencies. Notice that the performance with the noise hint is close to that without any hint (Figure 15.1), which is consistent with the notion of an uninformative hint. The regularisation effect seems to be negligible.

In the second experiment, we used a harmful hint, or 'false' hint, in place of the symmetry hint. The hint takes the same examples used in the symmetry hint and asserts anti-symmetry instead. Figure 15.10 contrasts the performance of the false hint with that of the real symmetry hint. As we see, the false hint had a detrimental effect on the performance. This is consistent with the hypothesis that the symmetry hint is valid, since its negation results in worse performance than no hint at all.

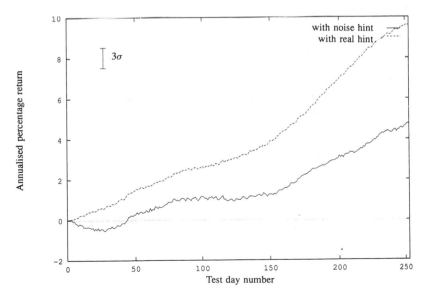

Figure 15.9   Performance of the real hint versus a noise hint

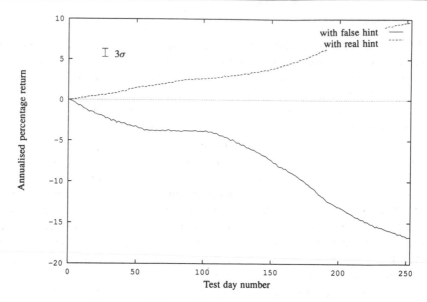

Figure 15.10 Performance of the real hint versus a false hint

Notice that the transaction cost is taken into consideration in all of these plots, which works as a negative bias and amplifies the losses of bad trading policies.

CONCLUSION

We have explained learning from hints, a systematic method for combining rules and data in the same learning process, and reported experimental results of a statistically significant improvement in performance in the four major FX markets that resulted from using a simple symmetry hint. We have described different types of hint and simple as well as sophisticated ways of using them in learning, to enable readers to try their own hints in different markets.

ACKNOWLEDGEMENT

I would like to acknowledge Dr Amir Atiya for his valuable input. I am grateful to Dr Ayman Abu-Mostafa for his expert remarks.

16

Machine Learning for Foreign Exchange Trading

Marc E. Levitt, *Sunny Vale, California, USA*

INTRODUCTION

This chapter focuses on applying machine learning techniques to foreign exchange (FX) trading. The first part of this chapter reviews selected background material on machine learning techniques while also introducing a new technique. This technique is a synergistic combination of known techniques called genetic-based local learning (GBLL). The methodology for applying GBLL to the FX market is outlined. Input data, data preprocessing and the cost functions used for the genetic-based optimisation are discussed. Results are then presented for both the futures market and the interbank cross-rate market. Finally, some comments are made on the methodology, results, and the general issue of applying machine learning to the FX market.

MACHINE LEARNING TECHNIQUES

Many techniques are available in the machine learning field. One of the best known and most often used is neural networks — the primary focus of this book. While a few brief comments are made about neural networks, they are not a major focus of this chapter. Two other less emphasised techniques are described — nearest-neighbour and genetic algorithms. Then a combination of numerous techniques called genetic-based local learning is presented.

Neural Networks in the Capital Markets. Edited by Apostolos-Paul Refenes.
© 1995 John Wiley & Sons Ltd

Neural Networks

While neural networks can be applied successfully to financial markets, it should be noted that in general, and especially with fixed-topology networks trained with backpropagation, they are global nonlinear predictor functions. This global approach has a great advantage for some applications and can be a step forward with respect to linear models. The globalness of the neural network solution can also serve as a hindrance. In particular, if there is sufficient noise in the data a neural network may not converge or may never generalise. This can be a problem when using neural networks for financial applications. The way to overcome this problem is by proper data selection, data preprocessing, and determining a suitable target value for the network to learn. This can be a very time-intensive task for a developer, and if one is not careful very poor results are possible [OSulli93]. While the above is in no way a serious criticism of neural networks or their application to financial markets one should keep these facts in mind when considering their use.

Nearest Neighbour

Nearest-neighbour (NN) techniques have been around since at least the 1950s and are widely used in pattern-classification applications [Dasara91]. The general principal of NN techniques is first to have a data base of examples with known outcomes — the training set. When a new example is presented to the system for which we want to determine the output the 'distance' from the new example to each member in the example data base (over known inputs) is calculated. Then the nearest (1-NN) or K-nearest neighbours' (K-NN) outcomes are used as the predicted class or output for the new vector. Pseudocode for the 1-NN classifier is given in Figure 16.1.

As with any long-existing technique, numerous improvements and variations have been incorporated over the years. One change that has been made is the application of least-squares regression to the K-nearest neighbours. This has been presented in many forms over the years [Clevel79, FarSid87]. The basic technique is to determine the K nearest neighbours, where K must be greater than the input dimension, as previously described, but then use these data points to build a model via multivariate regression of the output on the inputs. This regression model is then used to predict the output for the new example. This technique has been

```
for all examples in the data base {
      calculate the Euclidean distance between the new input and the example
}
sort the data base in ascending order by distance
new output = the output stored in the first example in the data base
```

Figure 16.1   Pseudocode for 1-NN predictor

shown to be quite successful and fast, since there is no learning necessary, for a wide variety of problems. Another modification of the standard K-NN technique is to use a different distance measure than the standard Euclidean norm [StaWal86]. A modification in this spirit is to weight the contributions of each input when calculating the distance between the examples. For example, the magnitude of the correlation coefficient between each input and the output in the training set can be used to weight each input when computing the distance measure for a new example. To clarify these points a more detailed financial example is now presented. Suppose one is given as a data base the returns from a daily series of prices, $r_t = \ln(p_t/p_{t-1})$. An input data set can be the return for the last five days and the value that is to be predicted is the next day's return. The training set will look as follows:

$$(r_{t-4}, r_{t-3}, r_{t-2}, r_{t-1}, r_t) \rightarrow r_{t+1}$$

Next we would calculate the correlation between each of the inputs and the output (r_{t+1}) over the training set and store the five values. When a new example is presented to the system we will calculate the distance between its values for the previous five days' returns and all the values stored in the training set, weighing the contribution of each previous day's return by its stored correlation coefficient. The K-NN are then chosen for estimating the next day's return. Experiments run by the author have shown that weighted distance schemes can improve the accuracy for both the standard K-NN and the local linear version of K-NN for numerous data series.

Genetic Algorithms

Genetic or evolutionary strategies, commonly referred to as evolutionary algorithms (EAs), are a very powerful search and optimisation procedure based on the principle of natural selection and evolution that has operated on living species for millions of years. While there are many different types of EA, among them genetic algorithms, genetic programming, and classifiers, they all share a common framework. The main components of the framework are as follows:

- a population of solutions;
- a fitness function to rank each solution in the population;
- the ability to combine various members of the population into a new solution (cross-over).
- the ability to change a current solution member to a new member (mutation).

The various ways these components are implemented and the strategies for them differ for each EA. Pseudocode for a generic genetic algorithm is presented in Figure 16.2.

```
generate initial population
while not done {
    evaluate all members of the population for fitness
    rank each member
    new population = null
    while new population not full {
        select two members for mating
        combine the two individuals to form a new solution
        mutate the solution
        add the member to the new population }
}
```

Figure 16.2   Pseudocode for a simple genetic algorithm

For more details on what are the variations for performing the mutation, cross-over, selection, population replacement, etc., for each EA strategy one should consult detailed references on the subject [Goldbe89, Hollan92].

One application of genetic algorithms that is of particular interest in the trading environment is their ability to create trading rules automatically. A genetic algorithm can be used to generate and evolve rules such as: if$((r_{t-2} > 0)$ and $(r_t > 0))$ then buy the market, that is, $r_{t+1} > 0$. This ability to evolve rules to partition the data or grow a rule tree will be of particular interest for the next section.

Genetic Based Local Learning

While the above three methods are very powerful in their own right, combining them yields a more powerful technique, referred to as *genetic based local learning* (GBLL). GBLL combines genetic algorithms with local predictor functions to yield a two-phase solution to a problem. The genetic algorithm decides on an input state space (selects inputs to use and determines how they are transformed); develops a partition scheme for the data (builds a rule/decision tree); and determines the local predictor for each leaf of the rule tree.

When it comes to the learning technique, the most important of the tasks are the first two. Given a file with various inputs, step one might determine that the ADX technical indicator today and yesterday and the percentage change in the market for the last five days are a candidate representation for building the model. Step two might determine that the data should be partitioned into groups based on yesterday's ADX level. Once this is done, step three determines a predictor for each partition of the data set. These predictor functions can be as simple as the outcome with the highest probability in a leaf of the tree or as complex as a neural network to pick up any nonlinear effects in a partition.

For example, take the input space of the ADX indicator and a moving-average cross-over (MAC) system trading signal. A tree shown in Figure 16.3 can be built

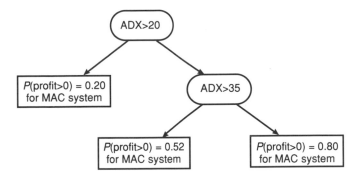

Figure 16.3 Decision tree for input data

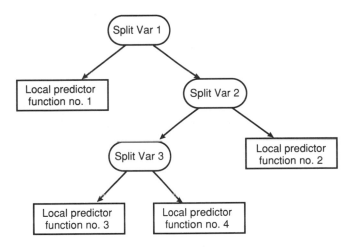

Figure 16.4 General genetic-based local learning solution structure. The genetic algorithm determines the splits for the tree and determines the best local predictor function for each leaf. The genetic algorithm uses a global cost measure to evaluate the tree

to describe the data. What this tree represents is that when ADX < 20 the moving-average strategies are not profitable. When ADX > 20 (and, more specifically, when ADX > 35) then the moving-average strategy is very profitable. Now that we have such a tree a trading strategy needs to be designed for it. Two possibilities are: (a) when ADX < 20 be neutral; and (b) when ADX > 20 take the MAC system's signal.

Of course, there are numerous other strategies like only trading when ADX > 35. What the GBLL algorithm does is to determine the best local predictor for each leaf node based on a global cost function. Figure 16.4 shows the basic structure of a GBLL solution. There are a few things to know about the GBLL methodology.

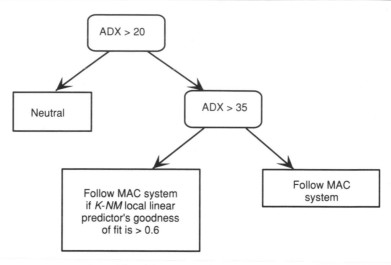

Figure 16.5   Genetic-based local learning solution for the trading system problem

First, the local predictors for each leaf in the tree do not have to be the same. Second, the tree is produced via a genetic algorithm, although more traditional techniques could be used. Third, predictions can be thresholded and weighted. And finally a global, but potentially nonlinear cost function, is used for determining the goodness of a solution. Taking the example, we could get the solution shown in Figure 16.5. The tree is explained as follows:

- If ADX < 20 go neutral.
- If ADX > 35 follow the MAC system's signal
- If 20 < ADX < 35 then fit a K-NN local linear model to the data in the leaf, and if this model's goodness of fit is greater than 0.6 then use the prediction as a trading signal, otherwise go neutral.

The model shown in Figure 16.5 has two types of local predictor: the largest class is used unconditionally (ADX < 20 and ADX > 35 leaves); and local linear regression with a threshold (20 < ADX < 35 leaf)

One may be wondering at this time, if there was data to do a K-NN local linear fit, why not just build the tree deeper in this branch? This can be done, but it should be noted that the data used for splitting in the tree and building the local linear model may be different, that is to say, variables in the input space may be exempt from the distance calculation for the K-NN or as a decision variable in the tree. This allows the tree to concentrate on more global macro features of the data while the local predictor can build a detailed model of the micro-linear or nonlinear interactions. A final difference between GBLL and most other techniques is the ability to use a global nonlinear cost function. This allows the system to ignore predictions that are not economically justified as specified by the user. This can be seen in the example for the K-NN model leaf. In many standard techniques one would most likely trade the MAC system, since P (profit > 0) $= 0.52$ for the leaf or if the tree were treated as a class probability tree one might be neutral. Instead GBLL says that under certain circumstances our cost function has a positive expectation for the cell so trade the cell under the correct conditions.

With such a powerful technique, the reader may be wondering whether we are just going to learn the training set. This is an important issue in any trading system design, since if we do not generalise from the training data our system will not be profitable when used on new data. To circumvent the overfitting problem three steps are taken:

- We do not allow the solutions to grow to too many parameters.

- Cross-validation techniques are used in the model-building.

- Data-replication techniques such as bootstrapping [Efron79] are used to check the significance of the models when they are run out-of-sample.

To facilitate comparison to other published learning/prediction techniques, GBLL was run on the Makey–Glass delay differential equation, commonly used in the dynamical systems literature to compare prediction techniques [Casdag89]. It should be noted that success with the Makey–Glass time series does not guarantee the success of a technique on the financial markets (to the chagrin of many hopeful physicists). These data are only presented for comparison purposes. The four techniques that GBLL has been compared with are:

- global polynomial fitting;

- K-NN local linear with a Euclidean distance measure;

- radial basis functions [Casdag89];

- neural networks trained with backpropagation.

The error measure is $\log_{10}$ (NRMS), where NRMS is the normalized root mean squared error. The results are presented in Table 16.1, from which it can clearly be seen that GBLL is comparable to or better than the other techniques.

Table 16.1 Results of various learning/prediction techniques on the Makey–Glass delay differential equation. The figure of merit is $\log_{10}$ (NRMS).

	Polynomial	Local linear	Radial basis functions	Neural nets	GBLL
MG17	−1.95	−1.48	−1.97	−2.0	−2.15
MG30	−1.40	−1.26	−1.60	−1.5	−1.70

METHODOLOGY

Now that the basic machine learning technique has been described, our attention will focus on its application to the FX markets.

Input Data

Input data constitute one of the most important parts in building a system. While the GBLL technique searches through the input variables for significant ones and will not be thrown off by noise variables, one must at least have some variables that are of significance. The following five categories have been found to be useful by either the tree-generation phase or the local predictors.

- Price data. These can be the first difference in closing prices, the percent return, raw values, etc., of a time series we wish to trade or some related intermarket data. For example, the change in the DEM/USD rate could be used when building a model for trading the CHF/USD rate.
- Volume and open interest. For futures data this information can be very useful. Many technicians hold the belief that price moves on heavy volume are much more meaningful than when volume is light.
- Technical indicators. In general these are transformations of price, volume or a combination of both. Some examples include moving averages, ADX, DM+, DM−, %D, %K, volatility, etc.
- Technical trading system signals. Many of the above indicators have been used in conjunction with price to develop trading systems which indicate when to be long, short or neutral. An example is a simple moving-average system which will go long when the price is above the moving average and go short when the price is below the moving average. This signal, long, short or neutral (for some trading systems), can be one of the inputs.
- Time-series diagnostics. This category of inputs is usually based on the price series but may be based on other indicators. These inputs can be simple pass/fail tests or the level of significance for a test. Some tests that can be used are: correlation/autocorrelation; checks for stationarity; checks for independence; checks for randomness; and checks for runs in the data

For example, a market can have two modes of operation, trending and random walk. These modes may be determinable by computing the time-series diagnostics over some past window. When we are trending up or down we would expect the number of runs to be statistically less than for a random series.

Data Transforms

Depending on how and when the input data are used, some transformations may be necessary. In general the following data transformations are used:

- Categorical data are changed to an integer representation or a one-off binary encoding.
- Real values are most commonly standardised (autoscaled), though linear scaling and other transforms can be used.
- Operators (such as look-back, average, rate of change or absolute value) are applied to the data.

These transforms allow the algorithm to create a higher-dimensional input data set from lower dimensional data without the user having to create a new data set every time.

Cost Functions

An important part of a GBLL system is the cost function that is optimised when searching or learning. It is widely known that techniques that minimise the RMS or NRMS error are not necessarily profitable as trading strategies. Sometimes just getting the direction correct can lead to a better system from a trader's point of view, even though RMS may not be minimal. Due to the above observations, numerous cost functions can be used in GBLL. These functions can be nonlinear and encompass a user's preferences. Some types of cost function that have been used in GBLL include:

- RMS or NRMS error;
- percentage of the predictions that have the correct market direction;
- total profit;
- ratio of the profit to a perfect trading strategy's profit;
- combinations of percentage correct, profit and a minimal number of trades;
- profit given a maximal accepted drawdown;
- matching swing filters on the time series;
- whether the technical analysis strategy was profitable for a given time-span;
- Sharpe ratio.

Some of the above cost functions can be used with stops in the evaluation procedure. An example function's pseudocode is given in Figure 16.6. As one can see, we want the system to trade on at least 10% of the days, be greater than 50% correct, and profitable before we consider it a candidate trading system. Setting such minimal values is useful for two reasons

- keeping diversity in the population during genetic optimization;
- a system whose profit is greater than 0.0 but which very rarely trades is undesirable since its statistical significance cannot be verified.

```
if (% of the time in market < 10%) then
    return(0.0)
else if ((% correct > 50%) and (profit > 0.0)) then
    return(profit)
else
    return(0.0)
```

Figure 16.6   Pseudocode for the cost function

This helps keep the balance between overtrading and the ability of the system to determine entry and exit points.

RESULTS

This section presents the results for both the FX futures and interbank cross-rates trading using a GBLL-based system. Interbank rates with the dollar as the base are not presented since their results were similar to the futures trading for the data examined.

The raw inputs used for each model consisted of: daily return for the currency we wish to trade; the MAC system's trading signal; the ADX indicator; the number of runs significance test; the daily return for the other currencies we are not currently trading; interest rate differentials.

Each system was developed with four years of data and traded out-of-sample for three years. For each series we compute five criteria for the trading system which are sightly different for the futures and interbank results:

- The return for the trading strategy. For the futures market this is the average yearly profit in dollars per contract. In the interbank market we assume a $125 000 nominal amount.
- The maximum drawdown for the trading system. In the futures market this is reported as a percentage of an assumed margin amount, which is equal to three times the exchange's minimum. For the interbank market a leverage factor of ten to one was assumed when computing drawdown.
- A T-test to determine if the returns are greater than zero.
- A T-test to determine if the returns at the predetermined leverage will be greater than 20% per year. For the futures market the leverage is based on three times the exchange's minimum margin and for the interbank market the leverage factor is ten to one.
- The number of 10 000-bootstrap-simulations whose return is greater than the GBLL trading system.

The results for the futures contracts are presented in Table 16.2. All T-test results are significant at the 10% level or better. The bootstrap simulations follow in the

Table 16.2 Results for the GBLL-based trading system for the futures contracts. For the T-statistics the number in parentheses is the significance level for the test.

	Yen	Sterling	Deutschmark
$-return/year	$5,000.0	$5,980.00	$5,112.00
Drawdown	17%	11.0%	28.0%
T-test for	2.8	2.3	2.4
return > 0	(0.5%)	(2.5%)	(1.0%)
T-test for	2.0	1.6	1.65
return $> 20\%$	(2.5%)	(10.0%)	(5.0%)
Bootstrap	65	325	116

Table 16.3 Results for the GBLL trading strategy for the spot interbank cross-rates. For the T-test the number in parentheses is the significance level for the test.

	Yen/sterling	DM/sterling	DM/Yen
Return/year	5.0%	6.2%	2.5%
Drawdown	25.6%	26.0%	16.5%
T-test for	1.75	3.0	1.77
return > 0	(5.0%)	(0.5%)	(5.0%)
T-test for	0.65	1.4	-1.4
return $> 20\%$		(10.0%)	(10%)
Bootstrap	299	10	621

same order as the T-tests and the actual out-of-sample return ranks near the top for the 10 000 simulations. The interbank spot cross-rate results are in Table 16.3. These results show that the GBLL-based systems do have statistically significant positive returns. The only drawback is that the statistical significance of a greater than 20% return per year for the defined leverage is not as high for the yen based cross-rates as one would like.

SUMMARY

This chapter has presented a new machine learning technique, GBLL, which is a synergistic combination of genetic algorithms and local prediction techniques that are evaluated based on a global nonlinear cost function. When GBLL was applied to the FX trading problem, it was shown to produce statistically significant returns greater than zero over a long period of time for all the markets examined. These results are very encouraging, demonstrating the bright future machine learning techniques have in the FX trader's toolbox.

17

A Neural Network Procedure for Selecting Predictive Indicators in Currency Trading

W. Hsu, L. S. Hsu and M. F. Tenorio,
Purdue University, USA

INTRODUCTION

One of the major problems in forecasting currency returns is the selection of technical indicators. Over the years researchers have proposed many such indicators, including moving averages, oscillators and mean value. However, many are believed to carry redundant information, while the usefulness of others is unclear.

Nevertheless, many successful attempts have been reported [KimAsa90, WeHuRu91, Refene93]. Weigend and Refenes reported successes with the foreign currency exchange-rate prediction problem using two variants of the backpropagation algorithm. Their methods take as input the full set of training patterns obtained from the time series by a technique known as *windowing* [Refene93]. A problem with using these unprocessed training data is that noise can result in slow training and degraded prediction performance. This chapter focuses the attention of neural network researchers on the need for a systematic preprocessing methodology on the universe of indicators for the purpose of improving predictability. The approach taken here is to select only subsets of indicators from the universe of available indicators. Two algorithms for selection are described. The first algorithm, the *penalty feature selection algorithm*, evaluates each indicator in the universe independently, assigning a value of penalty to each indicator and removing indicators with large

Neural Networks in the Capital Markets. Edited by Apostolos-Paul Refenes.
© 1995 John Wiley & Sons Ltd

penalty. The set of indicators obtained using the first algorithm is called the *penalty feature set*, denoted by **p**. The second algorithm, the *feature elimination algorithm*, evaluates a set of indicators as a whole and only removes an indicator from the set if removing it improves the criterion. The set of indicators obtained using the second algorithm is called the *eliminated feature set*, denoted by **e**.

The indicator selection problem has practical importance because in many financial applications, the universe of indicators is large typically, with over 200 potentially useful indicators. Using all the indicators typically results in unnecessary complexity, long training time and degraded performance.

RELATED WORK

Several neural network researchers have looked at this problem of improving prediction by removing undesirable features or vectors. For example, Wong [Wong92] used a genetic algorithm to search the space of subsets of the universe of indicators. The fitness criterion used for evaluation is the actual prediction error made. This is an expensive operation since, to evaluate each subset of indicators, training has to be done from scratch.

A different approach to this problem is to remove some training samples (as opposed to features) from the training set. The candidate training samples to be removed belong to the 'malicious' category [TuvRef93].

Another approach is to extract features by making linear combinations of the features in the full feature set. We propose a decision boundary method for doing this. Our method favours features that discriminate between the classes of interest rather than the fidelity of representation as principal component analysis does. This technique works well if none of the indicators in our universe confuse the predictor.

Several related techniques exist in the pattern recognition field [MozSmo90, DudHar73, Fukush88] dealing with feature subset selection. All of the existing methods handle the case when the features in the full feature set are all useful to the classification task. The motivation there is to select features until any further increase in prediction is not justified by the added complexity of having an extra feature. However, in our application the problem is quite different. We are typically given a large set of features constituting the full feature set where not all of the features help and some features may confuse the predictor.

Another related technique is the well known analysis of variance (ANOVA). This technique computes the sum of squares between classes SS(between) and the sum of squares within each class SS(within). This technique is described for situations where each class is characterised by only a single quantity or feature. The ratio of SS(between) to SS(within) can be used as an alternative criterion for both of the proposed feature selection algorithms. Our approach in this chapter uses the number of mismatches as our criterion. The advantage is that our criterion can handle cases when each class is characterised by more than one feature, as is typical in many prediction tasks.

The organisation of this chapter is as follows. In the next section the universe of indicators is explained. Following that, the indicator selection algorithms based on SupNet are described. Then the Deutschmark–dollar exchange-rate prediction problem is formulated and we demonstrate an improvement in prediction performance using the subsets of indicators obtained with both of our algorithms.

THE UNIVERSE OF INDICATORS

Many different indicators have been proposed for financial prediction applications over the years [Brown63]. We include in this section the definitions of several commonly used indicators for economic predictions.

The *k-day trend* at day t is the running mean of the returns of the k last days:

$$d_{k,t} = \frac{1}{k} \sum_{t-k+1}^{t} r_t = p_t - p_{t-k+1} \tag{17.1}$$

Similarly, the *k-day volatility* is the running standard deviation of the returns of the k last days:

$$v_k = \sqrt{\frac{1}{k-1} \sum_{t-k+1}^{t} (r_t - d_{k,t})^2} \tag{17.2}$$

The k-day tangent slope indicator is computed from a time series by fitting a straight line $y = mx + c$ to the current day t from day $t - k$. The tangent slope indicator is the value of m obtained. The ratio of two k-day tangent slope indicators with different k captures the turning characteristics of the time series.

Some financial experts believe that the foreign currency market can be predicted from itself. Thus, a substantial portion of our universe of indicators is devoted to delayed samples of the foreign currency markets. These are typically obtained using the technique of windowing.

The universe of indicators used in our experiments contains inputs for several past weeks of daily Deutschmark returns, the Monday values of five major currencies and the returns of the five major currencies. Both the volatilities and trends are computed for various window sizes between one week ($k = 5$) and three months ($k = 65$). The prices themselves are also input in case they, too, play a role in the dynamics of the returns. Trends for the other currencies are also input. Three tangent slope k-day indicators for $k = 2, 5, 10$ on the Deutschmark price are also input. In typical financial applications, the number of features given for a prediction task may be even larger because we simply do not know which features may help the system and would include rather than risk throwing away a potentially useful feature. In the next section, we briefly describe the SupNet architecture that we will use to describe the two indicator selection algorithms.

THE INDICATOR SELECTION ALGORITHM BASED ON SUPNET

The Supervised Clustering Network

The input of the network is the universe of indicators denoted by **f**. The supervised clustering network SupNet is a neural network that classifies a given set of n delayed vectors $\mathbf{z}^p$ into N clusters, according to their corresponding values of y_p. Its architecture is shown in Figure 17.1.

The network consists of two layers. The bottom layer is the input layer. It consists of L nodes, each representing a feature. The last node represents the desired prediction y. We assume in this chapter that y is a scalar.

The top layer is the cluster layer. Its size is determined dynamically by the learning algorithm described in the next subsection. With this architecture, each cluster node conceptually represents input vectors with similar values of y.

The weights connecting a given cluster node c to the input nodes are the components of the weight vector $\mathbf{W}^c$. The values of these weight vectors are determined by the learning algorithm which will be described in the next subsection.

The Learning Algorithm

The learning is done in two stages. During the first stage, each input vector **f** is masked to appear to be a zero vector and only the value of its corresponding y is presented. We follow the algorithm used in ClusNet [Whu92] to determine the $(L + 1)$th component of the weight vectors for all the clusters. The first L components of $\mathbf{W}$ remain at zero. After this stage, the input vectors are grouped into clusters with respect to the desired prediction y.

During the second stage, the input vectors are presented a second time. Let us assume that when the pth input vector $[\mathbf{f}^p, y^p]$ is presented, the cth cluster node has the lowest activation among existing cluster nodes. The activation of node c

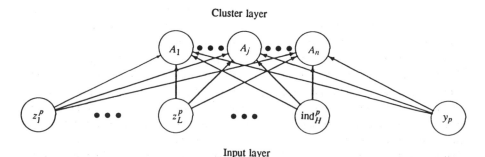

Figure 17.1 The SupNet architecture

with respect to this input is

$$A_c = \left(y^p - W_{L+1}^c\right)^2 \qquad (17.3)$$

where W_{L+1}^c is the $(L + 1)$th component of the weight vector. We say that the cth node is the *winning node* and the first L components of its weight vector are updated to:

$$W_i^c = \frac{1}{n_c}\{(n_c - 1)(W_i^c + z_i^p)\}, \quad 1 \leqslant i \leqslant L \qquad (17.4)$$

where n_c is the number of input vectors belonging to cluster c including the input vector $[\mathbf{f}^p, y^p]$. This procedure is repeated for all the input vectors. At the end of this stage, the weight vectors $\mathbf{W}$ of the network are known. Each cluster is represented by its weight which is the mean of all input vectors that belongs to it.

Using the described algorithm above, each input vector $\mathbf{f}^p$ is clustered with respect to its corresponding values of y_p. Consider two of these vectors, $\mathbf{f}^i$ and $\mathbf{f}^j$, belonging to a single cluster. The distance between them may be large even though they are in the same cluster, because the clustering was done with respect to y. The basis of the two proposed feature subset selection algorithms is to eliminate features that have different values within a single cluster. The motivation is that the resulting feature subsets will enable better prediction. For our experiments, we use a criterion called *MisMatch* to evaluate a particular set of indicators.

The Feature Selection Methodology

First, we describe how the proposed feature subset selection algorithms can be used in a specific prediction task.

1. Choose a set of *full feature vectors* $\mathbf{f}$. A portion of these is used as the training set, the rest are used as a prediction set.
2. Choose a small positive number ε. Using ε, the full feature vectors in the training set are separated into three categories:
    (a) category A consists of vectors whose corresponding $y > \varepsilon$;
    (b) category B consists of vectors whose corresponding $y < -\varepsilon$;
    (c) category C consists of all other vectors.
    The motivation for this particular set-up will become clear in the application section.
3. Using SupNet, the sets of training vectors in categories A and B are separately clustered according to the y-value. The corresponding weight vectors for each cluster are also calculated.
4. After training, if a training vector that belongs to category A is predicted to be in categories B or C, or a vector that belongs to category B is predicted to be in categories A or C, then we say that a mismatch has occurred.

5. The penalty feature selection and elimination algorithms which will be described in the next subsections are applied to **f** to obtain feature subsets **p** and **e**, respectively.

6. **p** or **e** is then used as input to a prediction algorithm.

The Penalty Feature Subset Selection Algorithm

The penalty feature subset selection algorithm starts with the universe of indicators **f** containing L components/features. Each feature is associated with a penalty which is computed as the number of mispredictions due to the single feature. Features with penalty greater than a user-specified threshold are removed from **f**. The resulting subset of the universe of indicators is called the penalty feature vector **p**.

Single Cluster per Category

In the case when there is only one cluster in a category, the penalty is calculated as follows:

Step 1:   Initialize penalty $[1, \ldots, k]$ to zero

Step 2:   Cluster the L components of the full feature
          vectors **f** into N clusters and compute the weight vectors
          $\mathbf{W}^c$ for $c = 1, \ldots, N$

Step 3:   Select component $k = 1$
          Select cluster $c = 1$
          Select vector $i = 1$

Step 4:   If vector $i \in c$ but $d \neq c$
          /* vector i is misclassified to cluster d */, i.e.
          $(\mathbf{f}_L^{c,i} - \mathbf{W}_L^c)^2 > (\mathbf{f}_L^{c,i} - \mathbf{W}_L^d)^2$ then
          add 1 to penalty $[k]$
          end

Step 5:   Repeat Step 4 for $i = 1 : N_c$

Step 6:   Repeat Step 4 for $c = 1 : N$

Step 7:   Repeat Step 4 for $k = 1$ to L

Multiple Clusters per Category

In the case when there are multiple clusters in a category, the penalty is calculated as follows:

Step 1:   Initialize penalty $[1, \ldots, k]$ to zero

Step 2:   Cluster the L components of the full feature vectors **f**
          into N clusters and compute the weight vectors $\mathbf{W}^c$ for $c = 1, \ldots, N$

Step 3:   Select component $k = 1$

Select cluster $c = 1$
Select vector $i = 1$

Step 4: If vector $i \in c$ but d and c belong to different category
/* vector i is misclassified to different category */, i.e.
$(\mathbf{f}_L^{c,i} - \mathbf{W}_L^c)^2 > (\mathbf{f}_L^{c,i} - \mathbf{W}_L^d)^2$ then
add 1 to penalty $[k]$
end

Step 5: Repeat Step 4 for vectors i belonging to cluster c

Step 6: Repeat Step 4 for clusters c

Step 7: Repeat Step 4 for features k

The Feature Elimination Algorithm

The feature elimination algorithm starts with the universe of indicators $\mathbf{f}$ containing L features. The number of mismatches (*MisMatch*) due to $\mathbf{f}$ is computed and stored. Subsequently, $L - 1$ feature subsets each containing $L - 1$ features are computed from $\mathbf{f}$ by removing one different feature at a time from $\mathbf{f}$. These feature subsets are then evaluated to obtain the number of mismatches due to each one of them. The subset resulting in the minimum number of mismatches as well as the number of mismatches are recorded. The process is then repeated until feature subsets containing only one feature are generated. When the process is terminated, the resulting feature subset, called the reduced set of indicators and denoted by $\mathbf{r}$, is the recorded feature subset with the minimum number of mismatches among all the recorded feature subsets.

The algorithm is explained in greater detail in the following pseudo code.

Function FindMisMatch(f)

Step 1: If $\mathbf{f}$ is of unit length, the base case of the recursion
is reached. Return.

Step 2: Evaluate the number of mismatches due to $\mathbf{f}$ as follows
CurrentMisMatch = ComputeMisMatch($\mathbf{f}$).

Step 3: Generate length($\mathbf{f}$) $- 1$ subfeatures denoted by $\mathbf{f}'_i$
where $\mathbf{f}'_i$ is obtained from $\mathbf{f}$ by removing feature i.

Step 4: Compute MisMatch$[i]$ = ComputeMisMatch($\mathbf{f}'_i$) for
$i = 1 : length(\mathbf{f}) - 1$.

Step 5: Let the index of the minimum of MisMatch$[i]$ be i_{min}.
Record the tuple (i_{min}, MisMatch$[i]$) in LIST.

Step 6: Call FindMisMatch with $\mathbf{f}'_{i_{min}}$.

Step 7: Let the index of the minimum of the MisMatch in LIST be LIST$_{min}$.

The eliminated feature vector **e** can be reconstructed from the associated i_{min} in LIST.

The algorithm returns the eliminated feature vector **e** found by the feature elimination algorithm. The algorithm is independent of the number of clusters. However, it makes use of the function **ComputeMisMatch(f)** which does depend on the latter.

Single Cluster per Category

In the case when there is only one cluster in a category, the function **ComputeMisMatch(f)** is as follows:

Function MisMatch(f)

Step 1: Initialize MisMatch = 0

Step 2: Cluster the L components of **f**
into N clusters and compute the weight vectors $\mathbf{W}^c$ for
$c = 1, \ldots, N$

Step 2: Select cluster $c = 1$
Select vector $i = 1$

Step 3: If $i \in c$ but $d \neq c$
/* vector i is misclassified to cluster d */, i.e.
$(\mathbf{f}_L^{c,i} - \mathbf{W}_L^c)^2 > (\mathbf{f}_L^{c,i} - \mathbf{W}_L^d)^2$ then
add 1 to MisMatch
end

Step 4: Repeat Step 4 for all vectors $i \in$ cluster c

Step 5: Repeat Step 4 for all clusters c

Step 6: Return MisMatch

Multiple Clusters per Category

In the case when there are multiple clusters in a category, the function **ComputeMisMatch** is changed to read:

Function ComputeMisMatch(f)

Step 1: Initialize MisMatch = 0

Step 2: Cluster the L components of **f**
into N clusters and compute the weight vectors $\mathbf{W}^c$ for
$c = 1, \ldots, N$

Step 2: Select cluster $c = 1$
Select vector $i = 1$

Step 3:   If $i \in c$ but $d \neq c$
          /* vector i is misclassified to a different category */, i.e.
          (1) c and d belong to a different category and
          (2) $(\mathbf{f}_L^{c,i} - \mathbf{W}_L^c)^2 > (\mathbf{f}_L^{c,i} - \mathbf{W}_L^d)^2$ then
          add 1 to MisMatch
          end

Step 4:   Repeat Step 4 for all vectors $i \in$ cluster c

Step 5:   Repeat Step 4 for all clusters c

Step 6:   Return MisMatch

THE USD/DEM TUESDAY RETURNS PREDICTION TASK

The primary purpose of this example is to demonstrate improved prediction using one of the feature subsets compared to that obtained with the universe of indicators. Our experimental set-up follows closely that used by Weigend *et al.* [WeHuRu91].

The foreign currency exchange data are taken from the *Monetary Yearbook* of the Chicago Mercantile Exchange. They are daily closing bids for five currencies (Deutschmark, Japanese yen, Swiss franc, pound sterling and the Canadian dollar) with respect to the US dollar. The DEM/USD rate is shown in Figure 17.2 for the period from September 1973 to May 1987.

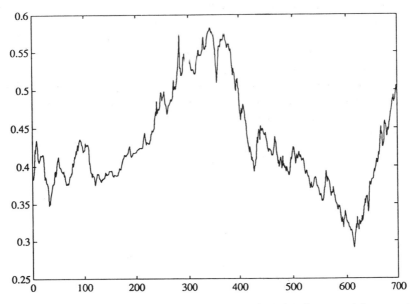

Figure 17.2 The DEM/USD exchange rate on Tuesdays for the period from 14 June 1977 to 20 May 1987

Instead of predicting the actual value of the DEM/USD time series itself, our forecasting experiment predicts a quantity of particular interest to a currency trader called the next-day returns, denoted by r_{t+1}. In order to make profitable moves in the foreign currency markets, the trader must predict the sign of the next-day return which we define as

$$r_{t+1} = p_{t+1} - \text{ave}(p_{t-k}, \ldots, p_t) \tag{17.5}$$

where k represents a number of days which are averaged. This quantity r_{t+1} represents the movement of the price p_{t+1} in relation to the average of the past k days, i.e.,

$$\text{sign}(r_{t+1}) = \begin{cases} 1 & \text{if } r_{t+1} > \varepsilon \\ -1 & \text{if } r_{t+1} < -\varepsilon \\ 0 & \text{otherwise} \end{cases} \tag{17.6}$$

We preserve the 'day of the week' effect by predicting only the returns on Tuesdays in order to avoid averaging the dynamics of different days of the week. The data set is split into two sets: the training set, of size 500, runs from September 1973 to April 1983; and the test set, size 212, from April 1983 to May 1987.

We group the next-day returns into the categories shown in Table 17.1. Category C patterns are those occasions when the price hardly moves from one day to the next. There is not much to be gained or lost by trading on such days. Category A patterns represent days in which the price is going up significantly. This class of days is of interest to the trader because there is profit to be made. Category B patterns represent days when there is significant downward movement of the market price. This class of days is equally important because traders with this information can short positions in the market. The decision between category A and category C patterns is based on the value of the parameter ε.

Some of these features represent completely different quantities measured using unrelated scales. To prevent one feature from overwhelming the contributions of other features, we normalize feature j by the quantity n_j, computed as

$$n_j = \sum_c \sum_i \left(\mathbf{X}_j^{c,i} - \mathbf{W}_j^c \right)^2$$

where c represents clusters and i represents the vectors belonging to cluster c.

Table 17.1 Classification of the time-series patterns into three categories.

Category	$\text{sign}(r_{t+1})$	Remarks
A	1	Uptrend
B	−1	Downtrend
C	0	—

The SupNet Prediction Procedure

The prediction procedure is described as follows:

1. The feature subset is presented to SupNet and we compute D_A and D_B as the activation of the winner node in category A and category B, respectively.
2. If $\|D_A - D_B\| \leqslant \varepsilon_m$, we predict X as belonging to category C.
3. If $D_A > D_B$, we output a prediction of category B.
4. Otherwise, if $D_B > D_A$, we output a prediction of category A.

The parameter ε_m is related to the choice of ε. For all our experiments, we compute ε_m as follows:

$$\varepsilon_m = \frac{1}{N_C} \sum_C \sum_{i=1}^{N_C} \left(X^{i,c} - W^c \right)^2 \delta \left(X^{c,i}, C \right) \qquad (17.7)$$

where

$$\delta \left(X^{c,i}, C \right) = \begin{cases} 1 & \text{if } X^{c,i} \in \text{ category C} \\ 0 & \text{otherwise} \end{cases}$$

and N_C is the number of $X^{c,i} \in$ category C. If the value of ε_m is too large, patterns belonging to category A and B will be drawn into category C. If the value is too small, then patterns in Category C will be predicted as belonging to category A or B. In our experiments, a procedure is used to seek a suitable value for ε_m dynamically.

Single Cluster Per Category

For a specific ε, the patterns in the data are broken down into categories as shown in Table 17.2.

From Table 17.3, using all the features in the universe of indicators, chance prediction is recorded. Using the penalty feature subset **p**, and the eliminated feature subset **e**, improved prediction is observed.

In this experiment, the best prediction percentage for each category is 83.3, 52.4, 94.5, for A, B and C, respectively. Another measure of error that is appropriate for these data is the *critical misprediction error count* defined as the number of vectors

Table 17.2 Grouping the returns data into categories.

Category	Training set	Testing set
A	134	78
B	136	61
C	230	73

Table 17.3   Prediction performance for the single cluster per category approach.

Feature set	Length	Category A	Category B	Category C
The universe of indicators **f**	71	47	28	35
The penalty feature vector **p**	32	50	27	48
The eliminated feature vector **e**	11	65	32	69

associated with uptrends but predicted to be associated with downtrends and vice versa. In this experiment, the critical misprediction error count is 7 for **f**, 2 for **p** and 0 for **e**.

Multiple Cluster per Category

In this method, we allocate multiple clusters per category. The results are as shown in Table 17.4. There, we observe that the best prediction percentage for each category is 82.1, 67.2 and 84.9, for A, B and C, respectively. In this experiment, the critical misprediction error count is 10 for **f**, 9 for **p** and 0 for **e**.

The eliminated feature vector **e** obtained in the multiple cluster experiments contains the following indicators that are important for this predicting task:

- the two- and five-point tangent slopes;
- the past one-week returns of the Deutschmark;
- the trends for 5, 10 and 65 days on the Deutschmark;
- 65-day trend on the swiss franc;
- the 20- and 40-day volatility;
- the Monday returns on sterling;
- the Monday returns on the Japanese yen.

Upon closer analysis, we notice that indicators associated with the Canadian dollar are often being eliminated by both of our subset selection algorithms. This finding is consistent with the observations of other researchers [LeBaro90, WeHuRu91]. This could be due to the strong coupling between the Canadian and US economies.

In this chapter, we described and demonstrated the use of the indicator selection and elimination algorithm for prediction. Several factors favour our prediction methodology.

Table 17.4   Prediction performance for the multiple clusters per category approach.

Feature set	Length	Category A	Category B	Category C
The universe of indicators **f**	71	37	13	46
The penalty feature vector **p**	32	52	34	33
The eliminated feature vector **e**	14	64	41	62

- Our assumption that patterns associated with small values of y for this particular prediction task appear to help remove some undesirable examples from the training set.

- The proposed penalty feature subset selection and elimination algorithm is effective in removing redundant or confusing indicators for improved prediction ability.

- The built-in parameter ε_m allows us to fine-tune the trade-off of the accuracy of the predictions in the various categories as required by different prediction tasks.

CONCLUSIONS AND FURTHER WORK

Current neural network approaches to financial applications typically use variants of the backpropagation algorithms. In practice, these methods have several difficulties, including long training time due often to the large size of the training set and because the stopping condition is not known for each application. Perhaps the main obstacle to the use of neural network techniques in actual financial applications is its 'black-box' nature which makes it difficult to understand why a certain decision or prediction is made. Our proposed network, called ClusNet, represents an alternative training method for financial applications.

   In this chapter, we use the SupNet architecture to learn to predict the sign of the returns of the USD/DEM exchange rate. In our experiments, both subsets of indicators obtained with our algorithms result in more accurate prediction performance on the exchange-rate prediction task than the unprocessed universe of indicators. The feature elimination algorithm requires more execution time but its resulting feature subset enables more accurate prediction performance. Further research is ongoing to develop and compare other indicator subset algorithms. An important contribution of this work is to focus the attention of neural network researchers on the need for a systematic feature preprocessing methodology for the purpose of improving predictability.

PART FOUR
BOND APPLICATIONS

18

Criteria for Performance in Gilt Futures Pricing

Jason Kingdon, *University College London, UK*

INTRODUCTION

Since the early 1990s considerable research interest has focused on the use of neural networks (NNs) in financial forecasting. In particular, the prospect has been raised that such techniques present a significant and real challenge to the efficient market hypothesis (EMH) [Falma70, Shille87]. To date, much of this work has concentrated on the design of NNs, the training algorithm used, the comparison between NNs and linear techniques, or establishing the equivalence or superiority of NN forecasting performance to traditional time-series forecasting techniques [GroWur91, Foster91, HiCoRe92, KimAsa90, ReFrZa93, Schoen90, White89]. This has mostly been applied to either benchmark chaotic time series or financial indicators. However, little has been reported in the way of detailed experimental results, in which precise consideration is given to the experimental procedure.

In this chapter the emphasis is shifted to the actual experimentation and the analysis of the results. We present a detailed description of an extended series of experiments, in which an NN is used to forecast trends in a gilt futures price series. Some of the pitfalls and dangers that exist in using NNs, particularly with regard to the inherent complexity of an NN solution, are examined. It is demonstrated how some of the seemingly less important parameters (such as data preprocessing and the number of training cycles) have profound effects on the solution obtained, and that as a consequence careful safeguards within the experimental procedure must be ensured to avoid biases in the results obtained. This is emphasised not just for the more usual negative instances, when a network's performance can

Neural Networks in the Capital Markets. Edited by Apostolos-Paul Refenes.
© 1995 John Wiley & Sons Ltd

suffer, but also in the positive instances when a network's performance is overly generous.

By taking this approach a set of criteria for a fair and rigorous test of a network's forecasting performance is established. We then apply this to an extended series of out-of-sample forecasting experiments (over 1700) for the long gilt futures contract (LGFC). It is shown that a fixed network isolates a deterministic signal within the LGFC, to a confidence level of over 99%, yielding a prediction accuracy of 57%. We show that this cannot be explained by a simple bias within the series, and that for any given day the probability of a price rise, or a price fall, over the forecast horizon is 0.5. These results are then analysed in terms of their trading significance. It is shown that the network could form the basis of a profitable trading system, but that certain weaknesses exist in terms of a bias in the network's trading profile. This is discussed in terms of the EMH and possible improvements to the forecast accuracy that might be available.

To sum up, the chapter is organized as follows. In the next section we outline NN design and training. We demonstrate some of the dangers in NN forecasting, and derive conditions for a fair and rigorous testing. In the third section we give an introduction to the data, describing how the price series is formed, and how it is traditionally interpreted. In the fourth section we describe the experimental set-up, the NN design and the NN performance criteria. In the fifth section we present and analyse the results. Finally we present some conclusions and outline the direction of current research.

DESIGN CONSIDERATIONS

Network Set-up

The learning algorithm that was used was a variation of standard backpropagation with a fully connected three-layer network architecture, using a dynamic learning rate for each weight update, with hyperbolic tangent activation functions, no momentum term and batch learning. Batch learning updates the weights from a single point in the weight space. That is, it calculates the cumulative weight change for each weight for the entire training set before adjusting the weights. This variation is not untypical and is described in detail in many of the standard texts [Wasser90].

For univariate time-series analysis the network's input layer corresponds to lagged values of the target series. Lagged values at the input layer can then be matched against future values at the output layer. This technique, so-called *windowing*, attempts to build a relationship between past and future values as a function of time. For example, a time series T takes values t_n at time step n. Here t_n could be the closing prices of a particular asset, with t_n representing the closing price on day n. The net can be trained on input values $t_n, t_{n-1}, t_{n-2}, t_{n-3}$ and output value t_{n+1}. A contiguous series of such values can then be grouped to form the input–output patterns required for network training.

Data Ranging

In almost all non-trivial applications of NNs some form of data preprocessing is necessary. Regardless of the form this takes, safeguards must be present to ensure that the validation set does not become corrupted. This is particularly important when the net is being used for forecasting trends. An example of the problems that can be encountered is shown in Figure 18.1. Here a 6-4-1 totally connected feedforward network has been trained on values in the range (-5,+5) of the symmetrically bounded ramp function given by:

$$f(x) = \begin{cases} 10 & \text{if } x > 10 \\ x & \text{if } -10 \geqslant x \leqslant 10 \\ -10 & \text{if } x < 10 \end{cases}$$

Using hyperbolic tangent activation functions for all nodes, the net has a functional range $(-1, +1)$. Three networks were trained for exactly the same number of training cycles, with exactly the same training parameters, the only factor that was changed being the scaling of the training set for each of the nets. Using different

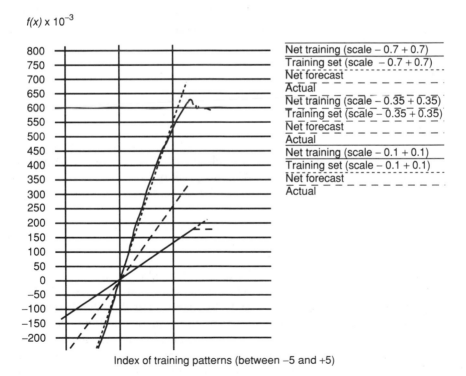

Figure 18.1   Network trained on symmetric ramp

scaling values for the training set Figure 18.1 shows how the network's forecast is forced to dip as the output values approach the limit of the activation function's range. This effect can essentially be produced at will by selecting an appropriate scaling of the training set. This type of turning point can produce false negative as well as false positive results. This makes it imperative that the validation sets are not included in any of the preprocessing, and that forecasts should not be made from points close to the activation function's limit. If the data are made stationary this becomes less of a concern, provided that future values of the series do not violate the bounds set on the training data. For the work reported here the training set is scaled to within a fixed range ± 0.5 and the validation set is ignored for the purposes of this calculation.

A similar method of forecast adjusting can be achieved via the number of training cycles. That is, the forecasts for each of the net's output in Figure 18.1 can be made to coincide by adjusting the amount of training each of the networks receives. This is another factor that has to be strictly regulated in the large-scale validation tests.

THE DATA: THE LONG GILT FUTURES CONTRACT

The long gilt futures contact (LGFC) is a gilt instrument giving the option to buy or sell government issues at some time in the future. The size of the contract is a nominal £50 000 and the price is expressed in terms of a national 9% long-dated stock. The minimum step by which the price can move is $\frac{1}{32}\%$ (one tick). The buyer of a contract is theoretically buying a nominal £50 000 of gilt-edge stock for delivery in the future, all return being direct capital gain on the instrument itself. If interest rates fall, the value of the contract is likely to rise because gilt-edge stocks will rise in value. The initial margin of the LGFC is £500, so each tick represents a potential profit or loss of approximately £15. Financial futures contracts very rarely result in physical delivery. The purchaser of a contract simply closes his position by selling an identical contract and taking his profit or loss.

The contract can be used in a number of ways. A trader might buy simply as a gamble based on the hunch that interest rates will go down. Alternatively, a buyer may have £50 000 to invest in gilt-edge stock in the future and may fear a price rise. From a forecasting point of view there are many factors that will account for price movement in the series. Since gilt prices are taken as economic indicators for the economy as a whole, a variety of different indices are thought to be relevant in driving the price series. Gilt futures on the back of this are thought to be driven by speculation as to the likely strength or weakness of the future economy. For this reason public sector borrowing requirement (PSBR), the exchange rate, unemployment levels and interest rates are all seen as contributory factors in the movement of gilt-based stocks. This conventional description of gilt pricing apparently all but rules out the possibility of the LGFC price series having some internal dynamic based on past price movement. In fact, due to the discrete

Table 18.1 Sample dataset

Trading day		TUE 2 MAR 1993		
	Opening range	Settle change	Floor daily	Est floor volume
Long gilt				
Mar93	105−02 105−02	105−06−0−05	105−08 105−00	4259
Jun93	106−02 105−31	106−05 −0−02	106−05 105−27	25899
Sep93	105−00 105−00	105−05 −0−02	105−00 105−0	50

nature of contract trading, the idea that past price values of old contracts have any effect on new contracts seems, if anything, most unlikely.

This brings us on to the first technical problem associated with forecasting the LGFC. Somehow a continuous time series must be created from the various contracts that exist. The series itself can be obtained from the London International Financial Futures and Options Exchange (LIFFE), and will typically list the opening range, settlement price, and the volumes traded for a number of contracts, for example March 1993, June 1993 and September 1993 (see Table 18.1). The series constructed here used the lowest price of the opening range of the most traded contract — the contract currently trading with the highest volume. These values were then decimalised (to remove the tick pricing) and concatenated to form a single series. Even though this produced a single series, marked discontinuities occur between contact changes. To alleviate some of this movement, a moving average of the series was also taken. Doing this meant that the forecast horizon had to be extended to a point beyond the length of the moving average.

EXPERIMENTAL DESIGN

The LGFC price series is given in Figure 18.2. The series was constructed from all contracts for the period from 18 November 1982 to 23 February 1993, this gave 2596 trading days, with 124 changes of contract. In order to smooth the contract change-overs a 34-day moving average was taken. This meant that the network was to forecast the moving average of the series, and therefore the forecast horizon would have to extend beyond 17 days to make a genuine forecast for the raw data. To select the precise forecast period some match between the moving-average price movement and raw series movement had to be decided. Figure 18.2(a) gives the relationship between raw price movement and moving-average price movement. What Figure 18.2(b) shows is how price movement in the moving average corresponds to movement in the raw series. It can be seen that at about 40 days the correspondence between the moving average and raw series stands at about 88%; this means that a price rise (fall) in the moving average over a 40-day period will signify a corresponding price rise (fall) in the raw series about 88% of the time. Before the 40-day period the correspondence quickly deteriorates, and after this

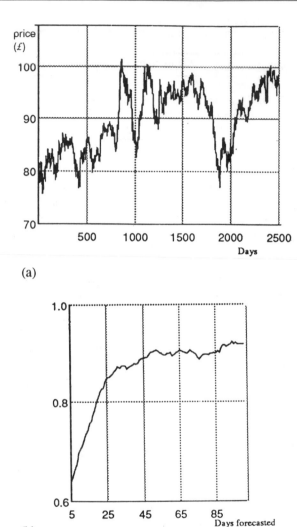

Figure 18.2 (a) The LGFC price series after concatenating contract prices between 18 November 1982 and 23 February 1983. (b) Correspondence between moving-average and raw LGFC movement

period the correspondence levels off, rising to 92% for a 100-day forecast. The 40-day horizon signifies the turning point of the relationship, and affords the shortest forecast horizon with the highest likelihood of predicting the raw series movement. For this reason a 39-day forecast horizon was chosen. It should be pointed out that Figure 18.2(b) is characteristic of the relationship between the moving average and the raw series over the whole ten years, but for the purposes of the experiment Figure 18.2(a) was produced for the contract prices between 30 January 1989 and the 23 January 1991. These two dates represent the training set that was used for network design and validation. It gives a price series of about 500 data entries all of which served to test topologies and training algorithms. The reason for choosing this period was simply that these values were the first to be made available to the author. The validation periods preceding and succeeding these dates were obtained later once encouraging results had started to emerge. Over the training set a great many experiments were conducted, varying network topology, activation functions, training cycle limits, momentum terms, learning rates, stochastic learning parameters, training-set size and data representations. The experiments consisted of selecting some setting of all of the above, training a network and then making forecasts over a validation period within the 500-day limit. Essentially this replicated the jackknifing technique used to validate statistical models. Moody and Utans [MooUta92] have described a similar process for network selection in which multiple cross-validation tests are conducted. Here small segments of the data are excluded from training and are then used for network validation. Two main criteria for network selection were used. The first was the network performance on the validation set. This consisted of simply counting the number of successful predictions over a series of 20 validation tests. A successful prediction meant that the network correctly identified the direction of the raw data over the forecast horizon taken from the first day outside of the moving-average window, that is, the first day that live trading would be possible. The second criterion related to the smoothness of the training profile of the net. This took into account several factors: the root mean square error (RMSE) of the training error profile; the RMSE forecast error profile; and finally, the convergence characteristics. It is worth describing the last two factors in greater detail.

The RMSE forecast error profile was created by taking the RMSE of the forecast error every ten cycles of batch training over a validation set. That is, the forecast was made as if the network was completely trained and was being tested. The RMSE was then summed for each day of the 39-day iterated forecast. This gave a single figure which could be plotted against the number of training cycles to give a measure of forecast performance to training cycles, the idea being that if the net was capturing some element of the series, and was likely to produce good generalisation, then the forecast error profile should smoothly start to approach zero. Note, this profile was not being used as a control parameter and therefore could not directly contribute to any form of overfitting. It was used simply as a way of discarding certain network configurations, and therefore could only indirectly effect the outcome of training. The convergence was similarly calculated and judged. The only difference was that this is measured within the training set, and therefore produced satisfactory profiles most of the time. What was looked for here was the additional signs of possible overtraining, this being characterised by a smooth decrease in the error profile for many cycles followed by a sudden and marked increase. The increase for some configurations would disappear after further training, but as a heuristic this was judged undesirable behaviour. Note that this does not refer to the small oscillations in training error caused by dynamic learning rates. These are perfectly expected and sit on top of the overall profile. Figure 18.3 gives both these curves for a randomly chosen net. Both these heuristics proved very powerful, to the extent that good forecast performance over many data sets could be predicted for networks that had these properties.

Several other points are worth mentioning in terms of experimental experience. On-line training was found too slow ever to be useful. On-line training is where the network updates the weights after each pattern, as opposed to batch training which takes an aggregate weight update for all patterns. This seems reasonable in that on-line training always has the danger that a set of patterns can exist which mutually contradict each other's movement in the weight space. For example, a pathological case would be where one pattern's weight update is immediately undone by the succeeding pattern. This sort of effect is cancelled out in batch training. The situation is improved by using momentum terms (where a proportion of the previous weight update is retained in any subsequent weight update) and randomising the presentation of the patterns. However, for all of the experiments conducted in this instance neither of these techniques was needed for batch training, and a momentum term served to slow down convergence.

Another factor that slowed convergence was the choice of activation function. This has been reported elsewhere [LeCun85, RefAli91, ReFrZa92]. It was found that an asymmetric sigmoid produced far worse results than the symmetric version, not so much in eventual network performance, but in terms of the number of training cycles needed.

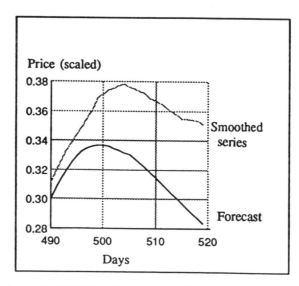

Figure 18.3　Forecast of LGFC against actual values

Stochastic training schemes were also tested; this included a Cauchy machine [Wasser90], and the combined backpropagation and Cauchy machine. The Cauchy machine is based on the Boltzmann machine, where weights are adjusted stochastically according to the Cauchy distribution. Both of these proved less robust than backpropagation with a dynamic learning rate.

The set-up phase finally produced a fixed set of parameters which gave a good performance over the 500-day set, and had the highest proportion of good training profiles. The network consisted of a fixed, totally connected topology of 15-4-1, trained with a dynamic learning rate which was bounded below by 0.1, with a success multiplier of 1.1, and divisor of 2.0. The network training set was held at 250 days, trained for a fixed 750 batch cycle, giving 750×250 presentations of individual patterns. After training the net made an iterated 39-day forecast. All of these parameters were then fixed and the large-scale testing of the network started.

RESULTS

The full-scale validation test consisted of testing the fixed network design and training parameters over the full series. For each test the network was trained on 250 days of smoothed LGFC past prices. Once trained, the network made an iterated 39-day forecast, the direction of which was logged and compared with the target series (the smoothed LGFC series) and the raw price series. The days between 30 January 1989 and 23 January 1991 were removed from the experiment; these were part of the network set-up phase, and were therefore judged to be corrupted. This gave a total of just over 1790 completely unbiased experiments, i.e., no element of network training was changed, and all preprocessing was fixed on the basis of each of the 250 training days each network received. There were two reasons why the network was trained for each successive window of 250 days before making its forecast: first, during the set-up phase this technique proved the most effective; second, it seemed reasonable that characteristics within the data would change. Table 18.2 gives an example of an output file, and Figure 18.4 gives an example forecast as compared to the smoothed time series. Note, in Figure 18.4, that even though the forecast follows the target series well, the ultimate direction of the forecasts is a fall in price, as opposed to a rise in the smoothed series. This would count as a miss. Figure 18.5 gives an extended set of such results showing 36 forecasts that were made over a 600-day period between 12 January 1990 and 17 March 1991 (this diagram therefore includes forecasts from both the set-up phase and the actual experiment). It shows how the forecasts compare to the underlying smoothed series. Table 18.3 gives a breakdown of the results as compared to the raw series (calculated on the basis of possible trading days) and as against the moving average (taken as a straight comparison over the whole 39-day forecast period).

What is interesting about Table 18.3 is just how bad the results appear to be. In terms of target series movement the network seems to have very little idea as to how much prices will change. The correlation between target series and forecasts, and

Table 18.2   Sample output

Key	Tdir	Rdir	Fdir	Tmv	Rmv	Fmv	Hit
88	−1	−1	−1	−3.5771	−2.7914	−0.2211	1
89	−1	−1	−1	−3.6679	−2.6935	−0.2895	1
90	−1	−1	−1	−3.7183	−2.4731	−0.1975	1
91	−1	−1	−1	−3.7874	−2.4486	−0.1749	1
92	−1	−1	−1	−3.8638	−2.62	−0.1909	1
93	−1	−1	−1	−3.9077	−2.2282	−0.1098	1
94	−1	−1	−1	−3.894	−2.8649	−0.0686	1
95	−1	−1	−1	−3.9127	−4.5054	−0.0009	0
96	−1	−1	−1	−3.9509	−4.0891	−0.041	1

Tdir = Target direction
Rdir = Raw direction
Tmv = Movement in target
Rmv = Movement in raw series
Fmv = Forecasted movement
Hit = Forecasted trend correct = 1

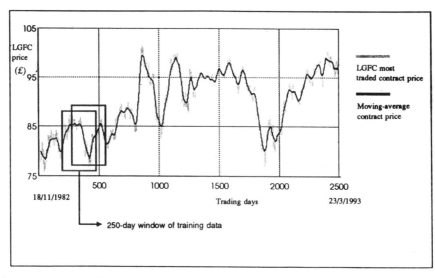

Figure 18.4   Neural network training windows for the LGFC between 18 November 1982 and 23 March 1993

between raw series and forecasts are significantly bad, to the extent that forecasted movement and raw movement are negative as well as being almost zero. The mean movement in all three series is also interesting; here again the forecast movement is biased towards negative price movement, whereas both target and raw are positive. However, what is also apparent is the high accuracy (relatively) with which the network attains the direction of the series. For the target series and raw series

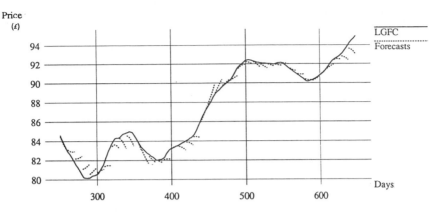

Figure 18.5   Neural network trend forecasts for the LGFC

Table 18.3   Forecast statistics

Mean target movement	0.25
Mean forecast movement	−0.24
Mean raw movement	0.13
Variance of target movement	9.19
Variance of forecast movement	6.11
Variance of raw movement	6.86
Correlation target and raw movement	0.74
Correlation target and forecast movement	0.15
Correlation raw and forecast movement	−0.005
Forecast target series trend correctly	58%
Forecast raw series trend correctly	57%

Movement = price change over 39-day forecast horizon.
Results based on 1790 independent experiments of an NN trained
on the LGFC.

the network achieves approximately 57% accuracy. The first question is how to reconcile these two sets of statistics. Why is the movement so poor in comparison to the actual direction? And, perhaps most significantly, does it suggest that the network is picking up a simple bias within the series that makes direction simple? If this is so, does it mean that for trading purposes this information is worthless in that when the network is wrong it so wrong as to wipe out any potential gains that may have been achieved when it is correct? This relates to the drawdown, or the maximum amount lost on a bad forecast. To answer some of these questions we first probe the raw and target series to establish some performance criteria. For the 1790 experiments the probability of a raw series price rise was given by 0.4966, and a rise in the target series by 0.51; for these figures we can test the following:

Null hypothesis: $p = 0.5 = p_0$

Alternative hypothesis: $p \neq 0.5$

Test statistic: $z = (\bar{p} - 0.5)/\sigma_{\bar{p}}$, where

$$\sigma_{\bar{p}} = \sqrt{\frac{p_0 q_0}{N}}$$

with $q_0 = 1 - p_0$.

For this we take p to be the probability of a price rise in the raw series over the forecast horizon. Taking values for the raw series, we obtain $z = 0.8463$, which is well within the first standard deviation from 0.5, and thus we overwhelmingly accept H_0. This gives a 0.5 chance of a price rise or price fall in the raw series over the forecast horizon. The same holds true for the target smoothed series. If on each occasion there is a probability of 0.5 of a price rise, or a price fall, over the forecast horizon then to calculate the probability of the net scoring 57% by chance we take as null hypothesis $p = 0.5 = p_0$ and as alternative hypothesis $p \neq 0.5$. For the network, we obtain $z = 5.923$ which means that the probability of the network scoring 57% by chance is less than 0.001. This means not only that we have dispelled any simple bias in the series which might explain the high level of correct trend forecasts, but also that we have extremely strong statistical evidence that the network is picking up some form of determinism within the series. This seems even more remarkable considering the contract basis on which the raw series is formed. However, this still does not account for the negative mean price movement in the forecast, and what this implies in terms of trading.

Figure 18.6 shows four histograms which go some way towards explaining the negative mean movement in the forecast. The first histogram (Figure 18.6(a)) represents the frequency of raw series movement over the forecast horizon. The frequency is calculated on basis of 0.1 price movement intervals. That is, price movements of approximately 3 ticks form the frequency bands. The raw movement is approximately normal with mean 0.13. Figure 18.6(b) gives the frequency of incorrectly forecasted movement, this again is approximately normal with a mean absolute of incorrectly forecasted movement of 0.84 points, or 26 ticks. Figure 18.6(c) give the frequency of correctly forecasted movement. Here we have a mean absolute correctly forecasted movement of 1.15, or 36.8 ticks. This means that an average loss trading with the system would be about £390, compared to an average gain of £552, giving an average profit of £162, or 32% of invested. This represents a genuine profit, even with trading expenses. To investigate this further, Figure 18.6(d) shows correctly forecasted movement minus incorrectly forecasted movement for each frequency band. What can be seen is a system that on the whole does very well, being profitable almost everywhere over the price-movement spectrum, except for the region between 0.2 and 0.7 positive price movement. That is, the net seems to do very badly when a rise in the LGFC occurs of between 6 and 22 ticks, or equivalently between £90 and £330. This would seem to imply that the network is slightly biased towards forecasting a price fall when the raw

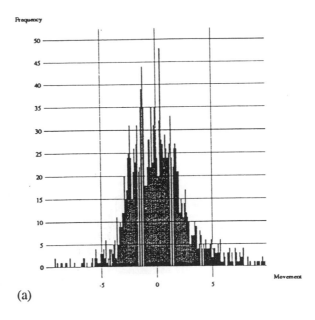

(a)

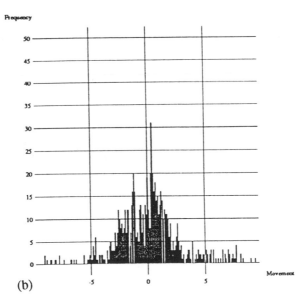

(b)

Figure 18.6 Frequency of (a) LGFC movement; (b) incorrectly forecasted LGFC movement; (c) correctly forecasted LGFC movement; (d) correctly minus incorrectly forecasted LGFC movement

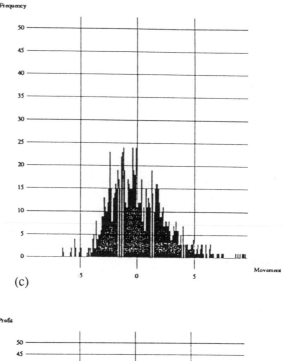

(c)

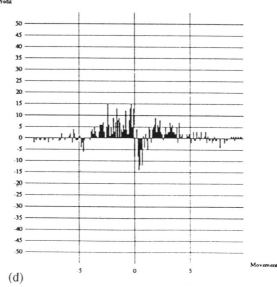

(d)

Figure 18.6 *(continued)*

series actually has a slight rise. This behaviour tails off as the actual price movement increases, until at about 31 ticks, or a £480 rise, the network's performance becomes solid again. The identification of a slight downward bias in the forecast accounts for the negative mean movement. This would seem to imply that the network's parameters could be further optimized. Ideally the profit profile should be smoothly distributed around zero, giving an equal probability of the net scoring with slight price rises, as well as slight price falls. The bias in forecast direction is borne out by the number of price falls as opposed to price rises forecasted by the net. The results give a 0.53 probability of the net forecasting a price fall, which is a significant bias given the number of experiments. This compares with a 0.503 probability of a price fall in the raw series.

Lastly, we examine the relationship between the target series forecasts and the raw series forecasts. First, there appears to be a discrepancy between the network's performance on the target as compared to the raw series. The forecast horizon of 39 days was picked because over this period the target, or smoothed series, has an 88% chance of corresponding to a raw series movement. However, the network scores 58% and 57%, respectively, for the target and raw series. The reason for this apparent discrepancy is the way the forecast has been calculated for the two series. The success rate for the target series has been calculated on the basis of the full 39-day forecast, whereas the raw series is calculated on the basis of the real 22-day forecast (the movement taking place on possible trading days). If the 17-day movement is taken into account for the target series, so that the forecast is then over the 22 days as for the raw series, the network's score can be made to rise to 70% for the moving average. This gives a theoretical score of approximately 61% (0.7 × 0.88) on the raw series. This again would suggest that the network's performance can be improved.

CONCLUSION

There are good reasons why the machine learning community has taken such an interest in the use of adaptive techniques in financial and economic forecasting. This goes beyond the fact that they provide a pragmatic demonstration of the potential of learning systems, or the more obvious potential for making money (although these may be contributory factors). A genuine interest comes from the fact that the EMH guarantees the absence of any *a priori* model on which to base the computational solution. From this point of view, the algorithm (perhaps with the aid of the programmer) has discovered aspects within the target system that have not been available to other techniques. More explicitly, traditional economic theory holds that for any asset price the following relationship best describes the price movement:

$$x_{t+1} = x_t + \varepsilon \qquad (18.1)$$

where x_t is the price of any asset at time t, and ε represents some noise factor. This is the equation of a random walk; it says the best guess for tomorrow's price is today's [Shille87]. The justification for this model forms the basis of the EMH; it is the assertion that the price level of an asset fully reflects all current information relating to that asset, and that accordingly price movement is driven by the arrival of new information, which is inherently random. Further, it implies that it is impossible to design an automated procedure for profit-making based on past values of such a series. Any ability to refute this argument would have obvious consequences within economics; it would challenge the basic principles underlying the EMH interpretation of capital market dynamics. Moreover, if the technique used is based on adaptive machine learning principles, it represents one of the most significant applications of such techniques.

In the work reported here an extensive series of experiments has been conducted on one particular price series, the LGFC. The idea was to analyse the performance of an NN on an extensive set of validation tests. Particular care was taken to set a fair and unbiased reckoning of the NN's performance. This meant careful safeguards on data preprocessing, and for the network training parameters. What has been shown is that an NN trained exclusively on past values of a smoothed LGFC series has a probability of 0.57 of predicting a price trend. This figure, established in 1790 independent experiments, represents at least some evidence against the weak form of the EMH. It was shown that the network's success had no simple explanation in the form of a bias in the series, and that the probability of the network achieving this score by chance is less than 0.001. It was also shown that the success rate is just high enough to sustain some form of trading strategy, giving a positive expected profit for each trade. This in conjunction with the fact that the net makes forecasts on the basis of past price movement alone, and that the original series is a concatenation of contract prices seems a significant achievement.

The results reported here are a firm starting point for a forecasting and trading system for the LGFC. In particular, the bias in the network's forecasted direction is addressed along with the introduction of further price series in the training procedures, all of which has given a much improved trading capability. However, as an extended series of unbiased experiments the results reported here will remain significant in that the network was designed and fixed on 500 days' data; for the remaining 1790 days a fixed procedure was employed and the results reported.

19

Architecture Selection Strategies for Neural Networks: Application to Corporate Bond Rating Prediction

John Moody and Joachim Utans,
Oregon Graduate Institute, USA

INTRODUCTION

This chapter investigates strategies for selecting a good neural network architecture for modelling any specific data set. The approach involves efficiently searching the space of possible architectures and selecting a 'best' architecture based on estimates of generalisation performance. Since an exhaustive search over the space of architectures is computationally infeasible, we propose heuristic strategies which dramatically reduce the search complexity. These employ directed search algorithms, including selecting the number of nodes via sequential network construction (SNC), sensitivity-based pruning (SBP) of inputs, and optimal brain damage (OBD) pruning for weights. A selection criterion, the estimated generalisation performance or prediction risk, is used to guide the heuristic search and to choose the final network. Both predicted squared error (PSE) and nonlinear cross-validation (NCV) are used for estimating the prediction risk from the available data. We apply

Neural Networks in the Capital Markets. Edited by Apostolos-Paul Refenes.

these heuristic search and prediction-risk estimation techniques to the problem of predicting corporate bond ratings.

NONPARAMETRIC MODELLING WITH LIMITED DATA

Many data modelling problems in finance, economics and other fields are characterised by two difficulties: the absence of a complete *a priori* model of the data-generation process (such as the models frequently available in physics, say); and a limited quantity of data. When constructing statistical models for such applications, the issues of model selection and estimation of generalisation ability or prediction risk are crucial and must be addressed in order to construct a near-optimal model. The prediction of corporate bond ratings has both of the above problems.

When a complete *a priori* model for the data-generation process does not exist, one must adopt a nonparametric modelling approach. In nonparametric modelling, elements of a class of functions known to have good approximation properties, such as smoothing splines (for one- or two-dimensional problems) or neural networks (for higher-dimensional problems), are used to fit the data. An element of this class (for instance, a particular neural network) is then chosen which 'best fits' the data.

The notion of 'best fit' can be precisely defined via an objective criterion, such as maximum *a posteriori* probability (MAP), minimum Bayesian information criterion (BIC), minimum description length (MDL), or minimum prediction risk. In this chapter, we use the prediction risk (defined as the expected performance of an estimator in predicting new observations) as our selection criterion for two reasons: first, it is straightforward to compute; and second, it provides more information than MAP, BIC, or MDL, since it tells us how much confidence to put in predictions produced by our best model.

The restriction of limited data makes the model-selection and prediction-risk estimation problems more difficult. A limited training set results in a more severe bias–variance (or underfitting versus overfitting) trade-off (see, for example, [GeBiDo92]), so the model-selection problem is both more challenging and more crucial. In particular, it is easier to overfit a small training set, so care must be taken not to select a model which is too large.

Also, limited data sets make prediction-risk estimation more difficult if there is not enough data available to hold out a sufficiently large independent test sample. In such situations, one must use alternative approaches which enable the estimation of prediction risk from the training data, such as data resampling and algebraic estimation techniques. Data resampling methods include nonlinear refinements of v-fold cross-validation (NCV) and bootstrap estimation, while algebraic estimates (in the regression context) include generalised cross-validation (GCV) [CraWah79, GoHeWa79], Akaike's final prediction error (FPE) [Akaike70], Akaike's information criterion, and other estimates of predicted squared error (see discussion in [Barron84]) for linear models, and the recently proposed generalised prediction error (GPE) for nonlinear models [Moody91, Moody92, Moody94b]).

Neural Network Architecture Selection

For the discussion of architecture selection in this chapter, we focus for convenience' sake on the most widely used neural network architecture, the two-layer perceptron (or backpropagation) network; our approach can be easily generalised to networks with multiple outputs and multiple layers. For two-layer perceptrons, the architecture selection problem is to find a good (hopefully near-optimal) architecture for modelling a given data set. The architecture is characterised by the number of hidden units H_λ; the number of input variables I_λ; and the subset of weights which are nonzero. If all of the weights are nonzero, the network is referred to as *fully connected*. Note that, for brevity of exposition, we denote weights and biases in either layer of the network generically by w.

Complexity of Exhaustive Search

If we consider a set of two-layer perceptrons up to some maximal size determined by I_{max} and H_{max}, then the maximal fully connected network has

$$M_{max} = 1 + H_{max}(I_{max} + 2)$$

weights, where I and H denote input variable and hidden units, respectively. All smaller two-layer networks can be obtained from the maximal network by setting weights and thresholds to zero. The total number of resulting network topologies (treating the ordering of the hidden units as unique and thus not considering permutations of them) is

$$N_{max} = 2^{(M_{max})}$$

For a set of networks with $I_{max} = 10$ and $H_{max} = 12$, for example, we obtain $N_{max} = 2^{145} \approx 4.46 \times 10^{43}$. Even though the maximal network in this example is modest in size, N_{max} is a prohibitively large number of network topologies to search exhaustively. Even if exhaustive search for an optimum were computationally feasible, it is likely that it would prove to be pointless, since, based on our experience, many network architectures are likely to provide similar performance (see, for example, Figure 3 of [MooYar92]). Moreover, the model variance for networks trained on small, noisy data sets will make the near-optimal models indistinguishable from the asymptotically optimal model. The term 'asymptotic' refers to the limit of infinite training-set size. Thus, we are compelled to consider restricted search strategies over the space of network architectures. This is the subject of later sections.

Corporate Bond Rating

The corporate bond rating problem served as our motivation for developing the approach which we describe in this chapter. It is a typical example of a problem which lacks a complete *a priori* model and for which data sets are of limited size.

We performed our original work on corporate bond rating at Yale University from June to December 1989 at the request of a major Wall Street bank. The data set provided by the bank consisted of the most recent Standard & Poor (S&P) bond ratings (the targets) and a set of ten carefully selected input variables (time-averaged financial ratios) for 196 industrial firms. The set included exemplars (firms) over a range of 16 S&P sub-ratings. Several of the sub-ratings had only three or four exemplars associated with them, so the data set was rather thin in these cases.

Since the S&P rating categories are an ordered set, bond rating can be treated as a regression problem by mapping the ratings onto a set of integer values. Analysts at the bank had already developed a 'state-of-the-art' linear regression model based on this data set, and our task was to develop a neural network bond rating predictor which would outperform the linear regression model. As our results, described below, indicate, the data set has significant nonlinearity which the linear regression model could not capture.

HEURISTIC SEARCH OVER THE SPACE OF PERCEPTRON ARCHITECTURES

Given the impossibility and futility of exhaustively sampling the space of possible networks in search of an optimum, we propose an efficient heuristic search algorithm. First, we select the optimal number of internal units from a sequence of fully connected networks with an increasing number of hidden units. We use an efficient algorithm, sequential network construction (SNC), for training this sequence. Then, using the optimal fully connected network, we prune input variables via sensitivity-based pruning (SBP) and weights via optimal brain damage (OBD).

Figure 19.1 depicts two search strategies. After selecting the number of hidden units H_λ, the input removal and weight elimination can be carried out in parallel (Figure 19.1(a)) or sequentially (Figure 19.1(b)). The parallel strategy (which was used for the bond rating simulations) allows a comparison of the results of the input and weight-pruning steps but requires a final step of combining the resulting networks to obtain the final network architecture. On the other hand, the sequential approach is less costly to implement since, for the weight elimination stage, the network is already reduced in size by removing inputs. This alternative corresponds to a *coarse to fine* strategy, that is, pruning inputs removes groups of weights while the final weight elimination is concerned with individual weights. A refinement of the sequential approach is to redetermine the optimal number of hidden units after a good set of input variables has been selected or after the removal of each unnecessary input variable. This results in an iterative procedure (dashed line in Figure 19.1(b)).

For determining an appropriate (hopefully optimal or near-optimal) number of hidden units, we construct a sequence of networks with increasing numbers of units. This sequence is trained using an efficient algorithm which we call sequential

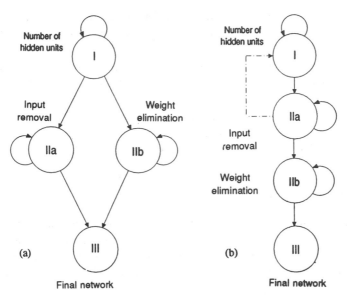

Figure 19.1 Heuristic search strategies. After selecting the number of hidden units H_λ, the input removal and weight elimination can be carried out (a) in parallel or (b) sequentially. In (b), the selection of the number of hidden units and removal of inputs may be iterated (dashed line)

network construction (SNC). Each network in the sequence is fully connected and uses all available input variables.

The SNC Algorithm

The SNC algorithm constructs a sequence of networks as follows. First, a network with a small number of hidden units H_{min} is trained using random initial weights. Then, for $H_J > H_{min}$, a larger network is obtained by adding units in clumps of size C to the largest current net in the sequence. When a larger network is constructed, a four-step retraining procedure is used.

1. The weight values of the previous network with H_λ hidden units are used to initialise the weights of the first H_λ units of the network with $H_\lambda + C$ hidden units.
2. The weights of the new clump of units are initialised to small, random values.
3. These new weights are then trained to a local optimum while keeping the weights of the first H_λ units fixed.
4. Finally, all weights of the $H_\lambda + C$ hidden units are retrained from their previous values until a local optimum for the whole network is reached.

This procedure of adding clumps and retraining is iterated until a network with H_{max} units is obtained. (In our bond rating work, we usually chose $H_{min} = 2$, $H_{max} = 12$ and $C = 1$.)

The SNC algorithm is designed to solve two problems. First, it substantially reduces computation time compared to what would be required if larger networks were trained from scratch. Second, the sequence of networks constructed comprise a nested set. This second point is discussed below.

Before proceeding, we would like to note that many authors have independently proposed iterative network construction algorithms (see Chapter 3).

Nested Models and Inverse Pruning

A nonlinear model in general has many local minima, and each local minimum corresponds to a different set of parameters and thus to a different model (see Figure 19.2). The SNC algorithm, on the other hand, provides some continuity in model space by constructing a nested sequence in which larger networks contain the smaller networks.

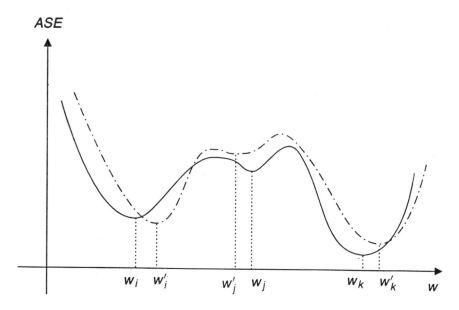

Figure 19.2 A nonlinear model can have many local minima in the error function. Each local minimum w_i, w_j and w_k (solid curve) corresponds to a different set of parameters and thus to a different model. Training on a different finite sample of data or retraining on a sub-sample, as in nonlinear cross-validation, gives rise to a slightly different error curve (dashed) and perturbed minima w'_i, w'_j and w'_k. Variations due to data sampling in error curves and their minima are termed *model variance*

The sequential construction accomplishes this nesting as follows. As larger networks are constructed, the features discovered so far by the smaller network's hidden units will continue to be used by the larger networks. In effect, this means that as the sequence grows, the networks are trained to learn corrections to the mappings discovered so far. Moreover, we have found that the effect on existing hidden units of adding a new hidden unit once the model is big enough is likely to be small. (A related effect can be observed, for example, in Figure 19.4, where the training error decreases only gradually after the third node is added.)

Because of the resulting continuity in model space, SNC can be thought of as an *inverse pruning* procedure. Since the most recently added clump of units serves only to correct a mapping learned already, it is highly likely that a node-pruning method would prune these units first. Also, it is clearly less expensive computationally to construct a sequence of networks from small to large than it is to train large networks first and prune from large to small.

Three advantages are obtained by constructing a nested set of models. First, the sequence will have monotonically decreasing (or non-increasing) training error. Second, the sequence is likely to have an easily identifiable minimum of prediction risk. Third, architecture selection via prediction risk has a formal connection to the hypothesis-testing approach to pruning when the set of models is nested (see, for example, the discussion in [Akaike74]). This last point formalises the inverse pruning interpretation described above.

Note that, in spite of these advantages of SNC, it is possible that pruning nodes from a larger network may give rise to a better fit to the data and better generalisation for a given final number of nodes. This is not to say, however, that a larger network obtained via SNC might not perform as well or better. Resolving the issue of whether SNC or node pruning is more effective in general requires a systematic study.

Our heuristic search procedure, as we implemented it for the bond rating problem, thus selects the number of nodes as follows. For each network in the sequence produced by SNC, an estimate of the prediction risk is computed. The network selected at this stage for further refinement via input and weight pruning is the one with the smallest estimated prediction risk.

PRUNING INPUTS AND WEIGHTS VIA DIRECTED SEARCH

After the optimal number of hidden units of the fully connected network with all available input variables is determined, the next steps of our heuristic search are to select input variables and remove individual weights from the network. As before, we evaluate a candidate network architecture by computing an estimate of the prediction risk. In order to avoid a search over the very large range of architectures obtained by considering all possible combinations of inputs and all possible connection structures, we propose a directed search strategy using the SBP and OBD algorithms. With these algorithms, candidate architectures are constructed by evaluating the effect of removing an input variable or an individual weight from the fully connected network (see Chapter 3).

Pruning of Input Variables via Sensitivity Analysis

In [UtaMoo91, MooUta92], we proposed a simple sensitivity-based pruning method for input variables (SBP). The SBP algorithm computes a sensitivity measure to evaluate the change in training error that would result if input x_i were removed from the network. The sensitivity of the network model to variable i is defined as:

$$S_i = \frac{1}{N} \sum_j S_{ij} \tag{19.1}$$

where S_{ij} is the sensitivity computed for observation x_j. Since there are usually many fewer inputs than weights, a direct evaluation of the sensitivity S_{i0} is feasible:

$$S_{ij} = SE(\bar{x}_i, w_\lambda) - SE(x_{ij}, w_\lambda) \tag{19.2}$$

where $\bar{x} = N^{-1} \sum_{j=1}^{N} x_{ij}$. S_i measures the effect on the training squared error (SE) of replacing the ith input by its average for all observations. Replacement of a variable by its average value removes its influence on the network output.

Note that in computing the sensitivity, no retraining is done in evaluating the first term of (19.2) and selecting which input to prune. Also note that it is not sufficient just to set $x_{ij} = 0$ for all j, because the value of the bias of each hidden unit was determined during training and would not be offset properly by setting the input arbitrarily to zero. Of course, if the inputs are normalised to have zero mean prior to training, then setting an input variable to zero is equivalent to replacing it by its mean.

If the number of input variables I_λ is large, S_i is expensive to compute and can be approximated. For a small change of the ith input of the jth observation, ∂x_{ij}

$$dSE = \sum_i \frac{\partial SE}{\partial x_{ij}} dx_{ij} + \frac{1}{2} \sum_{i_1 i_2 j} \frac{\partial^2 SE}{\partial x_{i_1 j} \partial x_{i_2 j}} dx_{i_1 j} dx_{i_2 j} + O(\|x_{ij}\|^3) \tag{19.3}$$

The linear term in (19.3) approximates S_{ij} as

$$\hat{S}_{ij} = \frac{\partial SE}{\partial x_{ij}} dx_{ij} \tag{19.4}$$

where $dx_{ij} = \bar{x}_i - x_{ij}$, and the derivative information can be efficiently computed as a minor extension to the backpropagation algorithm used for training.

Note that the SBP algorithm neglects possible correlations between inputs. An improvement of the method would be to first orthogonalise the inputs (for example by a KL transform) and perform the sensitivity analysis using the transformed inputs. The pruning would be performed on input eigennodes rather than the actual input variables. This approach has been explored recently by [LeLeMo94]. A related input pruning algorithm based on a different approximation of the sensitivity measure has been proposed by [ReFrZa93].

Other Pruning Methods

A number of other pruning methods besides the one we have described here are potentially effective and should be considered when constructing neural network models (see Chapter 3 for a review). Several of these were developed after our original bond rating work was completed.

ARCHITECTURE SELECTION VIA THE PREDICTION RISK

Prediction Risk

The notion of generalisation ability can be defined precisely as the prediction-risk, the expected performance of an estimator in predicting new observations. For comprehensive discussions of prediction-risk estimation, see [Eubank88, HasTib90, Wahba90]. We present a brief description here.

Consider a set of observations $D = \{(\vec{x}_j, t_j); j = 1, \ldots, N\}$ that are assumed to be generated as

$$t_j = \mu(x_j) + \varepsilon_j \tag{19.5}$$

where $\mu(x_j)$ is an unknown function, the inputs x_j are drawn independently with an unknown stationary probability density function $p(x)$, the ε_j are independent random variables with zero mean and variance σ_ε^2, and the t_j are the observed target values. The learning or regression problem is to find an estimate $\hat{\mu}_\lambda(x; D)$ of $\mu(x)$ given the data set D from a class of predictors or models $\mu_\lambda(x)$ indexed by λ.

In general, $\lambda \in \Lambda = (S, A, W)$ where $S \subset X$ denotes a chosen subset of the set of available input variables X, A is a selected architecture within a class of model architectures, and W are the adjustable parameters (weights) of architecture A. Here we make explicit the dependence of the estimator $\hat{\mu}$ on the available data D used for training, and its sample size N.

The prediction risk $P(\lambda)$ is defined as the expected performance on future data:

$$P(\lambda) = \int dx p(x)[\mu(x) - \hat{\mu}(x)]^2 + \sigma_{-\varepsilon}^2 \tag{19.6}$$

(here we have used the squared error, but the prediction risk can be defined for other loss functions as well). This can be approximated by the expected performance on a finite test set:

$$P(\lambda) \approx E\left\{ \frac{1}{N} \sum_{j=1}^{N} (t_j^* - \hat{\mu}_\lambda(x_j^*))^2 \right\} \tag{19.7}$$

where (x_j^*, t_j^*) are new observations that were not used in constructing the estimator $\hat{\mu}_\lambda(x)$. In what follows, we shall use $P(\lambda)$ as a measure of the generalisation ability of a model. Our strategy is to choose an architecture λ in the model space Λ which minimises an estimate of the prediction risk $P(\lambda)$. The set of networks considered is determined by the heuristic search strategies described already.

Prediction Risk for Nonlinear Models

The training error functions of nonlinear models, such as two-layer perceptrons, often contain many local minima (see Figure 19.2). Each minimum should be viewed as defining a different predictor. In order to seek out good local minima, a good learning procedure must therefore include both a gradient-based optimisation algorithm and a technique such as random restart which enables sampling of the space of minima.

Since the models we use as predictors are trained to a particular 'good' local minimum in weight space, we are interested in estimating the generalisation ability or prediction risk associated with that minimum and not others. This point is important for the estimation procedures described in the next section.

Note that different realisations of a finite training set will result in slightly different error surfaces in the weight space. This is illustrated in Figure 19.2 by the difference between the solid and dashed curves. Note that the minima of the dashed curve differ slightly from the minima of the solid curve. This effect gives rise to model variance.

ESTIMATES OF THE PREDICTION RISK

Since it is not possible to calculate the prediction risk $P(\lambda)$ exactly given only a finite sample of data, we have to estimate it. The standard method based on test-set validation is not advisable when the data set is small. The prediction of 16 corporate bond ratings from a database of only 196 firms as described in the next section is such a case.

Cross-validation (CV) is a sample reuse method for estimating prediction risk; it makes maximally efficient use of the available data. We have developed a nonlinear refinement of CV called NCV. Algebraic estimates, such as generalised cross-validation (GCV), the final prediction error (FPE), the predicted squared error (PSE), and the generalised prediction error (GPE), combine the average training squared error (ASE) with a measure of the model complexity. These will be discussed in the next sections.

Test-Set Validation

If enough data are available, it is possible to use only part of the data for training the network. The remaining exemplars form a test set that can be used to estimate the prediction risk. The obvious disadvantage of this method is that not all the data are used for training. Even in cases where the data set is large one would like to use as many data as possible for training, since the estimation error associated with model variance becomes worse as the training-set size is reduced. However, if the test set is too small, an accurate estimate of the prediction risk cannot be obtained. Test-set validation becomes practical only if the data sets are very large or new data can be generated cheaply.

Cross-Validation

Cross-validation is a method that makes minimal assumptions on the statistics of the data. The idea of cross-validation can be traced back to [MosTuc68]. For reviews, see [Stone74, Geisse75, Stone78, Eubank88, HasTib90, Wahba90]. For our presentation of the general method, we follow [Eubank88]. We then present a refinement of the method for nonlinear models called NCV.

General Formulation

Denoting a predictor trained on all N data samples by $\hat{\mu}_\lambda(x)$, let $\hat{\mu}_{\lambda(j)}(x)$ be a predictor trained using all observations except (x_j, t_j) such that $\hat{\mu}_\lambda(x)$ minimises

$$ASE_j = \frac{1}{N-1} \sum_{k \neq j} (t_k - \hat{\mu}_{\lambda(j)}(x_k))^2 \qquad (19.8)$$

For $\hat{\mu}_\lambda(x)$ we can treat the jth omitted datum as a test set, and repeat this for all j. Then, an estimator for the prediction risk of the model trained on all observations is the cross-validation average squared error

$$CV(\lambda) = \frac{1}{N} \sum_{j=1}^{N} (t_j - \hat{\mu}_{\lambda(j)}(x_j))^2 \qquad (19.9)$$

This form of cross-validation is known as *leave-one-out* cross-validation. However, $CV(\lambda)$ is expensive to compute for neural network models; it involves constructing an additional N networks, each trained with $N - 1$ observations.

For the work described in this chapter we therefore use a variation of the method, v-*fold* cross-validation, that was introduced by [Geisse75] and [WahWol75]. Instead of leaving out only one observation for the computation of the sum in (19.10), we delete larger subsets of D.

Let the data D be divided into v randomly selected disjoint subsets D_j of roughly equal size:

$$\overset{v}{\underset{j=1}{\overset{\cdot}{\bigcup}}} D_j = D$$

$$D_i \cap D_j = \emptyset \qquad i \neq j$$

Let N_j denote the number of observations in subset D_j. Let $\hat{\mu}_{\lambda(D_j)}(x)$ be an estimator trained on all data except for $(x, t) \in D_j$. Then, the cross-validation average squared error for subset j is defined as:

$$CV_{D_j}(\lambda) = \frac{1}{N} \sum_{j,(x_k,t_k) \in D_j} (t_k - \hat{\mu}_{\lambda(D_j)}(x_k))^2$$

$$CV(\lambda) = \frac{1}{v} \sum_j CV_{D_j}(\lambda) \qquad\qquad (19.10)$$

Typical choices for v are 5 and 10. Note that leave-one-out CV is obtained in the limit $v = N$. Note that CV is a nonparametric estimate of the prediction risk that relies only on the available data.

NCV: Cross-Validation for Nonlinear Models

The frequent occurrence of multiple minima in nonlinear models (see Figure 19.2), each of which represents a different predictor, requires a refinement of the cross-validation procedure. This refinement, *nonlinear cross-validation* (NCV), is illustrated in Figure 19.3 for $v = 5$.

A network is trained on the entire data set D to obtain a model $\hat{\mu}_\lambda(x)$ with weights w_0. These weights are used as the starting point for the v-fold cross-validation procedure. Each subset D_j is removed from the training data in turn. The network is retrained using the remaining data starting at w_0 (rather than using random initial weights). Under the assumption that deleting a subset from the

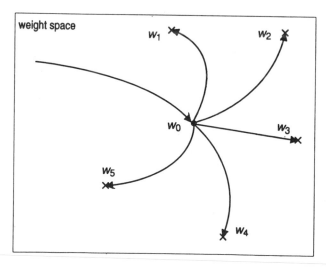

Figure 19.3   Illustration of the computation of 5-fold nonlinear cross-validation

training data does not lead to a large difference in the locally optimal weights, the retraining from w_0 'perturbs' the weights to obtain w_i, $i = 1, \ldots, v$. The $CV(\lambda)$ computed for the 'perturbed models' $\hat{\mu}_{\lambda(D_j)}(x)$ according to (19.10) thus estimates the prediction risk for the model with locally optimal weights w_0 as desired, and not the performance of other predictors at other local minima.

If the network were trained from random initial weights for each subset, it could converge to a minimum corresponding to w_i different from the one corresponding to w_0. This would correspond to a different model. Thus, starting from w_0 assures us that the cross-validation estimates the prediction risk for a particular model in question corresponding to $w \approx w_0$.

In Figure 19.2, the unperturbed model could be one of the minima of the solid error curve, and a perturbed model would be the corresponding minimum of the dashed curve with weights w'_k. Our NCV algorithm attempts to avoid finding a 'wrong' perturbed model with weights, say w'_i. NCV has the additional benefit of requiring much less computational load than would be incurred by retraining from random initial weights. Note that the same perturbation procedure described here yields nonlinear refinements of the bootstrap and jackknife algorithms as well [EfrCom83].

Algebraic Estimates

Predicted Squared Error for Linear Models

For linear regression models with squared error loss function, a number of useful algebraic estimates for the prediction risk have been derived. These include the well-known generalised cross-validation (GCV) [CraWah79, GotteWa79] and Akaike's final prediction error (FPE) [Akaike70].

$$GCV(\lambda) = ASE(\lambda) \frac{1}{\left(1 - \dfrac{Q(\lambda)}{N}\right)^2}$$

$$FPE(\lambda) = ASE(\lambda) \frac{1 + [Q(\lambda)/N]}{1 - [Q(\lambda)/N]}$$

(19.11)

$Q(\lambda)$ denotes the number of weights of model λ. A more general expression for the *predicted squared error* (PSE) is:

$$PSE(\lambda) = ASE(\lambda) + 2\hat{\sigma}^2 \frac{Q(\lambda)}{N}$$

(19.12)

where $\hat{\sigma}^2$ is an estimate of the noise variance in the data. Estimation strategies for (19.12) and its statistical properties have been analysed by [Barron84] and elsewhere (see [HasTib90] and [Wahba90] for tutorial treatments).

Generalised Prediction Error (GPE)

The PSE, and therefore the FPE, are special cases of the *generalised prediction error* (GPE) [Moody91, Moody92, Moody94]. GPE estimates prediction risk for biased nonlinear models which may use general loss functions and include regularisers such as weight decay. The algebraic form (written here for squared error) is:

$$GPE(\lambda) \equiv ASE(\lambda) + \frac{2}{N}\text{tr}\hat{\mathbf{V}}\hat{\mathbf{G}}(\lambda) \qquad (19.13)$$

where $\hat{\mathbf{V}}$ is the estimated noise covariance matrix of the observed targets and $\hat{\mathbf{G}}(\lambda)$ is the estimated *generalised influence matrix*, a nonlinear analogue of the standard influence or hat matrix. Under the assumption that the noise in the target variables is independent with uniform variance, GPE can be expressed as:

$$GPE(\lambda) = ASE(\lambda) + 2\hat{\sigma}^2 \frac{\hat{Q}_{\text{eff}}(\lambda)}{N} \qquad (19.14)$$

where $\hat{\sigma}^2$ is an estimate of the noise variance in the data, and $\hat{Q}_{\text{eff}}(\lambda) \equiv \text{tr}\hat{\mathbf{G}}$ is the estimated *effective* number of model parameters. For nonlinear and/or regularised models, $\hat{Q}_{\text{eff}}(\lambda)$ is generally not equal to the number of weights $Q(\lambda)$. Note that replacing $\hat{Q}_{\text{eff}}(\lambda)$ with $Q(\lambda)$ gives the expression for PSE. Also, various other special cases of (19.13) and (19.14) have been derived by other authors and can be found in [Eubank88, HasTib90, Wahba90].

At the time that we performed the original work described in this chapter, GPE was not yet available. Thus, we used

$$\hat{P}(\lambda) \equiv ASE(\lambda)\left(1 + 2\frac{Q(\lambda)}{N}\right) \approx GCV(\lambda) \approx FPE(\lambda) \qquad (19.15)$$

as our algebraic estimator.

CASE STUDY: PREDICTION OF CORPORATE BOND RATINGS

In this section, we describe the bond rating problem and present a neural network bond rating predictor which we developed using the architecture selection methods described in the previous sections. The experimental results we present here are more detailed and slightly better than those which we presented originally in [UtaMoo91] and [MooUta92]. (Although we used the same data set as before, we obtained performance improvements by eliminating the non-standard 'AAA−' rating from the rating scale.)

A Description of Bond Ratings

A bond is a debt security which constitutes a promise by the issuing firm to pay a given rate of interest on the original issue price and to redeem the bond at face value at maturity. The firm is in default if it is not able make the promised interest payments. For an introduction to the subject of corporate bonds, see [ShaAle90].

Bonds are rated according to the default risk of the issuing firm by independent rating agencies such as Standard & Poor (S&P) and Moody's Investor Service.[1] The bond rating thus characterizes the risk for the investor and affects the cost of borrowing for the issuer. Some investors, such as pension funds, are prohibited by law from investing in a bond where the default risk, as indicated by the bond rating, is too high. Bonds with low default risk are termed *investment grade*, while bonds with high risk are called *speculative grade* or *junk* bonds (see Table 19.1).

S&P and Moody's determine the rating from various financial variables and possibly other information, but the exact set of variables is unknown. The financial data considered important by the agencies appear to be related to leverage, coverage and profitability. The method used for assigning the rating based on the input variables is not publicly disclosed. Furthermore, the agencies have publicly stated that the assessment of the rating requires expert judgement in addition to statistical analysis of financial data [Standa79]. In particular, Moody's appears to rely less on historical data and places more emphasis on expected future performance [PeaSco86].

It is thus generally believed that ratings are to a certain extent judged on the basis of subjective factors which are not easily quantifiable and on variables not directly related to a particular firm. Subjective factors could, for example include the firm's willingness to pay or the firm's ability to perform in a difficult situation based on past performance. Other factors that might be important could be the general economic situation, changes in management, currency fluctuations, and so on.

Due to these ambiguities in the bond rating process, the ratings cannot be independently reproduced with 100% accuracy, and financial institutions are thus dependent on the rating agencies for the 'official' ratings. However, it is none the less helpful to be able to evaluate the default risk independently for firms issuing bonds by estimating the ratings based on a model.

Independent ratings estimates are useful for two reasons. First, the rating agencies do not rate the bonds for every firm, and a financial institution might be interested in investing in a firm for which no ratings from standard sources are available. Second, changes in official ratings occur infrequently. Unless important

Table 19.1 Key to S&P bond ratings and our integer representation. Our data sample contained bonds with ratings from 'B−' up to 'AAA', and our corresponding integer scale ranges from 3 to 18. The rating below 'B−', denoted 'CCC', corresponds to 'very high default risk'. While 'AAA' means 'very low default risk'. Bonds with rating BBB− or better are termed 'investment grade' while 'junk bonds' have ratings BB+ or below. The change in the rating from one category to the next as referred to as a *notch*.

B−	B	⋯	BBB+	A−	A	A+	AA−	AA	AA+	AAA
3	4	⋯	11	12	13	14	15	16	17	18

developments that affect a firm's default risk occur, ratings are reviewed only peri-odically. Therefore, there is considerable value in being able to anticipate rating changes before they are announced. A predictive model which maps fundamental financial factors onto an estimated rating can accomplish this.

Prediction of S&P Bond Ratings

The problem we are considering here is to predict the S&P rating of a bond based on publicly available fundamental financial information about the issuer. For our purposes, we assigned a integer number to each rating but neglected to distinguish between ratings below 'B−'. Our scale ranges from 3 to 18: 18 corresponds to a rating of 'AAA' and 3 represents a rating of 'B' or below. In contrast to most previous work, we thus attempt to predict the bond rating over a large range of categories (16) as shown in Table 19.1.

The input data for our model consists of time-averaged financial ratios reflecting the fundamental characteristics of the firms. The data base was prepared for us by analysts at a major financial institution. Since our data set did not include all information that could possibly be related to a firm's bond rating (for instance, all fundamental or technical quantitative factors, qualitative information such as quality of management, or other subjective or irrational factors intrinsic to the S&P rating process), we could only attempt to estimate an approximate S&P rating.

Note that our original work [UtaMoo91, MooUta92] used a scale from 3 to 19 with an additional non-standard rating 'AAA−'. The inclusion of 'AAA−' was suggested by the Wall Street firm which provided the data, but our prediction performance improved when we removed it for the results presented here.

A Linear Bond Rating Predictor

For comparison with the neural network models, we computed a standard linear regression model. All input variables were used to predict the rating (which is scaled to fall in the interval [0,1]). The rating varies continuously from one category to the next. This 'smoothness' is captured in the single output representation and should make the task easier. To interpret the model's response, the output was rescaled from [0,1] to [3,18] and rounded to the nearest integer. The input variables were normalised to the interval [0,1] since original financial ratios differed widely in magnitude. Table 19.2 summarises the results obtained with the linear regression model. The model predicted the rating of 21.4% of the firms correctly, for 37.2% of firms the error was one notch, and for 21.9% two notches (thus predicting 80.5% of the data within two notches from the correct target). The RMS training error was 1.93 and the estimate of the prediction risk was 2.038.

Table 19.2 Results for the linear regression model using all input variables. The top part of the table presents the predictive performance of the model by a histogram. The column labeled '$|E_{notch}|$' indicates the error in the number of rating categories (notches), while the columns labeled 'Firms', '%', and 'Cum. %' correspond to the number of firms, the percentage of firms, and the cumulative percentage of firms with a given value of $|E_{notch}|$. Various model diagnostics are indicated. The standard deviation and the mean absolute deviation are computed after rescaling the output of the network to [3,18] and rounding to the nearest integer (notch). The RMS training error is computed using the rescaled output of the network before rounding.

$|E_{notch}|$	Firms	%	Cum. %
0	42	21.4	21.4
1	73	37.2	58.6
2	43	21.9	80.5
>2	38	19.5	100.0

Number of weights	11
Standard deviation	1.165
Mean absolute deviation	1.311
Training error	1.930

Prediction by Two-Layer Perceptrons

In the following sections, we present the results obtained with the neural network predictor and the effects of the methods we used to reduce the network size and to improve the predictive ability of our model. We trained two-layer sigmoidal networks with logistic hidden units (that is, asymmetric sigmoids) and a single piecewise linear output unit.

Selecting the Number of Hidden Units

Following the heuristic search strategy outlined earlier, we initially trained fully connected networks with all ten available input variables but with the number of hidden units varying from two to a maximum of 12. Figure 19.4 shows the training error for networks of increasing size as measured by H_λ; as expected, it decreases as the number of hidden units increases (but the decrease in error is small for less than eight hidden units).

The result of the pruning procedure for hidden units is given in Figure 19.5. The results of the two estimates $\hat{P}(\lambda)$ and NCV(λ) are consistent, having a common minimum for three internal units.

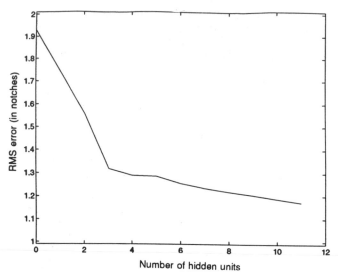

Figure 19.4 Training error versus number of hidden units H_λ ($H_\lambda = 0$ corresponds to linear regression)

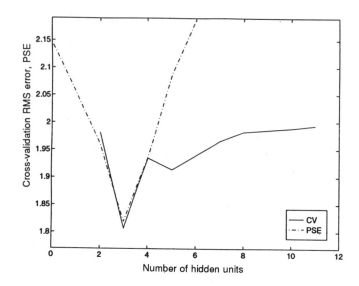

Figure 19.5 Cross-validation error $CV(\lambda)$ as computed via NCV and predicted squared error $PSE(\lambda)$ versus number of hidden units. Both have distinct minima at three hidden units. The discrepancy between $CV(\lambda)$ and $PSE(\lambda)$ for five and more units may be due to the number of model parameters $Q(\lambda)$ used in the PSE formula exceeding the *effective* number of parameters $Q_{\text{eff}}(\lambda)$ of the networks. Under this assumption, the $CV(\lambda)$ estimate is more accurate than $PSE(\lambda)$ for larger networks. An alternative to $PSE(\lambda)$ which is based on $Q_{\text{eff}}(\lambda)$ is $GPE(\lambda)$

Table 19.3 Results for the network with three hidden units. The standard deviation and the mean absolute deviation are computed after rescaling the output of the network to [3, 18] and rounding to the nearest integer (notch). The RMS training error is computed using the rescaled output of the network before rounding. The network with three hidden units significantly outperformed the linear regression model. On the right cross-validation results for the network with three hidden units are shown. In order to predict the rating for a firm, we choose among the networks trained for the cross-validation procedure the one that was not trained using the subset the firm belongs to. Thus the results concerning the predictive ability of the model reflect the expected performance of the model trained on all the data with new data in the cross-validation sense.

Training error				Cross-validation error			
$|E_{notch}|$	Firms	%	Cum. %	$|E_{notch}|$	Firms	%	Cum. %
0	68	34.7	34.7	0	58	29.6	29.6
1	87	44.4	79.1	1	78	39.8	69.4
2	31	15.8	94.9	2	33	16.8	86.2
>2	10	5.1	100.0	>2	27	13.8	100.0
Number of weights		37					37
Standard deviation		1.206					1.630
Mean absolute deviation		0.898					1.148
Training error		1.320		Cross-validation error			1.807

Table 19.3 (left four columns) shows the results for the network trained on the entire data set. A more accurate description of the performance of the model is shown in Table 19.3 (right), where the predictive ability is calculated from the hold-out sets of the nonlinear cross-validation procedure.

Pruning of Input Variables via Sensitivity Analysis

Next, we attempted further to reduce the number of weights of the network by eliminating some of the input variables. To test which inputs are most significant for determining the network output, we performed a sensitivity analysis. For each input we computed the sensitivity by eliminating each input variable in turn. Inputs were ranked in increasing order of sensitivity. $I_\lambda - 1$ candidate models are obtained by progressively removing an increasing number of inputs from the original model according to the ranking.

After an input has been removed, the network is retrained using the remaining inputs only. Then the inputs are ranked again, and another input variable is selected for removal. For our simulations we used a simplified procedure where the input variables are ranked only once using the initial model with all inputs. This assumes that the effect on the training error of those inputs that will be discarded is small, and that therefore the rank order of those inputs will not be changed using the heuristic. When compared to the ranking obtained by retraining the network after removing an input, we found this to be the case for the problem studied here. However, since the network should be retrained in any case after removing an input variable, the speed-up of using this simplification is small, and the assumptions made might not hold in general.

Again, we use 5-fold nonlinear cross-validation and $\hat{P}$ to estimate the prediction risk $P(\lambda)$. Figure 19.6 shows the results. A minimum was attained for the model with eight input variables (two inputs were removed). This reduces the number of weights by six. Table 19.4 shows the performance of this network. The cross-validation error as well as the standard and mean absolute deviation have decreased and the predictive ability of the model has improved when compared to the network using all input variables (Table 19.3).

Weight Pruning via 'Optimal Brain Damage'

In parallel with the input elimination, the effect of removing individual weights was studied (see Figure 19.1(a)). As with the sensitivity analysis, we remove an increasing number of weights from the network to obtain the candidate models for this step. NCV and $\hat{P}$ were computed to select the optimal model. We found that both are minimised when nine weights are deleted from the network using all input variables (see Figure 19.7 and Table 19.4).

Combining both Methods

The sensitivity analysis and the weight removal both started from a fully connected network with all inputs. Comparing the results obtained using each method separately, we find that some overlap exists. Five of the weights removed using OBD

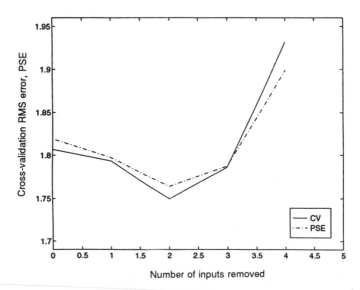

Figure 19.6 Cross validation error $CV(\lambda)$ as computed via NCV and $\hat{P}(\lambda)$ for the sensitivity analysis

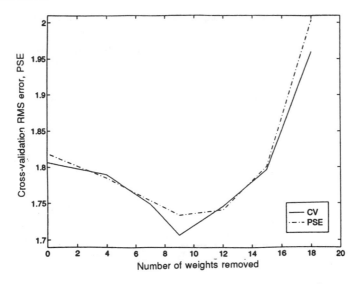

Figure 19.7 Cross-validation error $CV(\lambda)$ as computed via NCV and $\hat{P}(\lambda)$ for 'optimal brain damage'

Table 19.4 Left four columns: cross-validation results for the network with three hidden units with two inputs removed. Right: cross-validation results for the network with three hidden units with nine connections removed. Note that although the cross-validation error for the network with nine weights removed is lower than that for the network with two inputs removed, the cross-validated classification performance (measured in notches) is actually slightly higher. This is an artefact of our treating the bond rating problem as a regression rather than a classification problem.

$|E_{notch}|$	Firms	%	Cum. %	$|E_{notch}|$	Firms	%	Cum. %
0	63	32.1	32.1	0	59	30.1	30.1
1	79	40.3	72.4	1	78	39.8	69.9
2	30	15.3	87.7	2	36	18.4	88.3
>2	24	12.3	100.0	>2	23	11.7	100.0
Number of weights		31				28	
Standard deviation		1.605				1.539	
Mean absolute deviation		1.129				1.111	
Cross-validation error		1.750				1.707	

would also have been removed by the sensitivity method. Three weights were additionally removed and the methods differed with respect to one weight that OBD would not remove. This weight connects an input unit to a hidden unit, and the sensitivity analysis resulted in the removal of this input. Weight removal alone would keep the input variable, because one weight from this input unit remains.

We obtained our final model by combining both methods and removing weights from the network that either method (but not necessarily both) would remove.

Except for one weight as mentioned above, this model corresponds to the one obtained from the weight removal method alone. However, in general we expect the two methods to complement each other, with the sensitivity analysis used first to remove groups of weights by removing inputs and the weight removal used afterwards to delete individual weights. Since OBD is more expensive to compute than sensitivity analysis (since the network in general has fewer inputs than weights), our results suggest that one apply weight removal to the best model selected by the sensitivity analysis (as in Figure 19.1(b)).

Table 19.5 shows the overall performance of our model when the two techniques were combined to yield the final architecture. Note the improvement in estimated prediction performance (CV error) in Table 19.5 relative to Table 19.3.

Table 19.5 Results for the final network with three hidden units, two inputs and nine weights removed, with both sensitivity analysis and OBD applied. Note the improvement in *CV* error performance relative to Table 19.3.

$|E_{notch}|$	Firms	%	Cum. %	$|E_{notch}|$	Firms	%	Cum. %
0	71	36.2	36.2	0	60	30.6	30.6
1	83	42.3	78.5	1	78	39.8	70.4
2	29	14.8	93.3	2	34	17.3	87.7
>2	13	6.7	100.0	>2	24	12.3	100.0
Number of weights		27					27
Standard deviation		1.208					1.546
Mean absolute deviation		0.882					1.117
Training error		1.356	Cross-validation error				1.697

The error bars in Figure 19.8 suggest that with the available data the model cannot reliably distinguish the rating categories. We tested the model using fewer categories. For a five-class model, the sub-categories '+' and '−' are dropped and 'AAA' is combined with the 'AA' category. The categories for the three-class model are 'B−'–'BB+' (low grade), 'BBB−'–'A+' (medium grade), and 'AA−'–'AAA' (high grade). Table 19.6 shows the classification results.

Table 19.6 Cross-validation performance for the final model when only five (left) or three (right) distinct classes are considered. For the five-class model, the sub-categories '+' and '−' are dropped and 'AAA' is combined with the 'AA' categories. The categories for the three-class model are [B−, BB+] (low grade or 'junk'), [BBB−, A+] (medium grade), and [AA−, AAA] (high grade).

Five Classes				Three Classes			
$|E_{class}|$	Firms	%	Cum. %	$|E_{class}|$	Firms	%	Cum. %
0	125	63.8	63.8	0	167	85.2	85.2
1	65	33.2	97.0	1	29	14.8	100.0
2	6	3.0	100.0	2	0	0.0	100.0
>2	0	0.0	100.0	>2	0	0.0	100.0

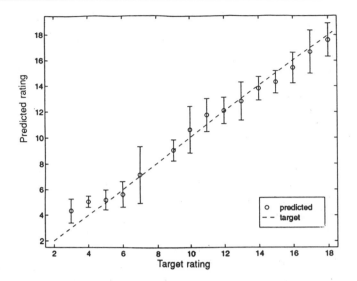

Figure 19.8 Predicted rating versus target rating for the final model (trained on all data). The error bars show the standard deviation

FINAL WORDS

At a very basic level, our bond rating study has shown that nonlinear networks can outperform a linear regression model on an interesting financial application (see Table 19.7). More interestingly for us, however, our bond rating results have demonstrated that substantial benefits in performance can be obtained by the use of the principal architecture selection methods we have proposed. Specific conclusions supported by our empirical results include the following:

- Architecture selection via heuristic search is effective and computationally feasible.
- Sequential network construction offers an efficient means for selecting the number of hidden units.
- Sensitivity-based pruning of inputs and weight elimination via optimal brain damage are effective at reducing network complexity.
- Predicted squared error and our nonlinear refinement of cross-validation enable the estimation of the prediction risk at specific local minima.
- PSE and NCV are effective selection criteria for guiding the heuristic search.

While we have formally tested these conclusions only on the bond rating example, the results presented here suggest that our approach merits consideration for other application problems.

Table 19.7 Comparison between the linear regression model and the best neural network model.

	Linear model	Best network
Number of parameters	11	27
Prediction RMSE	2.06	1.70
Training RMSE	1.93	1:36
Standard deviation	1.66	1.21
Mean absolute deviation	1.31	0.89

We wish to emphasise that the heuristic search procedures which we have presented here are not intended to be rigid, but are rather suggestive of a general approach to architecture selection. Furthermore, many other authors have proposed a variety of network construction and pruning strategies, and we are not claiming that our approach is necessarily unique or optimal. For example, SNC, SBP and OBD could each be replaced by other network construction or pruning algorithms, and PSE and NCV could be replaced by other estimates of prediction risk or other model selection criteria. (We have not attempted a complete review of the literature in this rather broad area. However, see Chapter 3 on other pruning methods.)

Finally, the model developed here for rating bonds should not be interpreted as a complete production model, since a number of aspects of the problem were not represented by the available input variables. However, the problem has proven very attractive as a case study of architecture selection procedures, since it is characterised by the limited availability of data and the lack of complete *a priori* information that could be used to impose a structure on the network architecture.

A more complete description of the methodology used in this chapter can be found in [Moody94b].

ACKNOWLEDGEMENTS

We thank Richard Timbrell for suggesting the bond rating problem, for providing the data, and for his expert advice. We thank Apostolos-Paul Refenes for inviting us to contribute this chapter to this volume and Steve Rehfuss for a careful reading of the manuscript. We gratefully acknowledge support for our recent work from ARPA under grant N00014-92-J-4062.

NOTE

1. The first author of this chapter has no known relationship to the John Moody who founded Moody's Investor Service.

20

Bond Rating with Neural Networks

J. Clay Singleton, *University of North Texas, USA* and
Alvin J. Surkan, *University of Nebraska-Lincoln, USA*

INTRODUCTION

Commercial bond rating agencies publish bond ratings to help investors assess default risk. Moody's, Standard and Poor, Fitch, Duff and Phelps, and Dun and Bradstreet earn fees for evaluating the creditworthiness of entities that issue new bonds. These agencies also rerate existing bonds when they detect changes in the credit quality of the issuing companies. Market yields correspond to bond ratings, indicating an association between rating and risk. Furthermore, regulators commonly accept bond ratings as indicative of suitability for institutional holdings. Consequently, the study of the rating process is of interest to bond issuers, investors and regulators.

Neural networks are commonly used to recognise complex patterns in deterministic variables. The search algorithm implicit in training and optimising neural networks makes them ideal for many of these applications. Before neural networks are generally applied to bond ratings, however, there should be both reason to believe the approach should be suitable and some evidence that it is at least as effective as other techniques.

Applying neural networks to bond ratings requires more justification than for the more common pattern recognition because ratings are the combination of analysts' judgement and the financial condition of bond issuers. While neural networks are often introduced as being somewhat analogous to a simple model of biological nervous systems, expanding the metaphor to claim the technique can mimic

Neural Networks in the Capital Markets. Edited by Apostolos-Paul Refenes.

inductive reasoning is a significant step beyond decoding or recognising patterns. No one would suggest that neural networks are nearly as sophisticated as complex neurological systems. However, neural networks may be successful in capturing disciplined expert reasoning in a highly structured problem such as bond ratings.

Moody's and Standard and Poor have publicly announced that their analysts consider leverage, coverage and profitability as prime determinants of bond quality. They also claim that statistical analysis lacks the sophistication necessary to model the expert judgement required by the bond rating process. If these claims are true, bond rating provides a suitable test case for the simulation of expert judgement by neural networks.

Bond ratings are not a perfect application, however, because ratings are sometimes ambiguous. Bond rating agencies rerate bonds in response to changes in capital structure, management or market conditions. Changes in ratings suggest that bond ratings are not based on absolute values but rather reflect a range of acceptable conditions within each rating category. When companies are close to the boundary of their assigned class, training sets will contain ambiguities or errors which make model development difficult. Repeated experiments will be necessary before preliminary conclusions can be drawn about the suitability of neural networks to the bond rating problem.

Assuming that the neural network metaphor can be applied to bond rating, their effectiveness still needs to be demonstrated. Even if neural networks could mimic analysts' judgements, simpler techniques have successfully classified bonds. The most common means for classifying bonds into their rating categories is multiple discriminant analysis (MDA). MDA is often applied in the finance literature to develop classification models and determine which variables contribute most to the classification. At present, neural networks do not give the same kind of information about the relative importance of the variables. If classification alone is the goal, however, the empirical evidence suggests that neural networks can be a superior tool. However, each application determines whether the complexity of the neural network model justifies the added computational expense.

PREVIOUS STUDIES

Dutta and Shekhar [DutShe88] were the first to investigate the ability of neural networks to classify bonds. They developed both multiple regression models and neural networks to detect AA bonds (as rated by Standard and Poor) from a set of AA and non-AA rated bonds. They used both ten- and six-variable models developed by Horrigan [Horrig66] and Pinches and Mingo [PinMin77]. These variables were: liabilities/(cash + assets), debt proportion, sales/net worth, profit/sales, financial strength, earnings/fixed costs, past five-year revenue growth rate, projected next five-year revenue growth rate, working capital/sales and the subjective prospect of the company. The authors selected 47 bonds at random. They used 30 patterns for training and 17 for testing. They did not report using a filter to improve sample homogeneity other than selecting bonds with approximately the same maturity (13-18 years). Experience from previous bond rating studies with linear statistical models suggests that both regression models and neural networks might have performed better had the sample been restricted to bonds from homogeneous industries. Although the authors do not report the range of bond ratings in their sample, previous research also suggests that the further apart or distinct the bond ratings are, the more successful classification results from both models will be. Nevertheless, the regression correctly classified 64.7% of the bonds in the test set as AA. This success rate is typical of most linear statistical bond rating models. Under several different architectures studied, neural networks were more successful, classifying between 76.5% and 88.3% of the test set correctly. While the authors did not address whether neural networks replicated expert judgement, they did differentiate between recognition (pattern) and generalisation (induction) problems. The authors concluded that in 'generalization problems (like rating bonds) ... neural networks perform much better than classical mathematical modeling techniques such as regression' [Deutsch88, p. 450]. While this statement may have been a bit premature, Dutta and Shekhar were the pioneers in applying neural networks to bond ratings.

Singleton and Surkan [SinSur91] also studied the bond rating abilities of neural networks and linear models. In their study Singleton and Surkan extended earlier research by Peavy and Scott [PeaSco86] which used MDA to investigate the ratings of the Bell Telephone companies divested by American Telephone and Telegraph (AT&T) in 1982. The Peavy and Scott study was selected because it had achieved the highest classification accuracy of published linear statistical models. Following Peavy and Scott, Singleton and Surkan used 18 companies and seven financial variables. The variables were: debt/total capital, pre-tax interest/income, income/shareholders' equity (ROE), coefficient of variation of ROE over past five years, logarithm of total assets, construction costs/total cash flow and local toll revenue/long distance toll revenue. With only one year of data and a limited number of companies, Peavy and Scott could use only two variables to construct their models.

Singleton and Surkan compared Peavy and Scott's MDA model with a neural network. Because so few observations were available, the neural network was repeatedly trained on $n - 1$ observations and used to classify the complementary test sets of single patterns. Using this procedure the neural network classified 17 out of 19 bonds correctly (89.5%) for Standard and Poor's ratings and 11 out of 18 correctly (61.1%) for Moody's ratings. Peavy and Scott's model classified 16 out of 19 (84.2%) for Standard and Poor's and 10 out of 18 (55.6%) for Moody's.

Singleton and Surkan then collected data for the same companies from 1982 to 1988. With more data, Singleton and Surkan used both two- and seven-variable models with two rating classes (AAA and AA for Standard and Poor's and Aaa and A for Moody's). They also used MDA as their linear statistical model. Their neural network was trained over a test set of ten bonds from each rating class in stages to ensure the network represented the different output classes. Their neural network correctly classified 73% of the bonds into their Standard and Poor's ratings (versus 40% for MDA) and 97% of the Moody's ratings (versus 39% for MDA).

Singleton and Surkan's neural networks appear to be more successful than Dutta and Shekhar's in classifying bonds. However, several differences between the two studies should be noted. Singleton and Surkan's sample was more homogeneous than Dutta and Shekhar's as all the firms were part of AT&T before divestiture. This homogeneity would have introduced less noise into the training set and could account for the neural network attaining better classification of the test set. The Singleton and Surkan neural networks also appear to outperform the linear models by a wider margin than in the Dutta and Shekhar study. Singleton and Surkan had a larger test set for their linear analysis. They also used cross-validation (jackknifing) rather than Dutta and Shekhar's hold-out sample approach to compute the linear classification results. However, Singleton and Surkan's classification accuracy was lower than those typically reported for linear models and the contrast between the two studies is somewhat illusory. Dutta and Shekhar's results are supported and strengthened by the Singleton and Surkan study.

When Singleton and Surkan extended their rating classes to the agencies' sub-classifications, their neural network model did not converge. These results leave open the question of whether a neural network model can detect the differences between adjacent bond rating classes. They also suggest that there is a minimum size for the sub-populations necessary to adequately represent sub-classes.

Adjoining or boundary bond rating classes are a problem for techniques that rely on a training set with potential misclassifications. While accommodating errors in the test set is one of neural network's distinct advantages, errors in the training set can seriously retard or even misdirect training especially when the number of training patterns is small (see [SinSur90] for more discussion of this point). Bond ratings change as conditions change. All the bonds in a sample might be in a border zone between adjacent classes. The next section considers the ability of neural networks to forecast changes in bond ratings. This ability is at least as important to investors as replicating a stationary rating.

BOND RATING CHANGES

Bond rating agencies often revise existing bond ratings when the company issues new bonds or when its creditworthiness changes. Bond investors and corporate financial managers are concerned about rating changes. Reclassification usually affects the firm's interest rate and stock price [PinSin78] as well as the bond's price [GriKat76].

In 1988 Moody's upgraded 12 and downgraded 22 investment-quality (Baa or better) bonds from companies which did not issue new debt in 1988. Financial data were collected from year-end 1987 accounting reports. Each of these bonds was then paired with another firm with the same four-digit SIC code and calendar year-end but which did not have its debt rerated. The bond pairs were divided into training and test sets (six upgraded and 11 downgraded pairs for a total of 34 bonds per set). To provide some measure of generalisation, the roles of the training and test sets were then reversed.

MDA was applied to both sets. Peavy's [Peavy84] six-variable model was used; involving total assets; long-term capital turnover; return on investment; financial leverage; earnings stability; and earnings coverage. The differences between these variables and Peavy and Scott's choices reflect the larger, more heterogeneous sample in the Peavy study. Peavy's research derived rating change forecasts by comparing the MDA predictions for two adjacent years. Different predictions were interpreted as forecasts of rating changes. In this study, actual rating changes that post-dated the data were used. A linear rather than quadratic classification rule was applied based on tests of the sample. Tables 20.1 and 20.2 show the results of the MDA model from two perspectives: estimation on the training set and classification of the test set, and with the role of the sets reversed. The overall forecast accuracy of Peavy's model applied to this data (57% correct) is similar to that of the original study of about 55% correct. The similarity between the two panels indicates that the model is robust for the entire data set.

Two neural networks were developed — one for the training set and one for the test set. The network had six elements in the input layer and three in the output layer. The hidden layer contained five elements. Experiments varying the length of the hidden layer between three and ten elements did not change the classification ability of the network. The network algorithm employed a standard backpropagation approach with a sigmoid transfer function.

The classification results are shown in Tables 20.3 and 20.4. The neural network correctly predicted bond rating changes in both the test and training sets in 73%

Table 20.1 Discriminant classification results: function estimated over training set and applied to test set.

from	Down	Up	No change	% correct	Total
Down	7	1	3	63	11
Up	2	4	0	67	6
No change	5	4	8	47	17

Table 20.2 Discriminant classification results: function estimated over test set and applied to training set.

from	Down	Up	No change	% correct	Total
Down	8	1	2	72	11
Up	1	4	1	67	6
No change	5	4	8	47	17

Table 20.3   Neural network classification results: network trained on training set and applied to test set.

from	Down	Up	No change	% Correct	Total
Down	10	0	1	90	11
Up	1	5	0	83	6
No change	6	1	10	58	17

Table 20.4   Neural network classification results: network trained on test set and applied to training set.

from	Down	Up	No change	% Correct	Total
Down	9	0	2	81	11
Up	0	4	2	67	6
No change	5	0	12	71	17

of the 68 cases. Peavy's model identified only 57% correctly. The neural network also misclassified only one bond (in the test set) as a downgrade when in fact it was an upgrade. The Peavy model misclassified two downgrades as upgrades and three upgrades as downgrades. The network also did better in identifying bonds without rating changes but these bonds proved difficult for both models to classify.

Neural networks were better in this instance of predicting which bonds would be reclassified. While further research is needed to improve the neural network's ability correctly to resolve rating differences between adjacent rating classes, these results are encouraging.

DRAWBACKS TO NEURAL NETWORKS IN THE CAPITAL MARKETS

One major difficulty with neural networks is the lack of replicability. Scientific inquiry has always insisted that experiments be replicated before their results are accepted. Unfortunately, neural networks are not easy to duplicate. Different random sequences in the initial values of the weight matrices will produce networks with comparable performance but different results. The transfer or threshold function will affect the outcome, as will the learning algorithm. Unless every element is identical, each neural network is unique and there is no guarantee that another researcher would attain the same results with the same input data. Unfortunately, neural networks offered commercially as tools for investment decision-making cannot be independently validated. Until more advanced techniques are available, the best way to establish the ability of neural networks to solve any problem is by repeated independent experiment.

CONCLUSION

Neural networks have demonstrated that they can recognise patterns in complex economic series. This chapter has reviewed a few applications to expert analysts' judgements about credit quality. Neural networks' success in classifying bonds and predicting reclassifications based only on financial information suggests that neural networks may have captured some of the judgement exercised by these analysts.

PART FIVE
MACROECONOMIC AND CORPORATE PERFORMANCE

21

Bankruptcy Prediction: A Comparison with Discriminant Analysis

Thorsen Poddig, *Universität Bamberg, Germany*

INTRODUCTION

Financial statement analysis is necessary for various purposes. One of the most important purposes is to analyse the sources and the potential of corporate success. For many practical purposes, a simple discrimination of successful and non-successful firms is sufficient. Probably the most important example for such a simple discrimination is credit rating. Every bank has to carry out a careful examination of any firm before giving credit to it. But this can be generalised further. Any investor should perform such a careful examination in order to avoid poor returns on invested capital or — even worse — capital losses. The most severe kind of non-success is the bankruptcy of the firm, and it is necessary to predict this event in advance.

There is a quite long history in financial statement analysis of the application of more objective methods such as discriminant analysis in the effort to overcome the problems mentioned above. Although a lot of research has been done in this area, the rates of incorrect classification are still often at a high level. Thus the practical use of such methods has been controversial.

Since their first applications to financial analysis, neural networks have shown very promising results. So there is reason to hope that they will perform better on this task than the multivariate statistical methods which are traditionally used here. As mentioned above, powerful prediction capability in this area not only helps the

Neural Networks in the Capital Markets. Edited by Apostolos-Paul Refenes.
© 1995 John Wiley & Sons Ltd

investor to avoid capital losses. Neural networks could signal to the managers of the firm that there is danger of bankruptcy and that action to rescue the firm is necessary. This in turn may prevent more unemployment and hence may help the economy as a whole.

In this chapter, we take a brief look at recent applications of neural networks to bankruptcy prediction and compare them with discriminant analysis which can be viewed as the most advanced application in this area to date. We start with some brief historical remarks which reflect the application of quantitative analysis to bankruptcy prediction. Then we briefly examine previous and parallel studies where the application of neural networks and discriminant analysis is compared. The major concern of this chapter is to present our own study as an example. Here, two types of neural network (multi-layer perceptron and learning vector quantiser) were used and compared to the application of factor and discriminant analysis. From the results presented in the literature and in our own study, one can conclude that neural networks may become the successor of discriminant analysis in this area, but there are still some open questions which need further research.

A BRIEF HISTORICAL REVIEW AND OTHER STUDIES

The first comparison of discriminant analysis with neural networks in this area was presented by [OdoSha90]. They took a sample of 65 firms which went bankrupt between 1975 and 1982, and 64 non-bankrupt firms matched on industry and year. The sample was divided into a training sample (38 bankrupt firms and 36 non-bankrupt firms) and a hold-out sample (27 bankrupt firms and 28 non-bankrupt firms). Five financial ratios were computed from the last financial statement issued before the firms declared bankruptcy. In this study, the multi-layer perceptron proved to be superior. It correctly classified 81.81% of the hold-out sample while multiple discriminant analysis only achieved 74.28%.

There are some problems concerning this first comparison. The number of cases is obviously very small, so that the results presented may vary considerably with a larger sample size. In addition, the five financial ratios were selected in advance according to the study by Altman. So neither discriminant analysis nor the multi-layer perceptron could select the most significant financial ratios from a larger pool. It is not possible to judge which method was advantaged by this preselection, but the comparison is biased anyway. Therefore, the results presented may only provide weak evidence for better performance by the multi-layer perceptron.

A very interesting study was presented by [ErxKoc91] and [Erxleb92]. Here, an extraordinarily large data base was used. The training sample consisted of 112 firms in each group. The available financial statements covered the period from one to three years before the firms declared bankruptcy. Seventy-two financial ratios were computed from the financial statements. Thus there were a total of $2 \times 112 \times 3 = 672$ data records. The hold-out sample contained 2020 data records of non-bankrupt firms and 847 data records of bankrupt firms from different

Table 21.1 Rates of incorrect classification for several years before bankruptcy.

Years before bankruptcy	Multi-layer perceptron	Discriminant analysis
1	20.89%	20.04%
2	21.64%	20.37%
3	27.09%	21.12%

periods before bankruptcy. Of the latter, 172 data records concerned firms one year before bankruptcy, 312 data records concerned firms two years before bankruptcy, 222 data records concerned firms three years before bankruptcy, and 141 data records concerned firms four or five years before bankruptcy. Table 21.1 shows the (unweighted) rate of incorrect classifications for several periods before bankruptcy in the hold-out sample. It provides weak evidence that the discriminant analysis is superior. Later, [Erxleb92] modified the comparison slightly because the results presented in Table 21.1 were not entirely comparable. Now, there was no difference between the multi-layer perceptron and discriminant analysis.

The major problem concerning this study was the selection of the financial ratios again. Due to computational limitations and hardware problems, factor and discriminant analysis were first used to determine the four most relevant financial ratios. These four financial ratios which proved to be best for discriminant analysis were then used as input for the multi-layer perceptron. Given the problems they had, this approach was reasonable. But from the viewpoint of a fair comparison, this study again has to be viewed as biased.

The study was continued by [Krause93]. He tried to construct a fairer comparison where the multi-layer perceptron was not forced to use the same financial ratios. In addition, the application of counter-propagation networks was tested. He now obtained better results for both types of neural network than for discriminant analysis. The counter-propagation network showed the best performance. A lot of work was done here and the development of the study by systematic variations in network parameters can be viewed as very time-consuming. The extraordinarily large data base (526 data records for bankrupt firms and 5340 data records for non-bankrupt firms in the hold-out sample) allows to view the superiority of neural networks as valid. But there are still some problems left. This study did not use modern procedures for the development of optimal networks. In particular, the comparison of the multi-layer perceptron with counter-propagation networks may be biased because of the lack of modern methods.

There are other studies in this area [BeRiVe90, TamKia90] which cannot be looked at in detail here. Nevertheless, these brief historical remarks on previous and parallel studies illustrate the development in this area. We will now turn to our study as an example where modern methods for the development of optimal networks were used for a comparison of discriminant analysis with neural networks in this area.

BANKRUPTCY PREDICTION USING DISCRIMINANT ANALYSIS AND NEURAL NETWORKS

The Data Base

The following study [RehPod92] was carried out in co-operation with a German bank. The main purpose of this ongoing study was a comparison of discriminant analysis with neural networks. The results were intended to serve the French office of the bank. So the financial statements of 150 French firms which went bankrupt were collected from publicly available sources. They covered the periods from one until three years before the firms declared bankruptcy. An equal number of financial statements from 150 non-bankrupt firms were chosen randomly from the same periods. The firms had a turnover of more than FF 30 millions.

The financial statements were collected by the bank and transformed into a record of 45 financial ratios which were commonly used by that bank and had proved to be useful in previous studies. Due to the source of information, the raw data showed numerous missing values and could not be viewed as very reliable. At this early stage of the study it became obvious that we had to deal with quite noisy data.

The total sample was partitioned by the bank, which we accepted in order to compare classification results between them and us. One hundred firms of each group were used for training, while the remaining 50 firms of each group served as a hold-out sample. So the training sample contained $2 \times 100 \times 3 = 600$ data records, the hold-out sample $2 \times 50 \times 3 = 300$ data records.

The Benchmark: Application of Discriminant Analysis

As mentioned above, the main purpose of this study was to compare discriminant analysis, which can be regarded as the standard tool in this area, with neural networks. So the results of the discriminant analysis served as a benchmark for the whole project. While there is a long tradition in the application of discriminant analysis in this area, it is necessary to mention that there are still several approaches possible. The first benchmark was obtained from the bank, which used a combination of factor and stepwise discriminant analysis to determine the most relevant financial ratios and to compute the discriminant function. This analysis only used the data from three years before the firms declared bankruptcy. The main assumption behind this approach is that the discrimination between bankrupt and non-bankrupt firms becomes easier as the event of bankruptcy approaches. Therefore, a suitable discriminant function should be computed from data which are furthest away in time from the event of bankruptcy. The resulting discriminant function contained only three financial ratios and achieved the rates of correct classification shown in Table 21.2.

Table 21.2 does not discriminate between two types of error. The first type of error (α error) occurs when a bankrupt firm is classified as non-bankrupt.

Table 21.2 Benchmark 1.

Years before bankruptcy	Training sample	Hold-out sample
3	70.5%	78.0%
2	78.0%	81.0%
1	83.0%	86.0%
Average	77.2%	81.7%

Table 21.3 Benchmark 2.

Years before bankruptcy	Training sample	Hold-out sample
3	68.5%	80.0%
2	81.0%	88.0%
1	84.0%	90.0%
Average	77.8%	86.0%

Correspondingly, the second type of error (β error) occurs when a non-bankrupt firm is classified as bankrupt in the future. There is a deep discussion in literature on how to treat these types of errors. On the one hand, α error is more severe because significant capital losses may follow. On the other hand, a β error causes only opportunity costs (because of the credit denied or retracted), but the *a priori* probability of the occurrence of non-bankrupt firms is much higher than that of bankrupt firms. In general, it is impossible to calculate the net effect because it also depends on the kind of investor. For example, the two types of cost might be quite different for a loan bank than for an insurance company where the credit risk can be insured. Therefore, many researchers treat both types of error as equal for convenience; this was also done in this study. Due to the different types of error, they are usually reported separately. In the following study, the two types of error were almost always well balanced, so that we suppress a more detailed report for convenience' sake. In the following, we still report only total rates of correct classification. This was also the objective of our co-operation where only total classification rates were measured in order to keep all different approaches comparable.

The approach of the bank had a severe disadvantage because only a part of the available training data was used to compute the discriminant function. So we used a combination of factor and stepwise discriminant analysis on the whole training sample to obtain a second benchmark. Here, there were still only three financial ratios in the discriminant function. We obtained the results shown in Table 21.3.

Surprisingly, both benchmarks showed a better performance in the hold-out sample than in the training sample, which is due to the random partition. In addition, the classification rates did not appear to be homogeneous regarding the results in the training and hold-out sample. Therefore, one might think about a new partition of the total sample. But for this project, we accepted the original partition done by the bank. So the main purpose was now to see whether neural networks could reach the high rates of correct classification in the hold-out sample and whether they were able to produce more homogeneous results.

The Application of the Multi-layer Perceptron

Two types of neural network were used during this project. Like most applications of neural networks to financial analysis, we used a multi-layer perceptron (also called a 'backpropagation network'; see Part I of this volume). The second type was an extended variant of the learning vector quantiser which we will treat in the following section. One of the most important advantages of the multi-layer perceptron is the long experience with this type of neural network. Many powerful techniques concerning this type of neural network have been developed which we will review only briefly.

Probably the most relevant task in the application of neural networks to certain problems in financial analysis is the development of the 'optimal' network. This covers three important sub-tasks: identification of the most relevant inputs; identification of the necessary number of weights; and identification of the necessary number of hidden units. These sub-tasks are accomplished by weight-pruning techniques, which are treated in detail elsewhere in this book. The general idea behind these techniques can be described as follows. One starts with an oversized network where weights and units are pruned by several methods during training until overfitting can no longer be observed. Well-known techniques are reviewed in Chapter 3 and include stopped training [Weigen90], weight cost [WeHuRu91] and weight decay [HanPra89]. A newer technique is used in conjunction with stopped training and based on the calculation of statistical test values for each living and dead weight in a multi-layer perceptron [FinZim91, HeFiZi92] studied these techniques on various nonlinear problems with noisy data and small data sets, which reflect the circumstances in financial analysis. Although all techniques proved to be useful in dealing with this problem, statistical weight tests showed the best results.

The papers on statistical weight tests were published when a part of this project had already been done using the older techniques. Then we implemented the statistical weight test method and the whole study up to this point was redone. In the following, we have to distinguish between an early and an advanced state of the project where different types of technique were applied. Thus, we can also present a comparison of different weight-pruning techniques on a real problem in financial analysis. Not surprisingly, our results mostly reflect the insights already presented by Hergert *et al.* [HeFiZi92].

The main approach in the early state of this project is illustrated in Figure 21.1.

The major element of this development procedure is the systematic search in the weight space which is performed by a downhill simplex preoptimisation procedure and the training of several networks based on conjugate gradient descent procedures [Poddig92]. Here, weight cost and weight decay were applied. The development procedure could be significantly simplified when using statistical weight tests in

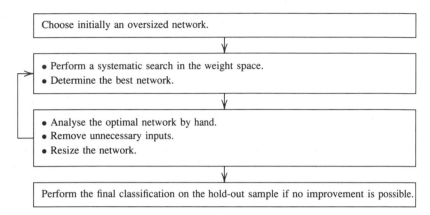

Figure 21.1   The development procedure using weight cost and weight decay

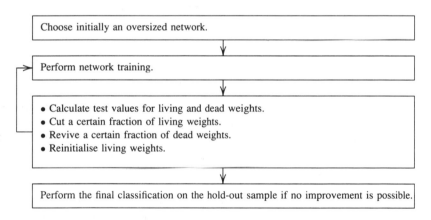

Figure 21.2   The development procedure using statistical weight tests

the advanced state of our project (see Figure 21.2). Here, the major element is the automatic pruning procedure which we call *auto-pruning*.

Another important question for both development procedures is when to stop the development and perform the final test on the hold-out sample. For the first development procedure in the early state of our project we always used the smallest network before the rates of correct classification in the training sample showed a significant decrease. The application of statistical weight tests is a little more complicated concerning this question. This procedure requires a permanent cross-validation in order to obtain an optimal stop-point of the network training so that reliable test values can be calculated. The optimal network was thus that which showed the highest number of correct classifications in the cross-validation sample.

When using this technique, the hold-out sample should not be used as cross-validation sample also although the cross-validation sample is only used to determine the optimal stop-point of the training procedure. The hold-out sample serves to simulate classification of unknown cases. Therefore, one should treat the hold-out sample as not available until the final test has to be done. So we further divided the original training sample (600 data records) randomly into a new training sample (510 data records) and a cross-validation sample (90 data records).

The data were used in three different ways. First, we used the original financial ratios without any preprocessing. Obviously, this may cause problems because the ratios have very different means and standard deviations. Therefore, a simple standardisation procedure was used as one kind of data preprocessing. It was always used in conjunction with a nonlinear transformation in order to weaken the impact from outlying data:

$$x_1 = \frac{x - \mu_x}{\sigma_x} \tag{20.1}$$

$$x_2 = \frac{1}{1 + e^{-x_1}} \tag{20.2}$$

Further data preprocessing was done by simply rescaling each financial ratio onto a unique interval:

$$x_1 = \frac{x - \min_x}{\max_x - \min_x} \tag{20.3}$$

The mean, standard deviation, maximum and minimum were computed only from the training sample for each financial ratio.

In the early stages of our project, the best results were obtained using the weight cost method and standardisation in conjunction with the nonlinear transformation of the input data. Table 21.4 shows the results obtained here.

Twelve financial ratios was used by the network. The weight decay method achieved inferior results and caused other problems so that there were no reasonable results to report. Nevertheless, the early stages of our project already showed good performance for the multi-layer perceptron in this area. The results were better and more homogeneous than the benchmarks. The main disadvantage was the time-consuming process of developing the optimal network. In addition, this process required optimisation steps to be done by hand so that the effort necessary to obtain these results was much higher than using discriminant analysis.

The first simulations using the statistical weight test procedure by [FinZim91] in conjunction with standardisation and nonlinear transformation of input data showed

Table 21.4 The best results obtained in the early stage of our project.

Years before bankruptcy	Training sample	Hold-out sample
3	83.5%	86.0%
2	85.5%	83.0%
1	91.5%	92.0%
Average	86.8%	87.0%

Table 21.5 First results obtained from using statistical weight tests.

Years before bankruptcy	Training sample	Hold-out sample
3	75.5%	82.0%
2	82.5%	88.0%
1	89.0%	89.0%
Average	82.3%	86.3%

Table 21.6 Results obtained using a logistic distance.

Years before bankruptcy	Training sample	Hold-out sample
3	76.5%	83.0%
2	82.5%	89.0%
1	86.5%	91.0%
Average	81.8%	87.7%

very promising results (Table 21.5). The results obtained were slightly better than the benchmarks, more homogeneous, and reached almost the benchmark results. But these results were obtained by an entirely automatic procedure in a fraction of the time. Several problems became clear at this stage which cannot be addressed here in detail. The most demanding problem was that the desired maximum in classification rates is reached long before the minimum error of the hold-out sample. This undesired phenomenon can be explained by the fact that the original cost function of the multi-layer perceptron is not well suited for this task. Classification rates are better related to a Hamming distance while the cost function normally used in the multi-layer perceptron is based on the Euclidean distance between target and actual network output. Therefore, it seemed necessary to apply other cost functions. Three different types of cost function were then tried [RehPod92]: the absolute distance; a kind of relative entropy; and a logistic distance measure. For example, using the logistic distance it was possible to improve classification rates without much effort (see Table 21.6).

Finally, it is necessary to point out that the statistical weight test procedure works best when the network optimisation is done by hand. In addition, the use of complementary tools such as sensitivity analysis on input data in order to determine the most relevant inputs helps considerably. So the automatic pruning procedure is helpful, but produces results which can be regarded as sub-optimal. Auto-pruning provides a reasonable base for further optimisation which then has to be done by hand. The best hand-optimised networks to date give classification rates as shown in Table 21.7.

Although the benchmarks showed very high correct classification rates in the hold-out sample, it was possible to improve the results further using a multi-layer perceptron. In addition, the results obtained from the multi-layer perceptron were more homogeneous. An important observation when comparing discriminant analysis with the multi-layer perceptron in this area is the number of financial ratios

Table 21.7 An example for results obtained from hand-optimised networks.

Years before bankruptcy	Training sample	Hold-out sample
3	81.0%	84.0%
2	85.5%	89.0%
1	91.0%	93.0%
Average	85.8%	88.7%

used. Discriminant analysis always used three financial ratios while the multi-layer perceptrons tended to use 10–13. Therefore, it seems that multi-layer perceptrons are capable of better using the information represented by the pool of 45 financial ratios.

The Learning Vector Quantiser

The second type of neural network applied was an extended version of the learning vector quantiser. Originally, in the parallel study done by Kerling [Kerlin92] it was intended to apply different variants of the *restricted coulomb energy network* (RCE) [Reilly82, ReiCoo90] and the *learning vector quantiser* (LVQ) [Kohone84]. These were first tested on several constructed problems which were supposed to reflect the problem structure of this study. Here, the RCE showed poor performance, and it seemed that there was no realistic hope of applying the RCE in this area with acceptable results. Therefore, we will confine ourselves to a brief look at the LVQ.

Nevertheless, the variant of the LVQ used (which we will call the *extended learning vector quantizer* (ELVQ)) made use of some of the ideas from the RCE. Like the RCE, our ELVQ has a variable layer of hidden units. While the network structure of the LVQ has to be determined in advance, our ELVQ can change its structure by dynamically allocating new hidden units as they are required. Again, the development of the optimal network structure proved to be the most important step. Because the neural network was of entirely different type, the development process was completely different, too. The development process for the ELVQ could be divided into two sub-tasks: input unit pruning and hidden unit generating.

In order to perform the pruning, it was first necessary to divide the training sample into a real training and a cross-validation sample. Fifteen firms from each group were randomly chosen from the original training sample to build up the cross-validation sample. By this means, the hold-out sample was reserved for the final classification test only and was not used in any other way. The input pruning procedure can be illustrated as shown in Figure 21.3.

The input pruning started with a network using all 45 financial ratios. After network training, the firms in the training and cross-validation sample were classified. Then, the input units were analysed and a certain fraction of the less relevant inputs removed. The network was reinitialised and trained again. If the resulting

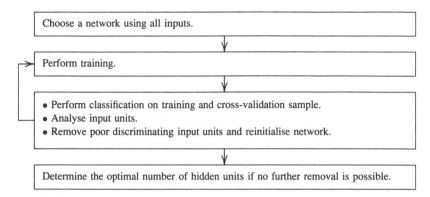

Figure 21.3   Input pruning for the ELVQ

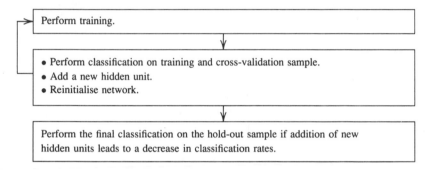

Figure 21.4   Hidden unit generation

classification showed a considerable decrease in classification rates, the previous pruning step was corrected. The input units removed were revived and other less relevant input units removed. If no further removal was possible without a considerable decrease in classification rates, the input pruning was stopped. The input units remaining were regarded as the optimum set of inputs. The next step had to determine the optimum number of hidden units. Here, a hidden unit generating procedure was used which can be illustrated as shown in Figure 21.4.

After network training, the network classified the firms in the training and cross-validation sample. Then, a new hidden unit was added, the network reinitialised and retrained. If the rates of correct classification in the cross-validation sample showed a decrease, the previous step of adding a new hidden unit was cancelled. The resulting network was now regarded as the optimum. It is necessary to point out that the LVQ had very seldom been applied to financial analysis and even now there is no comparable experience available as with the multi-layer perceptron. The ELVQ we used was a new development and its associated network development procedures can only be regarded as a first step. Therefore, results comparable with those of the multi-layer perceptron could never be expected.

Finally, we have to remark that data preprocessing is inevitable here due to the LVQ's use of Euclidean distance measure. We used the simple standardisation procedure in conjunction with the following nonlinear transformation as described in the previous section.

The development procedure finally identified only five relevant financial ratios. The optimal network achieved the rates of correct classification shown in Table 21.8. Although we did not expect to reach the high classification rates of the multi-layer perceptron, the results were disappointing. They did not reach the benchmarks and were considerably lower than the classification rates of the multi-layer perceptron. But one should not conclude from these results that the ELVQ is not suitable for such a task. There are theoretical reasons why the development procedure design presented could not work well which cannot be rehearsed in detail here. One could see, especially from the trace of the input pruning that there were problems in identifying the relevant inputs. In order to show that the development procedure caused the poor classification results, we took the financial ratios identified by factor and discriminant analysis in benchmark 2 and trained the ELVQ. The results shown in Table 21.9 were now obtained. These are nearly the same as for benchmark 2. Therefore, we think that the ELVQ is suitable for this task in principle, but we still have to work on the development procedure.

Although it might seem that the ELVQ is not of much interest, it has several advantages compared with the multi-layer perceptron. The ELVQ is much faster during training, easy to handle and simple in its structure. We still regard the ELVQ as more appealing than the multi-layer perceptron. But for practical use there is actually no doubt that the multi-layer perceptron is superior due to its powerful pruning techniques.

Table 21.8   Results for the ELVQ.

Years before bankruptcy	Training sample	Hold-out sample
1	not evaluated	70.0%
2	not evaluated	74.0%
3	not evaluated	84.0%
Average	77.9%	76.0%

Table 21.9   Results using the same financial ratios identified by discriminant analysis.

Years before bankruptcy	Training sample	Hold-out sample
1	not evaluated	80.0%
2	not evaluated	85.0%
3	not evaluated	89.0%
Average	79.4%	84.7%

CONCLUSIONS

From the results presented elsewhere in the literature and in this chapter, there is now strong evidence that neural networks are suitable for the task of bankruptcy prediction and that they are able to outperform traditional discriminant analysis in this area. But one has to look in detail. There are different types of neural network and not all of them are now able to outperform discriminant analysis. 'Neural network' is often used as a synonym for 'multi-layer perceptron' when considering applications to financial analysis. Indeed, it appears that the multi-layer perceptron might be best suited for bankruptcy prediction.

The study presented shows that the trial-and-error approach in the application of neural networks to a certain task should be history. There are now powerful development procedures which in turn significantly determine the performance of the neural network. Due to long experience with multi-layer perceptron, the most powerful network-developing procedures are available for this type of neural network. The superiority of the multi-layer perceptron in this study is due to this fact. Other types of neural network might show the same results, but as the case of the ELVQ illustrates, there is still a lot of research to do.

Obviously, a definitive judgement as to whether the multi-layer perceptron is superior to discriminant analysis in this area is not possible. The major problem here is that of collecting sufficient cases to enable valid conclusions to be drawn. Compared with other studies, the number of cases which could be used here can be viewed as extremely large. Nevertheless, the absolute number of cases still appears to be low for a definitive judgement. Only [Krause93] used sufficient cases in this sense.

Further, the results may vary significantly from country to country due to different accounting rules. While it appears that the application of the multi-layer perceptron is superior in this area for Germany and France, there may be different results for other countries. It is a challenging question to determine for which countries neural networks perform better and how this can be explained.

22

Predicting Corporate Mergers

Tarun K. Sen, *Virgina Tech, USA,* Robert Oliver,
Arthur Andersen & Co, USA and Nilanjan Sen,
Arizona State University, USA

INTRODUCTION

Mergers were extensively used in the 1980s as a strategy for corporate expansion, market stability, and in certain cases to provide windfall gains to the shareholders of acquired firms [DieSor84]. Although statistical merger prediction models seem to classify possible targets for mergers with a high degree of accuracy (ranging from 60% to 90%) [SimMon71, DieSor84, Palepu86] show that most of these studies have sampling biases. This bias occurs due to the manner in which the hold-out sample is selected in order to test the predictive ability of the model. Most studies use a random sample of target and non-target firms in which the number of non-target firms selected is far less than the number of non-target firms that exist in reality. Correcting for this bias, [Palepu86] shows that logistic regression is capable of predicting only about 45% of the targets and non-targets in a hold-out sample. Thus, any abnormal returns cannot be expected using logistic regression.

Our objective in this chapter is to compare the predictive and explanatory capabilities of neural networks and logistic regression. Tam and Kiang [TamKia90] observe that neural networks outperform logistic regression in a bankruptcy prediction task. Our results indicate that with data that is very noisy, neural networks model the data better than logistic regression. However, when the model is used

Neural Networks in the Capital Markets. Edited by Apostolos-Paul Refenes.
© 1995 John Wiley & Sons Ltd

to predict mergers based on a hold-out sample, neither model predicts very well. This is possibly due to the complexity involved in merger predictions.

One of the common criticisms aimed at neural networks is that their predictive behaviour cannot be explained — we cannot say which predictor variables, or combinations thereof, have a greater impact on the outcome. This is purported to be one of the advantages of statistical models. In this study we demonstrate empirically and theoretically that the predictive behaviour of neural networks can be explained by analysing the weights and using sensitivity analysis. The results using these methods are very similar to those obtained using logistic regression.

In the following section, we compare logistic regression and neural networks from a theoretical point of view, and show why neural networks should be better at such modelling and prediction tasks. We then provide a brief overview of the research done in the prediction of merger targets. Data collection and analyses are then described, followed by a discussion of the results. A section is devoted to interpretation of the neural network model using sensitivity analysis and a theoretical analysis of the weights.

LOGISTIC REGRESSION

To compare neural networks with statistical models, we chose logistic regression because most researchers have found it to be better than other statistical models when the dependent variable is binary [Palepu86, Myers90, TamKia92]. Here we use a logistic regression model (Figure 22.1(a)) for a binary response variable Y_i that can take values 1 and 0 (the value 1 indicating that the company is a target and 0 that it is a non-target). Let $p_i = P(Y_i = 1)$, $i = 1, \ldots, N$, where N is the sample size. The probability p_i is estimated by the logistic model:

$$\text{logit}(p_i) = \ln\left(\frac{p_i}{1 - p_i}\right) = B_0 + B_1 X_{i1} + B_2 X_{i2} + \cdots + B_n X_{in} \qquad (22.1)$$

where $X_{i1}, \ldots, X_{in}$ are predictor variables. The B_i are estimated by maximizing the log-likelihood function:

$$\sum_{i=1}^{N} L(\mathbf{B}; y_i) = \sum_{i} \ln\left(\frac{1}{1 + e^{-\mathbf{B}\mathbf{X}_i}}\right) \qquad (22.2)$$

where $\mathbf{B}$ is the vector of parameters to be estimated. The maximisation leads to a series of nonlinear equations that are solved for $\mathbf{B}$ using iterative mechanisms. Several methods are available, among them the Newton–Raphson method and the iteratively reweighted least squares (IRLS) method. Once $\mathbf{B}$ is estimated, p_i is estimated using (22.1) for a given set of predictor variables: $\mathbf{X}_i$. Note that (22.1) can be rewritten as:

$$p_i = \frac{1}{1 + e^{-\mathbf{B}\mathbf{X}_i}} \qquad (22.3)$$

Binary Response Variable = Y_i

Predictor Variables = $\mathbf{X}_1, \mathbf{X}_2, \ldots, \mathbf{X}_n$

$p_i = \text{Prob } (Y_i = 1)$

$\text{logit } (p_i = \log [p_i]/(1-p_i)$

$\qquad = B_0 + B_1 X_{i1} + B_2 X_{i2} + \cdots + B_n X_{in}\ .$

$P_i = 1/(1+\exp-(\text{logit}(p_i)))$

Maximise the log-likelihood function and solve for the B_i using iterative methods.

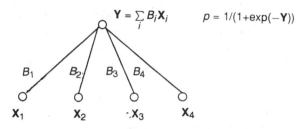

$$\mathbf{Y} = \sum_i B_i \mathbf{X}_i \qquad p = 1/(1+\exp(-\mathbf{Y}))$$

(a)

Optimisation method: gradient descent (minimise error)
Compute $\partial E/\partial w$ for each weight and change weights proportionally.
Repeat until convergence.

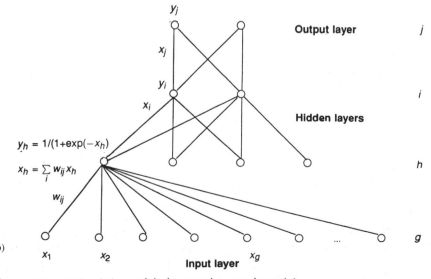

$y_h = 1/(1+\exp(-x_h))$

$x_h = \sum_i w_{ij} x_h$

w_{ij}

(b)

Figure 22.1 (a) Logistic model; (b) neural network model

The result obtained p_i is an estimate of the probability that the response variable $Y_i = 1$, that is, that the company is a target. Note the similarity with the transformation functions used in neural networks.

DATA ANALYSIS

Regardless of the quality of the prediction model, success in prediction is largely determined by the selection of the predictor variables. The variables chosen in this study are based on those found in the mergers and acquisitions literature [DieSor84, Palepu86]. This section will provide a brief description of the 12 predictor variables. A more complete description, including the COMPUSTAT data item numbers, can be found in Appendix 22A.

As hypothesized by Palepu [Palepu86], inefficiently managed firms are often acquired, that is, management is replaced by more adept managers. Average excess returns (AER), average return on equity (ROE), and average sales/asset turnover (AVTURNOV), are chosen as measures of a firm's management's performance.

[Palepu86] also indicates that firms with high growth and low resources or with low growth and high resources are likely to be acquired. In common parlance, these firms are considered as 'good deals'. Three intermediary variables, average sales growth (AVGROWTH), average liquidity (AVLIQUID), and average leverage (AVLEV), are combined to form a growth-resource dummy variable (GRDUMMY). Low-AVGROWTH, high-AVLIQUID, low-AVLEV, and high-AVGROWTH, low-AVLIQUID, high-AVLEV combinations are used to identify a growth–resource mismatch. For these cases, the value of GRDUMMY is set to 1.

[Palepu86] suggests that since economic disturbances tend to affect industries, acquisitions will cluster by industry [Gort69]. IDUMMY is a variable that is set to 1 if a takeover occurred in that industry a year prior to the observation year. This variable serves as a proxy for the economic disturbance phenomenon. [Palepu86] and [DieSor84] hypothesise that smaller firms are more likely to be acquired than larger firms. SIZE, as measured by net book assets, is also included as a variable.

[Palepu86] views with suspicion the popular hypothesis that firms with low market-to-book (MTB) ratios are likely takeover targets because the book value of a firm need not reflect the replacement value of its assets. He also questions the popular hypothesis that firms with low price-earnings (PE) ratios are more likely to be acquired. To test these hypotheses and to avoid leaving out any important variables, we included these two variables (MTB and PE).

Dietrich and Sorensen [DieSor84] hypothesise that if a firm's investment opportunities are scarce the firm is more likely to become a target. Lack of investment opportunities is indicated by high dividend payouts. Average payout (AVPAYOUT) is included in our study as a proxy for investment opportunities. Of the variables included in our study, [Palepu86] finds AER, ROE, GRDUMMY, AVGROWTH, AVLEV, IDUMMY, and SIZE to be significant. [DieSor84] found SIZE, AVTURNOV, and AVPAYOUT to be significant.

The data were obtained from the COMPUSTAT and CRSP tapes (see Appendix A) for two years (1984–5). Most of the data items were averaged over three to four years prior to the observation year. Thus, data were collected over the period 1980–85. Targets were identified by searching CRSP tapes for delistments from the New York Stock Exchange. The *Wall Street Journal* Index was used to verify whether the delistment was indeed due to a merger. The data obtained from 1984 were used to train the network and build the logistic regression model. Fifty targets were identified for 1984, of which 39 had complete data. In order to have an equal number of non-targets in the training set, 39 non-targets were randomly identified from the pool of 1260 non-targets that had complete data available for 1984. Data gathered from 1985 were used to test the neural network and the logit regression models. In 1985 a total of 78 targets were identified. Of the 2489 non-targets identified, only 1285 had complete data and were used in the hold-out sample.

Logistic Regression Analysis

Using the training sample of 39 targets and 39 non-targets in 1984, a logit model using the LOGISTIC procedure in SAS was run. The response variable in the logit model was a binary variable with the value 1 for target companies and 0 for non-target companies. The predictor variables were the 12 discussed earlier. The results of the analysis are shown in Table 22.1.

The table shows that only three of 12 variables, average excess return (AER), average growth (AVGROWTH), and market to book ratio (MTB) are significant in predicting merger targets. These results have some similarities with Palepu's results. Palepu observed that AER, GRDUMMY, AVGROWTH, IDUMMY, and

Table 22.1 Logistic regression results.

Variables	Parameter estimate	Chi-square	$P >$ chi-square
AER	7.54	3.86	0.04
AVROE	−1.1	0.71	0.4
AVGROWTH	6.41	6.1	0.01
AVLIQUID	2.04	0.97	0.32
AVLEV	−0.27	0.32	0.57
GRDUMMY	0.76	1.14	0.28
IDUMMY	−0.5	0.75	0.39
SIZE	−0.00003	0.14	0.7
MTB	−0.84	5.07	0.02
PE	−0.005	0.32	0.57
AVPAYOUT	−0.008	0.0003	0.98
AVTURNOV	0.38	1.02	0.31

Significance of the overall model: 0.0841
Goodman–Kruskall gamma coefficient: 0.50

SIZE were all significant in predicting whether a firm is a target or not. In this study, although we did not find GRDUMMY to be significant, one of its components AVGROWTH is found significant. IDUMMY and SIZE are not found significant in this study; however, MTB is found significant, confounding Palepu's suspicions.

Some variables were expected to be correlated in the model. For instance, GRDUMMY is obtained from AVLEV, AVLIQUIDITY and AVGROWTH. AVTURNOV and AER are both measures of a firm's management's performance. A reduced model obtained by dropping correlated variables was run. No difference in the results was obtained by doing so.

The differences in the results of the two studies can be partly explained by sample differences. In Palepu's study there were more non-targets (256) than targets (163) in the training sample. In this study, we had to use an equal-sized sample to allow comparisons with the neural network model. The difference in sample composition could have caused the difference in the significance of the predictor variables. An alternative explanation could be that it is difficult to identify predictor variables for merger targets and that it is a changing phenomenon. Thus, the variables that were important in predicting mergers during the period 1971–9 may not be the same for the 1980s.

The predictive ability of the model is fairly good, as indicated by the Somer's D and the Goodman–Kruskall gamma coefficients (0.50) indicated in the table. These coefficients are like correlation coefficients that measure the association of predicted probabilities and observed responses.

In order to determine how well the logit model performs in classifying the learning sample into targets and non-targets, a probability cut-off is determined. The cut-off is usually arbitrarily chosen to be 0.5, but Palepu criticises the arbitrary nature of this cut-off as being inappropriate for predicting mergers. It is argued that to derive the optimal cut-off, the context in which the predicted probability is of interest must be utilised. The purpose behind being able to predict targets for mergers is to make abnormal returns by investing in predicted targets. Using this objective it can be shown that the optimal cut-off is the point at which the distribution curve of the acquisition probability given that the firm is a target intersects the distribution curve of the acquisition probability given that the firm is a non-target. This method is explained in [Palepu86].

The marginal probabilities of the two distributions are computed and plotted. The plot is obtained by calculating the frequency distribution of the training sample over different prediction probability ranges (from 0 to 1.0 in increments of 0.2). This distribution is shown in Table 22.2. The percentage of sample firms in each probability range is plotted against the mid-point of the probability range (Figure 22.2). The two plots intersect at a probability of 0.6, which is selected as the cut-off for the logit model.

The predictive ability of the logit model was tested using the model estimation sample (1984) and the hold-out sample (1985) (Table 22.3). The logit model correctly classified 22 out of 39 targets and 34 out of 39 non-targets in the model

Table 22.2 Frequency distribution of acquisition probabilities.

Probability mid-point	No. of targets	No. of non-targets
0.1	0	10
0.3	7	9
0.5	10	15
0.7	13	5
0.9	9	0

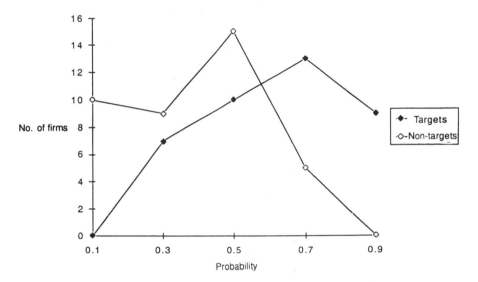

Figure 22.2 Distribution of acquisition probabilities for targets and non-targets

estimation sample. Its overall classification accuracy of the estimation sample is 71.8% (Table 22.3). It predicts 23 out of the 78 targets and 882 out of 1285 non-targets in the hold-out sample. This results in an overall prediction accuracy rate of 49.0%.[1] This compares closely with the 45.6% prediction accuracy obtained in Palepu's study. The model seems to predict nontargets better, but in doing so it misclassifies a large number of targets as non-targets.

The Neural Network Model

Using a commercially available package, the neural network model was obtained after several trials. It is difficult to determine the number of hidden layers and the number of nodes required in the hidden layers that would provide the best neural network model [GorSej88, Hirose91]. Many combinations of hidden layers and nodes are attempted before a satisfactory model is determined. This process takes a long time and an 'optimal' network can only be arrived at after many trials.

Table 22.3 Prediction accuracies of the models.

	Logit model			Neural network			Neural network with 23 nodes in hidden layer		
	Targets	Nontargets	Overall	Targets	Nontargets	Overall	Targets	Nontargets	Overall
Estimation Sample (1984)	22/39=56%	34/39=87%	72%	34/39=87%	37/39=95%	91%	37/39=95%	39/39=100%	97%
Hold-out Sample (1985)	23/78=29%	882/1285=68%	49%	28/78=36%	806/1285=63%	50%	38/78=49%	642/1285=50%	50%

Also, the activation function used need not be the logistic sigmoidal function. Other similar functions can be used — for instance, the hyperbolic tangent function. After several trials, we observed that a network that had two hidden layers, with four nodes in the first layer and two nodes in the second hidden layer with a hyperbolic tangent activation function produced good results.

This network was trained with 150 000 presentations of the observations (obtained by using randomised orderings of the training data set of 78 targets and non-targets of 1984). This network correctly classified 34 out of 39 targets and 37 out of 39 targets in the training set. This results in an overall classification accuracy of 91.0% (Table 22.3). It correctly predicts 28 out of 78 targets and 806 out of 1285 non-targets in the hold-out sample. The overall prediction accuracy rate is 49.3%.

Although the overall prediction accuracy rate for the neural network is higher than for the logit model for the estimation sample, this does not necessarily suggest that by using the neural network, abnormal returns from the stock market may be obtained. The neural network correctly predicts only 28 out of the 78 targets.

The neural network could be improved to make it learn the estimation sample pattern better by introducing more nodes in the hidden layer. In fact researchers [Funaha89, HiYaHi91] have shown that, given enough nodes, even one hidden layer can map any continuous function. Sietsma and Dow [SieDow91] show that networks with larger numbers of nodes generalise better when the data are noisy. However, unless the estimation sample is an exact representation of the expected behaviour of the phenomenon being predicted, perfect learning is not very useful.

To verify this for our data set, we trained another network with 23 nodes in the hidden layer. This network learned almost to perfection. Ninety-seven per cent of all targets and non-targets in the estimation sample were predicted correctly (Table 22.3). However, when this model was used to predict using the hold-out sample, only 38 of 78 targets and 642 of 1285 non-targets were predicted correctly. This resulted in an overall prediction rate of 49.3% which is the same as our previous result. Note that in predicting more targets accurately, it misclassifies many more non-targets as targets. Thus, obtaining the neural network with the highest prediction rate based on the estimation sample does not necessarily lead to a better prediction model.

To identify a good neural network model, the model-builder's knowledge about the problem domain is utilised. One way to do this is to do a sensitivity analysis of the predictor variables and observe their impact on the outcome. If the sensitivity behaviour is consistent with expectations, we have some validation of the model.

SIGNIFICANT PREDICTORS OF ACQUISITION LIKELIHOOD

One of the criticisms often made about neural networks is that they lack any explanatory capability, although some researchers have attempted to interpret the weights [GorSej88]. We attempt here to show how a neural network model can be explained. One method that is suggested [KlGuPe89] is to perform a sensitivity analysis.

Weights obtained from the neural network model are several and are spread over the multiple layers of the model. The relationship between these weights, the inputs, and the outputs, although complex, is clearly defined. This makes a sensitivity analysis possible.

Sensitivity Analysis

To perform the sensitivity analysis, the ranges for the predictor variable values are first determined. For each predictor variable, the minimum, maximum, and the mid-point of the range are determined. The value of each predictor is varied one at a time, holding the values of other variables fixed at the mid-points of their ranges. For each predictor being varied, the values are spread over ten equal intervals over its whole range. The neural network model is then used to compute the output. This output is treated as the likelihood of the sample being a target. Wan [Wan90] shows that the output of a multi-layer neural network pattern classifier can be considered to be a nonparametric estimate of the posterior probability of the sample belonging to a particular class.

For all of the 12 predictor variables, the neural network outcome (acquisition likelihood) is plotted against the value of the predictor variable. The plots are shown in Figure 22.3. The plots indicate the sensitivity of the network output to changes in the predictor variable. It should be noted that the absolute network output is not as important as the changes in the network output. As expected, the relationships between acquisition likelihood and the predictor variables are complex nonlinear functions.

The sensitivity plot for a predictor is interpreted to indicate that if all other predictors were held constant at around the industry average, changes in this predictor variable would affect the outcome in the manner shown by the plot. For instance, Figure 22.3(a) shows that if average excess return (AER) is either very low or very high the firm is very likely to be taken over. Logistic regression is unable to capture such information.

Some interesting observations can be made from the plots. When there is a growth–resource mismatch (GRDUMMY=1), the company is likely to be taken over. This is consistent with the growth–resource mismatch hypothesis found in the finance literature. Figure 22.3(d) indicates that, consistent with expectations, companies that are very large are unlikely to be taken over. Firms with low sales turnover (AVTURNOV) are unlikely to be taken over, whereas firms with higher turnovers are more likely to be taken over (Figure 22.3(d)). Also, firms with very low or very high dividend payouts (AVPAYOUT) are unlikely to be taken over (Figure 22.3(d)). Several of the plots indicate relationships that are consistent with general expectations.

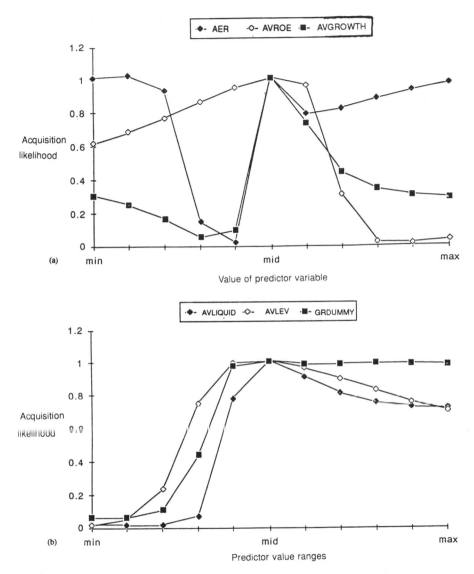

Figure 22.3 Sensitivity analysis for (a) AER, AVROE and AVGROWTH; (b) AVLIQUID, AVLEV and GRDUMMY; (c) IDUMMY, SIZE and MTB; (d) PE, AVPAYOUT and AVTURNOV

Thus, the neural network model is a fairly logical representation of the financial world of mergers. The justification of the sensitivity analysis approach lies in the argument that if the model captures the relationship between the predictor variables and the outcome accurately, then the relationship is very likely to be meaningful

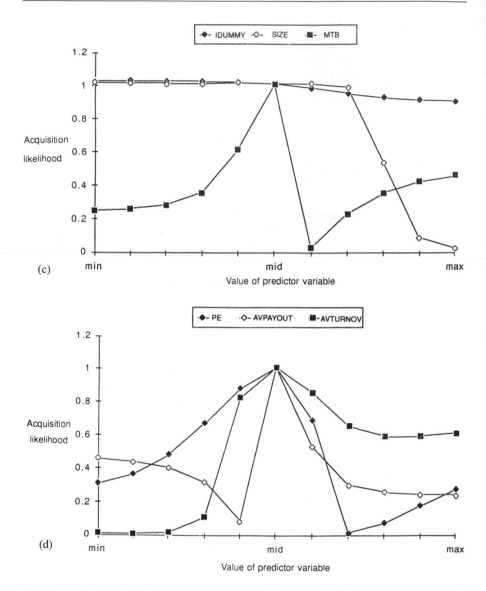

Figure 22.3 (*continued*)

at least for the estimation sample. The reliability of the model is enhanced further if the model behaviour displayed is consistent with expectations.

A sensitivity index was computed to find out the relative strength of the influence of a predictor variable on the outcome. This index was computed by averaging the deviations in outcome for decile changes over the whole range of values of the

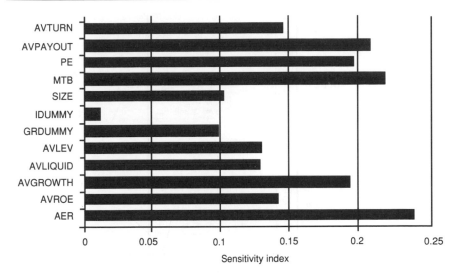

Figure 22.4 Sensitivity index for predictor Variables

predictor variable:

$$\frac{1}{10} \sum_{i} \left(P_{\mathbf{X}_{i+1}} - P_{\mathbf{X}_i} \right)$$

where $P_{\mathbf{X}_i}$ = acquisition likelihood for a given predictor $\mathbf{X}_i$. The sensitivity index provides a measure of 'significance' of the predictor variables in predicting the outcome. These indices are plotted in Figure 22.4 for comparison.

The five predictor variables that have a sensitivity index greater than 0.15 are AVPAYOUT, PE, MTB, AVGROWTH and AER. A sensitivity index of 0.15 was chosen as the cut-off, since the plot indicates a clear separation of high and low indices at this point. Recall that three of these variables, AER, AVGROWTH and MTB, were found significant predictors using logistic regression.

Analysis of Weights

Finally, the weights of each of the predictor variables in the neural network are interpreted. These weights are shown in Table 22.4. In order to interpret the relative importance of the weights of the predictors, the change in output relative to the change in an input variable, $\partial y_j / \partial x_g$, is determined by applying the chain rule of derivatives.

This methodology was first introduced by the authors and was subsequently adopted by several other researchers, including the editor of this book. A brief description of the rationale is given in Chapter 6 as adopted by the editor and his co-authors.

Table 22.4 Neural network weights.

	AER	AVROE	AVGROWTH	AVLIQUID	AVLEV	GRDUMMY	IDUMMY	SIZE	MTB	PE	AVPAYOUT	AVTURNOV
Hidden layer 2						-2.15	-1.7					
						2.15	1.7					
Hidden layer 1					2.91	2.86	-1.92	4.41				
					-0.38	-0.4	0.25	-0.6				
Input layer	6.88	0.16	1.1	2.22	-0.33	2.33	1.27	2.49	-3.25	0.76	3.2	-0.54
	2.31	1.24	-4.63	-1.37	-1.4	0.95	2.2	0.3	3.72	2.09	-4.43	-4.6
	-0.65	-0.54	0.08	-0.53	0.43	-2.59	0.53	-1.87	-1.5	-0.55	0.5	0.69
	-0.34	-1.44	2.14	-0.38	1.3	0.43	-1	-1.73	-0.49	-0.96	3.23	2.19
Sum of input layer weights (abs. value)	10.18	3.38	7.95	4.5	3.46	6.3	5	6.39	8.96	4.36	11.36	8.02

The absolute values of the input layer weights were summed for each predictor variable in Table 22.4. The five variables with the highest sum of weights are AVPAYOUT, AER, AVGROWTH, MTB and AVTURNOV. Four of the five variables match the sensitivity index analysis and all the variables found significant in the logit analysis are included in this set of five. Thus, combining the input layer weights in a linear fashion provides a good approximation of the degree of impact a predictor variable has on the outcome.

CONCLUSION

In this chapter neural networks are used to predict corporate targets for merger. The task of predicting which companies are suitable for mergers is not a simple one. The interaction of many factors is important in its prediction. Traditionally, research in this area has used logistic regression for prediction purposes. We showed that neural networks have better modelling capabilities than logistic regression. However, neural networks are still not capable of predicting mergers well. Although neural networks provide a good mathematical fit of the data, this does not necessarily lead to a good prediction model. Factors such as selection of predictor variables are vitally important in arriving at a good prediction model.

Neural networks have several advantages over statistical models. No assumptions regarding the distributions of the data need to be made. Neural networks are capable of fitting complex nonlinear models to the data. They are flexible and allow the modeller to use different model configurations by changing the number of hidden layers and the number of nodes in the hidden layers.

Its major disadvantage lies in its inability to explain the relative importance of its inputs. Consequently, it has had limited use compared to statistical models in empirical research in finance and accounting. In this chapter we have attempted to show that the significance of the inputs can be interpreted using simple techniques such as sensitivity analysis and graphical plots, and using a linear combination of the input layer weights provided by the neural network model. Nonlinear relationships between predictor and predicted variables that cannot be captured by statistical models are effectively captured by neural network models. Our approach shows results that are superior to those provided by statistical techniques.

ACKNOWLEDGEMENT

We would like to thank Raman Kumar for his assistance in data collection.

NOTE

1. The overall prediction rate is obtained by averaging the target and non-target rates. The prediction rate obtained by considering all correct predictions in sample is 66%. This is misleading since only 29% of the targets are correctly predicted, and predicting targets is the main objective of the model.

APPENDIX 22A

- AER = actual return − market model based return. Averaged for 4 years prior to observation year. (Obtained from CRSP tapes.)

- ROE = Income before extraordinary items (18)/(Preferred equity (10) + Common equity (11)). Averaged for 4 years prior to the observation year.

- AVTURNOV = Net sales (12)/Total assets (6). Averaged for 4 years prior to the observation year.

- AVGROWTH = (Net sales$_1$ (121) − Net sales$_0$ (120))/Net Sales$_0$ (120). Averaged for 3 years prior to the observation year.

- AVLIQUID = ((Cash (1) + Marketable securities (5)) − Current liabilities (5))/Total assets (6). Averaged for 3 years prior to the observation year.

- AVLEV = Long term debt (9)/(Preferred equity (10) + Common equity (11)). Averaged for 3 years prior to the observation year.

- GRDUMMY: calculated from AVGROWTH, AVLIQUID, AVLEV. Low-AVGROWTH, high-AVLIQUID, low-AVLEV, and high-AVGROWTH, low-AVLIQUID, high-AVLEV combinations result in a GRDUMMY value of 1. All other combinations of these three variables result in a value of 0.

- IDUMMY: calculated from SIC codes of targets for the year prior to the observation year. A firm is assigned an IDUMMY value of 1 if a takeover has occurred in the same industry one year prior to the observation year, otherwise IDUMMY is assigned a value of 0. The industry is identified by the COMPUSTAT SIC code.

- SIZE = Total net book value of assets (6). One year prior to the observation year.

- MTB = Stock price (24)/(Firm's book equity (60)/Outstanding shares (25)). One year prior to the observation year.

- PE = (Stock price (24)/Earnings per share (58)). One year prior to the observation year.

- AVPAYOUT = (Dividends per share (26)/Earnings per share (58)). Averaged for 4 years prior to the observation year.

*The numbers in parentheses are COMPUSTAT data item numbers.

23

Self-organizing Neural Networks: The Financial State of Spanish Companies

Bonifacio Martin-del-Brio and Carlos Serrano-Cinca,
Universidad de Zaragoza, Spain

INTRODUCTION

Many recent papers have dealt with the application of neural network architectures to financial forecasting or financial data analysis, most of them making use of feedforward layered neural networks with the backpropagation (BP) training algorithm or similar [DutShe88, White88, VarVer90, TriBer91, UtaMoo91, Hoptro93, Refene93]. As is well known, supervised networks require the output vector corresponding to every input pattern in order to learn. By contrast, there has been little work devoted to the application of unsupervised neural models to financial data [BliAll91, MarSer93]. Sometimes, the use of such models can be more suitable, for example when outputs are not available, or when we are interested in the clustering of the input patterns according to their similarity. These are the kinds of computation that an unsupervised or self-organising neural network is able to carry out.

The *self-organising feature map* (SOFM), also known as the *Kohonen map* [Kohone89, Kohone90] (see Chapter 1), is a well-known unsupervised neural model of widespread use in areas such as pattern recognition and robotics. SOFMs could be a very interesting tool for the representation and analysis of financial data, and to aid in decision-making, mainly on account of their ability to project multi-dimensional data onto a less-dimensional output space (usually one- or

Neural Networks in the Capital Markets. Edited by Apostolos-Paul Refenes.
© 1995 John Wiley & Sons Ltd

two-dimensional), that is to say, the map, where relationships between the patterns are easy to see.

The aim of this chapter is to explore the application of self-organising maps to economic data processing and representation. For this purpose, we apply this unsupervised model to two practical financial case studies taken from the Spanish economy: the Spanish banking crisis of 1977–85 and the financial state of Spanish companies in 1990 and 1991. In the first case study, without information being provided about the solvent or bankrupt state of every bank, the network has discovered the similarities between the patterns and has clustered them according to their solvency state (for example, healthy or bankrupt). In the second case study we have used financial data for two years (1990 and 1991) from 84 Spanish companies, showing the ability of self-organising maps to represent high-dimensional input data on a two-dimensional map. Several features can be inferred from such a map and, by analysing the synaptic weights, regions representing large liquidity, small profitability or large debt, where similar companies are clustered, can be delimited. The time evolution of the companies and other important conclusions can be drawn from the resulting maps. We have completed these results by using other statistical tools, such as hierarchical cluster analysis (HCA) and multi-dimensional scaling (MDS). Neural and non-neural systems (such as SOFM and HCA) can be integrated in a broader framework of decision-making aids with others tools.

PREPROCESSING OF THE INPUT DATA

An important aspect which has influence on the development and final appearance of the map is the preprocessing of the input data. Several preprocessing strategies are discussed in Chapter 4 of this book and elsewhere; see, for example, [EbeDob90]. The choice of the preprocessing strategy depends on the objective pursued in the study and on how the data are presented. On some occasions we must normalise or scale by variables (columns), on others by cases (rows), and there are situations where the selected preprocessing should be applied over the entire data file. In the present work we preprocess by variables.

When the input variables have very different ranges (for instance, one variable can be profits and another the number of employees), simple linear scaling is a way to initially equalise the importance of the input variables. Every component of the input vectors or input variable should be scaled to the same range, for instance $[0,1]$.

Normalising to unit length is a common method of preprocessing used with self-organising maps. As has been said above, when correlation is the similarity measure used, then it is mandatory to normalise both vectors to unit length. By contrast, when Euclidean distance is selected, normalisation to unit length is not strictly necessary, although it is commonly used when the norm of the vectors is big. Note that when vectors normalised to unit length are compared it is the shape, and not the magnitude, which is taken into account.

Another possibility (and the one used in our work) is standardisation of every input variable x to another dimensionless variable z of mean zero and variance unity, by subtracting its mean $\bar{x}_m$ and dividing by its standard deviation s:

$$z = \frac{x - \bar{x}_m}{s} \tag{23.1}$$

This is a common strategy followed in statistics, which keeps the values in a similar range and removes all effects of offset and measurement scale. The significance of this normalisation is that every variable is transformed into another one that measures its deviation in relation to the mean in units of its standard deviation; the new variable indicates the actual importance of a value with respect to the rest [Spiege88].

FINANCIAL DATA ANALYSIS WITH SELF-ORGANISING FEATURE MAPS

In this section we apply the SOFM model to two different financial case studies. The first case study is the data analysis of the Spanish banking crisis of 1977–85. We show how different regions, where solvent and bankrupt banks are located, are created on the map. The second case study is concerned with the financial situation of a large sample of Spanish companies in 1990 and 1991. We show how the map is able to cluster companies in several regions according to certain financial ratios, and discover interesting features in the input data.

The Spanish Banking Crisis 1977–85

The prediction of company failure is probably the most important function of financial analysis. Usually the analysis of the financial state of companies is made from ratios obtained from the accounting data published by the companies, to which conventional methods based on univariate or multivariate analysis are applied. The first study of this kind was carried out by [Beaver66]. In Spain, [Rodrig89, Pina89] carried out some interesting studies of the Spanish banking crisis of 1977–85. Most of the work on multivariate modelling of distress prediction attempts to get a Z-score that gives the probability of failure of a company. Linear discriminant analysis (LDA) [Altman68], (Logit Probit) and, more recently, the multi-layer perceptron, have been used for this task. An important characteristic of all these models is that they adjust their parameters in a supervised way. These methods have achieved a high percentage of success in the classification, but have been criticised because of several problems [Hartvi92]. In any case, the information provided by this kind of model, a single number, is quite poor. Recently, the use of unsupervised models has been proposed for the analysis of company failure, the advantage being that their results can be interpreted in a very intuitive way. This is the line we have followed in our work, specifically by using SOFMs, a very interesting unsupervised neural model. Other authors, such as [MarEzz91] and [MarSer93], propose the use of multi-dimensional scaling (MDS) in order to give a visual presentation of multivariate data.

During the Spanish banking crisis of 1977–85, no fewer than 58 out of a total of 108 Spanish banks were in crisis, involving 27% of the external resources of the Spanish banking system. This critical situation has been compared to the crash of 1929 in the USA. The data used in this study have been taken from the *Anuario*

Table 23.1   Banks used in the bankruptcy study. Bankrupt banks: 1 to 29. Solvent banks: 30 to 66. The Big Seven: 60 to 66.

Bankrupt banks	Solvent banks
1 B Unión	30 B de Progreso
2 B Mas Sardá	31 B Industrial Bilbao
3 B Levante	32 B Intercont. Español
4 B Catalana	33 B Comerc. Trans.
5 B Ind. Catal.	34 B De Comercio
6 B Barcelona	35 B Jover
7 B Gerona	36 B de Vitoria
8 B Alicante	37 B Pueyo
9 B Créd. e Inv.	38 B deCréd. Balear
10 B Pirineos	39 B Huesca
11 B Madrid	40 B Fomento
12 B de Navarra	41 B Pastor
13 B Cantábrico	42 B de Castilla
14 B Meridional	43 B Guipuzcoano
15 B Valladolid	44 B de Galicia
16 B Crédito Comercial	45 B Hisp. Ind
17 B Préstamo y Ahorro	46 B March
18 B Descuento	47 B Depósitos
19 B Comercial Occidente	48 B Herrero
20 B Occidental	49 B Sabadell
21 B Indust. Mediterráneo	50 B Bankpyme
22 B Catalán Desarrollo	51 B Interior de Comercio
23 B Promoción Negocios	52 B Zaragozana
24 B López Quesada	53 B Comercial Español
25 B Asturias	54 B Mercantil Tarragona
26 B Granada	55 B Abel Matutes
27 B Simeón	56 B Financición Industrial
28 B de Exp. Industrial	57 Sind. Banqueros
29 B Garriga Nogués	58 B de Europa
	59 B de Vasconia
	60 B Popular Español
	61 B Hispano Americano
	62 B Español Crédito
	63 B Santander
	64 B Central
	65 B Bilbao
	66 B Vizcaya

Estadístico de la Banca Privada (Private Banks Statistical Yearbook), published in Spain, as was the case in the earlier studies quoted above. The sample contains information from 66 banks (29 of them bankrupt, see Table 23.1). In the case of bankrupt banks, we use data from one year before their crisis, while for solvent banks we used data from 1982. The data used were published in [MarSer93]. The success of the model depends to a large extent on the selection of the input variables. In the present study we have made use of nine financial ratios (see Table 23.2), the same as those selected in [Pina89]. These ratios were selected from among many others by means of linear regression, because of its statistical significance. Every ratio has been standardised to have mean zero and variance unity. As stated earlier, the preprocessing of input data is a very important subject that deserves more attention, because it can modify the dynamics of recall and learning and the final results, but this is a matter which is outside the scope of the present work.

We have processed the data by means of SOFMs. The map used consists of 196 neurons arranged in a 14×14 square grid: Euclidean distance is used as a similarity measure (see Chapter 1). The synaptic weights are initialised at small random values. We use the whole data base for training the network, because we want it to give a visual image of the multivariate data. The 66 patterns, randomly ordered, are presented over and over again to the system. One presentation of the 66 patterns is called an *epoch*. The learning consists of 250 epochs in the first stage of training (until the learning rate reaches a value of 0.01 and the neighbourhood consists of the six nearest neighbours), and 50 epochs in the second stage (keeping these values constant), so that the number of total iterations is about 20 000 (about 100 iterations per neuron). It is worth noting that although this is a large number of iterations, the computing complexity of the algorithm is very simple compared to that of back propagation, and this results in a reduced training time. A simulation takes a few minutes in a 486-based PC. We have used a linear decreasing function for updating the neighbourhood radius $R(t)$:

$$R(t) = R_0 + (R_f - R_0)\frac{t}{t_{rf}} \tag{23.2}$$

Table 23.2 Ratios used in the bankruptcy study of Spanish banks.

Symbol	Ratio
R1	Current assets/Total assets
R2	(Current assets − Cash)/Total assets
R3	Current assets/Loans
R4	Reserves/Loans
R5	Net income/Total assets
R6	Net income/Total equity capital
R7	Net income/Loans
R8	Cost of sales/Sales
R9	Cash flow/Loans

where t is the present iteration and t_{rf} is the maximum number of iterations ($t_{rf} = 250 \times 66$) until reaching the final radius R_f ($R_f = 1$), and R_0 is the starting radius ($R_0 \bullet 10$). An accurate rule is not important, and other functions for updating $R(t)$ can be used. A similar linear decaying function has been used for updating the learning rate $\varepsilon(t)$:

$$\varepsilon(t) = \varepsilon_0 + (\varepsilon_f - \varepsilon_0)\frac{t}{t_{ef}} \tag{23.3}$$

where ε_0 is the starting learning rate (< 1.0), ε_f is the final learning rate (about 0.01) and t_{ef} is the maximum number of iterations until reaching ε_f. The neighbourhood is defined by a step function around the winning node.

Using different random initialisations of the synaptic weights, the maps developed are similar, but can present different orientations; Figure 23.1 depicts one of them. The numbers upon the neurons are the pattern labels (the number of the bank, see Table 23.1) that give a greater response, that is, the pattern to which this neuron has tuned. We can see two main areas, one consisting of neurons that

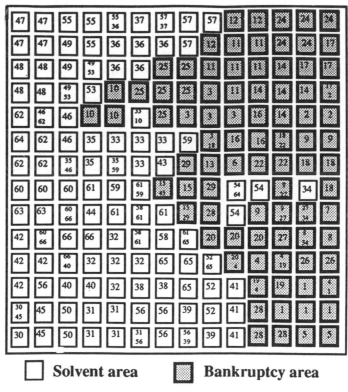

□ **Solvent area**   ■ **Bankruptcy area**

Figure 23.1   Solvency map of 14 × 14 neurons trained with data from 66 Spanish banks. The numbers represent the bank that every node has tuned to (see Table 23.1)

have tuned to the bankrupt banks, and the other of neurons that have tuned to the solvent ones. Almost all the solvent and bankrupt banks are in the same zone, but we can see that there are banks with similar data or ratios but that have had a very different fate, in that some went bankrupt but others did not. For instance, bank 54, which did not go bankrupt, has similar ratios to those of bank 6, which did; thus, they are neighbours on the map, but 54 is out of its actual area. There may be several reasons for this, for instance, the financial variables selected, which are the same as in [Pina89] in order to facilitate comparison, might not have enough information to explain all the cases; other reasons may be mistaken or false data, or non-accounting factors which are difficult to compute and that can lead similar companies to very different final results.

The unsupervised network has discovered similarities between patterns and has clustered similar patterns together, as we can see from Figure 23.1. Note that we have not provided information about the solvent or bankrupt state of every bank. The network itself, without any supervision, has found features in the input data that differentiate both situations. Because of the parallelism with the phonotopic maps or semantic maps [Kohone90, RiMaSc92], we have called these *self-organising solvency maps*; these have been discussed in [MarSer93]. An interesting feature that can be seen in Figure 23.1 is the clustering of the Big Seven (as the seven biggest Spanish banks, banks 60 to 66 in the figure, were then known), which occurs even if we do not provide information about bank size, as is the case with the present study carried out from financial ratios.

Usually, it is much easier to interpret the operation of unsupervised networks than that of supervised ones, through the analysis of the synaptic weights or weight analysis. In the present practical case, some interesting conclusions can be inferred from that analysis. In Figure 23.2 we depict the so-called weight maps, where every weight map is dedicated to one input variable, the weights that connect every input variable with all the neurons of the square output layer (14 × 14 neurons) are represented on every map (R1 to R9), their magnitude being coded in grey levels. From these maps the relationships between the input variables can easily be seen, allowing us to delimit several regions. Maps of ratios 1, 2 and 3 have a very similar appearance; we know that all these are liquidity ratios. The same occurs with ratios 5, 6 and 7, with all these being proportional to profits (net incomes). Comparing Figure 23.1 (location of bankrupt and solvent banks) and Figure 23.2 (distribution of synaptic weights), liquidity has not shown itself to be a good predictor of the crisis because, although the majority of banks in the bankrupt area present a small liquidity, there are solvent banks with a small liquidity and bankrupt ones with good liquidity. Good predictors of bankrupt situations have been (see Figures 23.1 and 23.2): profitability (ratios 5, 6 and 7, solvent banks present large profitability and bankrupt ones, small), cost of sales (ratio 8) and cash-flow to loans (ratio 9). It is worth noting that there is an old controversy between the use of profits or cash flow in the assessment of bankruptcy risk.

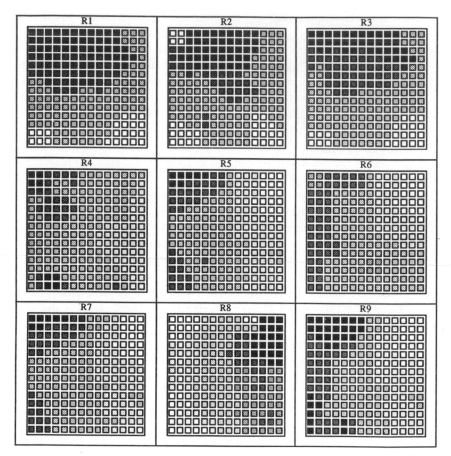

Figure 23.2 Weight maps of the solvency map (Figure 23.1). Weight magnitudes are coded in grey levels, from the large (black) to the smallest (white) weight

From the distribution of the synaptic weights shown in Figure 23.2, several regions can be delimited on the map, such as the large area of liquidity, that of small profitability and large debt, that of large profitability and so on (Figure. 23.3(a)).

By means of SOFMs we can see the financial situation of a company in a particular year or even the time evolution of its financial state. The financial situation of a bank can be seen by showing its pattern to the trained network and looking at the more activated neurons on the map. If these are located in the crisis zone, then that bank is in a critical situation; if they are in the solvent area, the bank is in a solvent one. For instance, bank 55 (Banco Abel Matutes), is located in the upper part of Figure 23.1, in the area of high liquidity and high profits of Figure 23.3(a). From the weight maps (Figure 23.2) it also has less cost of sales and large cash flow to loans. The conclusion is that this bank was healthy in 1982. It is important

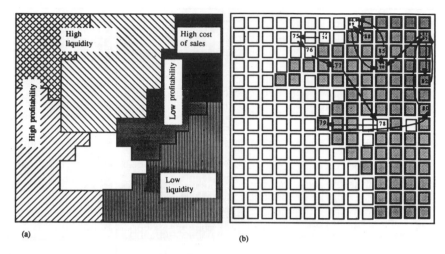

Figure 23.3 (a) Regions on the solvency map, delimited from the weight maps of Figure 23.2. (b) Evolution of the financial state of the Banco de Descuento on the solvency map of Figure 23.1 in the period 1973–90. This bank twice went bankrupt, in 1980 and 1990. The bankrupt area is in grey

that the response of the network be localised because, if not, the analysis is not clear, for example, if the activity bubble is distributed in a wide zone lying between bankrupt and solvent situations, we will not be able to make a clear diagnosis of the financial state of the bank being analysed.

The time evolution of the financial state of a firm can be seen by using a time sequence of data as input patterns, for example data for several consecutive years of a particular bank. As an illustration, we use the case of the Banco de Descuento, and show its trajectory on the solvency map (Figure 23.3(b)). Every input vector consists of the financial ratios of a year. We can see that between 1973 and 1976 it was in the solvent area. In 1977 it moved into the bankruptcy zone, and we know that this bank went into legal bankruptcy in 1980. In 1984 the bank was bought by an international trust, reorganised and renamed Bank of Credit and Commerce. We can see how the bank approaches the solvent zone of the map but, in the last few years, it has lain in a dangerous zone, with low profitability and high cost of sales (Figures 23.2 and 23.3(a)). As a result of this, the bank went bankrupt again in 1990. In studies of this kind we must take care when a pattern does not strongly excite any neuron because, in this case, the result might not be significant. If we show the same data from the Banco de Descuento to an MLP with BP learning as used in a previous work [SerMar93], the results achieved are consistent with those of the self-organizing solvency map in Figure 23.4. But with MLP we obtain a simple number as indicator, as occurs with many statistical models such as LDA or logit. However, from the solvency map, we obtain a more complete information on the state of the bank, because we

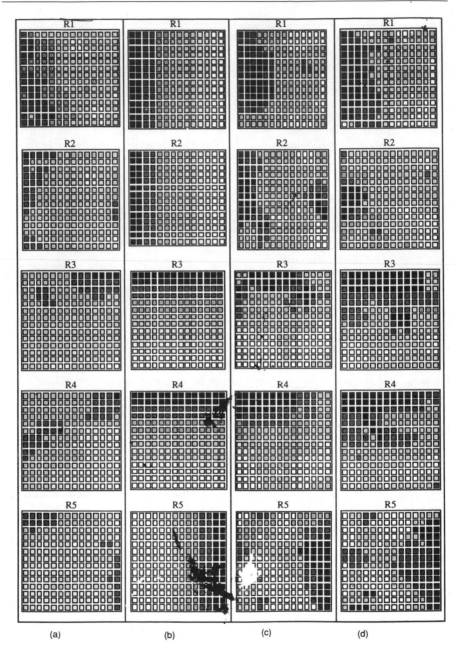

Figure 23.4   Weight maps of different networks (by columns) trained with data from 84 Spanish companies. (a) Network developed with data from 1990, starting with random weights. (b) Starting fixed weights. (c) Network of 1990 trained from the weight distributions of (b). (d) Network retrained with data from 1991, starting from the 1990 net of (c)

can see whether its situation is healthy, or healthy but near the danger zone, or in the high profitability area, and so on, depending on the location of the more excited neurons.

The Financial State of Spanish Companies in 1990 and 1991

The usefulness of financial ratios has been recognised in many areas, such as merger analysis, audit evaluation, evaluation of the creditworthiness of borrowers, security analysis, determining market return or rating bonds. One of the first works on the use of financial ratios is that of [PinMin73], where multivariate models are applied to analyse the Moody's bond rating. As a matter of fact, in one of the first neural network applications to the analysis of accounting data, that of [DudShe88], results attained with MLP and regression for Moody's bond rating are compared. In all these cases the rating given to the company, that is to say, the output, is known. Unfortunately, on many occasions the output is not available and in these circumstances an unsupervised model can be the solution.

In the present section we show the capabilities of self-organising solvency maps to show an image of the financial state of a wide set of companies; the maps developed can be used to make a visual diagnosis of the situation of the Spanish economy in 1991 in relation to 1990. In this practical case outputs are not available, because all the companies are solvent and have not been assessed. Therefore, it is not possible, in principle, to use supervised neural models (as MLP) in the modelling. We are interested in the unsupervised clustering of the input patterns (financial ratios of the companies) that allow us to delimit regions of interest on the map, such as liquidity zones, profitability regions or debt areas, where companies with similar features are located. We use data from 84 Spanish companies (from 1990 and 1991) most of them solvent and among the 250 biggest companies in Spain. Data have been drawn from the Spanish journal *El País* (issues of 15 December 1991 and 21 December 1992). Five financial ratios have been used as input data (see Table 23.3): ratios R1 and R2 are profitability ratios (profits to investments), R3 and R4 are short-term solvency ratios (current assets to current liabilities), and R5 is a debt ratio (loans to total assets).

As in the first case study, we use a self-organizing map of 14×14 neurons that is trained following a similar learning scheme with data from 1990. Previously,

Table 23.3 Ratios used in the study of the financial state of Spanish companies in 1990 and 1991.

Symbol	Name	Ratio
R1	Return on total assets	Operating profit/Total assets
R2	Return on equity	Net income/Total equity capital
R3	Acid test	(Current assets − Stocks)/Current liabilities
R4	Current ratio	Current assets/Current liabilities
R5	Debt ratio	Loans/Total assets

the input data have been standardised to mean zero and variance unity. Figure 23.4 depicts several weight maps corresponding to different trainings. Starting from small random synaptic weights, the resulting map is that in Figure 23.4(a), where we can see that the distribution of some weights is very fragmented. For instance, in R2, R3, R4 and R5 the large weights are separated into two main groups. The reason is that SOFMs project a high-dimensional input space onto a less-dimensional space which, in our problem, is two-dimensional (a plane). Hence, distortions are unavoidable. Compare the representation of when the Earth is on a plane: two near continents can be located on opposite sides of the map. Thus, the existence of fragmented regions in the weight space is revealed from the study of the synaptic weights. Different strategies can improve the appearance of the map, to obtain a map with smooth weight distributions. For this purpose, we start the learning phase from weight vectors fixed to predetermined values; thus, the global ordering of the map is given in advance and the regions of interest can be located in predetermined places. In this case, the learning is kept local by using a small starting neighbourhood radius, consisting of the adjustment of this initially globally ordered structure to fit the present data.

We can see from the weight maps in Figure 23.4(a), that the profitability ratios (R1 and R2) have a similar distribution on the map, as is also the case with the liquidity ratios (R3 and R4). Ratio 5 is a debt ratio which has a distribution approximately complementary to that of the profitability ratios (their large and small values are in opposite zones on the map). From these observations, the starting configuration of weights chosen is depicted in Figure 23.4(b). Weights are smoothly distributed in the interval $[-1, +1]$. The weights that connect input 1 (return on total assets) with every neuron on the map have a maximum value of $+1$ on the left-hand side of the map, descending towards -1 on the right-hand side (see Figure 23.4(b)). Similarly, ratios 3 and 4 have their maximum values at the top, descending towards -1 at the bottom side. Debt ratio (input 5), which was complementary to profitability ratios, is set to a complementary distribution. In this way, the profitability region is located on the left-hand side of the map, the liquidity region at the top and the debts area on the right-hand side. The learning starts from this new configuration. To preserve the initially stated global ordering, the learning is limited to a small starting neighbourhood. Thus, the starting radius chosen is of three neurons and the starting learning rate is 0.09. After 150 iterations, the resulting map is depicted in Figure 23.5(a) and the weight distribution of the final solvency map is that in Figure 23.4(c). After training, the synaptic weights have adapted to the actual data, and the problem of the existence of separated clouds of large weights has been solved for R3 and R4 (compare Figure 23.4(a) with 23.4(c)).

Figure 23.5(a) depicts the solvency map for 1990. In that figure the company number is on the neuron that gives the greatest response to the presentation of its pattern vector. The name of the company corresponding to every label has not been included here for the sake of brevity. Companies are distributed quite uniformly

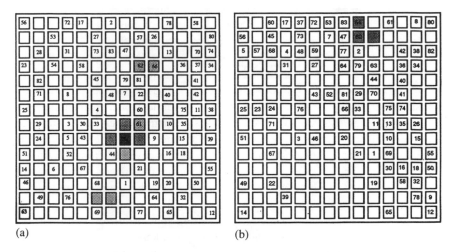

(a)   (b)

Figure 23.5   (a) Solvency map for 1990, developed by using, as starting weights, those of Figure 23.4(b). (b) New location of the same companies one year later. The company labels are on the node of greatest response. The response of every neuron to pattern no. 84 is coded in grey levels

over the map; this is a well-known characteristic of SOFMs that can be improved by using a 'conscience mechanism' [DeSien88]. If we present data from 1991 for the same companies to the previous net (trained with data from 1990), the new locations of the companies in 1991 are those represented in Figure 23.5(b).

From the weight map for 1990 (Figure 23.4(c)), several regions can be distinguished (Figure 23.6): an area of high profitability (left-hand side), another one of high liquidity (top half), an area of low profitability (upper right-hand side), a zone of large debts (on the right), an area of low liquidity (bottom half) and another one of low profitability, low liquidity and high debts (lower right-hand side). Looking at Figure 23.5(b), we can see that in 1991 there are regions with fewer companies than in 1990, as in the case, for example, of the profitability area. Many companies in that region have moved to the other side of the diagonal, leaving the profitability zone and moving into other regions, such as the high-liquidity area. Therefore, it seems that there are fewer companies with high profitability, but improving liquidity. This is easy to verify by looking at the mean value of profits and liquidity for these companies: R1 and R5 are the same in both years, but R2, a profitability ratio, has clearly decreased in 1991, and R3 and R4, liquidity ratios, have increased (the mean ratios in 1990 were 0.14, 0.12, 0.71, 1.10 and 0.56, versus 0.14, 0.07, 0.84, 1.18 and 0.56, in 1991).

The possibility of retraining a map with new data without needing to start from scratch is very interesting. For instance, we can retrain the self-organising map for 1990 (Figure 23.4(c)) with data from 1991. The weight map that results is seen

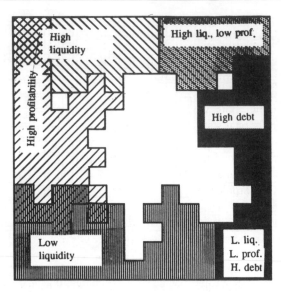

Figure 23.6 Regions on the solvency map built from data from 1990, delimited from the weight maps of Figure 23.4(c)

in Figure 23.4(d). Comparing Figures 23.4(c) and 23.4(d), the global aspect of the map has been preserved. In this map, we confirm that the area of large values of ratio R2 (return on equity) is smaller than that in Figure 23.4(c), and that the area of high liquidity (ratios R3 and R4) has grown. The area of high debt (ratio 5) is similar in both cases, but the area with extreme values (black squares) is smaller.

As in the previous section, we can trace the time evolution of a particular company on the map. For instance, let us examine the location of company 84, and let us compare its location on the map for 1990 (Figure 23.5(a)) and for that of 1991 (Figure 23.5(b)). In these figures, the more activated neurons for this pattern are shaded in grey levels. Note that in both cases this pattern strongly excites a group of neurons and that its activity bubble is small. We can see that this company moves from the central region in 1990 towards an upper zone in 1991, an area of less profitability but more liquidity. We can verify this conclusion by looking at the ratios of this company in both years: those of 1990 are 0.09, 0.04, 0.061, 1.01, 0.47 and those of 1991 are 0.01, 0.05, 1.25, 1.53, 0.48. Ratios R3 and R4 (liquidity ratios) have a higher value, and one of the profitability ratios (R1) is clearly smaller in 1991. The remaining ratios are similar in both years. Thus, the conclusions drawn from the solvency map agree with reality. The interesting thing about the SOFMs is that, by looking at the location of a company on the map, it is not necessary to take into account every input value, something which is difficult when the input space is of large dimension. In that case, the data compression carried out by the self-organising map can be very useful.

RELATING SOFM TO OTHER CONVENTIONAL TOOLS

Artificial neural networks can revolutionise data analysis in capital markets. Throughout this chapter it has been shown that SOFMs are in themselves of great usefulness in the study of accounting information. However, we must keep in mind that neural networks are not a panacea, but rather a large set of powerful and useful data-processing tools, which must be used appropriately [CroMas92]. There are many more traditional statistical techniques which can be more suited to solve a particular problem or some aspect of a problem. For developing a neural network application, the best method for solving each particular part of the problem should be chosen, merging neural and non-neural methods. For instance, in the study of the dimensionality of the problem and in feature extraction, a method commonly used is principal component analysis (PCA). The study of the relations of neural networks and statistical techniques is unavoidable for neural network researchers. In this section, we indicate some relationships between SOFM and several conventional techniques; this study does not pretend to be exhaustive, but is only a brief glance at the issue.

The similarity and relationships between SOFMs and clustering techniques have been pointed out on many occasions [Kohone89]. As an illustration, we have grouped the patterns from the Spanish banking crisis by means of hierarchical cluster analysis (HCA), a clustering technique used in exploratory studies in financial analysis. The result of the HCA is a dendogram that represents the extracted clusters. In our case, HCA has detected eight clusters, which have been superimposed on Figure 23.1 (see Figure 23.7). Notice that, although the patterns clustered together by HCA are also neighbours in the self-organising map, solvency and crisis situations have not been distinguished by HCA (there are clusters with both bankrupt and healthy banks). HCA could be used, for instance, to delimit regions on the map; this is an issue that requires further study.

The final results offered by the SOFM are similar to those of a statistical model, namely multi-dimensional scaling (MDS), a statistical algorithm that is able to represent multivariate data (vectors) as points on a map from a table of distances. Recently MDS has been proposed as an alternative to other multivariate methods in the prediction of company failure [MarEzz91, MarSer93]. In [MarSer93] MDS is applied to the same nine ratios of the Spanish banks, with similar results to those of SOFM, despite the fact that the algorithms appear to be very different. One of the differences between them is that SOFM results in a single map, while MDS provides several, depending on the statistical dimension of the problem. Both models are distribution-free, nonlinear and do not need to remove the outliers (patterns with extreme values) of the data set. But, in this last sense, SOFMs are better because the presence of outliers can cause many of the patterns on the map from the MDS to stand too close together, loosing all the interesting graphical information of the map. Instead, SOFMs are far more robust in the presence of outliers, because the Kohonen network distributes all the patterns uniformly on the map.

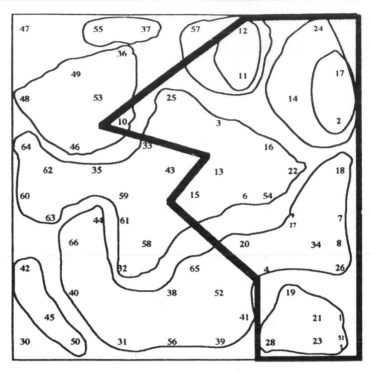

Figure 23.7   Results of the hierarchical cluster analysis superimposed on the solvency map of Spanish banks (Figure 23.1). The black line delimits the solvent and critical areas which are not distinguished by the clustering

There are relationships between MDS and more popular statistical techniques such as PCA. For instance, in [MarMol90] it is shown that MDA is equivalent to PCA when similarity measures are Euclidean. A comparison between PCA and SOFM has been carried out in [BlaDem91]. It is natural that more conventional techniques and neural models arrive at similar solutions, because they all try to solve similar problems. Establishing relationships between neural networks and traditional techniques is very useful for both, and much work is being carried out in this direction.

CONCLUSIONS

In this work, we have explored the capabilities of self-organising maps for the analysis and representation of financial data. For this purpose, SOFM has been applied to two financial data analyses, using real data from the Spanish economy: the analysis of the Spanish banking crisis of 1977–85; and a study of the financial state of 84 Spanish companies in 1990 and 1991. The idea has been to provide a method which is complementary to other mathematical models for the prediction of company failure based on Z-scores. Nevertheless, the conclusions drawn and the methodology used can be easily extended to data processing in other fields.

By means of the analysis of synaptic weights, we can infer how different input variables affect network operation and allow us to delimit regions on the map (profitability, liquidity, etc.) where similar companies are clustered, in an approximate way. Finally, if data for a financial entity from a series of years are shown to the trained network, the time evolution of this entity is traced on the map, by looking at the more activated neurons. An example of this has been given: the time evolution of the Banco de Descuento.

In conclusion, self-organising neural models present some features that, on some occasions, make their use more appropriate than other models in widespread use, such as backpropagation. This occurs mainly when outputs are not available, or when we require the unsupervised clustering of input patterns according to their similarity. Additionally, SOFM presents some special capabilities, such as dimensionality reduction and topological ordering of data, and their training algorithm is computationally very simple, which makes this model faster than BP. Several questions deserve wider study, such as how the development and final appearance of the map depends on the preprocessing which is selected.

One important issue is that SOFMs are intended to visualize relationships between patterns and represent high-dimensional input vectors in a low-dimensional space. For tasks such as pattern classification, if outputs are available, it is possible to increase the recognition rate by fine-tuning the map in a supervised way by means of the LVQ and LVQ2 algorithms [Kohone89, Kohone90].

We take the view that self-organising feature maps are a very interesting tool for studying the information contained in company accounting statements and capital markets in general. Our aim is to integrate SOFM in a complete financial decision-making system, which would also include different statistical tools, such as HCA or MDS.

ACKNOWLEDGEMENTS

The work of BMB is supported by the Research Consultant Council of the Aragon Government (CONAI-DGA), under grant BIT 2391, and that of CSC partly by the Fundación Caja de Madrid. The authors would like to acknowledge partial support from the University of Zaragoza.

Bibliography

[Abrams84] Abramson, I.S. (1984) 'Adaptive density flattening – a metric distortion principle for combating bias in nearest neighbor methods', *Annals of Statistics*, 12, 3, 880–86.

[AbuMos90] Abu-Mostafa, Y.S. (1990) 'Learning from hints in neural networks', *Journal of Complexity*, 6, 192–8.

[AbuMos93] Abu-Mostafa, Y.S. (1993) 'A method for learning from hints', in S. Hanson *et al.* (eds), *Advances in Neural Information Processing Systems* 5, Morgan-Kaufmann, San Diego, pp. 73–80.

[AcHiSe85] Ackley, D.H., Hinton, G.E. and Sejnowski T.J. (1985) 'A learning algorithm for Boltzmann machines', *Cognitive Science*, 9, 147–69.

[AffMcD89] Affleck-Graves, J. and McDonald, B. (1989) 'Nonnormalities and test of asset pricing theories', *Journal of Finance*, 44, 4, 889–908.

[Akaike69] Akaike, H. (1969) 'Fitting autoregressive models for prediction', *Ann. Inst. Statist. Math.*, 21, 243–7.

[Akaike70] Akaike, H. (1970) 'Statistical predictor identification', *Ann. Inst. Statist. Math.*, 22, 203–17.

[Akaike73] Akaike, H. (1973) *Information Theory and the Extension of the Maximum Likelihood Principle*, Akadémiai Kiadó, Budapest, pp. 267–810.

[Akaike74] Akaike, H. (1974) 'A new look at the statistical model identification', *IEEE Transactions on Automatic Control*, AC-19, 6, 716–23.

[Akaike77] Akaike, H. (1977) 'On entropy maximization principle', in P.R. Krishnaiah (ed.), *Applications of Statistics*, North-Holland, Amsterdam, pp. 27–41.

[Alspec87] Alspector, J.A., *et al.* (1987) 'Stochastic learning networks and their electronic implementation', *IEEE Conf. on Neural Information Processing Systems – natural and synthetic*, November.

[Altman68] Altman, E.I. (1968) 'Financial ratios, discriminant analysis and the prediction of corporate bankruptcy', *Journal of Finance*, September, 589–609.

[AmaArb82] Amari, S. and Arbib, M, (1982) *Competition and Cooperation in Neural Nets*, Springer-Verlag, New York.

[Anglui88] Angluin, D. (1988) 'Queries and concept learning', *Machine Learning*, 2, 319–42.

[AntBig92] Anthony, M. and Biggs, N. (1992) *Computational Learning Theory*, Cambridge University Press, Cambridge.

[AntHol93] Anthony, M. and Holden, S.B. (1993) 'On the power of polynomial discriminators and radial basis function networks', in *Proceedings of the Sixth ACM Conference on Computational Learning Theory*, ACM Press, New York.

[Ash89] Ash, T. (1989) 'Dynamic node creation in backpropagation neural networks', *Connection Science*, 1, 4, 365–75.

[Baba92] Baba, N. and Kozaki, M. (1992) 'An intelligent forecasting system of stock price using neural networks', in *International Joint Conference on Neural Networks – IJCNN, Baltimore, Maryland*, June 1992, Vol. I, pp. 371–77.

[BaBeFe92] Baetge, J., Beuter, H.B. and Feidicker, M. (1992) 'Kreditwürdigkeitsprüfung mit Diskriminanzanalyse', *Die Wirtschaftsprüfung*, 24, 749–61.

[Bailey64] Bailey N.T.J. (1964) *The Elements of Stochastic Processes with Applications to the Natural Sciences*, Wiley, New York.

[Bailey88] Bailey, David B., Thompson, Donna M. and Feinstein, Jerald L. (1988) 'Option trading using neural networks', in J. Herault and N. Giamisasi (eds), *Proceedings of the International Workshop, Neural Networks and their Applications, Neuro-Nimes*, 15–17 November 1988, pp. 395–402.

[BalHor89] Baldi, P. and Hornik, K. (1989) 'Neural networks and principal components analysis: Learning from examples without local minima', *Neural Networks*, 2, 53–8.

[Ballar86] Ballard, D.H, (1986) 'Cortical connections and parallel processing: structure and function', The behavioural and brain sciences, 67–120.

[Balsar92] Balsara, N. (1992) *Money Management Strategies for Futures Traders*, Wiley, New York.

[Band86] Band, R.E. (1986) *Contrary Investing*, Viking Penguin, New York.

[Barra91] Barra (1991) *Asset Allocation in the 1990's*, Barra International Ltd, London.

[Barron84] Barron, A. (1984) 'Predicted squared error: a criterion for automatic model selection', in S. Farlow (ed.), *Self-Organizing Methods in Modeling*, Marcel Dekker, New York.

[Bartle92] Bartlett, P.L. (1992) 'Learning with a slowly changing distribution', in *Proceedings of the Fifth ACM Conference on Computational Learning Theory*, ACM Press, New York.

[Bartle93] Bartlett, P.L. (1993) 'Lower bounds on the Vapnik–Chervonenkis dimension of multilayer threshold networks', in *Proceedings of the Sixth ACM Conference on Computational Learning Theory*, ACM Press, New York.

[Beaver66] Beaver, W.H. (1966) 'Financial ratios as predictors of failure', *Empirical Research in Accounting, Selected Studies*, Supplement to the *Journal of Accounting Research*, 71–111.

[BeRiVe90] Bell, T.B., Ribar, G.S. and Verchio, J. (1990) 'Neural nets versus logistic regression: A comparison of each model's ability to predict commercial bank failures', in R.P. Srivastava (ed.), *Auditing Symposium X, Proceedings of the 1990 Deloitte & Touche/University of Kansas Symposium on Auditing Problems*, Lawrence, KS, pp. 29–53.

[BiBlGr91] Bischoff, R., Bleile, C. and Graalfs, J. (1991) 'Der Einsatz neuronaler Netze zur betriebswirtschaftlichen Kennzahlenanalyse', *Die Wirtschaftsinformatik*, 5, 375–85.

[Biggs92] Biggs, N.L. (1992) 'Algorithms for learning and colouring', *LSE Mathematics Preprint* 28; to appear in the *Proceedings of the Conference on Graphs and Algorithms*, Kalamazoo, 1992.

[Bis93] BIS (1993) *Central Bank Survey of Foreign Exchange Market Activity in April 1992*, Bank for International Settlements (Monetary and Economic Dept.), Basel.

[BlaDem91] Blayo, F. and Demartines, P. (1991) 'Data analysis: How to compare Kohonen neural networks to other techniques', in *Proceedings of the IWANN®91, Granada, Spain*, Springer-Verlag, pp. 469–76.

[Blank91] Blank, S.C. (1991) ' "Chaos" in Futures Markets? A Nonlinear Dynamical Analysis', *Journal of Futures Markets*, 11, 711–28.

[BliAll91] Blinks, D.L. and Allinson, N.M. (1991) 'Financial data recognition and prediction using Neural Networks', in *Proc. Int. Conf. on Artificial Neural Networks ICANN'91, Espoo, Finland*, Elsevier, pp. 1709–12.

[Blum74] Blum, M. (1974) 'Failing company discriminant analysis', *Journal of Accounting Research*, Spring, 1–25.

[Blumer89] Blumer, A., Ehrenfeucht, A., Haussler, D. and Warmuth, M (1989) 'Learnability and the Vapnik–Chervonenkis dimension', *Journal of the ACM*, 36, 929–65.

[BluRiv88] Blum, A. and Rivest, R. (1988) 'Training a 3-node neural network is NP-complete', in *Proceedings of the 1988 Workshop on Computational Learning Theory*, Morgan-Kaufman, San Mateo, CA. (See also: *Neural Networks*, 5 (1992), 117–27.)

[Boller86] Bollerslev, T. (1986) 'Generalized autoregressive conditional heteroscedasticity', *Journal of Econometrics*, 31, 307–27.

[Boller92] Bollerslev, T., Chou, R.Y. and Kroner, K.F. (1992) 'ARCH modeling in finance: A review of the theory and empirical evidence', *Journal of Econometrics*, 52, 5–59.

[BowOco90] Bowerman, B.L. and O'Connell, R.T. (1990) *Linear Statistical Models: An Applied Approach*, PWS-Kent, Boston.

[Brown63] Brown, R.G. (1963) *Smoothing, Forecasting and Prediction of Discrete Time Series*, Prentice Hall International, NJ.

[Brock86] Brock, W.A. (1986) 'Distinguishing random and deterministic systems: Abridged version', *Journal of Economic Theory*, 40, 168–95.

[Brock87] Brock, W., Dechert, W.D. and Scheinkman J.A. (1987) 'A test for independence based on the correlation dimension', Working Paper, Department of Economics, University of Wisconsin, University of Houston and University of Chicago.

[Buse82] Buse, A. (1982) 'The likelihood ratio, Wald, and Lagrange multiplier test: An expository note', *The American Statistician*, 36, 3, 153–57.

[CarGro87] Carpenter, G. and Grossberg, S, (1987) 'A massively parallel architecture for a self-organizing neural pattern recognition machine', *Computer Vision, Graphics, and Image Processing*, 37, 54–115.

[Casdag89] Casdagli, M, (1989) 'Nonlinear prediction of chaotic time series', *Physica D*, 35, 335–56.

[CatMos94] Cataltepe, Z. and Abu-Mostafa, Y.S. (1994) 'Estimating learning performance using hints', in M. Mozer *et al.* (eds), *Proceedings of the 1993 Connectionist Models Summer School*, Erlbaum, Hillsdale, NJ, pp. 380–86.

[Caudill89] Caudill, M (1989) *Neural Networks Primer*, AI Expert, Miller Freeman, San Francisco.

[Chan88] Chan, K.C. (1988) 'On the contrarian investment strategy', *Journal of Business*, April.

[Chauvi89] Chauvin Y. (1989) 'A back-propagation algorithm with optimal use of hidden units', in D. Touretzky (ed.), *Advances in Neural Information Processing Systems* 1, Morgan Kaufmann, San Francisco.

[Chen86] Chen, N.-F., Roll, R. and Ross, S.A. (1986) 'Economic forces and the stock market', *Journal of Business*, 59, 3, 383–403.

[Clevel79] Cleveland, W.S. (1979) 'Robust locally weighted regression and smoothing scatterplots', *Journal of the American Statistical Association*, 74, 368, 829–36.

[Coats92] Coats, P. K. and Fant, L.F. (1992) 'A neural network approach to forecasting financial distress', *Journal of Business Forecasting*, 10, 4, 9–12.

[Cottrell90] Cottrell, G.W. and Thung, F.-S. (1990) 'Learning simple arithmetic procedures', in J.A. Barnden, and J.B Pollack (eds), *High Level Connectionist Models*.

[CraWah79] Craven, P. and Wahba, G. (1979) 'Smoothing noisy data with spline functions: Estimating the correct degree of smoothing by the method of generalized cross-validation', *Numer. Math.*, 31, 377–403.

[CroMas92] Croall, I.F. and Mason, J.P. (eds) (1992) *Industrial Applications of Neural Networks*, Springer-Verlag.

[Dasara91] Dasarathy, B.V. (1991) *Nearest Neighbor (NN) Norms: NN Pattern Classification Techniques*, IEEE Computer Society Press, Los Alamitos, CA.

[Deakin72] Deakin, E.B. (1972) 'A discriminant analysis of predictors of business failure', *Journal of Accounting Research*, Spring, 167–79.

[Deboec89] Deboeck, D. (1992) 'Preprocessing and evaluation of neural nets for trading stocks', *Advanced Technology for Developers*, 1, 2.

[DeBond91] De Bondt, W.F.M. (1991) 'What do economists know about the stock market?', *Journal of Portfolio Management*, Winter, 84–91.

[DeCost92] DeCoster, G.P., Labys, W.C. and Mitchell, D.W. (1992) 'Evidence of chaos in commodity futures prices,' *The Journal of Futures Markets*, 12, 291–305.

[DeGooi89] De Gooijer, J.G. (1989) 'Testing nonlinearities in world stock market prices', *Economics Letters*, 31, 31–5.

[DegWur91] de Groot C. and Wurtz, D. (1991) 'Time series analysis with connectionist networks', in *Proc. PASE 1991, Parallel Problem Solving Applications in Statistics and Economics, Zurich*, pp. 87–96

[DemCot93] DeMers, D. and Cottrell, G. (1993) 'Non-linear dimensionality reduction', in S.J. Hanson, J.D. Cowen and C.L. Giles (eds), *Advances in Neural Information Processing Systems 5*, Morgan Kaufmann, San Mateo, CA.

[Denker87] Denker, J.S. and Wittner, B.S. (1987) 'Network generality, training required and precision required', in *IEEE Conf. on Neural Information Processing Systems – Natural and Synthetic*, November 1987.

[DeSien88] DeSieno, D. (1988) 'Adding a conscience mechanism to competitive learning', in *Proc. Int. Conf. on Neural Networks*, Vol 1, IEEE Press, NY, pp. 117–24.

[DeSile92] DeSilets, L., Golden, B., Wang, Q., Luco, S. and Peck, A. (1992) 'A neural network model for the wire bonding process', Presentation, TIMS/ORSA Conference, Orlando 1992.

[Dicbol86] Diebold, F.X. (1986) 'Testing for serial correlation in the presence of ARCH', University of Pennsylvania.

[DieNas90] Diebold, F.X. and Nason, J.A. (1990) 'Nonparametric exchange rate prediction?', *Journal of International Economics*, 28, 315–32.

[DieSor84] Dietrich, J.K. and Sorensen, E. (1984) 'An application of logit analysis to prediction of merger targets', *Journal of Business Research*, 12, 393–402.

[DudHar73] Duda, S. and Hart, P. (1973) *Pattern Recognition and Scene Analysis*, Wiley, New York.

[DutSha88] Dutta, S. and Shashi, S. (1988) 'Bond rating: A non-conservative application of neural networks', in *Proc. ICNN-88, San Diego, CA*, 24–27 July 1988, Vol. II, 443–50.

[EbeDob90] Eberhart, R.C. and Dobbins, R.W (1990) *Neural Networks PC Tools*, Academic Press, San Diego, CA.

[EfrGon83] Efron, B. and Gong, G. (1983) 'A leisurely look at the bootstrap, the jackknife and cross-validation', *The American Statistician*, 37, 1, 36–48.

[Efron79] Efron, B. (1979) 'Bootstrap methods: Another look at the jackknife', *Annals of Statistics*, 7, 1, 1–26.

[Elman90] Elman, J.L. (1990) 'Finding structures in time', *Cognitive Science*, 14, 179–211.

[Engle82] Engle, R. (1982) 'Autoregressive conditional heteroscedasticity with estimates of the variance of U.K. inflation', *Econometrica*, 50, 987-1007.

[ErxKoc91] Erxleben, K. and Koch, H. (1991) 'Früherkennung von Unternehmenskrisen-ein Vergleich von neuronalen Netzen und Diskriminanzanalyse', Working paper, Universität Erlangen-Nürnberg, Abteilung Wirtschaftsinformatik.

[Erxleb92] Erxleben, K., Baetge, J., Feidicker, M., Koch, H., Krause, C. and Mertens, P. (1992) 'Klassifikation von Unternehmen. Ein Vergleich von neuronalen Netzen und Diskriminanzanalyse', *Zeitschrift für Betriebswirtschaft*, 11, 1237-62.

[Eubank88] Eubank, R.L. (1988) *Spline Smoothing and Nonparametric Regression*, Marcel Dekker, NY.

[FahLeb90] Fahlman, S.E. and Lebiere, C. (1990) 'The cascade-correlation learning algorithm', in D.S. Touretzky (ed.), *Advances in Neural Information Processing Systems 2*, Morgan Kaufmann, San Mateo, CA, pp. 525-32.

[Falma70] Falma, E. (1970) 'Efficient capital markets: A review of theory and empirical work', *Journal of Finance*, 25, 383.

[Fama65] Fama, E. (1965) 'The behaviour of stock market prices', *Journal of Business*, 34-104.

[FamGib84] Fama, E.F. and Gibbons, M.R. (1984) 'A comparison of inflation forecasts', *Journal of Monetary Economics*, 13, 327-48.

[FarSid87] Farmer, J.D. and Sidorowich, J.J. (1987) 'Predicting chaotic time series', *Physical Review Letters*, 59, 8, 845.

[FarSid88] Farmer, J.D. and Sidorowich J.J. (1988) *Can New Approaches to Nonlinear Modeling Improve Economic Forecasting? The Economy as Evolving Complex System*, SFI Studies in The Sciences of Complexity, Addison-Wesley, Reading, MA.

[FelBal82] Feldman, J. and Ballard, D. (1982) 'Connectionist models and their properties', *Cognitive Science*, March, 205-54.

[Feller50] Feller, W. (1950) *An Introduction to Probability Theory and its Applications*, Volume 1, Wiley, New York.

[FerHar91] Ferson, W.A. and Harvey, C.R. (1991) 'Sources of predictability in portfolio returns', *Financial Analysts Journal*, May-June, 49-56.

[FimZim91] Finnoff, and Zimmermann, H.G. (1991) 'Detecting structure in small data sets by network fitting under complexity constraints', in *Proceedings of the 2nd Annual Workshop Computational Learning Theory and Natural Learning Systems*, Berkeley, 1991.

[Fitzpa32] Fitzpatrick, P.J. (1932) 'A comparison of ratios of successful industrial enterprises with those of failed companies', reprinted in J.O. Horrigan (ed.), *Financial Ratio Analysis, A Historical Perspective*, New York, 1978.

[Foster91] Foster, B.F. *et al.*, (1991) 'Neural network forecasting of short noisy time series', presented at the ORSA TIMS National Meeting, May.

[Frank87] Frank, L.L. (1987) *Optimal Estimation with an Introduction to Stochastic Control Theory*, Wiley, NY.

[FraSte89] Frank, M. and Stengos, T. (1989) 'Measuring the strangeness of gold and silver rates of return', *Review of Economic Studies*, 56, 553–67.

[Frean89] Frean, M.R.A. (1989) 'The upstart algorithm: A method for constructing and training feed-forward neural networks', *Neural Computation*, 2, 198–209.

[Fukush88] Fukushima, K. (1988) 'A neural network for visual pattern recognition', *IEEE COMPUTER*, March, 65–75.

[Funaha89] Funahashi, K. (1989) 'On the approximate realization of continuous mappings by neural networks', *Neural Networks*, 2, 183–92.

[Gaines86] Gaines, B.R. (1986) 'Sixth generation computing: A conspect of the Japanese proposals', *ACM Sigart. News*, 95, 39–44.

[Gallan86] Gallant, S.I. (1986) 'Three constructive algorithms for neural learning', in *Proc. 8th Annual Conf. of Cognitive Science Soc.*

[Garava91] Garavaglia, S. (1991) 'An application of a counter-propagation neural network: Simulating the Standard & Poor's corporate bond rating system', in *Proceedings of the First International Conference on Artificial Intelligence Applications on Wall Street*, IEEE Computer Society Press, Los Alamitos, CA.

[Garava92] Garavaglia, S. (1992) 'Desperately seeking stability: Neural networks with insufficient data', in *Proceedings of the Second International Conference on Artificial Intelligence Applications on Wall Street*, Software Engineering Press.

[GarJoh79] Garey, M. and Johnson, D.S. (1979) *Computers and Intractability: A Guide to the Theory of NP-Completeness*, Freeman, San Francisco.

[GeBiDo92] Geman, S., Bienenstock, E. and Doursat, R. (1992) 'Neural networks and the bias/variance dilemma', *Neural Computation* 4, 1, 1–58.

[Geisse75] Geisser, S. (1975) 'The predictive sample reuse method with applications', *Journal of The American Statistical Association*, 70(350).

[GoHeWa79] Golub, G., Heath, H. and Wahba, G. (1979) 'Generalized cross validation as a method for choosing a good ridge parameter', *Technometrics* 21, 215–24.

[Goldbe89] Goldberg, D.E. (1989) *Genetic Algorithms in Search, Optimization, and Machine Learning*, Addison-Wesley, Reading, MA.

[GolLip88] Gold, B. and Lippmann, R.P. (1988) 'A Neural Network for isolated word recognition', IEEE ICASSP, 44–7.

[GorSej88] Gorman, R.P. and Sejnowski T.P. (1988) 'Analysis of hidden units in a layered network trained to classify sonar targets', *Neural Networks*, 1, 75–89.

[Gort69] Gort, M. (1969) 'An economic disturbance theory of mergers', *Quarterly Journal of Economics*, 83, 624–42.

[GriKat76] Grier, P. and Katz, S. (1976) 'The differential effects of bond rating changes among industrial and public utility bonds by maturity', *Journal of Business*, 49, 226–39.

[GroWur91] De Groot C. and Wurtz D. (1991) 'Analysis of univariate time series with connectionist nets', invited lecture at the Munotec-Workshop 1991.

[GruOsb93] Grudnitski, G. and Osburn, L. (1993) 'Forecasting S&P and gold futures prices: An application of neural networks', *Journal of Futures Markets*, 13, forthcoming.

[Hadady87a] Hadady, R.E. (1987) 'Using open interest to analyze price trends', *Futures*, 16, 7, 59–61.

[Hadady87b] Hadady, R.E., Finberg, I.L. and Rahfeldt, D. (1987) *Winning with the Insiders*, Weiss Research, West Palm Beach, FL.

[Hammer93] Hammerstrom, Dan (1993) 'Neural networks at work and working with neural networks', *IEEE Spectrum*, June–July.

[HanPra89] Hansen, S.J. and Pratt, L.Y. (1989) 'Comparing biases for minimal network construction with back-propagation', in D.S. Touretzky (ed.), *Advances in Neural Information Processing Systems 1*, Morgan Kaufmann, San Mateo, CA, pp. 177–85.

[Hartvi92] Hartvigsen, G. (1992) 'Limitations of knowledge-based systems for financial analysis in banking', *Expert Syst. Applic.*, 4, 19–32.

[HasSto93] Hassibi, B. and Stork, D. G. (1993) 'Second order derivatives for network pruning: Optimal brain surgeon', in S.J. Hanson, J.D. Cowan and C.L. Giles (eds), *Advances in Neural Information Processing Systems 5*, Morgan Kaufmann, San Mateo, CA, pp. 164–71.

[HasTib90] Hastie, T.J. and Tibshirani, R.J. (1990) *Generalized Additive Models*, Monographs on Statistics and Applied Probability, Vol. 43, Chapman & Hall, London.

[Haussl92] Haussler, D. (1992) 'Decision theoretic generalisations of the pac model for neural net and other learning applications', *Information and Computation*, 100, 78–150.

[Hawley90] Hawley, D.D., Johnson, J.D. and Raina, D. (1990) 'Artificial neural systems: A new tool for financial decision-making', *Financial Analysts Journal*, November–December, 63–72.

[Hebb61] Hebb, D. (1961) *Organisation of Behaviour*, Science Editions, New York.

[Hecht87] Hecht-Nielsen, R. (1987) 'Neurocomputer applications', in *Proc. National Computer Conf. AFIPS*, 239–44.

[Hecht91a] Hecht-Nielsen Corporation (1991) *ExploreNet Release 2.0*, Installation and Fast Track Manual, Hecht-Nielsen.

[Hecht91b] Hecht-Nielsen, R. (1991) *Neurocomputing*, Addison-Wesley, Reading, MA.

[HelLon91] Helmbold, D.P. and Long, P.M. (1991) 'Tracking drifting concepts using random examples', in *Proceedings of the Fourth Annual Workshop on Computational Learning Theory*, Morgan Kaufmann, San Mateo, CA.

[HeFiZi92] Hergert, F., Finnoff, W. and Zimmermann, H.G. (1992) 'A comparison of weight elimination methods for reducing complexity in neural networks', in *International Joint Conference on Neural Networks – IJCNN, Baltimore, Maryland, June 1992, Vol. III*, pp. 980–87.

[Hertz91] Hertz, J., Krogh, A. and Palmer, R.G. (1991) *Introduction to the Theory of Neural Computation*, Addison-Wesley, Reading, MA.

[HiCoRe92] Hill T., O'Conner, A.M. and Remus A.W. (1992) 'Neural network models for forecasting: A review', in *Proc of the 25th Hawaii International Conference on Systems Sciences*, Vol. 4.

[HinPat85] Hinich, M.J. and Patterson, D.M. (1985) 'Evidence of nonlinearity in daily stock returns', *Journal of Business and Economics Statistics*, 3, 1, 69–77.

[Hinton87] Hinton, G.E. (1987) *Connectionist Learning Procedures*, Technical Report, Computer Science Department, Carnegie-Mellon University, June.

[Hirose91] Hirose, Y., Yamashita, K. and Hijiya, S. (1991) 'Back-propagation algorithm which varies the number of hidden units', *Neural Networks*, 4, 61–6.

[Hollan92] Holland, J.H. (1992) *Adaptation in Natural and Artificial Systems* (2nd edn), MIT Press, Cambridge, MA.

[HonUhr89] Honavar, V. and Uhr, L. (1988) 'A network of neuron-like units that learns to perceive by generation as well as reweighting its links', in D. Touretzky, G. Hinton and T. Sejnowski (eds), *Proc. of the 1988 Connectionist Summer School*, Morgan Kaufann, San Mateo, CA.

[Hopfie82] Hopfield, J.J. (1982) 'Neural networks and physical systems with emergent collective computational abilities', *Proc. Nat. Acad. Sci*, 79 2554–58.

[Hoptro91] Hoptroff, R.G., Bramson, M.J. and Hall, T.J. (1991) 'Forecasting Economic Turning Points with Neural Nets', in *International Joint Conference on Neural Networks — IJCNN, Seattle, 1991*, Vol. 1, pp. 347–52.

[Hoptro93] Hoptroff, R.G. (1993) 'The principles and practice of times series forecasting and business modelling using neural networks', *Neural Computing and Applications*, 1, 59–66.

[Horrig66] Horrigan, J.O. (1966) 'The determination of long term credit standing with financial ratios', *Journal of Accounting Research*, supplement to Vol. 4, 44–62.

[Hsieh88] Hsieh, D.A. (1988) 'The statistical properties of daily foreign exchange rates', *Journal of International Economics*, 24, 129–45.

[Hsieh89] Hsieh, D.A. (1989) 'Testing for nonlinear dependence in daily foreign exchange rates', *Journal of Business*, 62, 339–68,

[Hsieh91] Hsieh, D.A. (1991) 'Chaos and nonlinear dynamics: Application to financial markets', *Journal of Finance*, 46, 5, 1839–77.

[Humper89] Humpert, B. (1989) 'Neurocomputing in financial services', *Expert Systems for Information Management*, 2, 3, pp. 172–98.

[Izenma91] Izenman, A.J. (1991) 'Recent developments in nonparametric density estimation', *Journal of the American Statistical Association*, 86, 413, 205–24.

[Jordan89] Jordan, Michael I. (1989) 'Serial order: A parallel distributed processing approach', in Jeffrey, L. Elman, and David E. Rumelhart (eds), *Advances in Connectionist Theory: Speech*.

[Kamijo90] Kamijo, Ken-Ichi and Tanigawa, Tetsuhi (1990) 'Stock price recognition – a recurrent neural network approach', in *International Joint*

Conference on Neural Networks — IJCNN, San Diego, California, 1990, Vol. I, pp. 215–21.

[Karnin90] Karnin, E.D. (1990) 'Simple procedure for pruning backpropagation trained neural networks', *IEEE Trans. on Neural Networks*, 1, 20.

[KarPra87] Karels, G.V. and Prakash, A. (1987) 'Multivariate normality and forecasting of business bankruptcy', *Journal of Business Finance and Accounting*, Winter, 573–93.

[Kaufma87] Kaufman, J. Perry (1987) *The New Commodity Trading Systems and Methods*, Wiley, NY.

[Kerlin92] Kerling, M. (1992) 'Anwendungsperspektiven der Handhabung betrieblicher Entscheidungsprobleme durch den Learning Vector Quantizer und das Restricted Coulomb Energy-Netzwerk' - Theoretische Betrachtungen und Anwendung auf das Problem der Kreditwürdigkeitsprüfung mittels Bilanzkennzahlenanalyse', Diplomarbeit, Universität Bamberg.

[KimAsa90] Kimoto, A.T. and Asakawa, A.K. (1990) 'Stock market prediction system with modular neural networks', in *Proc. of Int. Joint Conference on Neural Networks, San Diego, 1990*, Vol 1.

[KlGuPe89] Klimisauskas, C.C., Guiver, J. and Pelton, G. (1989) *Neural Computing*, Neural Ware Inc., Pittsburgh.

[KlKuMu87] Kleinbaum, D.G., Kupper, L.L. and Muller, K.E. (1987) *Applied Regression Analysis and Other Multivariate Methods*, PWS-Kent, Boston.

[Kohone84] Kohonen, T. (1984) *Self-Organisation and Associative Memory*, Springer-Verlag, Berlin, Chapter 5.

[Kohone87] Kohonen, T. (1987) 'State of the art in neural computing', in *Proc. Int. Conf. on Neural Networks*, IEEE, June.

[Kohone89] Kohonen, T. (1989) *Self-Organization and Associative Memory* (3rd edn), Springer-Verlag, Berlin.

[Kohone90] Kohonen, T. (1990) 'The self-organizing map', *Proc. of the IEEE*, 78, 9, 1464–80.

[Kon84] Kon, S. (1984) 'Models of stock returns – a comparison', *Journal of Finance*, 39, 1, 147–65.

[Kosaka91] Kosaka, Michitaka, Mizuno, Hirotaka, Sasaki, Toshiro, Someya, Ryuko and Hamada, Nariyasu (1991) 'Applications of fuzzy logic and neural networks to securities trading decision support system', in *Proceedings of the IEEE International Conference on Systems, Man and Cybernetics, October 1991*, pp. 1913–18.

[Kramer91] Kramer, M. (1991) 'Nonlinear principal component analysis using autoassociative neural networks', *AIChE Journal*, 37, 233–43.

[KraMez87] Krauth, W. and Mezard, M. (1987) 'Learning algorithm with optimal stability in neural networks', *J. Phys. A: Math Gen*, 20, 745.

[Krause93] Krause, C. (1993) *Kreditwürdigkeitsprüfung mit neuronalen Netzen*, Düsseldorf.

[KugLen90] Kugler, P. and Lenz, C. (1990) 'Sind Wechselkursfluktuationen zufällig oder chaotisch?', *Schweizerische Zeitschrift für Volkswirtschaft und Statistik*, 126, 113–27.

[Lakoni80] Lakonishok, J. (1980) 'Stock market return expectations: some general properties', *Journal of Finance*, 35, 4, 921–31.

[Larrai91] Larrain, M. (1991) 'Testing chaos and nonlinearities in T-bill rates', *Financial Analysts Journal*, September–October, 51–62.

[Lawler85] Lawler, E.L., Lenstra, J.K., Rinnoy Kan, A.H.G. and Shmoys, D.B. (1985) *The Travelling Salesman Problem*, Wiley, NY.

[LeBaro90] LeBaron, B. (1990) 'Forecast improvements using a volatility index', preliminary draft, University of Wisconsin.

[LeCun85] LeCun, Y. (1985) 'A learning procedure for asymmetric threshold networks', in *Proc Cognitiva 1985*.

[Lecun89] Le Cun, Y. (1989) *Generalisation and Network Design Strategies*, Technical Report CRG-TR-89-4, University of Toronto.

[LeDeSo90] LeCun, Y., Denker, J.S. and Solla, S.A. (1990) 'Optimal brain damage', in D.S. Touretzky (ed.), *Advances in Neural Information Processing Systems 2*, Morgan Kaufmann, San Mateo CA.

[LeLeMo94] Levin, A.U., Leen, T.K. and Moody, J.E. (1994) 'Fast pruning using principal components', in J. Cowan, G. Tesauro and J. Alspector (eds), *Advances in Neural Information Processing Systems 6*, Morgan Kaufmann, San Francisco.

[LeRoy89] LeRoy, S.F. (1989) 'Efficient capital markets and martingales', *Journal of Economic Literature*, 27, 1583–1621.

[Lippma87] Lippmann, R.P. (1987) 'An introduction to computing with neural nets', *IEEE ASSP Magazine*, April 1987, 4–22.

[Maass93] Maass, W. (1993) 'Bounds for the computational power and learning complexity of analog neural networks', in *Proceedings of the 1993 Symposium on the Theory of Computing*, ACM Press, New York.

[MacSon93] Macintyre, A. and Sontag, E.D. (1993) 'Finiteness results for sigmoidal 'neural' networks', in *Proceedings of the 1993 Symposium on the Theory of Computing*, ACM Press, New York.

[Malkie85] Malkiel, B.G. (1985) *A Random Walk Down Wall Street*, Norton, New York.

[Malkie87] Malkiel, B.G. (1987) *Efficient Market Hypothesis*, The New Palgrave, Macmillan, London.

[Mandel71] Mandelbrot, B.B. (1971) 'When can price be arbitraged efficiently? A limit to the validity of the random walk and martingale models', *Review of Economics and Statistics*, 53, 225–36.

[MarEzz91] Mar-Molinero, C. and Ezzamel, M. (1991) 'Multidimensional scaling applied to corporate failure', *OMEGA. International Journal of Management Science*, 19, 4, 259–74.

[MarMol90] Mar-Molinero, C. (1990) 'On the relationship between multidimensional scaling and other statistical techniques', research paper, University of Southampton.

[MarSer93] Martin-del-Brio, B. and Serrano-Cinca, C. (1993) 'Self-organizing neural networks for the analysis and representation of data: some financial cases', *Neural Computing and Applications* (In press).

[Marsha89] Marshall, J.F. (1989) *Futures and Options Contracting*, South-Western Publishing, Cincinnati, OH.

[Master93] Masters, T. (1993) *Practical Neural Network Recipes in C++*, Academic Press, San Diego, CA.

[Menden89] Mendenhall W. *et al.* (1989) *Statistics for Management and Economics*, PWS-Kent, Boston.

[Mervin42] Mervin, C.L. (1942) *Financing Small Corporations in Five Manufacturing Industries*, 1926–36, National Bureau of Economic Research, New York.

[MezNad89] Mezard, M. and Nadal, J. (1989) 'Learning in feedforward layered network: the tiling algorithm', *J. Physics A*, 22, 12, 2191–203.

[MilRei90] Miller, B. and Reinhardt (1990) *Neural Networks: An Introduction*, Springer-Verlag, Berlin.

[Minsky69] Minsky, M. and Papert, S. (1969) *Perceptrons*, MIT Press, Cambridge, MA.

[Moody89] Moody, J.E. (1989) 'Fast learning in multi-resolution hierarchies', in D.S. Touretzky (ed.), *Advances in Neural Information Processing Systems 1*, Morgan Kaufmann Publishers, San Mateo, CA.

[Moody91] Moody, J.E. (1991) 'Note on generalization, regularization and architecture selection in nonlinear learning systems', in B.H. Juang, S.Y. Kung and C.A. Kamm (eds), *Neural Networks for Signal Processing*, IEEE. Signal Processing Society, pp. 1–10.

[Moody92] Moody, J.E. (1992) 'The effective number of parameters: an analysis of generalization and regularization in nonlinear learning systems', in J.E. Moody, S.J. Hanson and R.P. Lippmann (eds), *Advances in Neural Information Processing Systems 4*, Morgan Kaufmann Publishers, San Mateo, CA, pp. 847–54.

[Moody94] Moody, J.E. (1994) 'The effective number of parameters and generalized prediction error for nonlinear regression', to appear.

[Moody94b] Moody, J.E. (1994) 'Prediction risk and architecture selection' in Cherkassky, V. et al. (eds) *From Statistics to Neural Networks*, NATO, ASI series F, Springer, 1994.

[MooUta92] Moody, J.E. and Utans, J. (1992) 'Principled architecture selection for neural networks: Application to corporate bond rating prediction', in J.E. Moody, S.J. Hanson and R.P. Lippmann (eds), *Advances in Neural Information Processing Systems 4*, Morgan Kaufmann Publishers, San Mateo, CA, pp. 683–90.

[MooYar92] Moody, J.E. and Yarvin, N. (1992) 'Networks with learned unit response functions', in J.E. Moody, S.J. Hanson and R.P. Lippmann (eds), *Advances in Neural Information Processing Systems 4*, Morgan Kaufmann, San Mateo, CA, pp. 1048–55.

[Morgan90] Morgan, M.S. (1990) *The History of Econometric Ideas*, Cambridge University Press, Cambridge.

[MosTuk68] Mosteller, F. and Tukey, J.W. (1968) 'Data analysis, including statistics', in G. Lindzey and E. Aronson (eds), *Handbook of Social Psychology*, Vol. 2, Addison-Wesley, Reading, MA.

[Moyer77] Moyer, R.C. (1977) 'Forecasting financial failure: A reexamination', *Financial Management*, Spring, 11–17.

[Mozer93] Mozer, Michael C. (1993) 'Neural net architectures for temporal sequence processing', in Andreas Weigend and Neil Gershenfeld (eds), *Time Series Prediction – Forecasting the Future and Understanding the Past*, Reading, MA, pp. 243–64.

[MozSmo90] Mozer, M.C. and Smolensky, P. (1990) 'Skeletonization: A technique for trimming the fat from a network via relevance assessment', in D.S. Touretzky (ed.), *Advances in Neural Information Processing Systems 1*, Morgan Kaufmann Publishers, San Mateo, CA.

[Myers90] Myers, R.H. (1990) *Classical and Modern Regression with Applications*, PWS-Kent, Boston.

[Narend90] Narendra S. Kumpati and Kannan Parthasarathy (1990) 'Identification and control of dynamical systems using neural network, *IEEE Transactions on Neural Networks*, 1, 1.

[Niehau87] Niehaus, H.-J. (1987) Früherkennung von Unternehmenskrisen, Düsseldorf University.

[OdoSha90] Odom, M.D. and Sharda, R. (1990) 'A Neural Network Model for Bankruptcy Prediction', in *IJCNN International Joint Conference on Neural Networks, San Diego, CA*, Vol. II, pp. 163–7.

[Ohlson80] Ohlson, J. (1980) 'Financial ratios and the probabilistic prediction of bankruptcy,' *Journal of Accounting Research*, 18, 109–31.

[OSulli93] O'Sullivan, J.W. (1993) 'Neural nets – A practical primer or … what I wished I knew four years ago', in *Second International Conference on AI Applications on Wall Street*, Software Engineering Press, Gaithersburg, MD.

[Palepu86] Palepu, K.G. (1986) 'Predicting takeover targets, a methodological and empirical analysis', *Journal of Accounting and Economics*, 8, 3–35.

[Pearce79] Pearce, D.K. (1979) 'Comparing survey and rational measures of expected inflation', *Journal of Money, Credit and Banking*, 11, 4, 447–56.

[Pearce84] Pearce, D.K. (1984) 'An empirical analysis of expected stock price movements', *Journal of Money, Credit and Banking*, 16, 3, 317–27.

[PeaSco86] Peavy, J.W. and Scott, J.A. (1986) 'The AT&T divestiture: Effect of rating changes on bond returns', *Journal of Economics and Business*, 38, 255–70.

[Peavy84] Peavy, J. (1984) 'Forecasting industrial bond rating changes: A multivariate approach', *Review of Business and Economic Research*, 19, 46–56.

[Perrid93] Perridon, Louis and Steiner, Manfred (1993) *Finanzwirtschaft der Unternehmung* (7th edn), Munich.

[Peters89] Peters, E.E. (1989) 'Fractal structure in the capital markets', *Financial Analysts Journal*, July–August, 32–7.

[Peters91] Peters, E.E. (1991) 'A chaotic attractor for the S&P 500', *Financial Analysts Journal*, March–April, 55–62.

[Peters92] Peters, E.E. (1992) *Chaos and Order in Capital Markets*, Wiley, New York.

[Pina89] Pina, V. (1989) 'Estudio empírico de la crisis bancaria', Revista Española de Financiación y Contabilidad, 18, 58.

[PinMin73] Pinches, G.E. and Mingo, K.A. (1973) 'A multivariate analysis of industrial bond ratings', *Journal of Finance*, 28, 1, 1–18.

[PinSin78] Pinches, G. and Singleton, J. (1978) 'The adjustment of stock prices to bond rating changes', *Journal of Finance*, 33, 29–44.

[Poddig92] Poddig, T. (1992) 'Künstliche Intelligenz und Entscheidungstheorie' Lehrstuhl für Finanzwirtschaft und Banken, Freiburg, Wiesbaden.

[PogSol69] Pogue, T.F. and Soldofsky, R.M. (1969) 'What's in a bond rating', *Journal of Financial and Quantitative Analysis*, 4, 201–28.

[Poli88] Poli, R., Cagnoni, S., Livi, R., Coppini, G. and Valli, G. (1988) 'A neural network expert system for diagnosing and treating hypertension', *IEEE Computer*, 21, 3, 64–71.

[Pollar84] Pollard, D. (1984) *Convergence of Stochastic Processes*, Springer-Verlag, New York.

[Ramsey90] Ramsey, J.B., Sayers, C.L. and Rothman, P. (1990) 'The statistical properties of dimension calculations using small data sets: Some economic applications', *International Economic Review*, 31, 4, 991–1020.

[ReBeBu94] Refenes, A.N., Bentz, Y. and Burgess, N. (1994) 'Neural networks in investment management', *Journal of Communications and Finance*, 8, April, 95–101.

[RefAli91] Refenes, A.N. and Alippi C. (1991) 'Histological image understanding by error backpropagation', *Microprocessing and Microprogramming*, 32, 3, 437–46.

[RefAze93] Refenes, A.N. and Azema-Barac, M. (1993) 'Neural network applications in financial asset management', *Neural Computing and Applications*, to appear.

[RefCha93] Refenes, A.N. and Chan, B. (1993) 'Sound recognition and optimal neural network design', in *Proc. Euromicro 92, Paris*.

[Refene90] Refenes, A.N., Azema-Barc, M. and Tehrani, A. (1990) 'An integrated neural network system for image understanding', in *Proc. Int. Conf. SPIE-90, Boston*.

[Refene92] Refenes, A.N. (1992) 'Constructive learning and its application to currency exchange rate prediction', in E. Turban and R. Trippi (eds), *Neural Network Applications in Investment and Finance Services*, Probus Publishing, Chapter 27.

[Refene93] Refenes, A.N., Azema-Barac, M. and Treleaven, P.C. (1993) 'Financial modelling using neural networks', in H. Liddell (ed.), *Commercial Applications of Parallel Computing*, UNICOM, London.

[ReFrZa93] Refenes, A.N., Francis, G. and Zapranis, A.D. (1993) 'Stock performance modeling using neural networks: A comparative study with regression models', *Neural Networks*, to appear.

[RefVit91] Refenes, A.N. and Vithlani, S. (1991) 'Constructive learning by specialisation', in *Proc. ICANN-1991, Helsinki, Finland*.

[ReZaBe93] Refenes, A.N., Zapranis, A.D. and Bentz, Y. (1993) 'Modeling stock returns with neural networks', in A.N. Refenes (ed.), *Neural Networks in the Capital Markets*, Proc. NnCM'93, London Business School, November.

[RehPod92] Rehkugler, Heinz and Poddig, Thorsten (1992) 'Klassifikation von Jahresabschlüssen mittels Multilayer-Perceptrons – Erste Ergebnisse und weiterführende Fragestellungen', Bamberger Betriebswirtschaftliche Beiträge, Nr. 87/1992, Otto-Friedrich-Universität Bamberg.

[ReiCoo90] Reilly, D.L. and Cooper, L.N. (1990) 'An overview of neural networks: Early models to real world systems', in *An Introduction to Neural Networks*, Academic Press, pp. 227–48.

[ReCoEl82] Reilly, D.L., Cooper, L.N. and Elbaum, C. (1982) 'A neural model for category learning', *Biological Cybernetics*, 45, 35–41.

[RiMaSc92] Ritter, H., Martinetz, T. and Schulten, K. (1992) *Neural Computation and Self-organizing Maps. An Introduction*, Addison Wesley, Reading, MA.

[Rissan78] Rissanen, J. (1978) 'Modeling by shortest data description', *Automatica*, 14, 465–71.

[Rodrig89] Rodriguez, J.M. (1989) 'The crisis in Spanish private banks: A logit analysis', *Finance*, 10, 1, 69–85.

[RosRos90] Ross, R.L. and Ross F. (1990) 'An Empirical Investigation of the Arbitrage Pricing Theory', *Journal of Finance*, December.

[Ross76] Ross, Stephen A. (1976) 'The arbitrage theory of capital asset pricing', *Journal of Economic Theory*, 13, 341–60.

[RuHiWi86] Rumelhart, D.E., Hinton, G.E. and Williams, R.J. (1986) 'Learning internal representation by error back-propagation', in *PDP: Elaborations in the Microstructure of Cognition*, Vol. I, Bradford Books, Cambridge, MA.

[Savit90] Savit, R. (1990) 'Nonlinearities and chaotic effects in options prices', *Journal of Futures Markets*, 9, 507–18.

[SchLeB89] Scheinkman, J.A. and LeBaron, B. (1989) 'Nonlinear dynamics and stock returns', *Journal of Business*, 62, 3, 311–38.

[Schoen90] Schoenenburg, E. (1990) 'Stock price prediction using neural networks: A project report', *Neurocomputing*, 2, 17–27.

[Schwar78] Schwartz, G. (1978) 'Estimating the dimension of a model', *Ann. Stat*, 6, 461–4.

[SenWad91] Sentana, E. and Wadwhani, S. (1991) 'Semi-parametric estimation and the predictability of stock market returns', *Rev. Econ. Studies*, 58 547–63.

[SeOlSe92] Sen, T., Oliver, R. and Sen, N. (1992) 'Predicting corporate mergers using backpropagation neural networks: A comparative study with logistic models', Department of Accounting, R.B. Pamblin College of Business, Virginia Tech.

[Servan89] Servan-Schreiber, David, Cleeremans, Axel and McClelland, James L. (1989) 'Learning sequential structure in simple recurrent networks', in D.S. Touretzky (ed.), *Advances in Neural Information Processing Systems 1*, Morgan Kaufmann, San Mateo, CA, pp. 643–52.

[ShaAle90] Sharpe, W. F. and Alexander, G.J. (1990) *Investments*, Prentice Hall.

[Sharpe63] Sharpe, William F. (1963) 'A simplified model for portfolio analysis', *Management Science*, 9, 277–93.

[Sharpe64] Sharpe, W. (1964) 'Capital asset prices: A theory of market equilibrium under conditions of risk', *Journal of Finance*, 19.

[Sharpe66] Sharpe, W. (1966) 'Mutual fund performance', *Journal of Business*.

[Shille87] Shiller, R.J. (1987) 'The volatility of stock market prices', *Science*, 235, 33–7.

[SieDow91] Sietsma, J. and Dow, R.F.J. (1991) 'Creating artificial neural networks that generalize', *Neural Networks*, 4, 67–79.

[SimMon71] Simkowitz, M. and Monroe, R.J. (1971) 'A discriminant analysis function for conglomerate targets', *Southern Journal of Business*, 6, 3–16.

[Simon82] Simon, H.A. (1982) *Models of Bounded Rationality*, MIT Press, Cambridge, MA.

[SinSur90] Singleton, J. and Surkan, A. (1990) 'Neural networks for bond rating improved by multiple hidden layers', in *Proceedings of the IEEE International Conference on Neural Networks*, Vol. II, 163–8.

[SinSur91] Singleton, J. and Surkan, A. (1991) 'Modeling the judgement of bond rating agencies: Artificial intelligence applied to finance', *Journal of the Midwest Finance Association*, 20, 72–80.

[SinSur93] Singleton, J.C. and Surkan, A.J. (1993) 'Bond rating with neural networks', in A.N. Refenes (ed.), *Proc. Neural Networks in the Capital Markets*, London Business School, November.

[Spiege88] Spiegel, M.R. (1988) *Statistics*, McGraw-Hill, New York.

[Standa79] Standard & Poor Corporation (1979) *Standard & Poor's Rating Guide*, McGraw-Hill, New York.

[StaWal86] Stanfil, C. and Waltz, D. (1986) 'Toward memory based reasoning', *Communications of the ACM*, 29, 2, 1213–28.

[Stein89] Stein, J. (1989) 'How commodity markets fit business cycle patterns', *Futures*, 18, 13, 34–8.

[Stone74] Stone, M. (1974) 'Cross-validatory choice and assessment of statistical predictions', *Journal of the Royal Statistical Society*, series B, 36, 111–47.

[Stone78] Stone, M. (1978) 'Cross-validation: A review', *Math. Operationsforsch. Statist.*, ser. Statistics, 9, 1.

[SurSin90] Surkan, A.J. and Singleton, J.C. (1990) 'Neural networks for bond rating improved by multiple hidden layers', in *Proceedings of IEEE International Conference on Neural Networks*, Vol. II, pp. 157–62.

[TamKia90] Tam, K.Y. and Kiang, M. (1990) 'Predicting bank failures: A neural network approach', *Applied Artificial Intelligence*, 4, 265–82.

[Taylor64] Taylor, S.J. (1964) 'Rewards available to currency futures speculators: Compensation for risk or evidence of inefficient pricing?', *Economic Record*, 68 (Supplement), 105–16.

[TewJon87] Teweles, R.J. and Jones, F.J. (1987) *The Futures Game* (2nd edn), McGraw-Hill, New York.

[TreFer86] Treynor, I. Jack and Ferguson, Robert (1986) 'In defence of technical analysis', *Journal of Finance*.

[TriBer91] Trigueiros, D. and Berry, R.H. (1991) *Neural Networks and the Automatic Selection of Financial Ratios*, Tech. Rep, INESC, Portugal.

[TuvRef93] Tuv, E. and Refenes, A.N. (1993) 'Removal of catastrophic noise in hetero-associative datasets', in *Proc. IJCNN 93, Nagoya Japan, Oct.*

[Tvede92] Tvede, L. (1992) 'What "Chaos" Really Means in Financial Markets', *Futures*, 21, 2, 34–6.

[UtaMoo91] Utans, J. and Moody, J. (1991) 'Selecting neural network architectures via the prediction risk: Application to corporate bond rating prediction', in *Proceedings of the First International Conference on Artificial Intelligence Applications on Wall Street*, IEEE Computer Society Press, Los Alamitos, CA.

[Valian84a] Valiant, L.G. (1984) 'A theory of the learnable', *Communications of the ACM*, 27, 1134–42.

[Valian84b] Valiant, L.G. (1984) 'Deductive learning', *Phil. Trans. Roy. Soc. London*, series A, 312, 441–6.

[VapChe71] Vapnik, V.N. and Chervonenkis, A. Ya. (1971) 'On the uniform convergence of relative frequencies of events to their probabilities', *Theory of Probability and its Applications*, 16, 264–80.

[Vapnik82] Vapnik, V.N. (1982) *Estimation of Dependences Based on Empirical Data*, Springer-Verlag, New York.

[VarVer90] Varfis, A. and Versino, C. (1990) 'Univariant economic time series forecasting by connectionist methods', in *Proc. Int. Neural Networks Conf., Paris, France*, pp. 342–5.

[Wahba90] Wahba, G. (1990) *Spline Models for Observational Data*, Regional Conference Series in Applied Mathematics Vol. 59, SIAM Press, Philadelphia.

[WahWol75] Wahba, G. and Wold, S. (1975) 'A completely automatic french curve: Fitting spline functions by cross-validation', *Communications in Statistics*, 4, 1, 1–17.

[Wan90]   Wan, E.A. (1990) 'Neural network classification: A Bayesian interpretation', *IEEE Transactions on Neural Networks*, 1, 303–5.

[Wasser90] Wassermann, P. (1990) 'A Combined Back-Prop Cauchy Machine', 1990, in Wassermann, P. *Neural Computing: Theory and Practice*, Van Nostrand, NY, 1990.

[WeHuRu91] Weigend, A.S., Huberman, B.A. and Rumelhart, D. (1991) 'Generalisation by weight-elimination applied to currency exchange rate prediction', *Proc. IJCNN'91*, IEEE 1991, pp. 837–841.

[WejTes90] Wejchert, Jakub and Tesauro, Gerald (1990) 'Neural network visualization', in D.S. Touretzky (ed.), *Advances in Neural Information Processing Systems 2*, Morgan-Kaufmann, San Mateo, CA, pp. 465–72.

[West70]   West, R.R. (1970) 'An alternative approach to predicting corporate bond ratings', *Journal of Accounting Research*, 7, 118–27.

[White88] White, H. (1988) 'Economic prediction using neural networks: The case of IBM daily stock returns', in *Proc. of the IEEE Int. Conf. on Neural Networks*, San Diego, vol. 2, pp. 451–459.

[White89] White, H. (1989) 'Learning in artificial neural networks: A statistical perspective', *Neural Computation*, 1, 425–64.

[Windso90] Windsor, Colin G. and Harker, Antony H. (1990) 'Multi-variate financial index prediction – a neural network study', in *Proceedings of the International Neural Network Conference INNC-90-Paris, Vol. 1*, pp. 357–60.

[WisCha78] Wismer, D.A. and Chattergy, R. (1978) *Introduction to Nonlinear Optimization*, North Holland, Amsterdam.

[Wong92]   Wong, Francis and Tan, Pan Yong (1992) 'Neural networks and genetic algorithm for economic forecasting', AI in economics and business administration.

[Zapran92] Zapranis, A.D. (1992) 'Stock ranking using neural networks', Project Report, Department of Computer Science, University College London.

[Zaremb90] Zaremba, T. (1990) 'Technology in search of a buck,' in R.C. Eberhart, and R.W. Dobbins (eds), *Neural Network PC Tools*, Academic Press, San Diego, CA.

Index